1968

HENRY JAMES
A Reader's Guide

HENRY JAMES
A Reader's Guide

S. GORLEY PUTT

with an introduction by
ARTHUR MIZENER

CORNELL UNIVERSITY PRESS
ITHACA, NEW YORK

CONTENTS

6

INTRODUCTION

Arthur Mizener

In this systematic commentary on Henry James's fiction, Mr. Putt has at last solved a problem that has existed ever since James's greatness was first recognized. James is one of the most notorious of the writers plain readers know to be important and yet find difficult and even irritating to read. Speaking for one group of plain readers, Mark Twain said that he would rather be confined to the Puritan Heaven than have to read one of James's novels. Henry James's favourite hero, what he called 'my poor gentleman', and this Mark Twain are the complementary 'innocents abroad' of American cultural history, its passionate pilgrim and its passionate provincial. Twain speaks for a formidable, though perhaps mainly American group of plain readers.

Henry James's brother William, who contributed so generously to what Mr. Putt calls the geminian split in Henry's sense of experience, speaks for the other great group of plain readers when he says that Henry's novels 'give a certain impression of the author clinging to his gentlemanliness though all else be lost, and dying happy provided it be *sans déroger*'. This judgement I imagine finds an echo in a good many English as well as American breasts. One of the interesting things about the relation between Henry and William James is the way Henry never argued against William's freely expressed objections to his novels and yet somehow managed to hold his own in their lifelong disagreement. How he did so is demonstrated by the story of a walk Henry once took, at William's urging, when he was staying with William in Vermont. When Henry returned, William, hopeful that Henry's interest in American life might have been aroused, asked if he had seen anything interesting, and Henry said, 'I saw a peasant gathering faggots'. It is a formidable insight that can produce spontaneously both this slyly William-esque parody of Henry's own manner and this destructive satire of William's ideological passion for the 'new man' of nineteenth-century American democratic theory.

It is obvious what causes the distress of the plain reader of Henry James. In the style of both his life and his work, James became throughout his long career steadily more mannered. By the end of it, his work—like the architecture of Vanbrugh or the lyrics of Hopkins—had a splendour so 'high', as Mr. Putt calls it, as to appear at first glance beyond ordinary comprehension. Only when one becomes familiar with it does one see the ironic, colloquial ease that controls it, and understand that, if James deliberately developed his famous manner because it was the best means available to him for saying what he had to, he was fully aware that artifice, though necessary to eloquence, is also absurd.

What stares out of James's great novels—even the early ones like *Roderick Hudson* and *The Portrait of a Lady* with which Mr. Putt rightly urges readers to begin—is a confounding extravagance of language, an apparently functionless luxury of decoration like that of an Edwardian drawing room. 'I can,' James once said, 'stand a great deal of gilt.' That may seem a judgement on him, unless the reader remembers that it is James's own judgement—the expression of his commitment to a style, to be sure, but also the expression of his awareness that when a style is mistaken for a moral commitment it becomes limiting and even vulgarizing. James did not make that mistake. He needed a special style to express his complicated vision of experience, what Mr. Putt (not, I gather, wholly approving) quite rightly calls the passionate pilgrim's hankering 'after his own notion of *quality*'. But no one knew better than James how easy it is to interpret a manner as a moral commitment and then to condemn it from the point of view of a different moral commitment, as gentlemen with solemn social or moralistic commitments have done with James's manner, from H. G. Wells to F. R. Leavis and Maxwell Geismar.

The first purpose of James's style is to express with poetic force those discriminations of quality that were for him an essential part of reality, just as the purpose of his equally strange dialogue—with its stylized diction, its extended metaphors, its leaps over the obvious,

its queer ellipses—exists to let his characters discuss such discriminations. At its best James's style is certainly very beautiful, as, for
example, in the description of Gloriani's pavilion, where Lambert
Strether of *The Ambassadors* first meets Mme. de Vionnet.

Far back from the streets and unsuspected by crowds, reached by a
long passage and a quiet court, it was as striking to the unprepared
mind, he immediately saw, as a treasure dug up; giving him too, more
than anything yet, the note of the range of the immeasurable town and
sweeping away, as by a last brave brush, his usual landmarks and terms.
It was in the garden, a spacious cherished remnant, out to which a dozen
persons had already passed, that Chad's host presently met them; while
the tall bird-haunted trees, all of a twitter with the spring and the weather,
and the high party-walls, on the other side of which grave *hôtels* stood
off for privacy, spoke of survival, transmission, association, a strong,
indifferent, persistent order. The day was so soft that the little party had
practically adjourned to the open air, but the open air, in such conditions,
was all a chamber of state.

This is Lambert Strether's great moment, and therefore it takes
place in what is, for a moment, a paradise, a place in the open air,
where all the Whitmans of America thought man should live, that
is also a chamber of state to delight all the Edith Whartons. (James
cherished an odd, reluctant respect for Whitman alongside his
admiration of Edith Wharton).

But except on properly solemn occasions like this, James's style
always includes his controlling sense of its own extravagance, a
qualifying element of deliberate self-parody that is almost as evident
as that of the frontier tall tale. This effect is most evident in his
conversation, for example in the little fancy Ford Madox Ford
produced in his description of James worrying over the hiring of a
'Lady Help' for Lamb House.

So the poor Master . . . had to spend long mornings and afternoons on
what he called 'the benches of desolation in purgatorial, if I may allow
myself the word, establishments, ill-named, since no one appeared there
to register . . . eminently ill-named: *registry-offices* . . .' And there would
be a sound like the hiss of a snake as he uttered the compound word. . . .
He would pass his time, he said, interviewing ladies all of a certain
age, all of haughty—the French would say *renfrognée*—expressions, all of

whom would unanimously assure him that the idea of entering the household of an untitled person like himself, in such a God-forsaken end of the world as the Ancient Town of Rye, they having passed their lives in the families of never anyone less than a belted earl in mansions on Constitution Hill in the shadow of Buckingham Palace . . . if they for a fleeting moment toyed with the idea, it was merely, they begged to assure him . . . 'forthegoodoftheirhealths'. Mr. James having dallied with this sentence would utter the last words with extreme rapidity, raising his eyebrows and his cane in the air and digging the ferrule suddenly into the surface of the road. . . .

How they come back to me after a quarter of a century . . . the savoured, half-humorous, half-deprecatory words, the ironically exaggerated gestures, the workings of the closely shaved lips, the halting to emphasize a point, the sudden scurryings forward, for all the world like the White Rabbit hurrying to the Queen's tea-party. . . .

James's seriousness is plain enough there: this was the way he lived, and he meant to make a success of his chosen mode of life however much trouble it might cost him. At the same time he was perfectly well aware that his anxiety might look ludicrous to those who had chosen other modes of life, and it is difficult to imagine a manner of speaking in which his sense of the ludicrous could be expressed more vividly than it is by those qualifying clauses and faintly exaggerated gestures—at the very moment that his seriousness was being quite as vividly expressed.

What I have been saying is, I hope, a fair summary of what the convinced Jamesian feels, but to talk in this way is to address oneself to the already persuaded. The problem is to talk usefully to the unpersuaded, and convinced Jamesians have up to now not succeeded in doing that. By a kind of infection from their author they fall into arguments in his defence more elaborate and tenuous than anything in James himself; they even begin to sound like imitations of him, meandering through the sunny byways of subordinate clauses and losing themselves in deliberately elaborate ellipses.

One of the ruefully comic aspects of Henry James's own commentary on his work—in the *Prefaces* to The New York Edition and in the *Notebooks*—is his constant reminder to himself that he must 'foreshorten', and his sad admission, after the event, that he had misplaced the middle of his story. This is no more than to say, as Mr. Putt notes, that James indulged himself in such leisurely elaborations of the beginnings of his novels that he had to hurry over—'heroically foreshorten'—the rest of them. The thing that distinguishes most of James's critics from James himself in this respect is their incapacity for heroic foreshortening: their conclusions are as generously elaborated as their beginnings.

The only critics I know who do not suffer to some extent from this defect are F. W. Dupee in his fine American-Men-of-Letters life of James, and Mr. Putt in this commentary on James's work. The first thing, then, that should be noticed about Mr. Putt's book is that, with unique brevity and rare good sense, he covers the whole range of James's fiction; it is, I believe, literally true that every novel and every short story James wrote is commented on by Mr. Putt, and what he considers James's important works are dealt with in some detail. Yet there is nothing mechanical about his discussion, no dull plodding from analysis to analysis. His arrangement is primarily thematic; he has defined with remarkable clearness the themes that dominated James's long career, worked out their relations for us, and shown us how they are embodied in the fiction. It tempts one to say that this is the ideal study of James for the student, and, since the argument is conducted at a fairly high critical level, most of all for the graduate student. It is; but to say just that is to ignore the extent to which all readers of James, even the most devoted, need the kind of help Mr. Putt offers. The bulk of James's work is so great and it is at once so elaborate and so refined in theme that the particularity of it—that 'felt life' by which James rightly laid such store—is extremely difficult to hold in the memory. It is, in fact, hard to imagine a reader of James who does not stand to benefit from Mr. Putt's commentary.

The intense common sense that gives Mr. Putt's ordering of James's work its lucidity is the product of a thorough-going and, I have no doubt, principled commitment to a particular view of what constitutes James's greatness. Richard Blackmur once remarked that 'the Henry James novel, the Joyce novel, the Kafka novel, the Mann novel, the Gide novel together will kill us yet if we do not realize soon that these novelists do not depend on what we think of as their "novels" except in the first instance'. Like Blackmur, Mr. Putt is impatient with the overemphasis in James's Prefaces on form, on the tactics of narration—and more than impatient with its repetition among his idolators. This is all to the good. When interest in James was first revived, in the thirties, criticism was struggling to come to terms with the modern novel's new forms and a preoccupation with the tactics of narration was almost inevitable. In these circumstances James's own account of the tactical ingenuity of his novels (a product of his perfectly natural delight in craftsmanship and perhaps also of his shyness about speaking of his passion and insight) was easily accepted as an explanation of his greatness. But we are now in a position to ask ourselves what it is *in* James's novels that makes the view of them first set forth with such clever vulgarity in H. G. Wells's *Boon* so wrong.

To this question too Mr. Putt has his answer, an answer that directs our attention to the solid reality of social insight on which James's work is founded. This answer points to a major value in James's work; it is also a badly needed corrective to the excessive attention recently given to the less solid reality in it, especially in the later novels. Toward such readings of James, Mr. Putt takes a bluff, no-nonsense attitude. He will accept none of the fine-spun subtleties of *The Golden Bowl*. 'For long stretches of *The Golden Bowl*,' he alleges, 'the reader loses his underlying interest in "the real" as seen through social eyes (as remains true even in *The Ambassadors*) and feels instead that he is called upon to do little more than *share* the social prying of the intolerable Assinghams.' Of James's late novels, in fact, only *The Wings of the Dove* escapes Mr. Putt's disapproval, logically enough from his point of view, since it contains relatively little indirect narration; though even here James is criticized for not showing us the final scene between Milly and Densher and for generally including a good deal of 'pother'.

No man of sense, I imagine, will disagree with Mr. Putt that, just as adulation of James's craftsmanship has distracted our attention from the substance of his novels, so the discovery of esoteric—and suspiciously contemporary—philosophical implications in his work has made him into a metaphysical grotesque. At the same time, I cannot help feeling Mr. Putt has been a little carried away by his quite proper anxiety to stress the novelist of manners in James. ' "The real" as seen through social eyes' is a crucial element in James and Mr. Putt does it clear justice. James was a great novelist of manners. That is what one might risk calling his 'English' side, assuming that Mr. Tony Tanner was right when he recently said that 'the English—perhaps because of their triumphant mastery of matter in the real world—tend to prefer novels in which the relationship between the author, his subject, and his language is firm, clear, and unproblematical. There is the writer on one side: on the other is his "story", that is, his selection of significant incidents from the real world. The writer's style is simply a tool, an efficient means of bringing the story in front of the reader.'

But James was an Englishman by adoption, the kind that perhaps only an American can become; and there is a substantial (not merely a tactical) reason, an 'American' reason, for his use of indirect narration. It is the same as the reason for James's elaborate dramatizations of tenuous states of the soul—in Lambert Strether and Merton Densher, in Milly Theale and Maggie Verver, even in Kate Croy and Charlotte Stant—that Mr. Putt describes with witty impatience as muddy morasses through which he is anxious to assist readers unspattered.

Considerably before Henry James's time, Hawthorne had noted in himself the consequences—equally present in James though not in so limiting a way—of being an American and a transcendentalist. In the comment on his own work that serves as a preface to *Rappaccini's Daughter*, Hawthorne observes that Hawthorne 'generally contents himself with a very slight embroidery of outward manners —the faintest possible counterfeit of real life—and endeavours to create an interest by some less obvious peculiarity of the subject'. James too was concerned with the less obvious peculiarities of his subjects, though not to the exclusion of outward manners and a counterfeit of real life. Nevertheless he was American as well as English: perhaps one ought to say he was American before he was English. He had his fair share of the characteristic American preoccupation with aspects of experience that are as dazzlingly meaningful to those who respond to them as they are irritatingly muddy to those who do not.

One consequence of this preoccupation is a perhaps exaggerated interest in subjective reality, and one consequence of that interest is a troubled uncertainty about objective reality, an uncertainty that makes the direct, authoritative narration of the conventional novel of manners hard to manage and indirect narration—what Mr. Putt calls the *voyeur* tendency habitual in the late James—so useful in dealing with the story. But that is not the only consequence for James of being American, for Lambert Strether is not 'the peripheral consciousness of a man of gentle temperament' through whose understanding we watch the story of Chad Newsome and Mme. de Vionnet unfold at what seems to Mr. Putt an unnecessary remove of reality, as if *The Ambassadors* were some badly blurred Edith Wharton novel (*The Age of Innocence* is the comparable case). The education of Lambert Strether, the development of his consciousness, is as central to the reality of *The Ambassadors* as is the social comedy of Chad and Mme. de Vionnet, which, in an important sense, exists to make that education possible. That education matters to James just as the education of 'Henry Adams' mattered to his friend Henry Adams. The necessarily subjective and personal apprehension of the quality of experience was as genuine a part of reality for James as was its social performance.

James is the first great novelist—and perhaps still the only one—to have fused the European's sense of the objective limits of life, which habitually expresses itself in the novel of manners, and the American's sense of its limitless conceivable possibilities, which habitually expresses itself in the so-called metaphysical romance (an unhappy term). The achievement of this fusion certainly contributes to the extravagance of his style, which had somehow to represent states of the consciousness and the accompanying uncertainties about objective reality in terms of the novel of manners. The cost was considerable; perhaps it was too great. But it was not paid for nothing, as Mr. Putt seems, in his mild way, to be suggesting, and as critics like F. R. Leavis sometimes quite ferociously suggest.

None of this is intended to imply that Mr. Putt is not absolutely right to insist that the solid reality of social comedy is the place for the plain reader to begin with James's novels, because it is the foundation of everything in them. Moreover, it is not simply the aspect of James's work with which the new reader should be concerned; it is the aspect no reader ought ever to forget—not even James himself if, as Edith Wharton suggested to his face, he did forget it in *The Golden Bowl*. It is to the enforcement of this 'nutritive truth' about James's work that Mr. Putt has directed himself in this book, with a success I believe unrivalled by any other critic.

Acknowledgments

In making a systematic survey of all James's novels and tales, I have naturally been indebted to a host of earlier commentators, and more especially to those listed in the Bibliographical Note; but the views and conclusions here expressed are an attempt to record the fresh impressions of the total impact of James's fiction on the mind of a single reader, namely myself. I am grateful to Messrs. Faber & Faber for allowing me to draw on the James essays in my book *Scholars of the Heart*, which form a basis for subjects treated in Chapters III, VI, X and XV. Here and there, paragraphs have been incorporated from contributions to *English* and the *Times Literary Supplement*.

S. G. P.

AUTHOR'S PREFACE

'NOWHERE had I condemned a luckless theme to complete its revolution, burdened with the accumulation of its difficulties . . . in quarters so cramped.' Thus Henry James (pruned) in his Preface to *The Wings of the Dove*. The wail may well be echoed by anyone rash enough to attempt a guide to his fiction. For it seemed to me that if this guide was to have any value, it would be as the simplest possible record of the impact of Henry James, as novelist and teller of tales, on a fresh mind. When I started reading James during the war, at first in my hammock and later as a shore-based sailor, the fresh mind was only too readily available. I had read Van Wyck Brooks's mainly antagonistic *The Pilgrimage of Henry James* (1928), the germinal Henry James number of the American magazine *Hound and Horn* (1934), the critical studies by Ford Madox Ford (1913) and Rebecca West (1916) and a few other scattered notes and articles; but none of these seemed to me to have the critical acumen displayed in brief *Scrutiny* articles by Dr. F. R. Leavis (later reprinted in *The Great Tradition*, 1948), or the illuminating personal testimony of Miss Theodora Bosanquet's *Henry James at Work* (1924), or the bracing quality of Percy Lubbock's introduction and commentary to his two-volume edition of the *Letters* (1920). For background information, I then relied solely on the *Letters* and on James's own autobiographical volumes, *A Small Boy and Others* (1913), *Notes of a Son and Brother* (1914) and the unfinished *The Middle Years* (1917).

But ever since the muted centenary celebrations of 1943, there has been a great outpouring of reprints and critical studies, the most useful of which are listed in the Bibliographical Note at the end of this volume. In seeking, therefore, to sketch an introduction to an author whose own immense output has scared away readers who might enjoy him if they once tasted him, it may well be that I have laboured points made more ably by other recent authorities. If so,

I can only offer my regrets to them and to their awakened readers. It is not to them that these chapters are addressed, but to the ordinary lover of good fiction who has yet to discover the rich merits of Henry James as a poet and scholar of the human heart.

This book is intended to be precisely what the title indicates: a guide. The reader I have ideally in mind would be someone who had read perhaps one novel and a couple of stories and wished to know a little about James's work before venturing deeper. That is to say, I shall assume some initial interest in Henry James the novelist, but no close familiarity with the vast output of 22 novels (two unfinished) and 112 tales, to say nothing of all the critical, descriptive and dramatic work for which there will be room here for barely a mention. This general stance will no doubt mean that some readers will be affronted by a synopsis, let us say, of a novel they already know well. I prefer to run this risk rather than infuriate my ideal reader by treating the James *oeuvre* as something already and immemorially *there*, like Stonehenge, and then enmeshing him in allusive discourses about a story he has not yet read. (And it may perhaps be admitted, even by the knowing, that a reminder of what actually *happens* in a James novel rarely comes amiss, even when our main attention is on some vexed moral or stylistic issue.) With this reader in mind, and conscious that thanks to the editorial labours of Professor Leon Edel and others, almost all James's important fiction is now readily available, I have introduced into this guide at least one reference to every one of the novels and tales.

May I, at this point, make two disclaimers for the benefit of readers of scholarly habit? The first is substantive, and seeks to excuse the absence, in this guide, of attempts to trace biographical parallels and literary 'influences'. There is, of course, a natural fascination in tracking down the 'originals' of a novelist's most successful characters. Those who read biographical studies of James (and especially Leon Edel's magnificent volumes) will be interested, for example, to follow speculations as to how many of his female characters may be documented as partial portraits of his cousin Minny Temple, whose death at the age of twenty-four ('There was too much life in her—it was this, this!' as one of William Gerhardi's characters is made to say) so profoundly affected the young writer.

Other scholars will find an equal interest in measuring James's debt to the novelists he himself read with pleasure: Hawthorne, Balzac, Dickens, George Eliot, Turgenev, and so on. But to the ordinary reader the unspoken question about a writer's characters must always be not 'Where do they come from?' but rather 'How well are they *now* presented?' Too many critical studies leave us, unwittingly, with the notion that it is all so simply explained: this character comes from Uncle Bert, that one from Becky Sharp, and that's all there is to it. At such a point, even the most naturally inquisitive of readers must be obliged to recall that we, too, have in our family a great 'character' in Auntie Flo, and that we, too, are fascinated by Falstaff. What comes of it? Nothing. Granted that the curious may find a few starting-points in Minny Temple for Milly Theale of *The Wings of the Dove;* the final presented form of that wonderful character succeeds or fails, as we read, whether or not we have ever heard of Henry James's unfortunate cousin. Milly Theale is memorable even without any knowledge of Minny Temple; just as Colonel Assingham would remain a boring convenience for the elaboration of the plot of *The Golden Bowl*, even if he could be shown to be a faithful transcript of a living person. My guide had just been completed when I came across a succinct statement of this point of view in a review, in the *Times Literary Supplement* of 5 August 1965, of the second volume of Mr. George Painter's life of Marcel Proust. What Proust's novel demonstrates, wrote the critic, 'is that almost from the cradle the potential writer is always "on duty", that everything is grist to his mill, but that the transformation of the raw materials is so radical that the hunt for "keys" is little more than an entertaining but irrelevant game'.

The second disclaimer is on a technical point. I am aware that by scholarly habit it is customary to refer to novels in italics (e.g. *The Bostonians*) and to stories in inverted commas (e.g. 'Eugene Pickering'). I have decided to break this rule in the present guide, in which the titles of novels and tales alike are italicized. I have done this partly because there is little real difference between them in most of the aspects I wish to emphasize; partly because the distinction between a short novel like *The Reverberator* and a long tale like *The Aspern Papers* is in any case meagre; and partly for the trite but humane reason that an endless jumble of inverted commas, such as must occur when quotations and titles are liberally scattered on the same page, is an unnecessary vexation to the eye.

It may be well to explain one other deliberate disregard of academic usage. Nothing is easier for a writer to produce, or more irritating for a reader to confront, than a text making no pretensions to scholarship and yet peppered with footnotes and page-references. In rigorous presentations of research, this habit may be unavoidable; but in a guide designed primarily to be useful to new readers of James, I have quoted freely from him without any attempt to nail sentences down to pages in the bewildering variety of editions in which his works are nowadays encountered. Similarly, I have eschewed footnotes when referring to works mentioned in the Bibliographical Note; only works not so listed are noted. In the case of citations from the nineteen volumes of *Scrutiny* and from the three volumes of Dr Leon Edel's biography of Henry James available to me, the references are further shortened in the text itself.

My arrangement of chapters, in an attempt to introduce so much wealth, may need a word of explanation. An unswervingly chronological survey would commend itself to a critic and make possible a developing view of James's scope and growth, but would be of small comfort to the ordinary student of fiction who might find himself baffled by the effort to keep so many threads in his hand at one time. A purely 'literary' treatment of the renowned style would offer much temptation, and the choice of illustrations of the early fresh flavour ripening to that famous 'highness' (as of pheasants) would automatically assemble a superb anthology—and please none but the converted, who do not need it. Again, *too* close an attention to plot, in dealing with a writer who progressively spurned external action, would be to display a skull when the chief glory is the bloom on the cheek—and yet a reminder of the underlying structure can only be merciful when an exasperated new reader of the later novels and stories is crying out 'Where *is* everybody, and what on earth are they *doing*?' I have had, in short, to strike a compromise; I have tried to draw out the main themes for examination, illustrating them from novels and stories which might at the same time illustrate many *other* themes; I have retained the comforting direction of chronology by taking these themes as they first began to achieve prominence in the long life-work; and as for James's style, I have hoped to display its overall quality by being liberal to the point of prodigality with quotations.

One example will indicate the type of problem and perhaps placate the reader who would have preferred a different solution. 'Mr. James is—and was from the first—the great master of the *nouvelle* in the Anglo-Saxon world.' Thus Ford Madox Ford—and no lover of James would disagree, or wish for a better text than the same critic's definition: 'It is rather no more and no less than the consideration of an "affair". The whole of the story, of the murder, of the liaison, of the bequest, might well be related in the opening of the first paragraph.' Very well; one could set out to study the Jamesian 'long-short' story in all its many aspects, and again Ford would provide a starting-point: 'Action ... in the sense of any-body's doing anything, is singularly rare in any of Mr. James's *nouvelles;* but what the French call *progression d'effet* is never absent from the almost apparently negligible of them.' Yet, in dis-cussing the germinal notion at the origin of one of these stories, how could one omit reference to a novel in which the same notion had been worked out in greater detail? Who could write about James's treatment of the marriage-market in, say, the short story *Glasses*, and not wish to bring in *The Awkward Age*? Or who could confine himself to the full-length study of the artistic temperament in *The Tragic Muse*, when a score of extra observations on art and society were jostling for attention, from stories as far removed as *The Author of 'Beltraffio'* and *The Tone of Time*? Over the whole span of James's writing career there is indeed little difference, either in texture or general effect, between his tales and his full-dress novels.

Limitation of space has preserved me from the danger of stumbling in the rear of those critics who, following the example of James himself (in the Prefaces, the *Notebooks*, his letters and sometimes even, distressingly, in the tales themselves), have paid special atten-tion to 'forms' and 'modes' and various dodges of the novelist's craft in which, to be brutally frank, he did not greatly excel. I may as well confess that a dogged re-reading of his fiction, with the minimum of side-references to his own and others' literary theory, leaves me with the impression that Henry James the man used the resources of a splendid intelligence to compensate for some crippling defects of experience; and that James the writer is most successful when, forgetting the 'tricks of the trade' in which he is quite often surpassed by lesser novelists, he allowed himself freedom to describe precisely what he saw and express, with an unparalleled exactitude of fine human judgement, precisely what he felt. Just as T. S. Eliot was penetratingly right when he suggested that James had a mind too fine to be violated by an idea, so James is most magnificently himself when, through the mouth of a character in *The Golden Bowl*, he asks—with full confidence in the reply—'What is morality but high intelligence?'

I

Apprenticeship in America

Watch and Ward; the first tales; *Washington Square;*
The Jolly Corner

'. . . the great idea that I am—oh,
ever so indigenously!—one of them.'
(Max Beerbohm cartoon: '*Mr. Henry*
James revisiting America.')

MANY critics seem to assume that James's first novel was *Roderick Hudson* (1875), perhaps because this was the earliest full-length work he included, late in life, in the revised New York Edition of his novels and stories. Together with this assumption goes the popular view that James did not start writing in earnest at all until his sensibilities had been liberated by his first adult experience of the continent of Europe. It is true, of course, that long before his first serious attempt to settle in London at the age of thirty-three he had partaken of the trans-Atlantic wanderings of his restless family; but it was as an American writer who had already written and published in America a substantial body of fiction that he arrived in the Old World. The Henry James who was to fling himself with such energy into the social and literary life of England and the Continent was by no means a beginner. With few exceptions, his early works have entirely American settings; yet in these works may be traced a first statement of almost all the major themes (including the international obsession) of his whole immense output. As a recent critic has put it,* 'when James as a young man left America virtually for good, he took with him a sane and capacious intellect, a progressively strengthening habit of fruitful and keenly relished social intercourse, and a counterbalancing devotion, necessarily lonely, to the service of major art'. He was also able to take with him in his luggage a published novel and over a score of published stories.

The novel was *Watch and Ward*, published serially in 1871. It is a charming and underrated story, written with careful prentice skill and yet possessing a mature wit in human assessments. The construction is poor: there are *longueurs* in the middle chapters and a hurried bustling towards a melodramatic climax quite out of keeping with the rest; yet the writing has an easy youthful confidence, based on some fifteen printed tales. Two recurring Jamesian themes make up, together, the whole plot: an obsessional timidity in the face of marriage (which in the 1870's, even more than today, provided the inescapable resolution for most fiction), and a tendency to distribute

* J. I. M. Stewart: *Eight Modern Writers*, 1963.

over two or more contrasting characters, often cousins, the split personality of the geminian author.

The opening of this strange day-dream of a story of cautious pre-arranged marital convenience is brilliantly professional, conveyed in speedy short sentences which would surprise a reader whose notion of James is based solely on the work of his later period. Roger Lawrence, a comfortable bachelor who has been repulsed by his first matrimonial choice, adopts a fatherless child, Nora: the father being a feckless Bohemian who had committed suicide after Lawrence, a complete stranger, had denied him a loan. This peace-offering to his vague feeling of guilt grows, with the years, to be Roger's main object in life; our sympathy is charmingly beguiled for this kind avuncular celibate who is as careful of his affections as of his property. 'He used to lie awake at night, trying hard to fix in his mind the happy medium between coldness and weak fondness. With a heart full of tenderness, he used to measure out his caresses.' This chaste domestic economy amuses his cousin Hubert, a fashionable clergyman who acts as foil to Roger in all things: 'each . . . seemed to find in the other an irritating counterpart and complement.' Nora, too, proves to have a cousin (or at least someone who claims that relationship to the now comfortable orphan)—a rascally George Fenton who recalls her shady antecedents and who smells in the snug relationship of guardian and ward a hopeful subject for blackmail.

The interrelations of these two pairs of cousins make up, rather too neatly, the plot. More effective than their plotted comings and goings, however, is the way in which the cousinly relationship serves to underline, by the antipathies and attractions of consanguinity, the contradictions in their own natures—more especially in those of Roger and his Nora. Thus, the petted Nora's vagrant cousin George represents—almost like a thumb-nail sketch of the strapping Basil Ransome of *The Bostonians*—a masculine version of what she might wish herself to be if she were not becoming a polite as well as a gifted young lady:

It must be said that Fenton was not altogether unworthy of her favours. He meant no especial harm to his fellow-men save insofar as he meant uncompromising benefit to himself. The Knight of La Mancha, on the

torrid flats of Spain, never urged his gaunt steed with a grimmer pressure
of the knees than that with which Fenton held himself erect on the hungry
hobby of success. Shrewd as he was, he had perhaps, as well, a ray of Don
Quixote's divine obliquity of vision. It is at least true that success as yet
had been painfully elusive, and a part of the peril to Nora's girlish heart
lay in this melancholy grace of undeserved failure. The young man's
imagination was eager; he had a generous need of keeping too many
irons in the fire.

If her kindly guardian is turning her into a New England blue-
stocking, Fenton specifically represents the freer manners of the
frontier—so pointedly so, in fact, that one wonders if Henry James
is not thinking of his own 'sociable' and 'improvident' brother
Wilky (the adjectives are Leon Edel's) out in the vague Wild West.
'He was invested with a loose-fitting cosmopolitan Occidentalism,
which seemed to say to Roger that, of the two, *he* was the provincial.'
Very self-illuminating words, these, written before James himself
had moved so far East across the Atlantic that the whole forsaken
Republic, and not just the part in which he lived, could be judged
provincial.

As for the cousins Roger and Hubert Lawrence, they do come to
make up, between them, the complete man to whom the adolescent
Nora would cheerfully surrender. Unhappily, the division of qualities
between the two men vexes her judgement, and vexes them too—
each wishing, at times, to be more like the other. Here, in three
snippets, is Roger:

In trifling matters, such as the choice of a shoemaker or a dentist, his
word carried weight; but no one dreamed of asking his opinion on
politics or literature . . .

He of course had no imagination, which, as we know, should always
stand at the right hand of charity; but he had a good store of that
wholesome discretion whose place is at the left . . .

He would now, he declared, cast his lot with pure reason. He had tried
love and faith, but they would none of him. He had made a woman a
goddess, and she had made him a fool. He would henceforth care neither
for woman nor man, but simply for comfort, and, if need be, for pleasure.

Beneath this gathered gust of cynicism the future lay as hard and narrow as the silent street before him. He was absurdly unconscious that good humour was lurking round the very next corner.

Cousin Hubert, whose more vigorous attractions are disguised by his Christian name and his profession as clergyman, expresses sentiments well below the surface in Roger who, poor prim fellow, had to be informed by his ward 'with a kind of desperate abruptness, that her mother had been a public singer'. Hubert's self-assurance arouses the suspicion of Roger's old flame, now a widow—who, incidentally, has her own antithetical light to shed upon the heroine herself: 'Between these two, though there was little natural sympathy, there was a wondrous exchange of caresses and civilities. They had quietly judged each other and each sat serenely encamped in her estimate as in a strategical position.' This competent lady objects to cousin Hubert on the following grounds:

'What is he, when you come to the point? ... He is neither fish nor flesh, neither a priest nor a layman. I like a clergyman to bring with him a little odour of sanctity, something that rests you, after all your bother. Nothing is so pleasant, at the sober end of one's drawing-room. If he doesn't fill a certain place, he is in the way. The Reverend Hubert is in any place and every place. His manners are neither of this world nor, I hope, of the next. . . . He finds the prayer-book rather meagre fare for week-days; so he consoles himself with his pretty parishioners. To be a parishioner, you needn't go to his church.'

The reverend gentleman himself reveals that he has enough of cousin Roger in his make-up to feel divided in himself:

'I only half live; I am like a purse filled at one end with small coin and empty at the other. Perhaps the other will never know the golden rattle! . . . I had the wit to see, but I lacked the courage to do—and yet I have been called reckless, irreverent, audacious ... There are men born to imagine things, others born to do them. Evidently I am not one of the doers. But I imagine things, I assure you!'

Readers alert to spot references in Henry's work to his relations with brother William may find a happy hunting ground in the early stories. In *Watch and Ward* itself, the parallel figures Roger and Hubert are merely and amicably content to differ:

They had between them a kind of boyish levity which kept them from lingering long on delicate ground; but they felt at times that they belonged by temperament to irreconcilable camps, and that the more each of them came to live his own life, the more their lives would diverge. Roger was of a loving turn of mind, and it cost him many a sigh that a certain glassy hardness of soul on his cousin's part was for ever blunting the edge of his affection. He nevertheless had a deep regard for Hubert; he admired his talents, he enjoyed his society, he wrapped him about with his good-will.

It is an early instance of the point wisely made by Professor Edel in his comment on the classic statement of twin personalities in the story *Benvolio*:* 'The two selves might be different, but they were different parts of an harmonious self. This suggests that in certain fundamentals Henry was an individual without conflict.' There was no real anguish of warring selves in him. One has only to recall the agonies of a Rimbaud or a Dostoevsky to realize how balanced (if limited) a personality the methodical creator of Roger and Hubert Lawrence was blessed with; and we should always remember, in reading James's later stories about contrasted types and clashing symbols, that these confrontations were usually carefully recorded in advance, as '*données*', in his notebooks. James himself was not deceived by any contrarieties and oppositions that could be so manageably contrived. As a character in *Madame de Mauves* remarks, 'an unhappiness that one can sit comfortably talking about, is an unhappiness with distinct limitations'.

In *Watch and Ward*, then, the cousinly contrasts and complements are structurally useful but not too obtrusive; the reader's attention remains fixed where the young author clearly intended it to be, on the rum but not unsavoury situation of Roger, as his ward, with whom he has become devotedly in love, grows towards marriageable age. The theme of the virtual imprisonment of a young person by an older lover, to be treated with such tension in the morbid relationship of Olive Chancellor and Verena Tarrant in *The Bostonians*, is

* *Henry James: The Conquest of London*, 1962, p. 194. Future reference to the first three volumes of Dr. Edel's four-volume biography will be by volume and page only.

in this earlier novel handled in bumbling innocence by Roger himself and by other characters with, at most, raised eyebrows. Even the opportunist Fenton does not, at first, express more than an impatient distaste: 'It seemed to him an extremely odd use of one's time and capital, this fashioning of a wife to order. There was a long-winded patience about it, an arrogance of leisure, which excited his ire.' Nora's virtue, and her ultimate freedom of choice, are never seriously in danger—either from the doting Godfatherly Roger, or the flamboyant preacher Hubert who turns her head for a while but keeps his own simply because 'to keep cool, morally, in a heated medium was, in fact, for Hubert a peculiar satisfaction', or even from the wordly widow Mrs. Keith, 'who had on hand a small capital of sentimental patronage for which she desired a secure investment'.

'Let us cast away nothing', said Shakespeare's Pandarus, 'for we may live to have need of such a verse.' Henry James, like Proust, was of Pandarus's point of view and carefully husbanded, as 'verses' not to be cast away, his notes and travel observations. When ward Nora is required by the plot to spend a year in Europe with her wordly chaperon the widow, her letters home to the self-sacrificing Roger are full of odd scraps from the author's own early wanderings, scraps which will appear to better effect before long: glimpses of convent life which will be expanded in *The American*; wide-eyed comments on the life of artists in Bohemia which will be echoed with more authority in *Roderick Hudson* and *Madame de Mauves*; an innocent girlish excitement of travel which will set the tone for *Daisy Miller*. Finally, Nora's return to America brings her 'followers' out from positional manoeuvring into open rivalry: her comings and goings are racy (if one believes in them) or melodramatic (if one doesn't), but hardly persuade the reader that the scales are ever seriously weighted against the long-suffering Roger. Hubert is found to have a fiancée already, and Nora shows herself a true Jamesian heroine by reacting with suitable fastidiousness to the squalor of cousin Fenton's fly-by-night *milieu* in New York City.

The author's own prudent fascination with products from 'a horribly vulgar soil' forms, indeed, one of the abiding impressions left by his first novel. Roger Lawrence is almost too pat in expressing his horror of his ward's antecedents: 'She barely knew that the earth is round, but she knew that Leonora is the heroine of *Il Trovatore*. She could neither write nor spell, but she could perform the most surprising tricks with cards.' All this love-hate feeling for the nineteenth-century American world of tumblers and mountebanks will reappear in *Professor Fargo* and notably in *The Bostonians*. Some are tempted to attribute these glimpses of the seamy side of life to the influence on the young novelist of his beloved French and English literary models; but a far more convincing source he supplied on his own account when he set down, in mature years, those wonderful reminiscences in *A Small Boy and Others*, redolent of the rich low life and child-haunting entertainments of New York. The pastoral New England setting of much of *Watch and Ward*, and of the early stories, should not cause us to forget that Henry James was *not* a Bostonian, *not* strictly a New Englander, but a native of New York City who spent his first years and recorded his first impressions in that brash thriving metropolis of the bouncing 1840's and 1850's.

Most studies of *Watch and Ward* have had something to say about the novel's sexual situation and its sexual imagery. Two passages in particular have caught attention: the scene where the attractive Hubert's watch-key fits Nora's little watch whereas poor Roger's was 'a complete misfit'; and Roger's thought that 'the petals of the young girl's nature, playfully forced apart' by Fenton's flirtations, 'would leave the golden heart of the flower but the more accessible to his own vertical rays'. I doubt whether these two images would have been considered noteworthy or problematical in the work of any *other* author in his twenties writing about the dawning love of and for a young girl. I agree with Professor Cargill (who confesses that to a modern taste Roger and Nora seem anyway 'a rather washed out pair') that those who consider James to have been unaware or unconscious, even in 1871, of the goings-on of the birds and the bees, must be themselves pretty naïve.

To readers of the later James it may come as a surprise to learn that his very first story, *A Tragedy of Error* (1864), includes such a phrase as: ' "Baffled! baffled!" hissed Madame ...' The tale, published anonymously and only recently disinterred by Professor Edel (I, 217–19), is the kind of imitative literary exercise one might expect from a studious bookworm of twenty-one, a neat plot involving mistaken identity and murder by mischance. The curious may indeed find here the very first hint of that taste for melodrama from which he never quite freed himself. And so throughout these prentice tales, simple or contrived, there are fascinating (or warning, according to one's viewpoint) signs of things to come. Thus, *My Friend Bingham* (1867) hinges on the manslaughter of a child, another melodramatic theme to be elaborated, years later, in *The Other House*. Similarly, the plot of *A Most Extraordinary Case* (1868), of a man who dies of love and leaves a legacy to his successful rival, dimly foreshadows *The Wings of the Dove*. Sometimes a mere scrap of dialogue from these early American tales will suggest notions which, fished out later from those famous 'deep wells of unconscious cerebration', emerged hardly recognizable in their encrusted form. The quasi-supernatural story *De Grey: A Romance* (1868), which first exposes James's obsession that the consequences of marriage are literally mortal, contains in a few words the germ of *The Sacred Fount*: 'As she blossomed and prospered, he drooped and languished. While she was living for him, he was dying for her'. And this same murky story by a twenty-five-year-old author offers in two lines the future lesson of that most elderly of parables, *The Beast in the Jungle*:

> 'My adventure?' said Margaret, 'I have never had any.'
> 'Good!' cried Paul; 'that in itself is an adventure.'

But it is not for their plots and foreshadowing themes alone that these steady outpourings from a young writer in his early twenties deserve special attention. True, one may trace the overt or sidelong effects of the American Civil War upon an uneasy young non-combatant; one may track down hints and sources in the French and English novels which the young writer was devouring; one may even raise an eyebrow to discover how very early in his writing career James played with such unprepossessing subjects as the corrupting power of money (particularly its sadistic use as a weapon of vindictiveness or torture), or of that lust for emotional domination which dresses itself up as kindness, or of the distorted face of envy, so hideous that only a dip into the most grisly guise of the supernatural could produce for the apprentice artist colours lurid enough for its presentation. Even as he recognizes and allows for them, a reader who has already dabbled in James will find these adumbrations of major themes of less interest than the wonderful freshness of style in which, for the most part, they are conveyed. The catalogue, nevertheless, is remarkably complete. It deserves a rapid survey.

Three stories have direct reference to the Civil War. *The Story of a Year* (1865) evades the marriage crux by letting the hero die, rather late in the day, a soldier's death. Our sympathies have been almost forcibly wrenched away from heroine Lizzie by such editorial comments as: 'I am afraid I should make the reader sneer, were I to rehearse some of this little fool's diversions.' In a passage of considerable imaginative power we are introduced to Lizzie's propensity for day-dreaming (a habit, incidentally, no young writer should ever scorn); then side by side with it we are invited to admire the more self-contained composure of an older woman, the first of a whole regiment of mature Jamesian 'companions' of whom, as of this one, it could charitably be said: 'Her occupation here below was to perform the forgotten tasks of her fellow men—to pick up their dropped stitches, as she herself declared.' In *Poor Richard* (1867), the stay-at-home lover is gallingly jealous of other suitors wearing the uniform and glamour of war; the feebleness of his courtship only flickers into life as the young woman herself, on his recovery from illness, begins to waste away. The first glimpse, in James, of emotional cannibalism? A heads-I-win, tails-you-lose escape, at any rate, from the normal mating process. And the off-stage Civil War is yet more distant in the third story of the group, *A Most Extraordinary Case*, where the dying hero celebrates, as with relief, his own sexual impotence by endowing his rival with his own money: a curious reversal of the Biblical pattern of 'silver and gold have I none, but what I have . . .' Professor Edel skilfully links this ineptitude with James's own famous 'obscure hurt'.* But psychosomatic backache or no, there is here a broad suggestion that even for the youthful James the notion of physical impotence as a way of solving or avoiding the marriage problem can be not only admitted but positively desired. For if it was one thing to credit a battered wounded soldier with intimations of delicacy as he enjoys convalescence

* See below, p. 89.

amid feminine solicitude ('I am saturated with whispers and perfumes and smiles, and the rustling of dresses. It takes a man to understand a man!')—it was quite another thing to call in this man, or any man, to do a man's office, so to say. An odd conclusion, one might suppose, for a story-teller of twenty-five. It is well known that Henry felt keenly the disparity between himself and his poor war-wounded brother Wilky; but his later life and writing suggest that the Civil War 'guilt' was a mere externalization of a tendency to withdraw from all physical encounters with life—a tendency later observable alike in his feeblest and most sublime literary creations. Yet—to anticipate at this sensitive point a fairly obvious conclusion to be drawn later in this chapter—those critics who draw from such observations the view that Henry James's *writing* must on this account alone be cast aside as emasculate or fraudulent, show themselves to have so little acquaintance with the creative process in *literature*, at least, as to rule themselves pretty effectually out of court.

In claiming this, of course, one may quite willingly go on to admit that there are some of James's stories where an almost frivolous frailty of grasp on reality can at times, when unredeemed by those flashes of direct observation which at happier moments vitalize the characters and diminish the importance of the plot, make one pray fervently that the novice explorer in James country will not chance upon *this*, or *this*, as his first sample! One casts about, sometimes, for exculpations almost as far-fetched as the plots themselves. Thus, with *De Grey* and other marriage-shy stories in mind, one is relieved to be able to recall that ever since Alcestis and Admetus there has been seen some merit in dying *for* someone as well as merely *of* someone. The odd incident described in *A Day of Days* (1866), however, is no more than an account of how two young people meet and part, the simplest possible version of what Professor Edel calls James's 'predilection for separating his people, instead of bringing them together'. But in *Osborne's Revenge* (1868), death again follows love, if only this time from simple incompetence, from innocent mistakes in trying to come to terms with the dangerous passion. The narrator seeks to avenge the suicide of his poor 'jilted' friend, only to discover that the 'guilty' woman was both innocent and ignorant. Ignorance of the laws of love is no defence.

Nor does death itself always wipe out the danger, when vague supernatural threats may be invoked. *The Romance of Certain Old Clothes* (1868) may be eerie enough to call for the explanation of Hawthorne's influence, but the ghostly 'horror' has that same chill of the fear of marriage which makes the other non-ghost stories clammy, too. Here, a jealous wife who pries into a locked trousseau which her husband's first wife, her own dead sister, had left for their child's use, is strangled by the ghost of her outraged predecessor. These Gilbertian perils of 'marriage with deceased wife's sister' are matched, in *Master Eustace* (1871), by the Hamlet-like doom spread by a young man who has been cradled in self-absorbed arrogance by a doting widowed mother from whom he develops the appropriate Oedipus-complex. James's almost charming study of the narcissism of a spoilt boy who struts as if he were 'the final morbid little off-shoot of a long line of despots' figures as a mild character-sketch of an explainable and forgivable type, when contrasted with the fearful goings-on when Master Eustace returns from a foreign tour to find his own private Queen Gertrude married to an unsuspected King Claudius, an innocent old admirer. He rages and attempts to murder his stepfather, whereupon his mother dies of shock.

In the flimsy sketch *A Problem* (1868), the death of a child, fore-told by a fortune-teller, is allowed to draw the stricken parents together: punished (for the crime of marriage, one supposes?) by both death and the supernatural, they have bought a kind of dejected companionship in what remains of their married life. A more elaborate story, *Gabrielle de Bergerac* (1869), brings hero and heroine together across the gulf of class-consciousness in pre-Revolutionary France—but at that moderately happy moment the tale abruptly fizzles out. The story was written as a 'French' exercise before James's really significant trip to Europe, and he later found it 'thin and watery'. A fairy tale with turgid passages might be a more accurate description. The life of the *farouche* young tutor Coquelin in his little lodge, *vis-à-vis* the stately social life of the Bergerac family up at the *château*, prefigures the contrasting appeals of the private and public life most purely stated in the emblematic situation of poor Benvolio in the tale of that name. The Bergerac heiress and her plebeian admirer come to terms (and almost to grief) very appro-priately among the ruins of an old castle. 'We don't live in a natural world, Coquelin', she informs her lover, and when finally she succumbs to him after a more acceptable suitor, the Vicomte de Treuil, has taken a pot shot at her, their situation becomes so socially unnatural that the story peters out.

Yet another bar to married bliss is money. James's third tale, *A Landscape Painter* (1866), has a pellucid New England setting and an amiable narrator, fit subject for a day-dreaming young scribbler of twenty-three, who, though the possessor of a handsome income, likes to think of himself as an artist 'not wholly unfit for a life of (moderate) industry and (comparative) privation'. Alas, he finds that it is for his (comparative) affluence that his chosen patient-Griselda figure marries him—and if *she* is devious, then surely *no* woman may be trusted! The other stories concerned with money are faintly or markedly unpleasant. In *A Light Man* (1869), even the imagery is coin-ridden: 'Assume that her fortune has the proper number of zeros and that she herself is one of them, and I can even imagine her adoring me.' Cheating and treachery weave the plot; money corrupts friendship; usurpation is the ugly motive; one of a pair of friends supplants the other in the affections (and the will) of an old father-figure. Viler still is the behaviour of a jealous elder brother in *Guest's Confession* (1872), who takes a sadistic revenge by exacting from the father of his younger brother's fiancée an actual on-bended-knee begging for release from a financial obligation. 'These tales are best read in the light of biography', writes Professor Edel in his Introduction to Volume II of the *Collected Tales*. The text-book reactions of brothers, the mingled love and hate, admiration and envy, seem indeed to have operated between brothers William and Henry James no less, and no more, than usual. For most of his writing career, Henry's diagrammatic use of brothers or cousins or other close-linked pairs was surely to illustrate his own geminian nature rather than nursery conflicts with actual siblings. And as if to check in advance such psychological speculations, this same unsavoury tale has one perfectly overt reference to the subject of guilt: 'Guilt is not the vulgar bugaboo we fancy it . . ., it has organs, senses, affections, passions, for all the world like those of innocence'. So that if one must admit that the youthful writer could tread at times deliberately in the mire, it must also be confessed that he kept his head remarkably well while doing so.

Just as the first-known fiction by Henry James (*A Tragedy of Error,* noted above) was plain unabashed melodrama, so, in *The Story of a Masterpiece* (1868), he makes use of one exceedingly un-promising theme which seems to have had an inexplicable fascination for later nineteenth-century writers (one thinks, for instance, of Wilde's *Dorian Gray* and Anthony Hope's *Father Strafford*)—namely, the revelation of character via a painted portrait. We are asked to believe that the narrator becomes aware of the ugly character of his lover only when he sees it displayed in a portrait—whereupon he stabs not the lady but the picture. It is indeed a relief, when confronted by such a plot from which no learned tracking-down of sources, or consideration of the expectations of the readers of magazines, can altogether exculpate a major writer even in his youth—it is a relief to invite attention, instead, to much subtler aspects of self-revelation embodied in the incidental commentary even of this otherwise unrewarding exercise. Two sentences will serve to show that the apprentice was working with wonderful material, even if he sometimes botched the design:

The ample justice moreover, which, under the illusion of sentiment, he had rendered to her charms and graces, gave him a right, when free from that illusion, to register his estimate of the arid spaces of her nature.

A woman, it seems to me, ought to desire no easier company, none less embarrassed or embarrassing, than a disenchanted lover; premising, of course, that the process of enchantment is wholly complete, and that some time has elapsed since its completion.

Not only does this sort of writing attest to an easy fluent confidence in a twenty-five-year-old apprentice tackling his sixth short story; it also betrays, far more significantly than the stagey plot for which we can find plenty of contemporary parallels, the world-weary pose of a sensitive youth who is anxious to persuade himself that, faced by life, he can 'take it or leave it'— and who best takes it, with immense and successful artistic industry, when he seems most obstinately to leave it.

What is so delightful about *Watch and Ward* and the earliest stories is the evidence that several main characteristics of the novelist's mature manner were already present, and often with assured mastery, in such youthful exercises. I would list three for illustration: first, the splendid economy of phrase, often in the form of an amusing metaphor, with which he pins down a character; secondly, the contrasting and highly comic use of deliberately inflated tongue-in-cheek verbosity; and thirdly, the first fresh confession of a love for the sights and sounds of Europe as they were discovered by the ardent young trans-Atlantic traveller—as young, let us remember, as the Rhodes and Fulbright scholars who rediscover them today, but rarely with such astonishing confidence of articulation.

Economy, in Henry James, of all people? Yes. A vignette from *A Landscape Painter* happens to use the word itself; and how this brusque comment by a twenty-three-year-old writer rings with the full timbre of his later style: 'When people have to economize with the dollars and cents, they have a right to be splendid in their feelings'. And what neater thumb-nail sketch could one desire than this, from the mawkish *Master Eustace* itself: 'He had the air of one for whom the moral of this fable of life has greater charms than the plot'? Or take a more extended though still simple image from the unsavoury *Guest's Confession*, which shows a characteristic combination of freshness and penetration:

. . . but there was another Mrs. Beck, visible chiefly to the moral eye, who seemed to me excessively wrinkled and faded and wordly-wise, and whom I used to fancy I could hear shaking about in this enamelled envelope, like a dried nut in its shell.

Inflation? Ah, yes; *that* is a quality one automatically expects from James. But how dismally some of his high-spirited *jeux d' esprit* have been misinterpreted! One way of avoiding this trap is simply to read James aloud. This habit should quickly establish acquaintance with his happy knack of tossing off precisely the sort of good-natured histrionic arrogance of phrase which, in the mouths of our wittiest friends, causes us to laugh aloud—and to laugh without any trace of that resentment or even sense of moral outrage which afflicts some critics when they meet it, in James, in print. Even the least considerable of these early tales may be found to hold passages of sheer delight for declamation aloud by those readers who remember that they are not the maunderings of a fat clubman soon to meet the Order of Merit and death, but the gleeful, exuberant fancies of an elegant young man still in his twenties and as lively, given his time and place, as any literate beatnik of today. Here are two short examples from an almost unknown story, *At Isella* (1871)—and if one cannot detect a teasing *joie de vivre* in these undergraduate-ish mockeries, then one may as well give up reading James altogether, for he never, to his very end, gave up the joys of eloquent mock-hyperbole:

... the peasants were straddling stolidly about the little central *place* in the hideous festal accoutrements of the rustic Swiss.

What was such a man as that doing up there on a lonely mountain top, watching the snow clouds from closed windows and doling out restorative cognac to frost-bitten wagoners?

There are splendid moments when these first two characteristics, economy and inflation, combine in one controlled phrase of sardonic social observation. Take, for example, again from the ugly story *Guest's Confession*, the terse description of Mrs. Beck's attitude towards a brash millionaire from the Western States whose wooing is, though welcome, a little crude: 'A silver-mine was all very well, but a lover fresh from the diggings was to be put on probation'. If one labels this sort of thing 'Wilde' or 'Firbank', there would be automatic assent. Label it 'James', and a fog of misremembered pomposities from the Rye years may intervene to dull the pleasure.

As for the third characteristic, the young writer's joyous reaction to his first travels in Europe, this may be reserved for full treatment in the next chapter. Here, it is enough, linking these first 'European' pieces to the other more numerous 'American' stories contributed to magazines at the same time, to put on record their simple excitement. As one of his characters in *Travelling Companions* (1870) exclaims of Milan: 'How it all wasn't Germany! how it couldn't have been Araminta, New Jersey!' Even the plodding American businessman in the same story is forced to admit: 'I want awfully ... to see if there is anything to be got out of a gondola'. For James's disillusionment, as in *The Spoils of Poynton*, with the sour acquisitiveness of much European culture, still lies far, far ahead. So, too, do the later stories in which concentration on the technique of presentation gradually obscures the fresh outline of the thing presented. Is there no passing hint, in all this prentice work, of the future change of stance? One might pluck from *Travelling Companions*, full as it is of innocent articulate love of Italy and its art, one snatch of dialogue which may point ahead to later complications:

> 'What is there here', I asked, 'that has moved you most, the painter or the subject?'
> 'I suppose it's the subject. And you?'
> 'I'm afraid it's the painter.'

How James's interest seemed to pass from the subject to the painter, from the painter to the canvas, and finally from the canvas to the easel and brush themselves, will appear all too soon. In squeezing the essence from *Watch and Ward* and the attendant stories of the youthful 'American' apprenticeship, it is important to recognize that long before James (and his later indiscriminate devotees) tried to persuade himself that his prime merit as a novelist lay in formal construction, he had given early proof of those finer qualities of human observation and verbal skill which bestow their incomparable stamp on every one of his tales and novels, however much they may differ in other respects. In staking this claim for James even in his earliest work, one gets singularly little formal help from the writer himself—the forbidding James of later legend. In his prefaces, in his letters, in his notebooks and critical essays, he was for ever patting and petting himself on the subject of themes and shapes, incidents and anecdotes, relationships and contrasts, dramatizations and confrontation. Most of his admirers have taken all this at face value and have shared, with a mesmeric professional interest, the endless musings and theorizings of this most self-conscious of novelists (until, of course, a critic like Mr. Maxwell Geismar, exasperated beyond endurance, invites us to empty out the baby with the bath-water).

But all this is of small concern to the general reader, who is interested only in results—as a *gourmet* rightly studies the menu rather than the cookery-book. And when one turns to the finished product, it is *not* in fact the much-lauded form that attracts one's attention, but rather the prime gift of perception. This gift James himself seems to have taken for granted, just as we all tend to take for granted those major benefits of brains, good looks or money with which we may have been endowed, perversely valuing much more highly some obscure acquired accomplishment. If an acquaintance with the work of the youthful James (the 'pre-James' James, almost) can help to establish his essential natural gifts, then it is easier, from the start, to grasp the nettle and admit that if the form of his stories is often too neat, balanced, artificial, inorganic, so too the actual subject-matter may at times be either grotesque or prim to the point of cowardice. Thus, an admittedly recurring theme in these earliest, as in all James's stories and novels, is the theme of withdrawal, non-attachment—call it what you will, but a reluctance, one way or another, to face life in general and the demands of love and marriage in particular. It is true that such pre-occupations do not necessarily detract, in themselves, from James's achievement, if only because of the uncomfortable fact that a goodly proportion of the human race *do* find in withdrawals and refusals their characteristic mode of self-expression. They remain, these sad creatures, raw material for a writer equally as valid as their braver colleagues. Yet the really important point is that the outer form and often restricted subject-matter of these tales, as of James's work as a whole, neither explain nor wholly detract from the vitality of his writing. If we insist on following James himself and most of his admirers in selecting these aspects of his work for special homage, then we are forced to take for granted (as he did) those other vivid qualities which make up the central body of his achievement, which illuminate everything he wrote, and which will alone give us patience to bear with him when, in mid-career, he first knots and then unravels the truly incidental business of 'presentation'.

Before turning to consider Henry James's rapturous literary treatment of Europe, we may glance at one 'American' story which he never collected in book form, perhaps because it represents his first direct onslaught on what he considered to be some of the provincial banalities of his homeland. This forgotten essay in social distaste, *Professor Fargo* (1874), presents in all his discreditable mock-finery a strutting charlatan who practises mesmerism and other 'manual blandishments' in the seedier country towns of New

England. 'The world has a horror of concentrated thought', shudders the narrator, whose own fastidiousness is not confined to the odious Professor Fargo who (sharing the narrator's country inn) was 'soon seated at a repast which indicated that the prophetic temperament requires a generous diet', but shrinks also from the hotel lobbies and other public places where 'the air seemed charged with that whimsical retention of speech which is such a common form of American sociability'.

In *Professor Fargo*, the young James's really vibrant horror of American vulgarity is unconcealed and unashamed. It is for this reason, I believe, that Professor Edel is mistaken in dismissing it as one of the 'recurrent potboilers' requiring 'no critical attention'. It has a freshness of observation—and more besides. The bogus 'professor' has a mild-mannered broken-down old scholar acting as a slavish stooge 'assistant', and this Colonel Gifford's mute daughter is an advance sketch for the full treatment of innocence flowering among squalid sectarians, Verena Tarrant of *The Bostonians*, just as Selah Tarrant, her father, will re-echo Fargo himself. The story quickly peters out once these rather touching characters have been portrayed. One remembers not the plot but the pathetic atmosphere of drab unsuccessful chicanery, of gullible farm-hands and of decrepit New York mission-halls, of ignorance and doomed innocence and the miseries of commercial failure in a community which has placed all its emotional capital in material success. It is raw, wounded, quite unlike the work of the apparently composed author of the next few years. *Professor Fargo* is the one early story in which Henry James embodied those strong negative reactions to America which are hinted at in an occasional letter. It offers a curious springboard for the passionate young pilgrim's leap towards his first full love-affair with Europe.

There would, naturally enough, be compensations and reappraisals later in his writing career. The novel *The Europeans* would celebrate, via the reluctant appreciation of visiting Europeanized sophisticates, all those virtues of New England civilization which are passed over in *Professor Fargo*. Nor would it be just to close the briefest account of James's American apprenticeship to the art of fiction without glancing ahead at one representative example of the way in which he was to embrace a critical but obstinate affection for

America within his capacious sympathy for all manifestations of culture (in the strictly anthropological sense of the word). As one of his first critics declared as early as 1879,* after some of his 'European' stories and the tell-tale *Professor Fargo* had had time to make some impact, 'to be really cosmopolitan a man must be at home even in his own country'. The immediate context of the remark was peevish, but the point is a sound one and James himself would have agreed with it. His most entertaining collections of aphorisms on America were to follow a year or two later, in the story *The Point of View* (1882). Story? Hardly. It is, rather, an animated series of exceedingly witty essays on contemporary America as viewed by different Europeans and Europeanized Americans. Many of the adverse comments are comic enough to make a reader laugh aloud, not once or twice but with repeated enjoyment. The sacred heart of the nation, Washington's Capitol, is described as 'a labyrinth of spittoons'; there are affrighted references to 'negroes who brush you with a big broom, as if they were grooming a horse'; there are shudders at American children and American hotels; there is yet another reference to a 'mesmeric healer' to prove that the special kind of fraudulence exemplified by Professor Fargo was still gnawing at the author's conscience and would continue to bother him until the full-scale treatment of the type in Selah Tarrant of *The Bostonians* would get it, for the moment, off his chest. But along with witticisms and blushes go some chastening home-truths of a more serious content. They are admissions of 'barbarous magnificence which in this country is the only alternative from primitive rudeness', and another character makes the charge even more specific: 'There is very little coarseness here—not quite enough, I think—though there is plenty of vulgarity, which is a very different thing.' There are, in this one brittle *jeu d'esprit* of *The Point of View*, scores of observations of the kind that still enliven debates over English-Speaking Union tea-urns on both sides of the Atlantic. One lady complains: 'In this country the people have rights, but the person has none', while another restores the balance with the observation that 'English girls, who know how to

* Thomas Wentworth Higginson, quoted in *The Question of Henry James*, ed. F. W. Dupee, 1948. In the Preface to his *Henry James: The Major Phase*, F. O. Matthiessen briefly but neatly disposed of later critical objections to James's deracination, notably by Van Wyck Brooks and V. K. Parrington.

speak ... don't know how to talk. My niece knows how to talk, but doesn't know how to speak'. All these harmless surface irritations are voiced in the spirit of the returning American traveller who was 'afraid she wouldn't like her native land, and that she shouldn't like not liking it'.

The counter-attack by other speakers in this cautionary tale, the more effective after so many surrenders to the contemporary European scale of values, shows that after his own saturation with Europe, James was still eminently capable of voicing the triumphs of his native land and not merely confessing that he 'shouldn't like not liking it'. No more loyal American sentiment could have been offered, in 1882, than the splendid definition: 'an aristocracy is bad manners organized'. How innocent, how virtuous does America sound when one has failed to be impressed by Europe's 'big, pompous armies'—'a pastime for children'. How proud is any New England farmer who can reflect on the 'stultified peasants of whom it takes so many to make a European noble'. And at least one returning American confesses, having 'got Europe off my back', 'how jolly it makes me feel'.

To trace these recurring spasms of American national loyalty throughout James's work would be a pleasant task but would encroach on the following chapter. It is enough to note the tendency, as an interim reminder that the young writer's début was made in America, on American themes, based often on American (as well as European) literary models, published in American magazines and praised, from the very beginning, by American readers.

The two best-known novels by James which have a wholly American setting are, of course, *Washington Square* (1880) and *The Bostonians*. The latter may more conveniently be studied, along with *The Princess Casamassima*, as a major statement of the author's concern to establish some workable balance between the claims of the public and the private life. *Washington Square* itself should be kept in mind, too, as one of the more striking examples of James's long preoccupation with the theme of escape—voluntary or involuntary—from marriage. Yet, coming as it does in the wake of three sustained efforts to come to terms, at novel length, with the contrasts of trans-Atlantic life (*Roderick Hudson*, *The American* and *The*

Europeans), the story is so steeped in the atmosphere of the New York of Henry James's youth that its charm of 'period' and 'atmosphere' are perhaps stronger, for a modern reader, than any moral problem posed by the plot. The near-passionate nostalgia for his New York childhood which glows in his late autobiographical work *A Small Boy and Others* (1913), was already present in *Washington Square*, written in the London of 1880 by an author already owning a sophisticated familiarity with Europe:

> It has a kind of established repose which is not of frequent occurrence in other quarters of the long, shrill city; it has a riper, richer, more honourable look than any of the upper ramifications of the great longitudinal thoroughfare—the look of having had something of a social history.
> ... it was here that your grandmother lived, in venerable solitude, and dispensed a hospitality which commended itself alike to the infant imagination and the infant palate; it was here that you took your first walks abroad, following the nursery-maid and sniffing up the strange odour of the ailanthus-trees which at that time formed the principal umbrage of the square, and diffused an aroma that you were not yet critical enough to dislike as it deserved. ... It was here, at any rate, that my heroine spent many years of her life; which is my excuse for this topographical parenthesis.

(Hardly, one might add, an excuse for dropping into the curious form of second-person narrative, as if half-way to the autobiographical first person!)

That irony which is rightly seen by Drs. F. R. and Q. D. Leavis as the prime characteristic of Dr. Sloper is by no means confined to him, but is also the tart and sometimes terrible flavour of the whole novel. Dr. F. R. Leavis, disagreeing with a comment by Matthiessen, wrote: 'I should have said that the whole point of the story depended upon the not obscurely presented datum that the father's ironic dryness covered something very different from "cruel egotism"' (*Scrutiny* XIV, 237). Mrs. Leavis shortly afterwards (*Scrutiny* XV, 74) reinforced the opinion, writing of *Washington Square* as 'a tragedy of the relations between an exceptionally brilliant father and a commonplace but worthy daughter'; it was the father's 'ironic tone' that acted as 'an insuperable barrier between them'. Yet Dr. Sloper's most cutting remarks (as when he comments, of Morris

Townsend's avowals, 'He is in love with this regal creature, then?') are not out of tone with his creator's sustaining narrative throughout this compact work of early maturity.* From the very first presentation of places and persons, the ironic tone is pervasive. Washington Square itself is not spared a sidelong sneer at its 'considerable quantity of inexpensive vegetation'. The ironic Dr. Sloper is himself introduced in merciless phrase: 'For a man whose trade was to keep people alive, he had certainly done poorly in his own family; and a bright doctor who within three years loses his wife and his little boy should perhaps be prepared to see either his skill or his affection impugned.' In the very same paragraph (the second paragraph of the novel) Catherine's future doom is sufficiently indicated: 'He had in hand a stock of unexpended authority, by which the child, in its early years, profited largely.' As for the Doctor's sister and Catherine's aunt, the addle-pated widow Mrs. Penniman, she collects throughout the novel a shower of poisoned darts under which a less lively creation would have succumbed altogether. Dr. Sloper, of course, views his sister and his daughter with equal distaste, intruding himself into a full-dress presentation of the lady which anticipates the set-piece portraits of Miss Birdseye and Mrs. Farrinder of *The Bostonians:*

Mrs. Penniman was a tall, thin, fair, rather faded woman, with a perfectly amiable disposition, a high standard of gentility, a taste for light literature, and a certain foolish indirectness and obliquity of character. She was romantic, she was sentimental, she had a passion for little secrets and mysteries—a very innocent passion, for her secrets had hitherto always been as unpractical as addled eggs. She was not absolutely veracious; but this defect was of no great consequence, for she never had anything to conceal. She would have liked to have a lover, and to correspond with him under an assumed name in letters left at a shop; I am bound to say that her imagination never carried the intimacy further than this. Mrs. Penniman had never had a lover, but her brother, who was very shrewd, understood her turn of mind. 'When Catherine is about seventeen,' he said to himself, 'Lavinia will try and persuade her that some young man with a moustache is in love with her. It will be quite untrue; no young man, with a moustache or without, will ever be in

* *Washington Square* is evidently too short to be considered a novel by Professor Cargill, who omits it from his otherwise complete survey of the novels.

love with Catherine. But Lavinia will take it up, and talk to her about it.
. . . Catherine won't see it, won't believe it, fortunately for her peace of
mind; poor Catherine isn't romantic.'

But by no means all these shafts are thrown by Dr. Sloper's hand:
there are enough left over for incidental pepperings:

Europe apparently had few surprises for Mrs. Penniman, who frequently remarked, in the most romantic sites: 'You know I am very
familiar with all this.' It should be added that such remarks were usually
not addressed to her brother, or yet to her niece, but to fellow-tourists
who happened to be at hand, or even to the cicerone or the goat-herd
in the foreground.

Nor is the doctor's presence required when use is made of his sister
to throw his daughter's character fully into relief:

If Catherine was quiet, she was quietly quiet, as I may say, and her
pathetic effects, which there was no one to notice, were entirely unstudied
and unintended. . . . But Mrs. Penniman was elaborately reserved and
significantly silent; there was a richer rustle in the very deliberate movements to which she confined herself, and when she occasionally spoke,
she had the air of meaning something deeper than what she said.

One unforeseen instance of irony, of course, is the present-day
popularity of *Washington Square* adapted for the stage (and later the
screen) as 'The Heiress'. For the theatrical success that eluded all
James's wooing has come, after his death, in the adaptation by other
hands of his non-dramatic stories—not only *Washington Square*, but
also *The Turn of the Screw*, *The Aspern Papers*, and even *The Wings
of the Dove*. That the quiet intensity of *Washington Square* can
sustain, with very little alteration, a full-length play and film, goes
to support Professor Edel's view that 'in the intensity of the narrative, the short scenes, the heightened dialogue, the clash of wills,
Henry James showed the mastery he had now attained'. One may
or may not follow Dr. Edel (II, 402–3) in seeing Dr. Sloper as
another fictional portrait of Henry's brother William, with Henry
himself, disguised as Catherine, 'trying to bide his time, avoiding
all overt action and hoping, by a kind of dogged persistence, to
triumph'.

The moral problem posed here is a direct outcome of a more imaginative treatment of the geminian author's old established habit of allocating antithetical characters between siblings disguised as cousins. Dr. Sloper's disapproval of Morris, the one of the Townsend cousins favoured as suitor by his daughter, drives that young man about his business when he discovers that the girl, whose dowry forms her sole attraction, would be disinherited by her father if he married her. The simple antithesis of character, adequately sketched in *Watch and Ward* nine years earlier against a similar American background, is here complicated by the intrusion of a more potent third party in the shape of Dr. Sloper (and thus, according to Dr. Edel, of brother William James). As a result, the reader is left not only with a handful of characters drawn with wit and economic irony, but also with a moral riddle larger than the book itself. Is it right to deny another person an experience which one supposes to be harmful? From one point of view, Dr. Sloper is right in estimating that the amiable good-for-nothing Morris would make a detestable husband:

'The sign of the type in question is the determination—sometimes terrible in its quiet intensity—to accept nothing of life but its pleasures, and to secure these pleasures chiefly by the aid of your complaisant sex. Young men of this class never do anything for themselves that they can get other people to do for them, and it is the infatuation, the devotion, the superstition of others that keeps them going. These others in ninety-nine cases out of a hundred are women.'

(In the hundredth case, says the unspoken corollary, it is a man: such a man as Rowland Mallet of *Roderick Hudson*, five years earlier; or, if we are to follow Dr. Edel's identification of Catherine, such a man as Henry James himself.)

Yet is Catherine any happier for being protected? Was it not wrong to prevent her natural impulses from flowering? She had all the patient equipment for 'helping' the handsome prodigal; perhaps, too, his probable ill treatment of her, much as it might have irritated the good Doctor to face competition in the polite exercise of sadism, would have supplied the missing significance in her life? In an indirect way, at any rate, the problem is resolved. Catherine's character, developed in spite of itself in the course of her sudden achievement of womanhood as she faces the implications of her choice, adjusts itself in the end quite naturally to spinsterhood. It might, but for a hair's breadth difference, have adapted itself equally easily to the lot of an ill-served wife. If characters are to be assessed not by what happens to them but by how they meet each accidental event and how they tread one or other of several possible paths, then it matters little what particular thing happens. This may seem no very fruitful doctrine for a teller of tales, and it is nowhere made explicit in *Washington Square*. Yet the full implication of James's antithetical approach to experience must be, in the end, that supremacy of personality over incident which, for all his endless manipulation of 'situations' and organization of 'ados', would become typical of his best work.

One thing is certain. The success of *Washington Square*, within its narrow and wholly American limits, shows that although James would come to win his distinctive fame as an 'international' novelist and would find reasons for preaching the doctrine that 'the flower of art blooms only where the soil is deep', yet the practice and the doctrine were *chosen* by him and not imposed upon him by artistic necessity. The Catherine Sloper whose own stubbornness in the face of parental bullying recalls the family likeness between Cordelia and King Lear, and who in the last words of the novel settles down to her spinster's fancy-work 'for life, as it were', owes nothing whatever to European models. Had he been so minded, Henry James could have remained, as he started, a purely American writer.

In 1908, nearly thirty years after writing *Washington Square*, Henry James published a story, *The Jolly Corner*, which was one of the fruits of his return to his homeland in 1904, after an absence of some twenty-one years. (The major literary harvest of that highly significant rediscovery, the collection of essays and sketches published in 1907 as *The American Scene*, is still immensely readable, but can claim no space in this present survey of his fiction.) It is a story which might be studied in the context of several of my succeeding chapters. Its confrontation of the hero with his ghostly *alter ego* makes it a prime instance of James's lifelong fascination with the notion of two twin-like personalities inhabiting one consciousness; its toying with the supernatural places it alongside such better-known essays in the macabre as *The Turn of the Screw*; the pointed contrast between its might-have-been stay-at-home American and its actual cosmopolitan returned prodigal gives it title to being one of the larger sops thrown to 'the international Cerberus'. But it demands notice at this point, as a coda to any consideration of the 'American' James, because it displays, only thinly disguised in semi-spooky form, his own notion of what he *might* have become if he had stayed at home.

The bare outline of the tale is simple enough: Spencer Brydon returns, after a long absence in Europe, to his childhood home in New York, where he meets the ghost of his *alter ego*, the 'other' Spencer Brydon of today who has developed, in America, from the point at which the actual Spencer Brydon departed. It is, on one level, a competent horror-story in a subdued key, for there is a sustained *tour de force* build-up of tension in that dark empty house when Brydon begins to feel certain that something, someone, is there, and realizes that the 'someone' is another version of himself. Even before this half-guilty, half-horrified confrontation with the true 'American' he might have become, however, Brydon has been shown reacting sharply to the impressions made by New York on his normal senses—'the differences, the newnesses, the queernesses, above all the bignesses . . .' He finds a nostalgic charm (as did James himself when, later still, he turned to write his autobiographical *A Small Boy and Others*) in those very scenes that had struck him, as an over-sensitive youth, as 'ugly'. It is not, any longer, the squalours and simple chicaneries of *Professor Fargo* that offend; what now fills him with loathing is the 'swagger' new city, typified by the 'dreadful multiplied numberings' which have turned the old Washington Square district into 'some vast ledger-page', or by the modern street-cars, 'terrible things that people scrambled for as the panic-stricken at sea scramble for the boats'. Assaulted by twin waves of nostalgia and revulsion, Brydon is already prepared to admit himself a prey to 'morbid obsession' by the time he falls to brooding, in the lonely shell of his old home, 'What would it have made of me?'

Strangely enough, he begins to feel for the first time in his life a stirring of interest in property, in urban development, in the possibility of money-making. Is *this* what he had so benignly missed by

running away to hide his old identity among new European values?
'It comes over me that I had then a strange *alter ego* deep down
somewhere within me, as the full-blown flower is in the small tight
bud, and that I just took the course, I just transferred him to the
climate, that blighted him for once and for ever.' His friend Alice
Staverton, to whom, like Lambert Strether of *The Ambassadors*
using poor Maria Gostrey as his sounding-board, Brydon retails
his New York self-communings, suggests that this other American
flower would have been 'quite splendid, quite huge and monstrous';
that Brydon, in short, would have tasted 'power'. Is it *this*, 'the
rank money-passion' of America, that Brydon—or Henry James—
is most piqued to have missed? If so, it would confirm 'the theory
of many superficially-judging persons ... that he was wasting his
life in a surrender to sensations'. We are back at the crucial watershed of James's own life, back at the point where parental scorn of
commerce allied with his own fear of engaging in physical competition to dictate his official future strategy. Whether that strategy
were now to be assessed as having been a cowardly retreat from
American reality, or a heroic advance into citizenship of a wider
spiritual and intellectual world, was the unresolvable problem Henry
James was now seeking, via Spencer Brydon and his *doppelgänger*,
to probe. When the mystical confrontation occurs, it is a melodramatic justification of the path Brydon had in fact trodden. For
his *alter ego*, when the ghostly figure lowers his hands from the face
which they had 'buried as for dark deprecation', reveals a countenance which the commercial life had rendered 'unknown, inconceiv-
able, awful'. Brydon faints, to awake in the nest-lap of Alice
Staverton—to whom in her sympathetic dreams the 'stranger ...
evil, odious, blatant, vulgar' had also made its horrible appearance.
Both Brydon and Miss Staverton had noticed, as he tried to screen
his ravaged features, that the ghostly or dreamlike figure was
missing two of his fingers. At the end of the tale, Brydon is reprieved:
he has Alice, he is *not* a hideous billionaire—*and* he has not lost
his fingers. I do not know whether this final proof of identity has
been spotted as an instance of long-forgotten castration-complex?
It seems to me too striking to be ignored. If *this* is the price the
young Henry James felt he would have to pay for full involvement,
like his brothers, in American life and particularly in full physical

life, then it is hardly surprising that his resolve to follow the intellectual rôle of observing rather than doing was to be buttressed by so many vehement protestations, in letters and notebooks and autobiographical exercises.

There is, at any rate, throughout this powerfully affecting late story a haze of self-hugging memory, not of the directly emotive Proustian kind or the straight evocative kind that James himself could release at other times, but rather a pampered, murky, guilty, nightmarish quality. Underneath all the long international obsession, the long devotion to art, was there to have lurked all this time in James's deepest 'wells of unconscious cerebration' a remorse that for the sake of 'the proved identity' of having kept all his fingers unsliced, he had somehow shirked his birthright?

II

The Passionate Pilgrim

The Sense of the Past

That was the way many things struck me at that time, in England—as reproductions of something that existed primarily in art or literature. It was not the picture, the poem, the fictive page, that seemed to me a copy; these things were the originals, and the life of happy and distinguished people was fashioned in their image.

The Author of 'Beltraffio'

So MUCH has happened to the Continent of Europe—including the British Isles—since Henry James began his methodical pilgrimage in the 1870's, that it is difficult to grasp, without some conscious effort of imagination, just why it was then so gem-studded a shrine for a sensitive young American. Pre-war Europe with its strident little nationalities and its goose-stepping children; the post-war Europe of ruin and desolation; these images rise up unbidden between us and the young traveller from the New World. And because we cannot hope to recall *his* Europe, it would probably help readers of my own generation to recall at least the notion of Europe in the 1920's: the Europe before the blackshirts and the bullies in dirty raincoats took over; when the London summer still called itself a Season and the name France evoked a picture not of sullen *gloire* but rather of villages dusty in the sunlight, of Proust's Balbec, Panama Hats and *brioches*.

It has often been suggested, and will be suggested again in later chapters of this book, that Henry James came to allow his interest in the predicament of Americans in Europe (and, to a lesser extent, of Europeans in America) to distort or divert the genius he had already shown, in his early tales and novels, for a loving preoccupation with the general human predicament. 'National' characteristics loom as large in much of the work of his early maturity as 'social' characteristics loomed large in the work of his latter years; and readers who happen by chance upon these stories rather than upon those in which his concentration on 'personal' characteristics is least distracted, may be forgiven if they find him tediously prone to national caricatures animated against a travelogue, or social caricatures animated (barely!) against a series of trivial complacent salons. It should, however, be a simple matter to show how his interest in society grew out of his interest in the conscious behaviour of individuals *in* society—and Proust could be adduced as a fashionable witness in sympathy. Similarly, it can readily be held that Henry James's preoccupation with the interrelations of the representatives of trans-Atlantic cultures sprang only from his attempt to externalize or universalize his own deep personal concern with his own reactions as an American plunging willingly into the European scene.

The notion of Henry James as a being enslaved from earliest childhood by a preternatural nostalgia for Europe is too well established to need much stress (people who have not ventured beyond *The Turn of The Screw* and the dramatized version of *The Aspern Papers* seem qualified to endorse this account), and in many important ways it is too accurate a notion to require much modification. His letters and autobiographical volumes are chock-full of references to 'that sense of "Europe" to which I felt that my very earliest consciousness waked'. His parents spent the summer of 1844 in Europe and took with them their baby sons William and Henry: Henry had been born in April 1843, but he claims that his memories of Paris date from this pilgrimage undertaken at the ripe age of one year and some few months. 'I had been hurried off to London and to Paris immediately after my birth, and then and there, I was ever afterwards strongly to feel, that poison had entered my veins.' When he was twelve, he returned to Europe with his family on a leisurely three-year trip which took him to Geneva, London, Paris, Boulogne; looking back on that wonderful experience nearly sixty years later, he could still conjure up indulgent memories of the rich inrush of impressions—as, to pick a random example, of 'the incomparable passage, as we judged it, of the Prince Imperial borne forth for his airing or his progress to Saint Cloud in the splendid coach . . . beside which the *cent-gardes*, all light-blue and silver and intensely quick jolt, rattled with pistols raised and cocked'.

The point of these and successive impressions, however, is not so much that they were impressions of Europe as that they were impressions of unusual quality and clarity. If it is important to recognize in the young James a quivering sensibility to European culture, it is still more important to recognize a similar sensitivity to everything else he saw, smelt, touched, tasted, or merely conjectured. When he attempted, late in life, to shake out 'the whole content of memory and affection in each enacted and recovered moment', he had to admit that from the first dawning of consciousness 'aspects began to multiply and images to swarm'. 'I saw my parents homesick', he wrote, 'for the ancient order'—but musing on those years he can recall not only the longing for Europe but also the minutest tinge and flavour of that old New York in which the longings came to him. He can give us glimpses of the city, scenes alive with accidental figures like those straw-hatted or long-skirted fauna who so oddly populate old picture-postcards, and scenes not only of a romantic vanished mid-nineteenth-century security, but also of dentists' waiting-rooms and of ice-cream parlours, of 'rank and rubbishy waterside quarters', of districts where 'the squalor was a squalor wonderfully mixed and seasoned, and ... I should wrong the whole impression if I didn't figure it first and foremost as that of some vast succulent cornucopia'.

This, then, is the primary motive for James's own passionate pilgrimage—a restless need ever to increase the scope of his awareness, the perimeter of his vast bland sensitivity to impressions. A secondary motive, easier to distinguish and fatally easy to misrepresent, is the narrower but cognate desire to turn away from the relatively meagre diet set before his complex sensibility by the American cultural scene in the 1860's and 1870's, and to seek out the richer nourishment of the European civilization he had but glimpsed for himself, but which was the daily preoccupation of his parents and which he was tasting in anticipation as he devoured European writing. This dissatisfaction with the American mental menu was acknowledged time and again throughout his life, and never more acutely than when it was accompanied by a feeling of guilt at his apparent ingratitude of response to the country of his birth and the people who were, after all, his comrades and compatriots. Quite early in life he was wondering, in the words of the Max Beerbohm cartoon, if he should 'find hard to swallow ... the great idea that I am—oh ever so indigenously—one of them!'

In the first pages of his study of Nathaniel Hawthorne (published in the English Men of Letters series, 1879), Henry James announced his view that 'the flower of art blooms only where the soil is deep, that it takes a great deal of history to produce a little literature, that it needs a complex social machinery to set a writer in motion'. He went on to make it thoroughly explicit that in his view America provided no such soil, no such machinery. As he saw it, Americans devoted to the world of business the energies which Europeans were still devoting to the world of ideas and perceptions. 'Before the

American business-man', he confesses in the Preface to Vol. XIII of the New York Edition, 'I was absolutely and irredeemably helpless, with no fibre of my intelligence responding to his mystery.' Henry James Senior, himself the scion of 'a prosperous man of business, whose successful career left him in a position to bequeath to his numerous descendants a fortune large enough to enable them all to live in complete independence of the commercial world',* encouraged his family to cultivate a studious aloofness from the clamorous demands of an age given over to bargaining and salesmanship. His son, writing after a lifetime of aversion from the mercantile, almost shudders with distaste as he pays the filial tribute: 'business in a world of business was the thing we most agreed (differ as we might on minor issues) in knowing nothing about.' Perhaps this horror had something to do with his confession that 'I so feared and abhorred mathematics that the simplest arithmetical operation had always found and kept me helpless and blank'. It certainly added vigour to his devastating comments on British commercialism when he discovered that the inhabitants of the Fortunate Isles had tended their immemorial lawns with avarice as well as with devotion, and that some owners of mellow libraries and time-hallowed master-pieces of painting looked upon their inheritance exclusively in terms of market value. But these disillusionments in particular instances in no way contradicted his own early longing for the old dispensation—indeed, they demonstrate, on the contrary, that the zeal of his pilgrimage never died.

He shared fully in the general restlessness of the James family. Between the years 1858 (when he returned to America, aged fifteen, at the end of the three-year tour) and 1876 (when he made his first serious attempt to settle in London, at the age of thirty-three), we can trace his passages to and fro across the Atlantic, follow him to Geneva, Harvard, Liverpool and the English country towns, Venice, Florence, Rome, America again, back to Switzerland, Paris, Homburg, Rome and Florence again, back to Cambridge (Massachusetts), Paris in the autumn of 1875, and so back to London where, writing steadily and leaping now and then to the Continent for some fresh or renewed impressions, he maintained his headquarters until late in 1881, when he returned to America. In the spring of

* Percy Lubbock, Introduction to Volume I of his edition of the *Letters* (1920)

1882 he returned to London, and did not visit America again for more than twenty years.

Add to the early passionate conscious greed for impressions ('such, in small very plastic minds, is the intensity, if not the value, of early impressions') a disposition—epitomized in the quotation from *The Author of 'Beltraffio'* at the head of this chapter—to view the world of nature through the world of art, and the complementary impulses behind Henry James's own pilgrimage are revealed. It is difficult to tear 'examples' from his writings, for the whole canon is bathed from first to last in the light of this conscious view of life. There are, however, in some of the earlier tales, passages which reflect this light at its purest, undimmed by social criticism or the carefully arranged filters of his later preoccupation with formal construction. Nowhere is the Promised Land more serenely and happily viewed than in the eager innocent tributes to England embodied in *The Passionate Pilgrim* itself (written in 1870, printed in the following year, and issued in book form with other stories in 1875).

The narrator meets the American traveller Clement Searle in the grounds of Hampton Court and:

> I foresaw that I should find him a true American full of that perplexing interfusion of refinement and crudity which marks the American mind. His perceptions, I divined, were delicate; his opinions, possibly, gross. On my telling him that I too was an American he stopped short and seemed overcome with emotion . . .*

* In all quotations from the tales, I have followed Mr. Leon Edel's sensible choice of 'the original book form of the story where there was one'. Such of the tales as were later revised for the New York Edition of 1907–9 suffered changes which, whatever else their merit, blur the freshness and occasional naïveté of the original version, which are precisely the qualities I wish to stress in this present chapter. The reader may be interested in a brief sample of the later revisions: the passage here quoted re-emerges, with small but subtle touches of elderly sophistication, thus:

> I foresaw that I should find him quite to the manner born—to ours; full of glimpses and responses, of deserts and desolations. His perceptions would be fine and his opinions pathetic; I should moreover take refuge from his sense of proportion in his sense of humour, and then refuge from *that*, ah me!—in what? On my telling him that I was a fellow citizen he stopped short, deeply touched . . .

Over 'a bottle of excellent Burgundy' (which in the New York Edition has become 'tolerable Burgundy', as befits a wiser author who had come to confront the privileged life on knowing terms), the allied pilgrims drink in the scene, 'the England of my visions' (which, again, was to become, world-wearily, 'the England of one's early reveries'):

> Over against us, amid the deep-hued gloom of its ordered gardens, the dark red palace, with its formal copings and its vacant windows, seemed to tell of a proud and splendid past; the little village nestling between park and palace, around a patch of turfy common, with its tavern of gentility, its ivy-towered church, its parsonage, retained to my modernized fancy the lurking semblance of a feudal hamlet. It was in this dark composite light, that I had read all English prose; it was this mild moist air that had blown from the verses of English poets; beneath these broad acres of rain-deepened greenness a thousand honoured dead lay buried.*

And when, later, the two friends venture into the English countryside, the careful balanced narrative glows with a warmth which could never be traced solely to the habit of reading English novelists and looking at English lithographs; there is a happy assurance about it all which is in significant contrast to the melodramatic motivation of these observers as 'characters'.

> The noble friendliness of the scenery, its subtle old-friendliness, the magical familiarity of multitudinous details, appealed to us at every step and at every glance. Deep in our souls a natural affection answered. The whole land, in the full, warm rains of the last of April, had burst into sudden perfect spring. The dark walls of the hedgerows had turned into blooming screens; the sodden verdure of lawn and meadow was streaked with a ranker freshness. We went forth without loss of time for a long walk on the hills. Reaching their summits, you find half England unrolled

---

* I cannot refrain from one final comparison with the New York Edition. The septuagenarian James, among other elaborations, makes the past no longer 'proud and splendid' but 'definite and massive'; the tavern is no longer 'of gentility' but merely 'of figurative names': the innocent 'feudal hamlet' becomes, to a historian who had experienced more harshly the material basis of Edwardian aristocracy, 'the property of a feudal lord'. Most significant of all, alike in its sadness and its still-besotted, still-palpable sense of beauty, is the new version of the last quoted phrase: 'I seemed to feel the buried generations in the dense and elastic sod.'

at your feet. A dozen broad counties, within the vast range of your vision, commingle their green exhalations. Closely beneath us lay the dark, rich flats of hedgy Worcestershire and the copse-checkered slopes of rolling Hereford, white with the blossom of apples. At widely opposite points of the large expanse two great cathedral towers rise sharply, taking the light. . . .

And going further yet we entered the town,—where surely Miss Austen's heroines, in chariots and curricles, must often have come a-shopping for swan's-down boas and high lace mittens;—we lounged about the gentle close and gazed insatiably at that most soul-soothing sight, the waning, wasting afternoon light, the visible ether which feels the voices of the chimes, far aloft on the broad perpendicular field of the cathedral-tower; saw it linger and nestle and abide, as it loves to do on all bold architectural spaces, converting them graciously into registers and witnesses of nature; tasted, too, as deeply of the peculiar stillness of this clinical precinct; saw a rosy English lad come forth and lock the door of the old foundation school, which marries its hoary basement to the soaring Gothic of the church, and carry his big responsible key into one of the quiet canonical houses; and then stood musing together on the effect on one's mind of having in one's boyhood haunted such cathedral shades as a King's scholar; and yet kept ruddy with much cricket in misty meadows by the Severn.

The 'story' of this early essay is of small consequence; the character of the English Miss Searle, the lady of Lackley Park, is merely the most precious item in the narrator's collection of curiosities:

Of all the old things I had seen in England, this mind of Miss Searle's seemed to me the oldest, the quaintest, the most ripely verdant; so fenced and protected by convention and precedent and usage; so passive and mild and docile. I felt as if I were talking with a potential heroine of Miss Burney.

Even the considerable dash of bitterness in the sketch of this good lady's brother is less an attempt at a character study than the personification of the pilgrim's consciousness, in the midst of so much garnered beauty, of his excluded state:

Our host, with great decency, led the conversation to America, talking of it rather as if it were some fabled planet, alien to the British orbit, lately proclaimed indeed to have the proportion of atmospheric gases required to support animal life, but not, save under cover of a liberal afterthought, to be admitted into one's regular conception of things. I, for my part, felt nothing but regret that the spheric smoothness of his universe should be strained to cracking by the intrusion of our square shoulders.

And social criticism, when it does appear, comes only as a pious version of this same disinherited objectivity:

Noblesse oblige: Oxford obliges. What a horrible thing not to respond to such obligations. If you pay the pious debt to the last farthing of interest, you may go through life with her blessing; but if you let it stand unhonoured, you are a worse barbarian than we!

There is, finally, a passage describing the Lackley peacock which brings together in small compass three aspects of the early James: first, his feeling for 'the genius of stately places' (to adopt the phrase with which he later replaced the words 'the very genius of antique gardenry' in the following quotation); secondly, his attempt to use his characters mainly as the exponents of a point of view; and thirdly, his tendency (as though to compensate for the passivity of the first two aspects) to rely on a stiff old-fashioned staginess to agitate his figures and animate his scene. (The modification of this third quality and the development of the other two—especially the second—would make up, in short, the main burden of James's own artistic pilgrimage). Here, with the three ingredients still awkwardly mixed, is the passage:

The scene had a beautiful old-time air; the peacock flaunting in the foreground, like the very genius of antique gardenry; the broad terrace, which flattered an innate taste of mine for all deserted promenades to which people may have adjourned from formal dinners, to drink coffee in old Sèvres, and where the stiff brocade of women's dresses may have rustled autumnal leaves. . . .

'The peacock has done for you, Mr. Searle,' said his cousin, 'what he does only for very great people. A year ago there came here a duchess to see my brother. I don't think that since then he has spread his tail as wide for anyone else by a dozen feathers.'

If we set *The Passionate Pilgrim* alongside *Flickerbridge*, a short story printed in 1902, we shall see that James's characterization has improved out of all knowledge during the thirty years' interval, that a tendency to melodrama has changed to a rooted habit of understatement, but that the glow of love for traditional England has not been extinguished by his experience of the seamy side of English social life. Indeed, *Flickerbridge* presents the old enchantment at its tenderest and subtlest, with just enough plot, mainly in the interplay of quiet characters, to sustain the mood. Frank Granger, who is engaged to be married to a competent young American publicist, comes to England and visits Flickerbridge, the ancestral home of his fiancée's distant cousin. He falls in love with the place. His respect for the peace of mind of its timid chatelaine, Miss Wenham, becomes so strong that he breaks off his engagement rather than run the risk of introducing his young lady to the place —her bright zeal would, he feels certain, spoil everything by making both the place and the owner self-conscious. It is, frankly, an incredible theme, and only a Henry James hero would behave with such wry sensitive self-effacement. But the theme is less notable than the mellowing of the author's regard for the England of his youthful dreams: he sticks to his view, but he is no longer unaware of the finer implications of a society maintaining a losing fight for the preservation of its heritage:

The scene was as rare as some fine old print with the best bits down in the corners. Old books and old pictures, allusions remembered and aspects conjectured, reappeared to him; he knew now what anxious islanders had been trying for in their backward hunt for the homely.

Nor is he unaware, now, of the danger of brushing the bloom by too sudden a snatch:

Supreme beauty suddenly revealed is apt to strike us as a possible illusion playing with our desire—instant freedom with it to strike us as a possible rashness.

The full measure of James's advance in his pilgrimage, however, is to be observed—along with the mastery of prose indicating a far milestone on that other pilgrimage to the perfection of his chosen medium—in the more assured manner in which *people* are examined as worthy or unworthy exponents of the culture on which they are nourished. Miss Searle of Lackley Park was merely 'the heroine of a last-century novel'; Miss Wenham of Flickerbridge is not only the living spirit of the rich reticences of her setting, she is also worthy to take her place in the author's gallery of English female gentility in its unmarried semi-eccentric and wholly timorous guise —the Pre-Raphaelite Miss Ambient of *The Author of 'Beltraffio'*, Lady Aurora Langrish in *The Princess Casamassima*, and a host of other sympathetic spinsters. The point is, I think, that just as James has 'seen through' his early romantic version of England and can still treasure, with the wiser valuation of experience, the real worth behind his dream, so in treating his living exponents he can now observe them with a detachment offering much scope for straight satire, and still reserve the right to lay aside the rapier and extend instead an understanding, a forgiving hand of friendship. He is now wise where once he was merely clever, compassionate in his disillusion where once he was trying to be 'knowing'. There is a lifetime of real appreciation between the Burgundy of *The Passionate Pilgrim* whether 'excellent' or 'tolerable', and the 'wafted gratitude' sanctifying the grotesque figure of Miss Wenham:

Miss Wenham, fifty-five years of age and unappeasably timid, unaccountably strange, had, on her reduced scale, an almost Gothic grotesqueness; but the final effect of one's sense of it was an amenity that accompanied one's steps like wafted gratitude. More flurried, more spasmodic, more apologetic, more completely at a loss at one moment and more precipitately abounding at another, he had never before in all his days seen any maiden lady. . . .

She wore on the top of her head an upright circular cap that made her resemble a caryatid disburdened, and on other parts of her person strange combinations of colours, stuffs, shapes, of metal, mineral and plant . . . she approached objects, subjects, the simplest questions and answers and the whole material of intercourse, either with the indirectness of terror or with the violence of despair. These things, none the less, the refinements of oddity and intensities of custom, her betrayal at once of conventions and simplicities, of ease and of agony, her roundabout, retarded suggestions and perceptions, still permitted her to strike her guest as irresistibly charming.

When Henry James died in 1916, he left among other unfinished works the opening sections of the third volume of his autobiography, *The Middle Years* (not to be confused with the story of the same name). He had set it aside at the onset of the Great War. Its opening pages hark back to the spring of 1869, to the Adelphi Hotel at Liverpool, to Half Moon Street in London, and to the intense joy of 'discovering' England, so intense that even his breakfasts of those days are vivid in recollection: 'I dare say it is the invitations to breakfast that hold me at this moment by their spell—so do they breathe to me across the age the note of a London world that we have left far behind . . .' As Professor Matthiessen has noticed, a parallel detailed nostalgia creeps into *The Sense of the Past*, that ambitious parable on which he was intermittently engaged at the same time. The last of all James's passionate pilgrims, Ralph Pendrel, links his first appreciation of such things as 'the inveterate muffin-plate that protected at breakfast the tepidity of his slop-bowl' with the excitement with which 'Columbus had caught on *his* immortal approach the spices of the Western Isles'. This astonishing novel must be studied in its proper place; but its beautiful relevance to the wide-eyed Clement Searle of forty-five years earlier, begs for brief acknowledgement here.

In *The Sense of the Past*, the unfinished novel on the revision of which Henry James was at work at the close of his long career, we are taken back into the old, old dream of the passionate pilgrim, the dream based on James's boyhood saturation in English history and English fiction, the dream of an inheritance which would allow a modern American 'to "come in" for something strange and storied, ancient and alien'. It is his most determined effort to burst through the barriers of geography and history, to grasp in his own hands that unattainable joy of inherited aristocratic consideration for which so many of his earlier heroes had sighed in vain. And at the same time, it is his most thoroughgoing renunciation of all that the dream entails—a disillusionment far beyond the more wary social judgements of *Flickerbridge*, a destructive, almost penitential, rending apart of the very fabric of romantic history. It is a renunciation that goes further than the simple desire to shrug off the weight of the past—the sort of release which caused Jung to remark, contrasting Zurich with Basle, 'here you were not weighed down by the brown fog of the centuries, even though one missed the rich background of culture'.* *The Sense of the Past*—or, rather, the extensive notes James had dictated for its unfinished chapters— attacks the very moral basis of the enchanted past and prefers, by implication, the standards of the more mundane present; the 'present', that is, of Edwardian London. Which, paradoxically, will strike most modern readers who have a social conscience as being quite immoral enough.

It was, after all, always the *legacy* of the past that had fascinated James as man and author. His efforts to rethink himself into the past by the conscious use of historical imagination were strangely rare, and even more rarely successful. What the opaque pages of *The Sense of the Past* make crystal clear is that James, as passionate pilgrim, hankered always after his own notion of *quality*.

Desmond MacCarthy, commenting on James's squeamish fasti- diousness, remarked: 'I do not think he could have sat without pain in a chair, the stuffing of which was visible in places.' The same critic, working like James himself from the surface downwards, goes on to make the splendid claim: 'He cared immensely for spiritual decency; nothing in life beguiled him into putting anything before that.' It is as if, in *The Sense of the Past*, James made his superhuman (super- natural, anyway) leap into the world of the perfectly stuffed and perfectly shapely chair, only to discover, by a more significant application of that same moral-aesthetic sensibility, that the world of the gracious chair was in essence as flawed as his own. In the early days of his pilgrimage the accent may well have rested, for a time, on the stuffing of the chair. His development as a novelist carried him to the use of that same discrimination as a touchstone for the subtlest overtones of human relationships. Indeed, it will be well to remember when one comes to tackle the last phase of James's work, that the spectacle of his fictional characters sniffing at one another with awed expressions like 'You're wonderful!' is no more, and no less, absurd to the uninitiated than the exclamations of a collector tapping a rare piece of china or—to revert to Sir Desmond's image—purring over a rare chair of which the stuffing remains intact. The genuine, the uncorrupted, was the object of James's lifelong quest. The James of legend may be easily derided as a man outraged

* *Memories, Dreams, Reflections* (1963), p. 113.

by the oozing stuffing of a chair. The James of literature became almost a professional assessor of spiritual decency.

Thus far we have considered only the English pilgrimage. But before casting on England as his spiritual home, Henry James experienced the enchantment of France and the intoxication of Italy. One or two of the other tales printed along with *The Passionate Pilgrim* in 1875 show attractive evidence of the impact of Europe, an impact acknowledged with reasonable directness and not tricked out in terms of debate by the manipulation of 'international' characters. *Madame de Mauves* (1874) has its sour comments and its uneasy balance between the over-sensitive withdrawal of the American narrator, Longmore, and the highly 'Continental' cruelties and sufferings of the de Mauves family; but when the rhetoric and the staginess have been forgotten, the impression of an idealized French culture still remains in the reader's mind.

Madame de Mauves brings together in one bunch most of the threads that, singly or intertwined, may be traced through the products of another forty years of James's writing life. There is the sensibility of the passionate pilgrim; there is one of the least blurred examples of what, when he came to muse and mumble over it in the Preface to Volume XIII of the New York Edition, he called 'sops instinctively thrown to the international Cerberus formidably posted where I doubtless then didn't quite make him out'; there is yet another variation on the theme of withdrawal from the entanglement of marriage; the whole contrived affair is presented by a disappointed observer. Of the plot itself, James tells us some thirty years later in the Preface, 'not a glimmer of attendant reference survives'—yet it is significant that he could recall with an almost narcissistic rapture the 'dampish, dusky, unsunned room' of an inn at Bad Homburg where, as he 'sat in crepuscular comfort', the thirty-year-old writer struggled to come to terms with himself, in prose glowing for pages at a time with a sunny fluent confidence.

The American narrator, Longmore, is as bewitched by his combined ideal and experience of France as was Clement Searle, the eponymous Passionate Pilgrim, by his combined ideal and experience of England. Yet when he is introduced to Madame de Mauves, a 'sweet American girl' who had married an 'unclean Frenchman', his American chivalry is aroused and he seeks to comfort her disillusion without getting so close as to be dragged himself into the machinery of her unhappy situation. For the gentle Euphemia had started out with Longmore's own romantic conception of the French aristocratic life into which she had married: as a young convent girl 'she had a mental image of that son of the Crusaders who was to suffer her to adore him, but like many an artist who has produced a masterpiece of idealization, she shrank from exposing it to public criticism'. The husband she actually landed is first presented as a villain of cruel infidelity, and Longmore is outraged when the cynical baron broadly hints that if the visiting American should care to make love to his prim wife, he for his part would be greatly relieved. Euphemia has been described as 'profoundly incorruptible, and she cherished this pernicious conceit as if it had been a dogma revealed by a white-winged angel'. We soon begin to feel that the baron, *l'homme moyen sensuel*, is not such a villain after all. His old mother may have been right in advising her stiff-necked daughter-in-law: 'if you don't take life as a fifty years' mass, the only way to take it is as a game of skill'. Euphemia, alas, has neither devotion nor skill—only her New England conscience. As for the easy-going baron, 'he was a placid sceptic, and it was a singular fate for a man who believed in nothing to be so tenderly believed in'.

All this is skilfully done—but James's real skill as a story-teller lies elsewhere. Before we have a chance to grow impatient with the temporizing Longmore, whose high-minded projection of his own timidity upon the object of his spiritual one-man rescue-party begins to look like sheer physical funk, the rich gallery of minor figures plus a masterly evocation of the French countryside have combined to hold us captive within a charmed atmosphere. The passionate pilgrim may be growing disillusioned, to the point of theatricality, with his story-book aristocrats; but his eye for landscape has not deserted him, nor his amused imperious intelligence grown too stale to pin down in a few ironic asides his comic view of social forms. He notes that the high-born family de Mauves had been 'obliged to balance dinner-table allusions to feudal ancestors against the absence of side-dishes'. He notes that the baron's sister 'had made a remunerative match and sacrificed her name to the millions of a prosperous and aspiring wholesale druggist—a gentleman liberal enough to regard his fortune as a moderate price for being towed into circles unpervaded by pharmaceutic odours'. He may seem at first to share his unfortunate heroine's early romantic belief that 'the enjoyment of inherited and transmitted consideration, consideration attached to the fact of birth, would be the direct guarantee of an ideal delicacy of feeling', but it is not long before he succumbs to the more sophisticated tolerance with which the baron's sister viewed the probable social braveries of her female ancestors who gaze down from the walls:

'How they did it—go and look at the dusky faded canvases and pastels and ask. They were dear brave women of wit. When they had a headache they put on a little rouge and came to supper as usual, and when they had a heartache they touched up that quarter with just such another brush. These are great traditions and great precedents. . . .'

The young novelist's powers are best displayed in a lengthy portrait of Baron de Mauves, an intelligent penetration into a potentially complex character who could well have been developed to fill a major rôle in a full-length novel. Slowly, one's sympathy veers in his direction and away from his wife's, whose beloved Wordsworth struck him as '*soupe aux choux*'. Longmore himself, the paralysed knight-errant, is not immune; while stumbling unwillingly into an awkward state of 'passion' for Euphemia, he recognizes that the baron 'would like to have the comfort of feeling that his wife was as corruptible as himself'. Fortunately for Longmore's peace of mind, the lady remains rigid; if her accomplished husband could not persuade her that 'one may bend a trifle without breaking', still less could her starchy countryman, who instead drew from this reluctant chatelaine an admission of 'sometimes wishing I was the daughter of a poor New England minister, living in a little white house under a couple of elms, and doing all the house-work'. She is, at this moment, a self-indulgent female Benvolio. One imagines the young writer, in his Homburg inn, looking over his shoulder towards Cambridge, Massachusetts. Euphemia was, certainly, an example of an American female type which was never quite to lose attraction for him, even though he can be savage at their expense. Now and again, Euphemia is given the kind of edged rectitude he will display at greater amplitude in Isabel Archer of *The Portrait of a Lady*, as when she confesses: 'if my conscience will prevent me from doing anything very base, it will effectively prevent me from doing anything very fine.' Technically, so to say, she need not have worried: Longmore, the James-like narrator, confesses to 'aching impotence' and indulges in a melodramatic soliloquy about his penchant for renunciation.

At this very point, where the wheels of the little plot creak to a standstill, James treats us to a quasi-autobiographical idyll so natural and yet so curiously personal that the reader feels, for a moment, almost like one of the author's own Peeping Toms. The distracted Longmore takes refuge in a long country walk and comes to rest at a village inn. Sap rises again in the flagging prose as the passionate pilgrim turns his attention from the engulfing possibilities of human intercourse and gazes again, fresh-eyed, at the France of his imagination and experience. And suddenly Longmore invents from his observation, as if on behalf of his reawakened creator, an entirely fortuitous little parable with which to confront his sense of cowardice. At the inn, he watches with envious interest the free uninhibited behaviour of a jolly young painter and his girl-friend. The youth, to Longmore's pompously self-conscious vision, is 'a member of that jovial fraternity of artists whose very shabbiness has an affinity with the element of picturesqueness and unexpectedness in life which provokes a great deal of unformulated envy among people foredoomed to be respectable'. The inflation of style, self-protective, warns us that the author is nearing the quick. Are we to confront yet another repetition of the toils of Benvolio? Are Roderick Hudson and Rowland Mallet poised for yet another dialogue? How—we are tempted to ask—will the young writer in the Homburg inn argue himself out of *this* confrontation?

The small *dénouement* from this miniature drama is as revealing as anything written by Henry James at this stage of his career as a writer who is begging himself to believe that observation *is* action, that art *is* life. Poor thwarted Longmore finds a way out. He need not envy the young artist his cheerful young mistress: that would be too blatant a contrast to his own frustrated preparations for flight. No; he will envy him something *else*, something he himself (and here it is James, not the non-artistic Longmore, speaking) *can* adopt. It comes almost as a cry of triumph, this resolution. 'Was it his work, Longmore wondered, that made him so happy? Was a strong talent the best thing in the world?' This was to be, at any rate, James's own order for release. It is just after this introduction of the young painter and the claims of art, at any rate, that Longmore enjoys the consolation of a Freudian dream in which he is separated from his mistress by a river, but when he crosses to her side of the dividing stream he finds—aha!—that she is now on the side he has just left. And the boatman—aha! again—was the Baron de Mauves.

From this point onwards, the story of *Madame de Mauves* takes its predestined course of withdrawal and factitious *finale*: Longmore, in a scene as vividly realized as if something were actually about to happen, is sent away by the suffering Euphemia; when he fails to take her in his arms it is as if he himself has willed her to remain steadfast at her post, so clearly relieved is he. (The curious may find in the second volume of Mr. Leon Edel's biography, *The Conquest of London*, that Henry James himself at about this time was disentangling himself from too close a relationship with Mrs. Sarah Butler Wister). After a long-drawn-out measure of soliloquy, Longmore, divested finally of that golden atmosphere of pilgrimage which bathed the otherwise wooden figures of the charade, returns to America where he later learns that the baron, chilled by his wife's unforgiveness of his infidelities, had blown out his brains. It is a contemptuous ending, quite out of character—but it does rub in the moral, now second nature to the bachelor author, that, one way or another, marriage kills.

There was material here for a novel; it was treated at greater length, a year or two later, when another more substantial sop to the international Cerberus was thrown in the form of *The American*. Meanwhile, if in *Madame de Mauves* there are uncomfortable traces of the highly-charged renunciations which were to render bleak so much of James's later fiction, there is still present the first fine glow of his own enthusiastic response, as a cultivated traveller, to people and places. Indeed, an appreciative re-reading of all these 'passionate pilgrim' type stories may even lead one to the conclusion that for all the squirmings of the elder James as he seeks to persuade himself and us of his subtle arrangements of psychological types in exquisitely dramatic sequence, his real qualities as a writer were, from the start, of a very different order—were, in fact, those of an ironic essayist and descriptive reporter who had also mastered the seventeenth-century art of brilliant set-piece unmoving 'characters'. It is perhaps over-easy to track down immediate models for his plots in the works of Hawthorne and Balzac and the rest. When the stage plots are disregarded, it will be found that his actual kinship, in the work of his youth and early maturity, is closer to Sir Thomas Overbury and John Earle, to Nicholas Breton, the first Samuel Butler, and to John Aubrey himself.

It is worth recalling that at this crucial phase in Henry James's development, when the first fine frenzy of the passionate pilgrim was becoming fixed in the confronted trans-Atlantic attitudes of his international obsession, he was in fact earning his living as accredited foreign correspondent of a New York newspaper. To latter-day fanciers of the later James style, this very notion will probably come as a signal for raised eyebrows and the promise of grotesque hilarity. How *could* he? And what would the newspaper editor, let alone his readers, make of it all? Recalling James's later inability to dictate even a telegram without overspilling into subordinate clauses, such readers might expect to settle down to enjoy his newspaper despatches* with the kind of awesome amusement with which, revisiting *The Mikado*, one awaits the discomfiture of Pooh-Bah.

There are, of course, dozens of quotable passages from these *Letters* to confirm this view and satisfy this specialist anticipation. Imagine James, conscientiously reporting a ludicrous melodrama at the Théâtre Historique in 1876, finding himself seated among 'that class of amateurs who find the suspense of the entr'actes intolerable without the beguilement of an orange'. Imagine, with still greater private wonder, any present-day New York (or London) editor allowing his foreign correspondent to write: 'The day had that soft, humid mildness which, in spite of the inveteracy with which you are assured here that every biting blast is "exceptional", and which consequently piles up your accumulated conviction that it is the rule—is really the keynote, the *fonds*, as they say, of the Paris winter weather.'

Yet when these expected diversions have been enjoyed, the impressions chiefly remaining from the perusal of his twenty sizeable

* Henry James: *Parisian Sketches. Letters to the New York Tribune 1875–76*, edited by Leon Edel and Ilse Dusoir Lind, Hart-Davis, 1958.

essays for the New York *Tribune* of 1875–76 are the imperturbable common sense of the author and the quite astonishing patience of his editor. It is true that poor Mr. Whitelaw Reid's mild request that 'the letters should be made rather more "newsy" in character, and somewhat shorter', together with his tactful comment that 'the difficulty has sometimes been not that it was too good, but that it was magazine rather than newspaper work', stung the hypersensitive young author to reply: 'If my letters have been "too good" I can honestly say that they are the poorest I can do, especially for the money!' It is true, too, that after his brief labours had petered out, James could never afterwards refer to newspapers, in his fiction or his correspondence or his conversation, without exaggerated loathing. But the amplitude of these sketches, the willingness of the *Tribune* readers to swallow pages and pages of detailed descriptions of pictures in the Paris Salon, of highly allusive dramatic criticism, of such un-newsy items as a sentence like this: 'I am sure M. Taine, for instance, never meets of an evening a flannel-shirted, pea-jacketed, soft-hatted son of Albion, followed by his robust feminine shadow, all blonde chignon and linsey-woolsey, without murmuring to himself that the "Vikings" and "Berserkers", the offspring of the north wind and the sea fog, are not extinct'—all these manifestations of tolerance and the power of absorption must surely make any foreign correspondent of today writhe with envy and question James's views as to the ineradicable vulgarity of the popular press of his day.

James's assignment as special correspondent had come about through the good offices of John Hay, who recommended him to the editor as a young writer with a 'wonderful style and keen observation of life and character'. *This*, of course, is the real point of relevance to the stories and novels upon which he was engaged at this same period. During his Paris year the young novelist met Turgenev and the members of the Flaubert circle; he was busy with his own private elaboration of the international obsession which was then producing *The American* and would be the theme of many later stories; he was tingling with impressions of every kind and he claimed to have found the *Tribune* chore a dreadful burden supportable only for the money earned, which he thought in any case insufficient. But the articles show not the slightest sign of weariness: they are alert, entertaining, beautifully contrived, bubbling over with knowing fun and tremendous verbal high spirits; they are the product of a creative energy of a very high order in full healthy spate. These transient pieces of a writer working, by his own confession, against the grain, provide collateral evidence for one's view that it was his natural observant high spirits, and *not* his overrated structural gifts, which makes his fiction of these years worth reading. Even James's cautious appraisal of not very interesting paintings can still glow with the competence of his word-juggling, although the art criticism falls pretty hesitantly on the modern ear: 'Two naked athletes, in a sort of flesh-colored cave, are interlocking their arms and legs and clinching their teeth; but neither of them is moving an inch—which indeed is quite natural, as they are composed, to all appearance, of rose-colored granite.' And when, as so often, his Parisian impressions lure him into further reflections and interim generalizations, we can hear in these unlikely paragraphs and this youthful tone of voice a kind of anticipatory echo of the rhythmic generalship of the later Master himself:

But certainly France occasionally produces individuals who express the national conceit with a transcendent fatuity which is not elsewhere to be matched ... I don't know how it affects people who dislike French things to see their fantastic claims for their spiritual mission in the world, but it is extremely disagreeable for those who like them. ... They read Victor Hugo's windy sublimities in the evening paper over their profanely well-cooked dinners. ... The aspect of the boulevards ... exhibits a number of features which are not especially provocative of 'veneration'. ... A good many other things are laid bare, but brain is not among them.

All this sort of thing is hardly James the First, let alone James the Second or The Old Pretender; it is a Bonny Prince laying about him with a fine careless swing. That same verve was to sustain him when, with the dogged professional skill of a celibate puppeteer determined to prove to himself that he could manipulate people on paper in preference to grappling with them at first hand, he sat down to arrange his *tableaux* showing the plight of Americans who, once they had passed through the passionate pilgrim phase, were striving to come to grips with the phenomenon of Europe.

In the same year 1874—the year before the publication of *Roderick Hudson*—there had appeared a tale which prefigured these stages almost as neatly as *Benvolio* itself (1875) was to prefigure the geminian theme. This was *The Last of the Valerii*. The plot, simply told, links it immediately with the tales of melodrama and the supernatural: a young Italian count becomes obsessed by the beauty of a statue of Juno excavated from the grounds of his villa, and neglects his charming young American wife until the narrator, her American Godfather, peeping at the count during his quasi-religious nocturnal adoration of the pagan relic, discloses the cause of the husband's neglect and thus ensures that with the reinterment of Juno he is freed from his obsession. But if the melodramatic and supernatural aspects of this story relegate it to a category fanciful, inferior and derived (Dr. Leon Edel recalls that James had earlier translated Merimée's *La Vénus D'Ille*, with its similar creepy plot of a statue coming to life), its unpleasantly necrophilic odour nevertheless arises from an early treatment of the 'art versus life' theme, summarized when the bewildered wife cries: 'His Juno's the reality; I'm the fiction!' At the same time, the enduring freshness and vitality of the descriptive prose of *The Last of the Valerii* has nothing whatever to do with any of these melodramatic, supernatural or professional-artistic aspects, but spring from the natural fluency of the thirty-year-old writer when he is *not* straining after patterns or symbols, but indulging the innocent passion of a pilgrim.

The set-piece presentation of Count Valerio as an example of 'the light, inexpensive, urbanity' of Italians is charmingly done; this two-dimensional portrait is rounded and animated with splendid economy when he is observed by his young wife—who 'thought her husband as handsome asleep as awake ... he was at least as entertaining, for the young man's happiness had not multiplied the topics on which he readily conversed'—or by her more cynical Godfather—who found him to be 'fundamentally unfurnished with "ideas". He had no beliefs nor hopes nor fears,—nothing but senses, appetites and serenely luxurious tastes'. The amused good-natured tone plays on places as well as on people; there are descriptions of Rome in which a beautifully controlled eloquence can still strike a modern observer of a very different Rome as fluent and sensitive. This freshness of the young writer's observation of the Roman scene coexists, in *The Last of the Valerii*, with an almost farcical early example of James's *voyeur* tendency, when the narrator scrambles up on a garden-seat to spy on the count prostrate before his Juno. It is enough, this freshness, to preserve the frail contrived little tale and project a reader forward in time, not so much to James's own later murky experiments in spooky peeping, as to the philhellenic clarities of Forrest Reid. And, as so often in James, along with the freshness goes the deliberate amused inflation: the count, about to kiss his fiancée's hand in St. Peter's, remembers in time that 'they were in a place unaccordant with profane passions'; and the wife in turn recalls, when she takes up the archaeological interests which were to have so strange an outcome, that 'this liberal process would help to disinfect her Yankee dollars of the impertinent odor of trade'. Taken solemnly, Count Valerio's posturing as Pygmalion makes him as ludicrous a figure as the character in *Rose-Agathe* (1878) who falls in love with a hairdresser's dummy; taken lightly, he figures as a caricature of the narrator's own enchantment with the romantic patina investing a passionate pilgrim's classical infatuations.

Another tale of the same period, *The Sweetheart of M. Briseux* (1873), is less successful simply because although the plot is not in itself more absurd, James seems to have worked harder at it, wasting more effort on the frame than on the picture. A young girl, engaged to a cultivated but sterile painter, allows a young Bohemian of genius to supplant her fiancé's still-born portrait of her with a masterpiece; her engagement is broken off, and she tells her story, late in life, to the narrator who surprises her sitting before the famous 'master-piece' in a French provincial gallery. No liveliness of presentation saves this awkward charade. The dashing artist may be a quick sketch for Roderick Hudson; the coldly mediocre fiancé may be a model for Gilbert Osmond of *The Portrait of a Lady;* but the momentary twitch of life comes not from him but merely from his mother, who 'was what is called a very superior person—a person with an aquiline nose, who wore gloves in the house, and gave you her ear to kiss'. The 'sweetheart' herself is a puppet acting out her emblematic part; there is more life in the stage-setting.

The story *Adina* (1874), like *The Last of the Valerii*, of the same year, might be classified among the early essays in the supernatural. There is at least one attempt at creepiness when a young Italian, cheated by an American traveller of a superb topaz once belonging to the Emperor Tiberius, steals in turn the robber's fiancée. We are intended to feel that the revenge is exacted by the topaz itself rather than by its simple owner. Indeed, when the young peasant takes to haunting the American's house, he strikes no particular terror: 'If Angelo confined his machinations to sitting about in damp gardens at malarial hours, Scrope would not be the first to suffer.' Yet one may forget the topaz and its message that the romantic past still holds us in thrall, while remembering the patient figure of Angelo who, like an avenging Pied Piper or one of Mr. E. M. Forster's Italians wreaking havoc in the hearts of English ladies, spirits away into his own private Golden Age the young woman who represents, for the travellers, a superior sophisticated modern culture. These particular passionate pilgrims try to outsmart the attractive simple-hearted offerings of European inheritance—but they lose by reason of their poor response to such treasures, whether gems or simple souls like Angelo's.

French scenes and French characters in James's tales of the next few years are (like the maturing paragraphs of his English observation) sketched with a rather more critical pen, but the enchantment is still alive behind that self-conscious cleverness of the semi-satirical 'knowing' view. Describing the little seaport of Blanquais-les-Galets, where the two young gentlemen of the short novel *Confidence* (1880) disport themselves, the author seems to be on his guard against a too-easy surrender to charm:

> There was evidently a great deal of nature about it, and at this moment, nature, embodied in the clear, gay sunshine, in the blue and quiet sea, in the daisied grass of the high-shouldered downs, had an air of inviting the intelligent observer to postpone his difficulties.

Moreover, to cite random instances from the same novel, there are passing twinges of that acid quasi-pompous humour of inflated phrase which James had so often affected to utter an Olympian judgement of the American scene: it is as though the author is still determined not to be 'had', however much the scene may attract him, however closely it may seem to approximate to his boyhood dreams:

> . . . it was one of those diminutive structures which are known at French watering-places as 'chalets', and, with an exiguity of furniture, are let

for the season to families that pride themselves upon their powers of contraction.

A fine day in Paris brings out a wonderfully bright and appreciative multitude of strollers and loungers, and the liberal spaces of the Champs Elysées were on this occasion filled with those placid votaries of inexpensive entertainment who abound in the French capital.

I have already suggested that James's freshly-excited or recalled impressions of American scenes, when placed alongside similar enthusiasms for European sights and sounds and smells, should cause an attentive reader to concentrate on the quality rather than the geography of his reactions. To continue the argument a stage further, I would suggest that these passages of mock-inflation should not so much be taken as evidence of a bitterness towards his beloved but exclusively self-sufficient Europe, but rather studied, in conjunction with innumerable parallel passages from his descriptions of American life, as giving us some clue to his *general* conscious attitude towards his own *general* immediate impressions. There is certainly a growing stiffness in his attitude towards Europe as the goal of the passionate pilgrim, and it would be idle to deny a certain surface disenchantment even while we seek to recognize the underlying faithfulness of his quest. But the *general* disinclination to place too implicit a trust in his impressions, or sink too much emotional capital in his longing to uncover the human heart-afflicting 'sympathy' in external surroundings, is a more rewarding theme. It is, at least, a more legitimate field for literary criticism, for it depends less upon the imagined coincidence of biographical data with narrative opinions than upon the author's attitude towards his own reactions as expressed impartially (and perhaps unconsciously?) in a trick of prose style occurring at every successive stage of his development as a writer, and in contexts American, European, or geographically unlocated.

Not to be recognized too easily as an excluded foreigner was clearly one aim in the young author's mind; enthusiasm let loose on some occasions must at other times be kept hidden, and the burgundy be appraised first as 'excellent' and later as 'tolerable'. It is always easier, of course, to be on one's guard against people than against art or nature: 'sales resistance' is naturally stronger against wares which have disappointed us in the past, than against wares which at worst arouse no more than disapproval or irritation, and at best can themselves give us a passing sense of personal unworthiness. And so (as we shall see when we come to discuss the 'international Cerberus') in the earliest pilgrimages we can detect mild instances of that savage penetration into European *moeurs* which would torment the later pilgrim even when the culture produced by such paltry specimens appears still to be rich and worthy of admiration. For American pilgrims of the 1870's, for example, the English peerage was a favoured shrine, but in *The American* (1876) we find Lord Deepmere's physiognomy exhibited as denoting 'great simplicity, a certain amount of brutality, and a probable failure in the past to profit by rare educational advantages'—a sketch closely resembling that of Sir Arthur Demesne in *The Siege of London* (1883). Similarly, when Christopher Newman, the passionate pilgrim in the same novel, meets the French lady who enshrines all his most cherished preconceptions, he 'wondered where, in so exquisite a compound, nature and art showed their dividing line. Where did the special intention separate from the habit of good manners? Where did urbanity end and simplicity begin?'

There will be lingering traces of the pilgrim's faithfulness to his quest, even in stories and novels which will be studied in succeeding chapters mainly as examples of James's concern with quite other matters. *The Portrait of a Lady* (1880), for instance, will offer us in the person of Gilbert Osmond a super-cultivated villain; but Isabel Archer, the poor girl who is lured into his chilly trap by her love of European life, does not have to revise her opinion of the setting of a leisured society but only of one or two deceitful denizens of the favoured scene. Her creator can still revel in 'a seat of ease, indeed of luxury, telling of arrangements subtly studied and refinements frankly proclaimed'. At the same time, he pauses to note how a connoisseur can turn sour, how Gilbert Osmond's cold frustration is not a quality set apart from his artistic sensibility but rather actively affected by it.

At times, the wariness of a more sprightly pilgrim than Isabel Archer will appear in a sarcastic comment on things as well as people. Mrs. Headway, in *The Siege of London*, 'wished to study English life so that she might take possession of it: and to pass in among a hedge of bobbing rustics and sit among the monuments of the old Demesnes would have told her a great deal about English life'. But more characteristic of the tales of this period is an uncritical backcloth to a critical examination of the behaviour of European people. Rotten Row, in *Lady Barberina* (1884), is as fresh and innocent as Hampton Court had been to the first passionate pilgrim fourteen years earlier:

> The wide long area of the Row, its red-brown surface dotted with bounding figures, stretched away into the distance and became suffused and misty in the bright thick air. . . . All this, however, was only a background, for the scene was before everything personal; quite splendidly so, and full of the gloss and lustre, the contrasted tones, of a thousand polished surfaces.

A mixed attitude is more apparent in later work, as that *self*-suspicion seems to grow and to shadow James's descriptive style with doubt. There is a significant instance in *The Tragic Muse* (1888), where the phrase 'all corn-fields and magistrates and vicars', set in the midst of a sincere attempt at a brief tribute to historical imagination, suggests that the author is afraid of being thought ingenuous and so puts at least one admiring reaction within invisible inverted commas in order that it could, if challenged, be discarded as a deliberate joke:

> It was simply the sense of England—a sort of apprehended revelation of his country. The dim annals of the place were sensibly, heavily in the air—foundations bafflingly early, a great monastic life, wars of the Roses, with battles and blood in the streets, and then the long quietude of the respectable centuries, all corn-fields and magistrates and vicars—and these things were connected with an emotion that arose from the green country, the rich land so infinitely lived in, and laid on him a hand that was too ghostly to press and yet somehow too urgent to be light.

It is a passage with all the glow of the authentic pilgrimage; there is in it, however, a trace of self-consciousness, suggesting that at any moment the passionate pilgrim may make himself and his passion the object of a piercing comment such as that which pins down for us the false dilettante Osmond: 'He has a great dread of vulgarity; that's his special line; he hasn't any other that I know of.'

There is one curious later story, '*Europe*' (1899), in which a 'passionate pilgrim' type longing for Europe is treated as a symbol not of hopes joyously realized but of hopes sadistically denied by a third party—in this case by a selfish old lady determined to deny her daughters the pleasure she herself had once enjoyed. Mrs. Rimmle, the immensely old widow of a famous author, lives with her three elderly daughters in New England. *Their* experience, under the mother's envious domination, is simply the experience of *not* visiting Europe. A quick sketch of one of the trio gives a malicious picture of them all: 'Jane . . . had to be described, for want of other description, as the pretty one, but it would not have served to identify her unless you had seen the others'. The comparatively normal Jane manages to escape the old vulture, goes to Italy with friends, and simply stays there. She has gained, in Europe, her symbolic freedom. The eldest sister Becky, left behind, grows to look as old as her mother. The mother, viciously sadistic, has been saying of the escaped Jane that she is 'dead'. When the aged Becky, too, dies in the New England home, the mother, now almost a mummy, says of her that she has gone to 'Europe'. It is, in its twisted way, as telling an example as James ever gave of the degree to which 'Europe' signified 'freedom'.

Finally, in taking formal leave, for the moment, of the passionate pilgrim theme which crops up throughout the whole of James's work, it is important to recognize that at its purest the pilgrimage is towards a state of mind rather than towards any habitable Atlantis. Indeed, there is no passage where Professor Matthiessen showed his insight into James's personality more clearly than when, after listing the various American characters (Roderick Hudson, Christopher Newman, Isabel Archer, Lambert Strether) 'for whom the symbol of abundance had been Europe', he went on to claim that 'a similar eagerness for liberation was to seize upon some of James's European heroes', notably Hyacinth Robinson of *The Princess Casamassima*, Nick Dormer of *The Tragic Muse*, and even the desolate and defeated John Marcher of *The Beast in the Jungle*. As in other writers, the passion could turn at times, of course, to a bitter scorn. There will be moments in James's writing when the wine of European culture will be found neither 'excellent' nor 'tolerable', but undrinkable. But quality of judgement, whether of places or people, was for Henry James an Attendant Spirit which rarely left him, and which he himself would never willingly betray. Paris or London, parklands or works of art, it all boiled down, in the end, to a hunt for some visible correlative for—to repeat once again Desmond MacCarthy's phrase—'spiritual decency'.

III

'Everyone Was a Little Someone Else'

Roderick Hudson, *Confidence*, and parables of the split personality

'Everyone was a little someone else'
The Great Good Place.

IT MUST come as a disappointment to amateur astrologers to note that Henry James was not born under the sign of The Twins; for few major writers have demonstrated, in writing of themselves and of their invented characters, a more consistent consciousness of the dual natures that so often seem to inhabit one body. When George Dane, central figure of that strange story *The Great Good Place* (1900), voices the realization that 'everyone was a little someone else', he is putting in the simplest terms a concept which intrigued his creator all his working life. To it, twenty-five years earlier, he had devoted two works of art: a sketchy parable of a tale, *Benvolio*, and the first of his novels to display unmistakable evidence of major quality, *Roderick Hudson*. During the quarter-century interval, there is hardly one novel or tale which does not to some degree strike the geminian notes of antithesis or parallel, dissonance or assonance, contradiction or compensation. The habit was so ingrained that whenever his creative power momentarily flagged, James dropped back into the expedient of creating yet another pair (or quartet or even sextet) of figures who seem, in their fascinated complementary matching unlikeness, to be different expressions of the same larger character, separate shoots from an identical parent plant. At their least inspired, these characters would reduce his plots to marionette shows; at their most successful, they would convey almost everything of value this novelist had to say about life. In the range of fiction from *Benvolio*, the least adulterated statement of the recurring theme in one diagrammatic figure, to the later mellower versions of that same diptych, representing again and again the hinged and self-confronting aspects of action and contemplation, the voyager and the stay-at-home, there may also be perceived the degree to which this same unresolved problem, like exasperated Siamese twins or the warring words of an oxymoron, first shapes, then develops, and finally comes near to disintegrating James's prose style.

Benvolio (1875), a sketch written immediately after *Roderick Hudson*, is fantasy at its most lucid. The young hero is as unreal, and as revealing, as a figure in a ballet. I am conscious, James seems to be saying, of two natures within me; let me construct a little marionette and make him jog to and fro to illustrate my discovery:

It was as if the souls of two very different men had been placed together to make the voyage of life in the same boat, and had agreed for convenience sake to take the helm in alternation . . .

Sometimes he looked very young—rosy, radiant, blooming, younger than his years. Then suddenly, as the light struck his head in a particular manner, you would see that his golden locks contained a surprising number of silver threads; and with your attention quickened by this discovery, you would proceed to detect something grave and discreet in his smile—something vague and ghostly, like the dim adumbration of the darker half of the lunar disc.

This young gentleman's double nature expresses itself in the simplest possible manner in his mode of lodging. The artless metaphor of Benvolio's two rooms provides a decorous early instance of James's intense love of 'settings', his power of putting on paper the 'feel' of a room or a landscape:

At home he lived in two chambers. One was an immense room, hung with pictures, lined with books, draped with rugs and tapestries, decorated with a multitude of ingenious devices (for of all these things he was very fond); the other, his sleeping room, was almost as bare as a monastic cell. It had a meagre little strip of carpet on the floor, and a dozen well-thumbed volumes of classic poets and sages on the mantleshelf. On the wall hung three or four coarsely-engraved portraits of the most exemplary of these worthies; these were the only ornaments. But the room had the charm of a great window, in a deep embrasure, looking out upon a tangled, silent, moss-grown garden, and in the embrasure stood the little ink-blotted table at which Benvolio did most of his poetic scribbling. The windows of his sumptuous sitting-room commanded a wide public square, where people were always passing and lounging, where military music used to play on vernal nights, and half the life of the great town went forward. . . .

His friends, coming to see him, often found the great room empty, and advancing, rapped at the door of the chamber. But he frequently kept quiet, not desiring in the least to see them, knowing exactly what they were going to say, and not thinking it worth hearing. Then, hearing them stride away, and the outer door close behind them, he would come forth and take a turn in his slippers, over his Persian carpets, and glance out of the window and see his defeated visitant stand scratching his chin in the sunny square. After this he would laugh lightly to himself—as is said to be the habit of the scribbling tribe in moments of production.

In that last paragraph there is more than a hint that poor Benvolio was whistling to keep his courage up, for when young men adopt a 'remote' and 'aloof' pose, it is a hundred to one that force of circumstance or some inner check is impeding their free social circulalation. Later, in *The Princess Casamassima*, James would turn to good effect the anguish of an excluded adolescent. Nor were his excluded persons always adolescent: the observer who sees most of the game is perhaps the best-known 'type' in James's fiction. That he saw himself in this light during the early years of his life (and perhaps even to the very end?) is more than an inference drawn from characters in his novels—always a dangerous game when played with prolific creators. In the autobiographies *A Small Boy and Others* (1913) and *Notes of a Son and Brother* (1914), in which he recreates—with septuagenarian meticulousness and a style elaborate to a degree sometimes well beyond the borders of mystification —his feelings as a child and a youth, Henry James admits that by contrast with his more active brothers he could at best try to be a trained observer of the sort of life *they* could live in real earnest. He was banned from active service in the American Civil War (which broke out when he was eighteen) by reason of an injury sustained when, helping to put out a small farmyard fire, he strained himself with the pump-handle. This incident, which I have translated to the best of my ability after a reasonable acquaintance with the style of 'the later James', is narrated with an obliquity so remarkable even in this master of the oblique that one suspects a deep inner reluctance of revelation:

Jammed into the acute angle between two high fences, where the rhythmic play of my arms, in tune with that of several other pairs, but at a dire disadvantage of position, induced a rural, a rusty, a quasi-extemporized old engine to work and a saving stream to flow, I had done myself, in the face of a shabby conflagration, a horrid even if an obscure hurt. . . .

It would be rash to relate the prolixity of Henry James Senior to a similar youthful accident, yet it is certain that when his son made reference to the father's mishap he wrote with an obscurity almost equal to that which enshrined his own: 'an accident received in early youth and which had so lamed him for life that he could circulate to any convenience but on even surfaces'. He had, in fact, one wooden leg.

Whatever part this accident may or may not have played in his decision, it is clear that young Henry James quite deliberately resigned himself, in the main, to the rôle of spectator. Like Benvolio, he seems to have accepted this rôle with a good grace touched with an irony which would be a sufficient preservative against self-indulgence:

Ennui was at the end of everything that did not multiply our relations with life. To multiply his relations, therefore, Benvolio reflected, should be the wise man's aim. Poor Benvolio had to reflect on this, because, as I say, he was a poet and not a man of action. A fine fellow of the latter stamp would have solved the problem without knowing it, and bequeathed to his fellow-men not rigid formulas but vivid examples. But Benvolio had often said to himself that he was born to imagine great things—not to do them; and he had said this by no means sadly, for on the whole he was very well content with his position. Imagine them he determined he would and on a magnificent scale. He would multiply his labours, at least, and they should be very serious ones.

The rest of his story is of no significance: that Benvolio should waver between the attractions of a wordly Countess and a retiring Scholastica is but another personification of the dichotomy already symbolized in the arrangement of his rooms. What *is* noteworthy is the persistence, in Benvolio's make-up, of the love of direct impressions and the sensuous appreciation even of his somewhat artificial austerities:

He flung himself on the grass, on the edge of the wood—not in the same place where he had lain at the Countess's feet, pulling sonnets out of his pocket and reading them one by one; a little stream flowed beside him; opposite, the sun was declining; the distant city lay before him, lifting its towers and chimneys against the reddening western sky. The twilight fell and deepened and the stars came out. Benvolio lay there thinking that he preferred them to the Countess's wax candles. He went back to town in a farmer's wagon, talking with the honest rustic who drove it.

Viewed as a symbolic self-portrait, Benvolio figures Henry James in his early thirties as 'a tissue of contradictions' and 'a mixture of inconsistencies', but he is endowed, like his creator, with a saving grace. 'He did possess the magic ring, in a certain fashion; he possessed, in other words, the poetic imagination.' For James, the poetic imagination was to be very largely a matter of seeing things from both sides: from the early tales to the final Prefaces his writing is full of images invoking the obverse and reverse, the back and the front, the passive and the active, the efficient and the visionary, the romance and the disillusion. Even Benvolio has his youthful senili-ties—it seemed to him at times that 'the gustatory faculty of his mind was losing its keenness'. That is no way for a young man to talk, we may tell ourselves. Benvolio heartily agreed: 'There is a way of never being bored, and the wise man's duty is to find it out.' And yet that is the way young men at times *do* think, becoming conscious like Benvolio 'of an intellectual condition similar to that of a palate which has lost its relish'. That complete honesty of the double vision in James's work explains much that is otherwise obscure; it elucidates his own brilliant elucidations of the young mind at odds with itself (Isabel Archer in *The Portrait of a Lady*, Hyacinth Robinson in *The Princess Casamassima*, and a score of others); it helps to explain the tortuosities of the 'high' style where he makes the reader dizzy by his conscientious efforts to be fair all round, to take every possible aspect into consideration.

From among the host of tales embodying James's obsession with the sensibilities of American tourists in Europe, in which for the most part—as we shall see—the contrast of cultures tends to over-shadow our interest in people as people rather than representative Americans and Europeans, one early *nouvelle*, *Eugene Pickering* (1874), may be selected for its presentation of the self-tormented 'split personality' in terms so bleakly familiar that they irresistibly suggest an autobiographical note. It is a version somewhere between the simple diagram sketched in *Benvolio* and the later patient un-ravelling of the complicated soul of Hyacinth Robinson of *The Princess Casamassima;* a version invested with a rhetorical sympathy echoing Henry James's own significant over-protestations concerning his choice of the spectator's rôle:

> I was like a poodle-dog that is led about by a blue ribbon, and scoured and combed and fed on slops. It was not life; life is learning to know one's self, and in that sense I have lived more in the past six weeks than in all the years that preceded them. I am filled with this feverish sense of liberation; it keeps rising to my head like the fumes of strong wine. I find I am an active, sentient intelligent creature, with desires, with passions, with possible convictions—even with what I never dreamed of, a possible will of my own! I find there is a world to know, a life to lead, men and women to form a thousand relations with. It all lies there like a great surging sea, where we must plunge and dive and feel the breeze and breast the waves. I stand shivering here on the bank, staring, longing, wondering, charmed by the smell of the brine and yet afraid of the water. The world beckons and smiles and calls, but a nameless influence from the past, that I can neither wholly obey nor wholly resist, seems to hold me back. I am full of impulses, but, somehow, I am not full of strength. Life seems inspiring at certain moments, but it seems terrible and unsafe; and I ask myself why I should wantonly measure myself with merciless forces, when I have learned so well how to stand aside and let them pass. Why shouldn't I turn my back upon it all and go home to—what awaits me?—to that sightless, soundless, country life, and long days spent among old books? But if a man *is* weak, he doesn't want to assent beforehand to his weakness. . . .'

The force of this outburst is certainly far stronger than anything called for by the relaxed Homburg setting or the mawkish contrived plot. There is little to engage the reader's feelings in an absurd rigmarole about Eugene's pre-engagement to a little girl, offering him a convenient escape when his maturing fancy is taken by a Homburg widow; we are offered a melodrama *manqué* when the widow sheers off and the child-fiancée is revived in Smyrna, of all places. Apart from the passionate statement of Eugene's double nature, the prose quickens only at occasional points of direct observation, as when the *fatale* Madame Blumenthal is described as a 'sincere attitudinizer' who enjoys 'fictitious emotions in perfect good faith'. It is an early example of the truth that James possessed a vivid sense of his own geminian balance plus a witty—sometimes devastating—gift of social judgement. Unless a reader learns to spot and to cherish them, both qualities tend to become submerged under a factitious plotting which, with peculiar persistence, James himself and some of his admirers claim to value above either the honesty or the skill.

That juvenile *ennui* which beset Benvolio and Eugene Pickering in their prescient imaginations is, of course, merely the 'other side' of their creator's intense love of life. The consistency of James's nature may be illustrated by a recognition of that same longing for life which irradiates his later parable of a single man weighed down not, this time, by a rejecting timidity but rather by the consequences of an over-eager acceptance of experience with all its hampering trivia. *The Great Good Place*, a riper version of the double nature in the single breast, is a moving rhapsody on the text 'the world is too much with us'. It is an appeal against the tyranny of affairs, of avoidable items of secondary importance as they afflict the social life of civilized man; it voices the desire of harried souls to seek peace from social demands in some retreat. The legend is as simple as that sketched in *Benvolio*. George Dane is a successful author— as close to Henry James's fantasy of himself in 1900 as Benvolio was in 1875. One day, he cannot cope any longer with the complexities of his social and literary life. He falls asleep, after greeting an unknown young man. He dreams that he is in 'The Great Good Place', a sort of lay monastery where quiet men in a spacious country hostel live remote from everyday life and win back their peace of mind—as Benvolio had won back his, twenty-five years earlier, by walking into his inner room. Waking from his long day-dream, Dane finds the young aspirant seated at his now tidied desk. He is greeted back to normal life with the comforting words: 'Everything's done'. He has gained the perfect confidential secretary. He has also caught a glimpse, one might add, of the ideal fantasy of university life such as Henry James himself had never experienced—a fantasy still shared by those who, nearly a century after Benvolio, forget Samuel Johnson and venture to 'dream ... life of toil and envy free' in such places as All Souls or the Institute for Behavioural Sciences at Stanford. One suspects that the day-dreaming part of Henry James which is enshrined in George Dane would have been happy, for a day or two, in either establishment. One can be quite certain that the ensuing portraits of his neighbours would quickly have demonstrated the longevity of his non-dreaming, conscious, clear-sighted counterpart.

The quintessence of the geminian theme is distilled in George Dane's discovery that 'everyone was a little someone else'. But the poor harassed fellow had, first, to experience the conviction that 'the real exquisite was to be without the complication of an identity'. The sensibility of a Benvolio survives even into this world-sated world-weariness. Only a man of great sensitivity could be brutal enough to long for this particular form of partial suicide:

To let them alone, these things, the new things, let them utterly alone and see if that, by chance, wouldn't somehow prove the best way to deal with them: this fancy brushed his face for a moment as a possible solution, giving it, as so often before, a cool wave of air. Then he knew again as well as ever that leaving was difficult, leaving impossible—that the only remedy, the true soft effacing sponge, would be to *be* left, to be forgotten. There was no footing on which a man who had liked life—liked it at any rate as *he* had—could now escape it. He must reap as he had sown. It was a thing of meshes; he had simply gone to sleep under the net and had simply waked up there. The net was too fine; the cords crossed each other at spots too near together, making at each a little tight hard knot that tired fingers were this morning too limp and too tender to touch.

Not until he had reached this extreme Dane could accept the truth of the other side of his nature, to admit that it was 'the inner life, for people of his generation, victims of the modern madness, mere maniacal extension and motion, that was returning health'.

When, 'at the height of his age', Henry James laboured over the Prefaces to those of his works considered worthy of inclusion in the great New York Edition, the first novel so honoured was not *Watch and Ward* but *Roderick Hudson*. It had been written in Florence in 1874 and published serially the following year. It is a novel of such mingled promise and achievement that it would be a significant work of fiction even if the thirty-one-year-old author had never written another. (Indeed, one may speculate, in passing, on the reputation of James if he had published only one or two early novels—say, *Roderick Hudson* and *The Europeans*. Certainly it would be high; perhaps even unassailable, like that of Howard

Sturgis for his *Belchamber*. For Gresham's Law can act in literature as cruelly as in economics, and James has suffered from it more than most writers). It is in *Roderick Hudson* that the genius of Henry James first blazed out through the talent; here that his pedantic scholarship of the human heart produced poetry as well as fine rhetoric. In the persons of Roderick the young sculptor and Rowland Mallet, his friend with a 'constitutional tendency to magnanimous interpretations', we are substantially introduced to one geminian theme to which James constantly returned but never with such simple heartache—the theme of the relationship between careless artist and careful consumer of art, between the adamantine hardness of the creator and the yielding sensibility of the apprecia-tor: the perennial problem, in short, of the Marys and Marthas of the world of the mind.

Some fifty years ago, Dame Rebecca West found *Roderick Hudson* to be 'crammed with local colour like a schoolmistress's bedroom full of photographs of Rome'. The raptures of James's young American sculptor on being introduced to nineteenth-century Italy may indeed tend to pall, though we have seen that his creator possessed for the feel and texture of that alien culture a romantic sensibility which could at times produce writing of flawless serenity. But the significance of the novel is not in outward setting but in its inwardness of apprehension of that selfish foolhardiness lying at the core of creative sensibility, which can first fortify and then destroy both the possessor and the fascinated benefactor of a certain type of artistic genius. It is true that Roderick's excited reactions to Italy, his meetings with other artists and *cognoscenti*, both Italian and expatriate, are based clearly enough on James's own Roman explorations and introductions; the curious reader will find them amply documented in the second volume of Professor Edel's bio-graphy. Yet whatever the details may have been, Dr. Edel is wise enough to add (II, 165) that James 'drew upon a view of life and art which seemed to have greatly enlarged itself in recent months, so that he felt he had in his grasp not merely certain precious moments of existence but a sense of living and feeling—and doing —that would carry him forward in all his future creations.'

The rôle of hero is divided between Roderick Hudson, the head-strong sculptor of inspired rightness of touch, and his older friend

Rowland Mallet who transplants him from a New England township, barren to his genius, to the richer artistic climate of Italy.*
Away in the background there is Mary Garland who loves in silence her affianced Roderick and in return is silently loved by the self-abnegating Rowland. Miss Garland fails to interest us deeply. We feel a compulsion to respect her reticence, sharing the view that 'it was not a disadvantage to talk to a girl who made one keep guard on one's composure; it diminished one's usual liability to utter something less than revised wisdom'. But if Mary is 'boiled suet' (Dame Rebecca's phrase), it matters surprisingly little, for she figures as the remotest corner of a conventional triangle. The tension of the novel is not triangular, not even when Christina Light, a livelier young lady of shady European antecedents, captivates a Roderick open to the appeal of beauty and adventure from whatever source. The tension is bilateral; it is between Roderick and Rowland as they exemplify, like twins or at least like cousins german, contrasted expressions of a basically similar response to life and to art.

It is at once clear that Rowland's avuncular affection renders him liable to unlimited hurt at the hands of his *protégé*. James allows him the one protective fibre of his type—an ironic familiar awareness of his own nature:

It often seemed to Mallet that he wholly lacked the prime requisite of a graceful *flâneur*—the simple, sensuous, confident relish of pleasure ... His was neither an irresponsibly contemplative nature nor a sturdily practical one, and he was for ever looking in vain for the use of the things that please and the charm of the things that sustain. ... Oftenest perhaps he wished he were a vigorous young man of genius without a penny.

No one could be less a *flâneur* than the man who could forget his own quite considerable grounds for grievance in the contemplation of the possible price Roderick would have to pay for the flowering of a genius which Rowland himself would die to possess:

He often felt heavy-hearted; he was sombre without knowing why;

* For a note on the structural significance of the Roderick-Rowland relationship, as contrasted with the Milly-Kate relationship in *The Wings of the Dove*, see below, p. 323.

there were no visible clouds in his heaven, but there were cloud-shadows on his mood. Shadows projected they often were, without his knowing it, by an undue apprehension that things after all might not go so ideally well with Roderick.

He wondered gloomily at any rate whether for men of his companion's large easy power there was not a larger moral law than for narrow mediocrities like himself, who, yielding Nature a meagre interest on her investment (such as it was), had no reason to expect from her this affectionate laxity as to their accounts. Was it not part of the eternal fitness of things that Roderick, while rhapsodizing about Christina Light, should have it at his command to look at you with eyes of the most guileless and unclouded blue, and to shake off your musty imputations by a toss of his picturesque brown locks?

A superficial inference drawn from the great mass of James's fiction might lead to the view that the Roderick in him was stifled and patted out of existence by the Rowland. Dr. Edel comments (II, 179) that 'James was sufficiently a Rowland to realize that he could never be a Roderick'. Recalling the unflagging creative power behind his writing life of half a century, one must also admit that there is at least one sense in which it takes something of a Roderick to *create* even a Rowland. The impression of *Roderick Hudson*, at any rate, lingers strangely as one reads James's other novels. As he developed more characters like Mallet, thoughtful, cultivated, debonair, the novelist yet managed to keep burning that flame of passion he had once displayed in his Roderick 'half', even while the Rowland 'half' lurked nearby with such extinguishing remarks, about James's later 'super-subtle fry', as the observation that Isabel Archer in *The Portrait of a Lady* 'was often reminded that there were other gardens in the world than those of her remarkable soul'. To reduce the matter to a sentence (supplementing Dr. Edel's just quoted): Gilbert Osmond, that 'sterile dilettante', could never have created *The Portrait of a Lady* in which he figures with so chill an air of superior sensibility. The warmth of that extra quality separating Gilbert Osmond from the Osmond-like *creator* of Gilbert Osmond is the quality of James's Roderick 'half', so to say —and it is the source of all that is best in his writing. One might juggle with the notions of conscious and unconscious identity, seeing in Rowland the outcome of the home teachings of Henry

James Senior, brimful of social conscience and magnanimity, and in Roderick the spark of an instinctive creator, self-engendered and owing nothing to conscious heredity. The tragic significance of the theme comes out in Rowland's appreciation of that 'genius' in Roderick which he himself understood but did not possess, and which the lucky owner used with little conception of its source or even of its results. One of Roderick's fellow-artists gives a good working image for that enviable quality—' "Complete", that's what he is; while we little clevernesses are like half-ripened plums, only good eating on the side that has had a glimpse of the sun.' It is left to poor talented Rowland to seize the implications:

Suddenly he felt an irresistible pity for his companion; it seemed to him that his beautiful faculty of production was a double-edged instrument, susceptible of being dealt in back-handed blows at its possessor. Genius was priceless, inspired, divine; but it was also at its hours capricious, sinister, cruel; and men of genius accordingly were alternatively very enviable and very helpless.

When, some thirty years later, Henry James wrote his Preface to the novel, he complained that 'the grounds of my young man's disaster was unquestionably meagre', and conceives of the reader as asking: 'On the basis of so great a weakness . . . where was your idea of the interest? On the basis of so great an interest, where is the provision for so much weakness?' To a sympathetic reader, this self-criticism is curiously beside the point. What Henry James had done had been simply to present an acutely moving picture of Rowland's 'constitutional tendency to magnanimous interpretations' expanding itself in love and pity upon a subject—the terrible loneliness of genius, whether genuine or illusory—wholly adequate to call forth that love and pity. There is no question of taking sides between the two friends. To the reader, both are sympathetic in the sense that both are credible, understandable; and although straight 'moral' sympathy can hardly be claimed for Roderick, the relationship built up between the two men is by no means one of simple give and take. For Rowland, indeed, it does at first seem all give and no take; yet when he came to look on the dead body of his friend and realized, like Othello, that his 'occupation's gone', he had grown in scope and stature. While Roderick claims the limelight and the pity, it is extraordinary how Rowland has grown in tragic stature as the novel pursues its unemphatic course. He had seemed to be so amiably long-suffering that a reader could apply to him unchanged, but for the proper names, any simple description of that comparatively simple character Roger Lawrence of *Watch and Ward*:

Roger felt that he was too doggedly conscientious; but abuse his conscience as he would, he could not make it yield an inch; so that in the constant strife between his egotistical purpose and his generous temper, the latter kept gaining ground, and Nora innocently enjoyed the spoils of victory.

His growth has been a direct outcome of his great outpouring of sensibility. It is for this very reason that Roderick, for his part, could not return in kind; his return was unconscious and consisted only, without intention, in providing an occasion for the release of the love and the pity. If Rowland was constitutionally the giver, he was also, at first unwittingly, the receiver too. For Roderick could not receive any more readily than he could give. His is the fundamental chill of the single-minded artist. Even his infatuation with Christina Light is an aesthetic and basically egocentric rapture.

All this emotional tension is so subtly achieved, with nothing pointed out and nothing falsified by placards, that it is plain (*pace* Dr. Edel) that James had not become so exclusively a Rowland as to lose *direct* touch with a Roderick. Yet although direct emotion is deeply worked into the design of *Roderick Hudson*, its effect is not immediate but rather progressive and implicit, as though Rowland's were indeed the reader's own experience. (One wonders, in a kind of Jamesian fantasy, if a 'genius', reading this novel, would find himself sharing the experience not of Rowland but of Roderick!) The book's serenity of tone is markedly superior to that of *The American*, his next novel. Everything is subdued to a uniform consistency, rich yet delicate. The novel's shock ending, with Roderick falling to his Alpine death after being spurned by Christina Light and having at last glimpsed something of Rowland's sense of grievance, is no less melodramatic than the ending of *The American*; yet it is far more moving, in spite of James's more

sustained efforts, at the close of the latter novel, to force the reader
to be moved. Nowhere in *The American*, for instance, does James
flick psychological truth on the raw with such deceptive economy
as in this single reaction of Roderick's when, goaded at last beyond
endurance, Rowland bursts out: 'It's a perpetual sacrifice to live
with a transcendent egotist.'

'I am an egotist?' cried Roderick.
'Did it never occur to you?'
'An egotist to whom you have made perpetual sacrifices?' He repeated
the words in a singular tone; a tone that denoted neither exactly indignation not incredulity, but (strange as it may seem) a sudden violent
curiosity for news about himself.

It is this confrontation, far more than Rowland's avowal of
his secret silent love for Roderick's neglected Mary Garland, far
more even than Roderick's own fatal infatuation for the worldly
Christina Light, future Princess Casamassima, that is the emotional
climax of the novel. For Rowland, the death of the young sculptor
that same day was the extinction of his own 'other half'. 'Now
that all was over Rowland understood how exclusively, for two
years, Roderick had filled his life. His occupation was gone.' He
had lost not only his occupation, but his twin. He and Mary, we
are told in a brief coda, remained friendly, and Rowland 'most
patient'. But their link—too late—is not love for one another,
but the consciousness of their shared love for the lost Roderick.

Most commentators ignore the short novel *Confidence* (1880)—
and its place in the James canon is incontestably minor. It was not
among the works chosen for revision in the New York Edition.
But, read at a sitting, it still has a 'period' charm. It could hardly
be bettered as a useful early text for the main theme of my present
interpretation: that James was a writer whose natural gifts for
visual description, high-spirited dialogue and an ebullient often
amusing magniloquence, were superior to his inventive capacity,
upon which he lavished so much will-power that he himself and
most of his admirers came to accept it—the result of so much
conscious effort—as his major asset. The basic plot pattern of
Confidence, so neat a diagram upon which to hang its many felicities

of phrase and judgement, is too preposterous in itself to hold any kind of psychological plausibility, much less profundity. The same could no doubt be said of *Love's Labour's Lost*. Shakespeare has, on the whole, been luckier in his admirers. The early comedies are praised for being everything *but* brilliantly constructed models of human truth. Read with an equal indulgence, with an eye for fresh observation and an ear for irrepressible verbal wit, the earlier minor works of James—*Confidence* among them—are still rewarding.

What the plot does reveal is another exercise in geminial juggling. The two friends Bernard Longueville and Gordon Wright represent, like Roderick Hudson and Rowland Mallet, the extension into two personalities of the conflicting natures of Benvolio. Gordon is the man of action. His friend Bernard is the kind of youngster of whom, when people asked the question 'why he didn't do something', it was generally accepted that 'he did more than many people in causing it to be asked'—and who, 'in spite of a great momentary appearance of frankness and a lively relish of any conjunction of agreeable circumstances', enjoyed the disadvantages as well as the advantages of his nature and 'had really little taste for giving himself up, and never did so without very soon wishing to take himself back'. There are, of course, a pair of young ladies to fabricate and entangle a plot; but throughout the various switches and 'betrayals' the reader's attention never strays far from what Gordon thinks of Bernard, and Bernard of Gordon. It is entirely in keeping with the level of treatment that the one character in *Confidence* who emerges as a truly lively person, observed with the utmost affectionate accuracy from outside and so revealing one or two quick penetrations into the working mechanism of motive, should be the slighter and sillier of the two puppet damsels. The two young American friends themselves are propped into grotesquely unlikely positions so that their likenesses and unlikenesses may be studied like a pair of dissimilar frogs on an amateur's dissecting bench; the ladies, left in their skins, are more lifelike to the casual glance.

The plot hangs on an absurd request from Gordon that his friend Bernard should visit Baden-Baden in order to assess the qualities of a young compatriot whom he is studying with matrimonial intent. The young gentlemen themselves have been carefully introduced in phrases which recall the more sensitive passages of referees' letters written by sympathetic college tutors. They are still, like their creator, in the 'passionate pilgrim' stage, so that the selective wit of their presentation is matched by tenderly sketched backgrounds of Siena and Baden. Bernard 'had a nature which seemed at several points to contradict itself'. Gordon, like Christopher Newman of *The American*, has clearer ideas of how Europe on the one hand and a carefully examined young lady on the other, may serve his conscious purposes: 'I want to marry with my eyes open.' There follows some elegantly light conversation, like mannered dialogue from a flirtatious play set in the sunny relaxed mood of nineteenth-century European spas, between the cool appraising friends and their willing victims, a group of American women who, like the inhabitants of the Pension Beaurepas and an ample handful of other Jamesian tourists, are blessed with more intelligence than money and a preference for cultivated friendship over unseasonable fervour. For pages at a time, there are agreeable exchanges of a type prevalent in the forgotten social comedies of the period, a type best recalled perhaps in Anthony Hope's *Dolly Dialogues*. Here are Bernard and his friend Gordon's fair Angela:

'To what else could one possibly attribute an indifference to compliments?'
'There is something else. One might be proud.'
'There you are again!' Bernard exclaimed. 'You won't even let me praise your modesty.'
'I would rather you should rebuke my pride.'
'That is so humble a speech that it leaves no room for rebuke.'

In a place like Baden, indeed, and among such people, it is clear that conversation *à la Love's Labour's Lost* slightly flavoured by Victorian phrase-books is a major source of entertainment. Even Angela's mother, 'a Puritan grown wordly, a Bostonian relaxed', can bat the ball to and fro, while the other *ingénue*, the frivolous Blanche Evers, whirls *her* conversational racquet with the prettiest arabesques.

Bernard, left alone on the field to quiz patient Griselda-Angela, reports on Gordon's return that in his view the young lady is interested only in the Wright fortune and would have allowed flirtatious advances from Bernard himself, had he been so minded.

Gordon Wright abruptly departs; the female trio also move their tents, and Bernard (in an almost buried sentence!) betakes himself to the East for two years of intelligent globe-trotting. One feels that the author was more interested in the passing observation, after Longueville had enjoyed a winning run at the casino, that 'it was extremely characteristic of Bernard Longueville that his pleasure should suddenly transform itself into flatness'. Meanwhile Gordon, forewarned against Angela, retires to America and marries the effervescent Blanche. It may be true that medieval tales had similar plot skeletons; it may be true that nineteenth-century tales (James's among them) could turn on such equally incredible third-party judgements as recognition of character only in oil portraits; but it is surely wise to admit these flaws as a sign of lack of narrative interest, rather than praise the fictive essayist for symmetry, still less for psychological insight. Let us admit, instead, the non-architectonic enjoyment of such good asides as the observation that it is always the 'strong, solid, sensible fellows' who marry flirtatious figures of fancy, since it is among their ranks that one finds the man who 'could afford, morally speaking, to have a kittenish wife'.

The second half of the story bring Bernard and Angela together again in an unfashionable Normandy seaside resort; cue for more travel notes about the *plage* 'inviting the intelligent observer to postpone his difficulties', seasoned with such consciously off-hand comments as 'there was evidently a great deal of nature about it'. The tone is never less than amusedly tolerant: 'The little world of Blanquais appeared to form a large family party, of highly-developed amphibious habits, which sat gossiping all day upon the warm pebbles, occasionally dipping into the sea and drying itself in the sun, without any relaxation of personal intimacy.' The plot requires, of course, that the hypercritical pair should admit their love and become engaged. In Paris, the betrothed are confronted by Gordon and his Blanche, whose 'irremediable triviality' is now as burdensome to her solemn spouse as it is still magnetic to her raffish *cavaliere servente*, Captain Lovelock. To mitigate the hurt occasioned to Bernard by friend Gordon's jealous fury at his engagement, Angela reveals that the latter had in fact proposed to her at Baden immediately after receiving Bernard's adverse report, but that she herself had turned down the reluctant prize: 'He hoped I would refuse him, yet when I had done so, he was vexed.'

This rupture between the friends brings real feeling, at long last, into the novel; but it is Angela who is allowed to make the discovery first that Blanche, behind her all inconsequential chatter, is 'intensely in love' with her sober husband who married her on the rebound, and secondly, after a theatrical scene of recrimination between the rival friends, that Gordon in turn is 'intensely in love with his wife'. In murmuring 'all's well that ends well', the reader may at this point remind himself that the whole masquerade has been in line with an Elizabethan tragi-comedy of errors. The novelist's practised ease of observation was still streets ahead, so to say, of any impulse to communicate important findings about the human plight. Only in the accelerated pace of the last few chapters, and in the vivid sketch of a pretty prattling woman (Blanche) whose conversational rain of sugared bon-bons serves to conceal a hurt to her own hidden pride, may one scent the authentic qualities of the future novelist. Meanwhile, *Confidence* need not be overlooked by readers who may enjoy without censure the pleasure of a writer—like Shakespeare and Proust and many another—who lingers a little long over experiments with his equipment, before he has discovered anything very remarkable to do with it.

The geminian or cousinly theme, so well established, will recur throughout James's fiction. Through the contrasts and likenesses of the cousins Julia Dallow and Nick Dormer of *The Tragic Muse*, or the terrible struggles between the cousins Olive Chancellor and Basil Ransome of *The Bostonians* as they outbid one another for the body and soul of a girl who feels the attraction of both sides of that double life so savagely torn apart and shared between them— text by text it would be possible to follow the developing theme right up to Milly Theale and Kate Croy of *The Wings of the Dove* and to the still later products of the full autumnal period. There would always be, for James, endless fascination in the contrast between those whose vocation was 'to be' and those whose ambition was 'to do'. We have seen that in the autobiographies he recalled how from the very first he classed himself among 'those whose faculty for application is all and only in their imagination and their sensibility'. Being, rather than doing, was *his* aim. Writing of himself as a child, he muses, as on some created character:

> For there was the very pattern and measure of all that he was to demand: just to *be* somewhere—almost anywhere would do—and somehow receive an impression or an accession, feel a relation or a vibration. He was to go without many things, ever so many—as all persons do in whom contemplation takes so much the place of action; but everywhere, in the years that came soon after, and that in fact continued long, in the streets of great towns, in New York still for some time, and then for a while in London, in Paris, in Geneva, wherever it might be, he was to enjoy more than anything the so far from showy practice of wondering and dawdling and gaping. . . .

How he dawdled and gaped at foreign cities we have already seen. But he was curious first of all about himself—and at the age of seventy he can still be curious about that early curiosity:

> I had rather a positive lack of the passion [jealousy], and thereby, I suppose, a lack of spirit; since if jealousy bears, as I think, on what one sees one's companions able to do—as against one's own falling short— envy, as I know it at least, was simply of what they *were*, or in other words of a certain sort of richer consciousness supposed, doubtless often too freely supposed, in them. They were so *other*—that is what I felt. . . .
> 'I never dreamed of competing—a business having in it at the best, for my temper, if not for my total failure of temper, a displeasing ferocity. If competing was bad snatching was therefore still worse, and jealousy was a sort of spiritual snatching. . . . A helpless little love of horizons I certainly cherished, and could sometimes care even for my own. (Chapter XIII.)

'They were so *other*'—but—'I never dreamed of competing'. Here, from long back, is the germ of George Dane's exhausted admission that 'everyone was a little someone else'. Here, rather than in his precocious zeal for Europe or his precocious mastery of language, was James's prime gift as a novelist. The quality that enables his own cherished created beings to step outside their inherited or conditioned bounds and greet, across chasms however deep, the personalities of their spiritual twins or cousins, is simply the gift of imagination (in the full Coleridgean sense of the word: a point established by James's similar control of fancy, when fancy is required). The gift is universalized as he employed it, while contemplating and writing about people rather than competing with them, to endow the creatures of that same imagination with reflected imaginations of their own.

Of course, there is a 'catch in it', if you want to look for one. The rhetoric and self-dramatization of a Benvolio may offer examples of wish-fulfilment, compensation, self-hallucination, impotence, withdrawal. Benvolio, Rowland Mallet, Bernard Longueville, Eugene Pickering and all the rest—they may all, to an unfriendly eye, be extensions of the author's own childish desire to shout: 'I'm the king of the castle because I can *imagine* myself to be you, and you're a dirty rascal because although you can *do* things you can't imagine them; so that I am two people and you are only one person.' The graver wisdom of *The Great Good Place* itself may be taken, in such a mood, as merely a spiteful retreat from the world of the doers, even if their doings are nothing more violent than indulgence in the more practical side of literary success.

There is, I am sure, much truth in such readings as these. Yet even so, they do not destroy the value of that compassionate imagination which enabled Henry James to bring renewed life, so to say, to the old discarded image of hendiadys, that figure of speech whereby one and one make three when the simple word 'and', by joining two contrasting nouns, turns the first noun into an adjective and thus transmutes the whole phrase from antithesis to compound. Much of his life and art, in short, was devoted to the belief that although, like the solitary islands of Matthew Arnold's poem, 'we mortal millions live alone', there may nevertheless be vivid to our imaginations the knowledge that we are still, however submerged our links, 'parts of a single continent'.

IV

'The International Cerberus'

The American; The Europeans; tales of trans-Atlantic discovery

'... sops instinctively thrown to the international Cerberus ...'
Preface to Vol. XIII of the New York Edition

'... the international young ladies, felt by me once more ... my appointed thematic doom ...'
Preface to Vol. XVIII

THERE is, of course, no clear division between those stories just grouped, for convenience, to illustrate the young Henry James in his 'passionate pilgrim' mood, and the novels and tales now awaiting survey from the point of view of his homage to 'the international Cerberus'. The freshness of observation made by the Europeanized visitors to New England, in *The Europeans*, no less than the vividly colourful Continental settings provided for Daisy Miller and her multitudinous American counterparts, bear the authentic stamp of the author as passionate pilgrim. Yet these new fictions, mainly the products of James's middle and late thirties, do tend to embody a common concern to grapple quite self-consciously with the 'appointed thematic doom', as he later called it, of the plight of transplanted persons. Some American critics, notably Van Wyck Brooks, soundly castigated James as a cultural deserter. Others, more recently, have defended him as a prophet or high priest of the international yearnings of our own days. Indeed, one recent authority has gone so far as to ask us to believe that the ambition which James shared with Whitman and Joyce was no less than 'the determination to forge or shape a changing world, to create a society, to take his place in a community-in-the-making by joining in the process of making it'.* This ambition is explained in terms of his expatriation, claimed as an exchange of territorial security for involvement with 'the middle-class world of change and crisis, with the culture of capitalism, which followed the American, French, and industrial revolutions'. Given the haphazard wandering habits of the James family, one does wonder whether the young Henry James was so consciously sociological a 'passionate pilgrim', so glumly determined to be slotted into the abstractions of future cultural history, when he strolled bright-eyed from one European resort to another, returning with a handful of tales and traveller's impressions not markedly more ponderous in intention than the ciné-camera records of his modern young counterparts.

* L. B. Holland: *The Expense of Vision:* Essays on the Craft of Henry James (1964), p. vii.

After examining other claimants, Professor Oscar Cargill has made an interesting case for *The American* (1876–77) as 'the first international novel', linking it to the Dumas play *L'Etrangère* (which presented a grossly unflattering version of American intrusion into French society) on which James had written an irritated review for the New York *Tribune* early in 1876. If Professor Cargill is right in his view that James was roused to action in 'justifying American ways against a European caricature of them', then *The American* may properly be considered as an early fruit of the novelist's international obsession, rather than as another treatment of the more innocent 'passionate pilgrim' theme. For Christopher Newman, 'The American', is never really sensitive to the lure of European cultural charm: his pride is hurt, his competitive instincts are aroused, and in some ways he figures as the innocent victim of European duplicity; but he is not, like Clement Searle and that pilgrim's innumerable James-like successors, a willing victim of infatuation. The Cargill detective work is of particular interest because it helps to explain the radical disappointment of *The American* as a novel. The early chapters, written soon after James arrived in Paris in 1875 with his contract to send back news-letters to the *Tribune*, are as fresh and witty as anything produced by his wonderfully vivid 'passionate pilgrim' mood. The later chapters are so melodramatic, so hectoring in tone, that it is difficult to think of them as coming from the same pen. It may very well be that annoyance with the Dumas play and other evidences of French contempt for American brashness, combined perhaps with vexation at his editor's reception of his over-elaborate articles, caused James to adopt a more sour and strident tone which in effect ruins the delicate promise of the first part of the book. Indeed, in Chapter XVI there is even a tell-tale repetition of his angry rejoinder to his *Tribune* editor ('If my letters have been "too good" I can honestly say they are the poorest I can do . . .'), when he makes Newman say, not very relevantly, 'I'm afraid it's the worst I can do'. If this nagging resentment is a clue to the young writer's state of mind, it explains much.

Nevertheless, another American critic, Professor Cleanth Brooks,* is undoubtedly also correct in citing Christopher Newman of *The*

* *Shenandoah*, Autumn 1964.

American (together with Jay Gatsby of Scott Fitzgerald's *The Great Gatsby* and Thomas Sutpen in William Faulkner's *Absalom! Absalom!*) as a prime exemplar of American innocence, the innocence that bases itself on self-made rather than acquired accomplishments, that strives in the face of sophistication to wrest reality from a dream. Dr. Leavis, on the other hand, whose comments on James are usually so penetrating, seems to me to be over-literal in holding it to be 'so preposterous an unreality' that 'Christopher Newman ... has rapidly made his pile in the West, and yet is offered to us as embodying a guileless integrity' (*Scrutiny*, XV, 102). What we are told, in a passage describing Newman's feeling that 'so fine an intelligence as Bellegarde's ought to be dedicated to high uses', is that 'the highest uses known to Newman's experiences were certain transcendent sagacities in the handling of railway stock'. Earlier, Newman has confessed to the American Mrs. Tristram that he had been 'successful in copper ... only so-so in rail-roads, and a hopeless fizzle in oil'. In the Bellegarde context, such specialized sagacity is comparatively guileless. Yet from one wry point of view, the misguided social loyalty of the corrupt Bellegardes does in the end prove less worldly than Newman's money-based security of conscience, since as his friend Mrs. Tristram points out to him, 'They wanted your money, but they have given you up for an idea'.

On the whole, then, it is not the moral structure of *The American* that makes it a less successful work of art than *The Europeans*. That Newman should be an 'innocent' among the near-Proustian social resonances of the Bellegardes and yet at the same time be known to have been a hard bargainer whose financial manipulations have brought him to the top of a more crudely competitive heap, surely makes him a more complex and plausible figure for the sort of international diagram his creator had in mind. It is a partial failure not of design but of execution: to compare the last few chapters with the opening pages is to see that a momentary decline in the actual quality of writing allows the melodramatic ending to stand revealed in all its unreality. In many another James novel or tale with equally stagey plot-endings, the accomplished sophisticated style serves to sugar the pill.

Newman, who 'had never reflected upon philosophical processes', feels a sudden revulsion against business tricks and comes to Europe to find 'the biggest kind of entertainment a man can get'. His compatriot in Paris, Mrs. Tristram (introduced with the customary *brio* of James's earlier set-piece style of character portraiture), has enough 'avidity of imagination' to wish to experiment socially with this clever man who boasts that 'I have never had time to feel things. I have had to *do* them, and make myself felt'. His social simplicity is extreme. He is determined to select a wife as cannily as if she were a financial investment: 'I want to do the thing in handsome style ... I want to make a great hit. I want to take my pick. My wife must be a magnificent woman ... I want to possess, in a word, the best article on the market.' In social and personal affairs, the naïve financial wizard wants to make a corner, a killing. With all his mercantile shrewdness, there is in this careful first presentation of Newman a sense of the inappropriate skills of a fish out of water, which in the Parisian world he now sets out to conquer do indeed reduce him to an unconscious 'guileless integrity' by no means 'preposterous'.

Newman's naïveté, indeed, is high-lighted for us even before his embroilment with the Bellegarde family, in his encounter in the Louvre with Noémie Nioche, the little copyist. He is not only unable to distinguish between old masters and Noémie's incompetent copies; he is curiously blind, too, to the barefaced determination of this coquette to sell her charms for social advancement. This not unattractive lack of sophistication is well established before we see how Newman, within his own limits as self-satisfied a manipulator as can be, advances into the life of Paris 'with all his usual appearance of slow-strolling leisure, and all his essential directness and intensity of aim'. 'He believed that Europe was made for him, and not he for Europe'—and in this state of rapacious innocence he will remain, through all his distresses, an essentially comic figure whose final renunciation, like Malvolio's, leaves one only half sympathetic.

It has been suggested that James's description of the aristocratic Bellegarde family, from whose ranks Newman selects his candidate to make him 'a first-class wife', shows the author no less than his hero to be a man staring from outside at the *beau monde* and never learning how it really behaves. Apart from a novelist's natural tendency to make the Marquis himself act consistently as spokesman for family pride, the charge seems wide of the mark. The old dowager Marquise is of British birth and upbringing, and in sketching her, James added but one more to his portraits of the English landed gentry whom, from his early 'passionate pilgrim' days, he had ample opportunity to observe closely at first hand. Nor was he by any means akin to his creature Newman in ignorance of French culture—indeed, more than once during the witty exchanges between Newman and the younger Bellegarde son, Valentin, a reader may find himself unconsciously retranslating sentences back into 'the original French'. Nor is Newman the sole social beneficiary of his friendship with Valentin; it is clear that the Bellegarde young sprig finds much to admire in his sister's strange suitor, in whose view American 'lads of twenty-five and thirty have old heads and young hearts, or at least young morals; here they have young heads and very aged hearts, morals of the most grizzled and wrinkled'. Valentin's own flighty (and finally fatal) rashness, his illusory 'safe spontaneity' within the loose bonds of privilege, certainly set him off in marked contrast to his brother the Marquis as anything but an awe-struck caricature drawn by an observer unfamiliar with the actual behaviour of contemporary noble families. And it should in fairness be admitted that even the inhuman stiffness of the Marquis is very deliberately accounted for; it is by no means a misreading due to distance of observation: 'Newman had never yet been confronted with such an incarnation of the art of taking oneself seriously; he felt a sort of impulse to step backward, as you do to get a view of a great façade.'

For all his 'essential directness and intensity of aim', Newman is, by the side of young Valentin, an inarticulate lover. As for women in general as a subject for conversation, 'to expatiate largely upon it had always seemed to him a proceeding vaguely analogous to the cooing of pigeons and the chattering of monkeys, and even inconsistent with a fully-developed human character'. (Valentin picks up the tell-tale Jamesian image later on, when discussing former Bellegardes who had made uncharacteristic mésalliances with lawyers' daughters: 'Horrible! One of us, in the Middle Ages, did better: he married a beggar-maid, like King Cophetua. That was really better; it was like marrying a bird or a monkey; one didn't have to think about her family at all.') Yet Newman is no fool. His growing distaste for Bellegarde social ethics is based on sound American principles in which the envy of an excluded outsider has little place. Many of James's wittier phrases are devoted to this aspect of his hero's confrontation, and themselves contribute to the composition of a character in which canniness and social integrity comfortably coexist. During the brief period when he is accepted, grudgingly, as suitor for the Bellegarde daughter, he not only distinguishes the Marquis as 'a man full of possible impertinences and treacheries', but enjoys the comedy provided by elderly French aristos who are invited to quiz him as a kind of tame monster, no less than he can appreciate the British-born mother's 'habit of unquestioned authority and the absoluteness of a social theory favourable to yourself'. Before long, he can profit, in the reader's mind, from his creator's connoisseur-like observation of 'that soft hardness of good society which puts out its hand but keeps its fingers closed over the coin', or he can share one's ironic impression of Lord Deepmere (a Bellegarde relation) as someone whose physiognomy 'denoted great simplicity, a certain amount of brutality, and a probable failure in the past to profit by rare educational advantages'. All this, be it remembered, is the James of 1876 speaking, and not the older, disillusioned, social surgeon of the last phase of his writing career. It is against such comparatively sophisticated 'placing' of his adversaries that one is invited, at times, to share such forthright examples of Newman's reactions as his unspoken equation of the Marquis's belief in 'the divine right of Henry of Bourbon, Fifth of his name, to the throne of France', with some such oddity as a dietary taste 'for fish-bones or nut-shells'.

The Bellegarde daughter, who should be, technically, the other central figure, is a pale uninteresting character beside brother Valentin. As Professor Cargill observes, 'the grounds for affection between Newman and Valentin are much more clearly exposed than those for deep attachment between Newman and Valentin's sister'. Melodrama takes over when Valentin dies after a duel provoked by Noémie Nioche (showing, incidentally, Valentin's folly of being 'wise' to her type, as contrasted with the wiser 'innocence' of Newman himself) and the fair Claire retires into a nunnery. Newman, armed by his dying friend with the secret that the old Marquis had been effectively murdered by his wife (by the withdrawal of medicaments), is now in a position to take his revenge on the family which had first presented him to their friends as a future son-in-law and then, finding the gilded pill too odious to swallow, jilted him. His noble revenge, of course, is to refrain from blackmail. The last word is left with Mrs. Tristram, who knocks his halo a little askew by guessing that the Bellegarde mother and elder son, faced by the threat of exposure, had summoned up ancestral courage and decided to trust his decency rather than ally themselves with Newman: 'Their confidence, after counsel taken of each other, was not in their innocence, nor in their talent for bluffing things off; it was in your remarkable good nature! You see they were right.'

There have been hints of other dark adulterous Bellegarde secrets which leave the reader unmoved. As Professor Cargill puts it, 'in correcting Dumas, James fell into the ways of the sensational dramatist', producing a 'conflict with the substantial realism of the materials of the story ...' There is little point in flinching, now, from a similar judgement of *The American* made in James's own life-time. Ford Madox Ford gently pointed out that James 'knew perfectly well that the matrons of the most corrupt of European aristocracies do not go murdering their husbands in order to secure eligible *partis* for their daughters', but that his 'comparative inexperience in the construction of novels led him into the paths of staginess'. It was this very fault, of course, that James came to defend or disguise most sturdily when he came to write the Prefaces to his revised edition.

The quartet of cousins who confront one another with their contrasting or complementary American and European view of life give *The Europeans* (1878) a set of characteristics including an assured serene treatment of both the geminian or cousinly theme and also the theme of trans-Atlantic discovery. This charming little book has an American setting, as *The American* had a European. One could hardly invent a more romantic cousin for the sober New England Wentworths than Eugenia, Baroness Munster, morganatic wife of Prince Adolf of Silberstadt-Schrenkenstein (a title with hints at farce or lampoon, fortunately groundless). This elegant lady, *née* Young, suddenly reappears with her brother Felix to ruffle in no uncertain fashion the quiet Wentworth dovecotes. Mr. Wentworth Senior is well equipped to brace himself against the Continental airs of these native-born members of his own family; nephew Felix promptly marks him down as 'a tremendously high-toned old fellow; he looks as if he were undergoing martyrdom, not by fire, but by freezing'. At the same time, Felix retains the reader's respect by a sincere appreciation of the Wentworth quality, just as James's most sympathetic American travellers show a sincere respect for European qualities:

> Felix had observed . . . his characteristic pallor; and now he perceived that there was something almost cadaverous in his uncle's high-featured white face. But so clever were this young man's quick sympathies and perceptions that he had already learned that in these semi-mortuary manifestations there was no cause for alarm. His light imagination had gained a glimpse of Mr. Wentworth's spiritual mechanism, and taught him that, the old man being infinitely conscientious, the special operation of conscience within him announced itself by several of the indications of physical faintness.

Professor Jefferson has neatly seized upon this attractive side of Felix by declaring that he 'has the American naturalness and good faith, combined with a European sophistication and vivacity of mind'. The same critic shows a rare degree of sympathetic insight when he later elaborates this particular observation and draws forth a general comment on the whole tribe of Jamesian expatriates: 'One of the ways in which they all manifest this aspect of Americanism is in the spirit with which they assimilate what they take to be its opposite; and our liking for them, or otherwise, depends largely on the degree of success with which they achieve a harmonious blend. In Felix Young, the best of the type, the result is civilized and delightful: his Europeanism qualifies him . . . to be a charming American.'

The Wentworth daughters, Charlotte and Gertrude, are open in their several ways to the affront from Bohemia: cousin Felix at once puts his finger on their New England similarities: 'They are sober; they are even severe. They are of a pensive cast; they take things hard. I think there is something the matter with them; they have some melancholy memory or some depressing expectation. It's not the Epicurean temperament.' Against their common background, the sisters have put forth some blossoms of individuality; but Charlotte and Gertrude are clearly blossoms on the same tree even if one should be a little less bud-like than the other. (It is because of this almost automatic quality of fraternal or sisterly closeness, even in contrarieties, that in many instances the *cousinly* relationship has been noted, in the last chapter, as a nearer approximation to that peculiar brand of close contradiction and distant affinity with which James was to make such reiterated and varied play.) When Mr. Wentworth warns his daughters that 'we are to be exposed to peculiar influences', the girls respond in contrasting tones, but they are both well within the charmed circle of home influences:

Gertrude was silent for a moment, in deference to her father's speech; then she spoke in a manner that was not in the least an answer to it. 'I want to see how they will live. I am sure they will have different hours. She will do all kinds of little things differently. When we go over it will be like going to Europe. She will have a boudoir. She will invite us to dinner—very late. She will breakfast in her room.'

Charlotte gazed at her sister again. Gertrude's imagination seemed to her to be fairly running riot. She had always known that Gertrude had a great deal of imagination—she had been very proud of it. But at the same time she felt that it was a dangerous and irresponsible faculty; and now, to her sense, for the moment, it seemed to threaten to make her sister a strange person, who should come in suddenly, as from a journey, talking of the peculiar and possibly unpleasant things she had observed. Charlotte's imagination took no journeys whatever; she kept it, as it were, in her pocket, with the other furniture of this receptacle—a thimble, a little box of peppermint, and a morsel of court-plaster.

Gertrude, in short, is beginning to experience, across the strong pull of sisterly likeness, the counter-attraction of the distant, different, yet fascinating magnetism of her strange cousins. Like so many of James's characters, she is being deliciously and dangerously nipped by sudden twinges in her 'other' self. The canny Felix observes, after a short time, that one sister at least feels the attraction of 'the other life', and noting her struggles as she feels herself drawn, counts it as yet another illustration of the general principle that 'nothing exceeds the licence occasionally taken by the imagination of very rigid people'. At such a point, a less subtle writer (and, to be fair, Henry

James himself in his less subtle exercises) could hardly have resisted the temptation to use Felix as a vehicle for straight satire—and so lose him the gained certainty of a reader's assenting concurrence. Once again, the distinction has been neatly made by Professor Jefferson: 'The moral for the reader, and it holds good more or less for the novel as a whole, is that we are not invited to arrive at a firm and settled opinion of how these various ingredients are combined in anything so stodgy or unlike James as "the total reality of the Wentworth way of life". Felix likes the Wentworths: he likes people generally. His view of his cousins is lively and hopeful; it is his nature to respond to the best in others, and the artist in him takes pleasure in displaying it to advantage.' A fair portrait, one may add, of Henry James himself at this time.

Felix's sister Eugenia is less successful. All her charms break in vain upon the bleak high-mindedness of the New England neighbour, Robert Acton, who had become her fascinated adorer. It is in terms of unfriendly coastal imagery that she admits her failure:

She found her chief happiness in the sense of exerting a certain power and making a certain impression; and now she felt the annoyance of a rather wearied swimmer who, on nearing shore, to land, finds a smooth hard wall of rock when he counted upon a clean firm beach. Her power, in the American air, seemed to have lost its prehensile attributes; the smooth wall of rock was insurmountable.

There has never been, however, the slightest suggestion that Robert Acton, who is no cousin by blood, is in any sense a cousin in spirit. In the different reactions of Gertrude and Robert Acton to the foreign visitors, there is the clearest possible illustration of the thesis that although they share a common and peculiarly self-confident New England culture and are therefore at first sight equally proof against the alien invasion, yet they are in an even more important sense *un*like, in that one has the imagination to feel the claims of cultural cousinship, and the other, unhelped by family leanings, has not.

If one wishes to introduce a new reader to James, and especially a reader who has been scared off by reports or even unlucky samples of the later style, *The Europeans* provides an admirable first text. It beautifully exemplifies his equipment as a novelist in the days before the famous manner grew so luxuriant that it covered the ground of everything he wrote with a tropical carpet of undergrowth so thick that it is often difficult to know exactly what lies beneath. (In some of the later fiction, as we shall see, there is so prodigious an expenditure of words describing, in the subtlest of *nuances*, precisely what the characters *don't* do and *don't* say, that even a practised reader is apt to fumble, now and then, not only for some indication as to what the ado is all about, but even for an anchoring clue as to the motives of the chief actors). The ground of this earlier work is covered by a rich but less obscuring verdure; the spring landscape reveals its contours, and Dame Rebecca West's fifty-year-old compliment to *The Europeans* is thoroughly in keeping with its pastoral air: 'that is the pure note of the early James, like a pipe played carefully by a boy'. The 'boy' was thirty-five when he played that particular tune, but the image will stand without hurt if we recognize in the novel a perfect example of writing so close-packed, so sinewy, that its lean simplicity is the simplicity of a manageable problem selected, posed, worked out, and resolved. In *The Europeans*, in short, one has a sample of how two simple recurring themes—the twin or cousin pattern, and the similarly magnetic-repellent theme of the fusion or clash of different national cultures—could in themselves provide James with almost all he needed for his distinctive contribution to literature when seen as, in Arnold's phrase, a 'criticism of life'. These same constituents, more crudely handled, could produce some of his wooden uninspiring tales of forced symmetry and glaring international confrontation. Here, they merge beautifully with James's other prime gifts of temperamental resonance and an unerring sureness of moral discrimination, to form a minor work of art within which, as Dr. Leavis has sensed, 'James is unmistakably feeling towards an ideal possibility that is neither Europe nor America' (*Scrutiny* XV, 209).

Four Meetings (1877) presents another aspect of the seamy side of trans-Atlantic relations; or rather, to be more accurate, the basic theme of a yearning for European experience is made to support one of the other obsessional Jamesian topics, the power of money to excite sadistic impulses. It is a cruel tale of how a wicked Europeanized American and his sordid French mistress cheat his poor simple

American she-cousin out of her savings the moment she sets foot at last on the Promised Land. She herself, pathetic passionate pilgrim, brings into the story yet another delicately phrased version of an informed nostalgia for the Old World; but it is difficult to retain sympathy for so naïve a simpleton, and the conjured atmosphere fails to redeem the over-dramatic confrontation of American innocence and European egotism. This time, the traveller's disillusion is complete: after her victimization, she neither cares, nor commands the means, to try her luck in Europe again. Ford Madox Ford considered that the concluding phrase of the story ('I reflected that poor Miss Spencer had been right in her presentiment that she should still see something of that dear old Europe') was 'one of the most pitiless sentences ever penned by the hand of man'.

The slow-moving but eminently readable story *An International Episode* (1878), with its long gentle mockery never concentrated to stagey wit, and its sad recital of Victorian Anglo-American incompatability neither forced into diagrammatic gestures nor falsified by any melodramatic trick-ending, is treated by James with a breadth and serenity suggesting the polite melancholy interviews between Isabel Archer and Lord Warburton in *The Portrait of a Lady*, a couple of years later. Lord Lambeth, the British 'hero' of the tale, is indeed not unlike a first version of Lord Warburton, as he strives with genuine goodwill to overcome his social bafflement in America. At first, in New York, where he figures as another spokesman for James's ferocious dislike for American hotels, he mildly observes:

a couple of hundred men sitting on divans along a great marble-paved corridor, with their legs stretched out, together with several dozen more standing in a *queue*, as at the ticket-office of a railway station, before a brilliantly illuminated counter of vast extent. These latter persons, who carried portmanteaux in their hands, had a dejected, exhausted look; their garments were not very fresh, and they seemed to be rendering some mysterious tribute to a magnificent young man with a waxed mustache, and a shirt-front adorned with diamond buttons, who every now and then dropped an absent glance over their multitudinous patience. They were American citizens doing homage to a hotel clerk.

Later, in the monied world of Newport, he watches 'pretty young girls, dressed as if for a *fête champêtre*, swaying to and fro in rocking-chairs, fanning themselves with large straw hats, and enjoying an enviable exemption from social cares'. In this first phase of his international education, Lord Lambeth comes, sees, and both conquers and is conquered—until, with a sudden creak of old-fashioned machinery, he is called home when his mother, the Duchess of Bayswater, learns that he is becoming interested in an American girl.

The second phase opens with the return visit to England of his charmer, Bessie Alden, and her married sister Mrs. Westgate. There, they are treated with the appallingly disproportionate lack of hospitality with which the Victorian English (as to a lesser but still shaming extent their modern successors) saw fit, in James's eyes, to reward those Americans who had lavishly entertained them on the other side of the ocean:

> 'We have been to Madame Tussaud's,' Bessie pursued . . .
> 'It did duty very well for a party,' said Mrs. Westgate. 'All the women were *décolletées*, and many of the figures looked as if they could speak if they tried.'

Yet it is not so much their casual reception that shocks the ladies, as the apparent indifference of aristocratic Britons to their own staggering privileges. Bessie tells her now infatuated lordling: 'I shall always think that, properly, you should have been a great mind —a great character', a view which his embarrassed lordship ascribes to 'Yankee prejudice'. We are left to conclude, in the end, when Bessie surprisingly turns down Lord Lambeth's offer of marriage, that her objection to him is not a consequence of her farcical interview with the Duchess (sister to Wilde's Lady Bracknell), but rather a last reluctant admission that he, and his like, are just not serious enough for the prime matters of life. We had already gathered that Bessie 'had a kind of ideal conduct for a young man who should find himself in this magnificent position, and she tried to adapt it to Lord Lambeth's deportment, as you might attempt to fit a silhouette in art paper upon a shadow projected upon a wall'. It is this, rather than superficial clashes between two branches of English-speaking culture, that interposes between a pair of sympathetic representatives. There is, James is saying, no common point of view. What a common point of view *means*, he sketched with beautiful economy when he first described Lambeth's amicable relations with his travelling-companion in America:

> The young Englishmen ... talked together as they usually talked, with many odd silences, lapses of logic, and incongruities of transition, like people who have grown old together, and learned to supply each other's missing phrases; or, more especially like people thoroughly conscious of a common point of view, so that a style of conversation superficially lacking in finish might suffice for reference to a fund of associations in the light of which everything was all right.

Of all James's stories, *Daisy Miller* (1878) gained the most immediate success—and it is easy to see why, even today when the mild activities of 'a pretty American flirt' could arouse no surprise in English, still less Italian, breasts. By one of those strange quirks of chance, Daisy became the 'type' for all James's trans-Atlantic heroines. Musing back on her success at the time of his New York Edition Prefaces (1907), he confesses indulgently that 'my supposedly typical little figure was of course pure poetry, and had never been anything else ...' She was presented, at any rate, in splendidly confident narrative prose, as fresh as the eponymous flower and unruffled by any awkward exigencies of plot. No stilted parallels, no tit-for-tat pairings and inversions, mar this simple tale: the innocent American girl blunders, still and always innocent, into situations of utmost child-like trustfulness, considered outrageously 'fast' by the American set in lakeside Switzerland and later in Rome. She finally runs the moral and medical risk of visiting the Colosseum late at night with her current Italian cavalier, and—poof! she succumbs to 'the Roman fever'. The tale is not even very moving: the self-unconscious flame of Daisy's life glows, flickers, is extinguished, and that is all. What remains of the story is its ring of truth, the clarity of its observation. Indulgent to his heroine, her creator is wittily tart with her compatriots: 'Mrs. Costello was a widow with a fortune; a person of much distinction, who frequently intimated that, if she were not so dreadfully liable to sick headaches, she would probably have left a deeper impress upon her time'. This is the good lady who remarks of Daisy: 'She goes on from day to day, from hour to hour, as they did in the Golden Age. I can imagine nothing more vulgar.') In the eyes of a more discerning American friend, 'there was always in her conversation, the same odd mixture of audacity and puerility'. He watched her sadly merely because 'it was painful to hear so much that was pretty and undefended and natural assigned to a vulgar place among the categories of disorder'. Did Daisy die of undeserved opprobrium, or merely of the Roman fever? Curiously enough, for the effect of her little history, it seems not to matter.

Anyone who is still taken in by the hoary legend of Henry James as an American renegade uncritically besotted by Europe, may be quickly undeceived by a reading of the story *The Pension Beaurepas* (1879). Nothing violent 'happens' in this quiet piece of observation of contrasted American expatriate types; but there is a violence of disgust, of outraged compassion, lying just beneath the surface of the limpid narrative prose and the light assured dialogue. Quiet though it is, the tale exposes a loathing for crude acquisitiveness on the one hand and cultural snobbery on the other, together with pity for the victims of both sets of false values.

The exposure assumes, of course, the possibility of a superior wisdom—and this is supplied in the inoffensive person of the unnamed narrator, a young American writer whose charmingly evocative picture of lakeside Geneva is a straight transcription from the travel notebooks of his creator, who was still, one recalls, in his mid-thirties. To the *pension* of this neutral recorder come two American families. The Rucks—father, mother and daughter—are comparatively fresh to the delights of travel; the Churches—mother and daughter—are irremediably steeped in the staler experiences of the European ethos. Both little groups are pathetically inadequate to respond naturally to their good fortune. Ruck is harassed by business worries while his womenfolk raid the shops for lace and jewellery: 'So, by way of not being mean, of being a good American husband and father, poor Ruck stands staring at bankruptcy.' The Rucks are, all three, immune to other cosmopolitan influences: 'He has spent his whole time in buying and selling; he knows how to do nothing else. His wife and daughter have spent theirs, not in selling, but in buying; and they, on their side, know how to do nothing else.' Meanwhile, Mrs. Church, equally armoured against the true European heritage while snatching at every inexpensive rag of intellectual and social superiority, is throttling the life out of her daughter who behaves with 'inscrutable submissiveness' but is seething, below the surface, with revolt. 'We have lived', the poor girl admits, 'at one time or another, in every *pension* in Europe.'

The full savagery of James's observant irony is reserved for the self-satisfied Mrs. Church: the Rucks are, by this time, mere sitting birds for him. This impoverished camp-follower of culture poses before her young countryman: 'The world seems to me to be hurrying, pressing forward so fiercely, without knowing where it is going. "Whither?" I often ask, in my little quiet way . . .' Later, when her daughter has admitted to the forbidden hankering to return to America, the dreadful woman repeats her smug apologia:

'Do you know my secret?' she asked, with an air of brightening confidence. And she paused a moment before she imparted her secret— 'To care only for the *best*! To do the best, to know the best—to have, to desire, to recognize, only the best. That's what I have always done, in my quiet little way. I have gone through Europe on my devoted little errand, seeking, seeing, heeding, only the best. And it has not been for myself alone; it has been for my daughter . . .'

The narrator, beset by sympathy for Ruck whose commercial training has left him with no inner resources, and for poor young Aurora Church who longs to shed her mother's load of fake gentility ('If I could tell you all the dull, stupid, second-rate people I have had to talk to, for no better reason than that they were *de leur pays*!'), can do no more than watch both families moving relentlessly to their doom—the Rucks to bankruptcy in New York, the Churches to another frugal *pension* at Dresden. Aurora, whose one harmless desire had been 'to do very simple things that are not at all simple— that is the American girl', fails in her protest. She is the other side of the medal of, and hence a sort of propitiation for, poor Daisy Miller who *did* succeed, and died for her success.

Another straightforward essay in national characteristics, somewhat less epigrammatic than *The Point of View* but with a similar amused impartiality undisturbed by the demands of plot, is *A Bundle of Letters* (1879). Another innocent girl, Miranda Hope, is alone in Paris on a culture-tour, picking up not only an acquaintance with French *mœurs* but also with the reactions of some fellow-

Americans. One of them, Leverett, who imagines Miss Hope, like another Daisy Miller, 'skirting the edges of obscure abysses without suspecting them', has the hungry art-starved appetite that had set in train the tragic *dénouement* of *Roderick Hudson;* he repeatedly expresses his faith in words which more significantly adumbrate the impassioned credo of Lambert Strether of *The Ambassadors*, that ultimate protagonist in James's long campaign to set down the full predicament of Americans abroad: 'the great thing is to *live*'. For full measure, the cultural essayist in James adds a set of other national prejudices, voiced by French and German boarders at Miss Hope's *pension*. It is a German who phrases the epigram which seems to have served, at about this time, to summarize European views of America as 'the arrival of a nation at an ultimate state of evolution without having passed through the mediate one; the passage of the fruit, in other words, from crudity to rottenness, without the interposition of a period of useful (and ornamental) ripeness'. Redeeming the balance, there are references to such examples of European vileness as the English lady who gives her governesses £5 a year extra to assume the same name—'they shouldn't have a nicer name than the family'. A curious instance of James's own benign neutrality in this war of words is Leverett's use of the word 'meagre' to describe Americans in Paris: precisely the word used by a character in *The Point of View* who objected to 'the meagreness, the stinginess' of London. Nobody, at least, could extend the concept of 'stinginess', also, to cover the behaviour of Americans in Paris!

The Siege of London (1883) is the full-scale treatment of a determined effort by a 'woman with a past' to crash into the topmost reaches of a society that in the 1880's, for all its licensed lapses, still closed its ranks pretty instinctively against interlopers. That this particular woman happened to be not only American but in addition a brassy product of the South-western frontier, added to the piquancy of the situation and allowed James to indulge yet another series of leisurely observations on current disparities in Anglo-American social customs—but the incompatibilities to be resolved are first a matter of social class, secondly an issue of conventional morality, and only in the third place a by-product of international differences. Mrs. Nancy Headway (ex-Mrs. Beck, ex-Mrs.—who knows who?) was as much a challenge to the classifications of her own countrymen as she was to the imagination of British hostesses: 'She was a charming woman, especially for New Mexico; but she had been divorced too often—it was a tax on one's credulity; she must have repudiated more husbands than she had married . . . She had gone in mainly for editors—she esteemed the journalistic profession . . . "The elegant and accomplished Mrs. Beck", the newspapers called her—the other editors, to whom she wasn't married.' It is made very clear, as she sets her cap at the Old World, that Mrs. Headway had never been 'received' in New York society. It is mainly for this reason that she declares: 'I have taken a great fancy to this old Europe; I feel as if I should never go back'. Her final success in becoming the wife of an English baronet is achieved against the resistance, partly active and partly passive, of her two American men friends, one a diplomat and one an old acquaintance from the frontier days. Class is stronger than morality in this tale, and moral judgement more severe than national pride.

The one unforeseen and almost crucial factor—and this is the real Jamesian touch in the plot—is that it is the comic side of Mrs. Headway's American-ness that makes her sought-after in the stiff but bored 'in-group' of London society, just as it is her questionable moral background that first excites their curiosity. One of her female compatriots can be cynical enough to say, of the London aristocracy: 'If they think there's something bad about you they'll be sure to run after you. It's like the decadence of the Roman Empire.' It is Mrs. Headway herself who admits, speaking of the polite world's infatuation with her Americanisms: 'They don't care for me; it's only to be able to repeat Mrs. Headway's "last". Every one wants to have it first; it's a regular race.' All these affronts she is prepared to endure simply because 'she had a very exciting life, and her vision of happiness at present was to be magnificently bored. The idea of complete and uncriticized respectability filled her soul with satisfaction; her imagination prostrated itself in the presence of this virtue'. James leaves us in little doubt that her object will be only too easily achieved.

In several earlier dramatizations of his mixed international cast of types, James had distributed an amused sympathy fairly evenly among the trans-Atlantic representatives. From the story of *The*

Siege of London, developed as a sizeable *nouvelle* and substantial enough for expansion to a light social novel, no character of either nationality emerges with much credit. Nancy has a certain brash daring, but there is calculation, too, in her use of her bizarre assets. 'She knew of course that as a product of fashionable circles she was nowhere, but she might have great success as a child of nature.' The shocked young gentleman from the American Legation felt revulsion at her notion of 'getting into society'—but he himself was already inside the charmed circle. Her male friend from the days when 'the circle of her activity was chiefly the Southwest' refuses to confirm Mrs. Headway's 'respectability' to her enamoured baronet and categorically denies it to his distraught mother. The fascinated baronet, Sir Arthur Demesne, does in the patched-up ending to the story marry the lady, but his anxious waiting upon events has been the reverse of heroic and such compliments as he collects from his creator are pitched in a minor key: 'If he was a little man in a big place, he never strutted nor talked loud; he merely felt it as a kind of luxury that he had a large social circumference. It was like sleeping in a big bed; one didn't toss about the more, but one felt a greater freshness.' Least admirable of all are the representatives of the set which the stupid greedy woman is so anxious to join. 'It's very distinguished to be dull,' she had said at the outset of her campaign; 'I'm ever so much too lively'. Just how mortally dull her new friends would be, is revealed at one of their ritual dinner-parties:

All those people seemed so completely made up, so unconscious of effort, so surrounded with things to rest upon; the men with their clean complexions, their well-hung chins, their cold pleasant eyes, their shoulders set back, their absence of gesture; the women, several very handsome, half-strangled in strings of pearls, with smooth plain tresses, seeming to look at nothing in particular, supporting silence as if it were as becoming as candle-light, yet talking a little, sometimes, in fresh rich voices. They were all wrapped in a community of ideas, of traditions, they understood each other's accents, even each other's variations. Mrs. Headway, with all her prettiness, seemed to transcend these variations; she looked foreign, exaggerated; she had too much expression; she might have been engaged for the evening. Waterville remarked, moreover, that English society was always looking out for amusement and that its transactions were conducted on a cash basis. If Mrs. Headway were amusing enough she would probably succeed, and her fortune—if fortune there was—would not be a hinderance.

Only the lingering sense of a romantic English tradition seems somehow to survive. There is a frail pathos in Lady Demesne's effort to keep her transmitted possessions in polite hands; but the other representatives of her class are already well on the road towards a rottenness that James himself would later reluctantly admit, and Marcel Proust, across the Channel, definitively expose. One simple index to the progressively critical attitude of Henry James to English society—to one aspect of the international sentimental tug-of-war, one holy object in the shrine of his passionate pilgrimage—is the nature of many of the minor verbal changes he would make to such tales as *The Siege of London* when he came to revise them for the 1907 New York Edition. In his first presentation of Lady Demesne, for example, he wrote: 'she was neither spontaneous nor abundant; she was conscious of herself, conscious of many things'. This was changed to: 'spontaneity had never come to her, and to express herself might have been for her modesty like the act of undressing in public'. Again, the sympathetic sentence: 'You might have pitied her, if you had seen that she lived in constant unrelaxed communion with certain rigid ideals', later becomes: 'You might have pitied her for the sense of her living tied so tight, with consequent moral cramps, to certain rigid ideals.'

One of the minor characters of *Lady Barberina* (1884), Lady Marmaduke, is an open spokesman for the Anglo-American marriages which were indeed occurring with increasing frequency at the time and doubtless created enough interest in British society to lend a topical interest to all James's variations on the theme. The lady herself was American— 'she had been for her conjugal baronet the most permanent consequence of a tour in the United States'—and she 'wished to add an arch or two to the bridge on which she had effected her transit from America'. Since 'reciprocity was the keynote of Lady Marmaduke's plan' and it was her belief 'that an ultimate fusion was inevitable', she voiced in London as a matter of public policy a social tendency which was already taking place, so to say, by private stealth. There were, at any rate, enough Anglo-American marriages in cold fact for James to count on his readers' interest in an almost complete catalogue of types and pairings. In *The International Episode*, a pleasant young American girl simply and shockingly turns down a pleasant young nobleman; in *The Siege of London*, a vulgar American divorcée forces her way into English society; in *The Modern Warning* (to be noted shortly), the violent dislike of a British aristocrat for the public manners of his American wife's native land will lead to a situation melodramatic to the point of farce. In *Lady Barberina*, a marriage between social equals— American millionaire on one side, daughter of a marquess on the other—skirts disaster simply because the poor girl cannot abide the social life of New York. But in this instance the story is wholly credible, the chief figures entirely acceptable and in the main sympathetic, the presentation admirably balanced, the outcome no more than a shrug of the knowing author's shoulder in face of the awkward, trivial, but nevertheless inescapable realities of social codes which nowadays look like the ritual dances of barbarians, but at the time of writing were as powerful a source of misunderstanding as, say, the ascription of sexual or extreme political deviation in our own socially more relaxed society.

That it should be necessary to call attention, apropos *Lady Barberina*, to the social stratifications of Victorian England (including the novelty of American marriages) is itself a tribute to the freshness of the story's narrative prose and its brisk intelligent dialogue. Contrasting the social rigidity of the characters with the liveliness of their speech, it is as if the staid posed photographs in an old family album, wearing clothes like James's Amazons in Rotten Row in their 'firm, tailor-made armour', or sporting beards like the eupeptic Lord Canterville's, 'of the richest growth, and of a colour . . . to which the coat of his admirable horse appeared to be a perfect match', suddenly looked up from the yellowing pages and spoke aloud in the light, allusive, comic, up-to-date speech of their own period, proving us the listeners to have been shamefully deficient in historical imagination. The opening scene in Hyde Park might be offered, indeed, to any young writer as a model of atmospheric setting and the economical introduction of characters, in a mood of high-spirited sophisticated social comedy. Nor, in this particular ballet, do the dancers harden into types as they pace out their international rôles. Jackson Lemon, the young American doctor who admits to the inherited possession of seven million dollars, is no vulgarian. 'Even after he learned that Lord Canterville's fortune was more ancient than abundant, it was still the mellowness of the golden element that struck him.' Nor is his Lady Barberina a freakish snob, nor her family a set of dragons of pride. When, in the early pages of this lengthy *nouvelle*, Jackson was considering 'whether such a marriage would square with his general situation', the reader feels that he had in mind his professional interests and his recognition that the girl herself was 'not strikingly clever', in addition to the rumness of marrying into the peerage plus his general hesitation, like all James's heroes, in the face of marriage of any sort.

Against this general background of mainly tolerant agreement to differ, the Americans can be American and the English be English without too rasping a contrast. Of course, some of the verbal exchanges are sharper than others—as they had been even in the debating-society amiability of *The Point of View*, and as they can be in similar exchanges even today. One still feels, for instance, James's pang of the not-quite-accepted pilgrim in the remark, descriptive of a pair of Anglophile Americans watching the cavalcade in Rotten Row, that 'people at once so initiated and so detached could only be Americans'. There is, too, a touch of pique in Lemon's view of himself: 'He was one of the most fortunate inhabitants of an immense, fresh, rich country, a country whose future was admitted to be incalculable, and he moved with perfect ease in a society in which he was not overshadowed by others. It seemed to him, therefore, beneath his dignity to wonder whether he could afford, socially speaking, to marry according to his taste.' And even the set-piece presentation of Lord Canterville was to have its tone noticeably sharpened in the revised version of 1907, where the concluding phrase 'he was a very imposing man indeed, and visibly, incontestably, a personage', becomes: 'he was, strikingly, a founded and builded figure, such as could only represent to the public gaze some Institution, some Exhibition or some Industry, in a word some unquenchable Interest.'

Yet the pathetic inability of Lady Barb to be culturally adaptable, when she is carried off to her husband's country, is very skilfully presented as a personal rather than a national failure. 'So long as she didn't hunt, it didn't much matter what she did.' Her nullity is encased in upper-class privilege, but it is an individual and not an anthropological insight that enables a professional friend of her husband's to see that 'Lady Barb, in New York, would neither assimilate nor be assimilated'. While she flinches ('it was not in the least of American barbarism that she was afraid; her dread was of American civilization'), her younger sister enjoys herself to the full and runs off to mingle her equally blue blood with that of a flashy lady-killer from the Wild West. If Lemon concludes that his wife's 'character, like her figure, appeared mainly to have been formed by riding across country', he is himself critical enough of Victorian modernity to add that 'striking cleverness was not a part of harmonious forms and the English complexion; it was associated with the modern simper, which was a result of modern nerves'. The one truly 'cultural' contest occurs when Lemon, seven times a millionaire, jibs at the Cantervilles' old-fashioned insistence on a marriage settlement. For the rest, when the baffled Jackson Lemon allows his wife to drag him back to England, to daily rides in the park and 'occasional scenes' during which 'the look of race is very visible' in his wife's countenance, the reader takes leave of them with the feeling (as flattering to James as a novelist as one's other reactions have been an acknowledgement of his felicities as an observant traveller) that international differences have simply helped to exhibit a radical miscalculation of personality.

Pandora (1884) returns, six years after *An International Episode* and four after *The Europeans*, to a treatment of America seen— ostensibly—through European eyes. The whole value of such a tale resides in the quality, the intelligence, of its observations. As a story, it is frail indeed. The young diplomat Count Otto Vogelstein meets Pandora Day, another Daisy Miller, on a trans-Atlantic liner. Two years later, he meets her in Washington, talking affably to the President as a 'self-made girl'. Vogelstein is interested in her, but discovers that she is still engaged to her original young man from Utica, who (thanks, one is given to suppose, to his fiancée's social charm) is appointed American Minister to Holland. And that is all. But as a social sketch offering James an opportunity for informed criticism of American manners in general and in particular the lack of cultural resonance in its political capital, the tone of *Pandora* is that of his more ambitious social novels and also of his best travel essays, with amusing vignettes such as that in the Jersey City customs shed where 'the few that had succeeded in collecting their battered boxes had an air of flushed indifference to their neighbours'—a human reaction as prevalent today as in 1884. The 'international' scales are not weighted, this time; any adverse observations by Vogelstein may be referred back to the introductory presentation of his mind as the container of 'several millions of facts, packed too close together for the light breeze of imagination to draw through the mass'. Again, though the Day parents are exhibited as exponents of 'the fascination of prosperity, the confidence of serenity, which sometimes makes people arrogant, but which had had such a different effect on this simple satisfied pair, in which further development of any kind appeared to have been arrested', and though 'the constant danger of marrying the American girl' is grasped by the young diplomat as 'something one had to reckon with, like the rise in prices, the telephone, the discovery of dynamite, the Chassepôt rifle, the socialistic spirit', yet it is left to an American lady to remind him that 'American life was full of social distinctions, of delicate shades, which foreigners are often too stupid to perceive'.

So that although Vogelstein decides that 'the only way to enjoy the United States would be to burn one's standards and warm one's self at the blaze', and looks with Olympian disdain at Washington senators as 'conscript fathers of invisible families, who had something of the toga in the voluminous folds of their conversation', it is clear enough that no particular 'international' objection is being voiced. The flippant reference to the dome of the Capitol 'looking as simple as a suspended snowball' is the tone of James's own voice, not that of a German diplomat. To match the ring of distaste for 'darkies and loafers and hackmen, and also individuals with tufts on their chins, toothpicks in their mouths, their hands in their pockets, rumination in their jaws, and diamond-pins in their shirt-fronts', one need go no farther afield than the passages of social loathing in *Professor Fargo*, written before Henry James had ever, as an adult, taken leave of his homeland.

The Modern Warning (1888) is as heavy and laboured an essay in trans-Atlantic misunderstandings as *The Point of View*, half a dozen years earlier, had been light and effective. After a promising opening in which Anglo-American social disparities are observed wittily against a charming backcloth of Lake Como, quite in the spirit of the assured opening of *Daisy Miller*, the tale is made to bear so heavy a burden of assorted portents—the clash between fraternal and marital love, the mortal effects of inter-cultural treachery, the writer's day-dream that the effect of a book can be overpowering—that it bursts apart in melodramatic absurdity. That such hideous symbolic effects as these may spring from a simple Anglo-American love-match is a proposition altogether too crude to be swallowed, especially from an author who had already handled similar themes with grace and penetration.

What seems to have happened to wreck the structure of this tale is that the highly-charged love-hate relationship with a brother (always a tender point in Henry James's make-up, which, when touched, could lead to agitations in his writing as violent as those recording on a seismograph the distant rumblings of an earthquake) was allowed to become superimposed upon a concocted and more easily ordered love-hate relationship between cultures. When the American Miss Grice is wooed by an amiable if high Tory ornament of the British ruling class who rejoices in the designation Sir Rufus Chasemore, K.C.B., M.P., the lady's brother opposes so vigorous an objection to the match as a blatant instance of 'moral treachery' that the poor girl takes to flight. However, after a lapse of years, she becomes Lady Chasemore and takes her husband to America. Her own passing observations on 'the misery and brutality of the English populace' as exemplified by the 'vice and wretchedness' she observes before they sail from Liverpool, are as nothing compared to Sir Rufus's view of the United States as 'a consummate illustration of the horrors of democracy'. On returning to England, he feels it his duty to convey these impressions to his endangered countrymen in a book entitled 'The Modern Warning'. Lady Chasemore, after reading the proofs, makes Sir Rufus promise to suppress the book. But after a year during which she imagines the full effect of his grievous sacrifice, she makes a thorough-going volte-face and urges him to publish it. At this point, her brother crosses the Atlantic to repay the visit of his sister and brother-in-law. The prospect of his reaction to the now imminent book, and to her own perfidy in encouraging its appearance, is too much for her, and she commits suicide.

Ritual murder via the printed word? We recall *The Author of 'Beltraffio'* and stare open-mouthed at yet another instance of a wife resorting to murder (in this case self-murder) in order to avert the consequences which might follow the reading of her husband's book. Of all the many direful consequences of marriage, as conjured up in the bachelor-novelist's pot-boiling (and hence perhaps most revealing) tales, this is perhaps the most nightmarish of all. It is, at any rate, the *reductio ad absurdum* of the 'sops thrown to the international Cerberus'.

A late skimpy story, *Miss Gunton of Poughkeepsie* (1900), briefly rehashes the old Daisy Miller-Bessie Alden recipe in order to present the grotesque egotism of a moneyed American flirt who, having attracted an Italian prince of ancient lineage, announces that 'unless he wants me more than anything in the world I don't want him'. She sets his family an outrageous social test, no less than a demand that the prince's mother, who is described by Lady Champer (a budding Fanny Assingham) as 'a most formidable personage', should write a letter welcoming her to the family, before the engagement may be formally announced. There is a pause while this monstrous demand is brooded over in the Roman palazzo. To please her son, the old dowager finally consents to 'write first'— but her humiliated letter crosses with one from America announcing Miss Gunton's engagement to a suitable American. In a vulgar and quite unprovoked way, European pride has been humbled.

One may faintly discern in the mistreated prince a sketch for Prince Amerigo, and in Miss Gunton a horrid caricature of Charlotte Stant, of *The Golden Bowl*. But the chief impression made by this pot-boiler is of surprise, and even of disappointment, that so late in his writing life James was still capable of picking again at the old—and, one had thought, healed—scab of the social *hauteur* of old European families when confronted by the magnetic yet repellent forces of American dollars and American lack of gentility. It is sad that the ghost of *The American* was still not finally laid to rest, nearly a quarter of a century after Christopher Newman had vengefully surrendered his own social revenge.

V

'Organizing an Ado'

The Portrait of a Lady

Millions of presumptuous girls, intelligent
or not intelligent, daily affront their destiny,
and what is it open to their destiny to *be*,
at the most, that we should make an ado
about it? . . . that was what one was in for
—for positively organizing an ado about
Isabel Archer.

Preface

ISABEL ARCHER of *The Portrait of a Lady*, Milly Theale of *The Wings of the Dove*, Maggie Verver of *The Golden Bowl*, and even their flighty little junior-league sister Daisy Miller, are all thought by various critics to bear marked traces of Henry James's beloved cousin Minny Temple, who died in 1870 at the age of twenty-four. Again and again, at any rate, in the slightest little international *nouvelle* and in the three masterpieces named above, we are asked to follow, as they 'affront their destiny', versions of the kind of brave yet stricken young American woman Minny Temple might have become.

Very early in *The Portrait of a Lady* (1880) there is a strange little scene which betrays a brooding indwelling of creator and created figure so intense as to be almost an effort at identification—and identification, I shall suggest, with benefit of transvestism. Mrs. Touchett, the independent-minded wife of a wealthy American living mainly in Europe, is revisiting New York State and 'takes up' her niece, Isabel Archer. This lonely intelligent girl has a mind 'a good deal of a vagabond' and an imagination 'by habit ridiculously active'. She accepts her aunt's fairy-Godmother offer of a new life in Europe, a considerable advance on the 'history of German Thought' which, like a youthful George Eliot, she is reading on the occasion of Aunt Lydia Touchett's irruption. Her late 'handsome much-loved father' had kept her in ignorance of the unpleasant sides of life; she and her sisters had 'no regular education and no permanent home—they had been at once both spoiled and neglected'. By the time Isabel was fourteen, she and her sisters had been 'transported . . . three times across the Atlantic'. Erratic indulgence and erratic education had given her an ambivalent view of the learned state: she was familiar with 'the London *Spectator*, the latest publications, the music of Gounod, the poetry of Browning, the prose of George Eliot'. She 'liked to be thought clever, but she hated to be thought bookish'. She was jealous of her socially more active sister. 'Her deepest enjoyment was to feel the continuity between the movements of her own soul and the agitations of the world.' She was inactive but excited throughout the Civil War. And suddenly we realize that in our first introduction to Isabel Archer we are gazing at a detailed portrait not of Minny Temple—but of young Henry James himself.

This, then, is the girl about whom James set himself to 'organize an ado'—and in doing so, created his first full-length masterpiece. In the end, Isabel is to face the most gruelling fate of all his 'international young ladies' as she resigns herself to life with a detestable husband, whom misjudgement in her zest for experience had brought her to marry, and to whom pride will keep her faithful. But until this happens, she represents the adventurous half of the old double nature, but the adventurous half much toned down and made wiser by liberal borrowings from the ruminative half: 'the agitations of the world', so thinks Isabel in her innocent if presumptuous folly, can be tamed to keep pace with 'the movements of her own soul'. In *The Portrait of a Lady*, the stay-at-home 'other side' is represented by Isabel's cousin, Ralph Touchett—for the old 'men must work and women must weep' adage is reversed in this novel, and it is Ralph who is called upon not only to give his cousin technical liberation, 'to put a little wind in her sails', but also to weep in prescient impotence as he watches her using that liberty to march into a prison far worse than any from which her uncle Touchett's generosity had released her. Ralph, perhaps the most thoroughly likeable and credible of all James's sensitive invalids, whose 'serenity was but the array of wild flowers niched in his ruin', is presented as being himself fully conscious of his *own* attempts, muted though they must necessarily be, to profit by a double nature. Recognizing in Isabel a similar but potentially more active sensibility, he quite explicitly reveals to his cousin his wry social deceptions:

'I keep a band of music in my ante-room', he once said to her. 'It has orders to play without stopping; it renders me two excellent services. It keeps the sounds of the world from reaching the private apartments, and it makes the world think that dancing's going on within.'

If this strikes the reader as a more mature version of poor Benvolio's innocent self-deception, then cousin Isabel, for her part, is like Gertrude of *The Europeans*: she 'was not accustomed to keep [her imagination] behind bolts'. Her complementary fault, from which a larger dose of Ralph in her make-up might have saved her, was that:

... she was always planning out her development, desiring her perfection, observing her progress. Her nature had, in her conceit, a certain garden-like quality, a suggestion of perfume and murmuring boughs, of shady bowers and lengthening vistas, which made her feel that introspection was, after all, an exercise in the open air, and that a visit to the recesses of one's spirit was harmless when one returned from it with a lapful of roses.

—and at this point there follows that ironic comment about her consciousness that 'there were other gardens in the world than those of her remarkable soul'.

Isabel's introduction to English country-house life, at her wealthy gentle uncle's house Gardencourt, is compassed in the mood, and the prose, of a passionate pilgrim beautifully mellowed. Though quite different in method and effect, it has something of the rare atmospheric quality one recognizes in the work of James's friend Turgenev—as in *A Month in the Country*, for example. Old Touchett, at his tea-table on the lawn, for all the world like Adam Verver of *The Golden Bowl* at his similar muted country retreat of Fawns, provides the appropriate tone of unflamboyant wealth: his face 'seemed to tell that he had been successful in life, yet it seemed to tell also that his success had not been exclusive and invidious, but had had much of the inoffensiveness of failure'. It is his wife (for in the Touchett family, the women wear the trousers) who has the sharper edge; indeed, 'the edges of her conduct were so very clear-cut that for susceptible persons it sometimes had a knife-like effect'. Launched gently into English society under these most favourable auspices, Isabel soon attracts the notice of the Touchett's eligible neighbour, Lord Warburton, one of 'the radicals of the upper class', with a hundred thousand a year.

Our backward glimpse of Isabel at her original home in Albany, New York, has already alerted us to the probability, which she herself records in the ampler atmosphere of Gardencourt, that she was 'very liable to the sin of self-esteem; she often surveyed with complacency the field of her own nature ...' and she had 'an unquenchable desire to think well of herself'. So far, so good; a very proper wish. But more specifically, 'it was one of her theories that Isabel Archer was very fortunate in being independent, and that she ought to make some very enlightened use of that state'. The arrival at Gardencourt of Isabel's friend Henrietta Stackpole, the loquacious American career-woman who is correspondent for the *Interviewer*, brings forward independence in its crudest possible form—but it is clear that Isabel's imagination encompasses possibilities far beyond Miss Stackpole's grasp. It is true that 'Isabel's chief dread in life at this period of her development was that she should appear narrow-minded; what she feared next afterwards was that she should really be so'; but that is merely her starting point. After a few terse words with her aunt over some minor social lapse, Isabel declares herself in words that promise all, and foreshadow her tragedy:

> 'But I always want to know the things one shouldn't do!'
> 'So as to do them?' asked her aunt.
> 'So as to choose,' said Isabel.

Having convinced himself that he is not himself in love with his fascinating cousin, Ralph Touchett finds a daily interest in watching her progress and imagining the chart of her boundless future. He is unsurprised when she gently rejects a proposal of marriage from the super-eligible Lord Warburton, for he has enough cousinly imagination to divine Isabel's view that 'the "splendid" security so offered her was *not* the greatest she could conceive'. She makes it clear to the baffled nobleman that to marry him would be somehow to escape her fate, even though the act of renouncing so magnificent a capture ('all I offer you is the chance of taking the common lot in a comfortable sort of way', is how *he* put it) made Isabel 'really frightened at herself'. Meanwhile the interfering Henrietta, noticing the *rapport* between cousins, tries to enlist Ralph's support for the claims of Caspar Goodwood, an American suitor who had pursued Isabel across the Atlantic. Isabel had earlier felt Goodwood's appeal, for he represented all that was most energetic and creative in the American commercial myth and had at times 'seemed to range himself on the side of her destiny ...' He was, certainly, a more active combatant than Lord Warburton: 'she saw the different fitted parts of him as she had seen, in museums and portraits, the different fitted parts of armoured warriors—in plates of steel handsomely inlaid with gold.'

Ralph obligingly accompanies his cousin and Henrietta to London for some sightseeing, and while the thick-skinned Miss Stackpole tries to come to grips with the Protean English upper classes (even though 'London at large suffered from her vivid remembrance of the strong points of the American civic idea', which relegates her to the level of poor Aunt Penniman of *Washington Square*), Ralph devotes himself to a deeper understanding of Isabel. 'You're exacting', he tells her, 'without the excuse of thinking yourself good'—and he adds: 'I shall have the thrill of seeing what a young lady does who won't marry Lord Warburton.' This sentiment is echoed in louder tones by Caspar Goodwood, who has pursued Isabel to her London hotel and is once again rejected, but only by Isabel's wilful swerve against his undeniable attraction. He is made to feel, in his straightforward sexual drive, 'a strong man in the wrong'. Isabel's sole reason for rejecting him is that 'I don't want to be a mere sheep in the flock; I want to choose my fate'. She is, at the same time, callously willing to treat him as a second-best reserve:

'You'll get very sick of your independence.'
'Perhaps I shall; it's even very probable. When that day comes I shall be very glad to see you.'

Triumphant in her second escape from a curtailment of her liberty and determined to set no bounds to her divine discontent, Isabel returns to Gardencourt. The temptations of aristocratic consideration and physical passion have been mastered—but for what? Ralph, more intrigued than ever, persuades his dying father to leave Isabel half his own inheritance. 'I should like to put a little wind in her sails,' he explains to the old man. 'She wishes to be free, and your bequest will make her free.' (It is for £70,000—and at the value of sterling in the 1870's!) It is a magnificent stroke of construction that James should present this scene guaranteeing Isabel's final financial liberation, immediately after the girl has met, and found herself strangely attracted by, a visiting friend of her aunt's, by name Madame Merle. For Madame Merle, sophisticated and generous, competent and manipulating, cultivated and rapacious, will be the one to act as representative of and temptress to the third and final impediment to Isabel's true freedom. In ignorance alike of her coming fortune (from old Touchett) and of her coming doom (via Madame Merle), Isabel awaits in apparent serenity, among her friends, the death of her kindly uncle. And with the heroine poised on her confident flight towards the unknown, the opening third of the novel is completed.

What is so striking about these eighteen chapters, quite apart from their effortless groundwork of plot, is their liveliness. There are long passages of ratiocination, but they are broken up by vivid dialogue and laced throughout with wit. At Gardencourt, the fortunate hosts and guests find plenty of entertaining things to talk about: they are not, like the Assinghams at Fawns, in *The Golden Bowl* a quarter of a century later, reduced to endlessly ingrowing personal gossip. The freshness of Gardencourt is in very marked contrast with the heavy *fin de saison* stuffiness of Fawns; though it must be conceded that in the first of these country-houses the plight of Isabel is as yet a matter of light interest, while the tangled lives of the quartet at Fawns will be already long past the stage of marginal appreciation, and well into that final trapped involvement which will affect Isabel only later in her story. In the mellow comfort of Gardencourt, at any rate, even such edgy characters as Mrs. Touchett and Henrietta Stackpole are softened by an amused tolerance. Her hostess may speculate that Henrietta 'has lived all her life in a boarding-house, and I detest the manners and liberties of such places', but Ralph and Isabel, who had more to fear from her inquisitiveness, see her in more indulgent imagery, borrowed from the careers in which this energetic feminist does, or might, channel her talents:

> She rustled, she shimmered, in fresh, dove-coloured draperies . . . she was as crisp and new and comprehensive as a first issue before the folding. From top to toe she had probably no misprint.
>
> She was wanting in distinction, but . . . she was brave: she went into cages, she flourished lashes, like a spangled lion-tamer.

As for Mrs. Touchett herself, she exhibits, even before the advent of the professionally competent Madame Merle, all those qualities of serenity which Henry James, from far back, had valued—and celebrated—in womankind. Later in the novel, these qualities will be summed up in one vigorous image:

Mrs. Touchett had a great merit; she was as honest as a pair of compasses. There was a comfort in her stiffness and firmness; you knew exactly where to find her and were never liable to chance encounters and conclusions. On her own ground she was perfectly present, but was never over-inquisitive as regards the territory of her neighbour.

It is in similar terms of civilized external correlatives of things, objects, accoutrements, that even Isabel herself is at this stage presented:

Vibration was easy to her, was in fact too constant with her, and she found herself now humming like a smitten harp. She only asked, however, to put on the cover, to case herself again in brown holland . . .

And it is in this mood of relaxed vigilance, in the paradoxical urbanity of country-house life, that Isabel makes her vitally important assessment of Madame Merle: 'She was in a word a woman of strong impulses kept in admirable order. This commended itself to Isabel as an ideal combination.'

Eighteen chapters have brought Isabel to the brink of possession of the key to her liberty; the next seventeen determine the identity of the man on whom she decides to bestow it. In a gingerly-leisurely fashion, first via his friend Madame Merle, then by the opinions of several other people and finally in the strangely won sympathy of Isabel herself, we are introduced to Gilbert Osmond. But first, we are to have many more aspects of Isabel Archer's nature steadily unveiled, as we overhear her talking with Madame Merle and her cousin, or are made privy to her long private musings. At one point she concludes that 'the supreme good fortune', 'the essence of the aristocratic situation', was 'to be in a better position for appreciating people than they are for appreciating you'—the word 'appreciate' denoting, in this freshly-observed novel of James's early maturity, an activity which in his later novels would come to be expressed more bitterly by some such concept as 'dominate' or simply 'devour'. She is uncritically impressed by Madame Merle's competence, all morning letter-writing and afternoon water-colours and evening piano-playing or embroidery, plus a general capacity for manipulation which seems at first to be entirely for the benefit of the persons manipulated. Isabel's observation of her produces some admirable judgements:

... she had rid herself of every remnant of that tonic wildness which we may assume to have belonged even to the most amiable persons in the ages before country-house life was the fashion. . . . She existed only in her relations, direct or indirect, with her fellow mortals. . . . One always ended, however, by feeling that a charming surface doesn't necessarily prove one superficial; this was an illusion in which, in one's youth, one had but just escaped being nourished.

At which point, a backward-looking reader may reflect that some of these maturing judgements sound more suited to Henry James than to Miss Archer (with, in the passage just quoted, the lingering presence of Henry James Senior), while a forward-looking reader may note how comparatively lightly the novelist deals with social cannibalism, in view of the ghastly excesses in that line to which the characters of *The Sacred Fount* and other country-house-haunters of later novels will become addicted.

Chatting of her cosmopolitan friends, Madame Merle promises Isabel an introduction to Gilbert Osmond, an American living in Italy, who is 'exceedingly clever' but 'very indolent'. Meanwhile, her scornful sweeping aside of the claims of straight boy-meets-girl affairs is in line with James's own persistent shrinking from the treatment of normal courtship. Just as Olive Chancellor in *The Bostonians* will show an envious contempt for Verena's probable liking for 'a young man in a white overcoat and a paper collar', so Madame Merle snorts about 'a young man with a fine moustache going down on his knees'—and it is precisely the tone of some of the early stories written when Henry James was clearly suffering feelings of inhibition. Yet when Madame Merle explicitly confesses her 'great respect for *things* . . . one's home, one's furniture, one's garments, the books one reads, the company one keeps—these things are all expressive', Isabel disagrees, and in her disagreement is economically pin-pointed the rigidity—the frigidity, almost—of a heroine too prudent—headstrong not to be felt by the reader, this time, to be courting disaster: 'I don't know whether I succeed

in expressing myself, but I know that nothing else expresses me.'
For a moment, 'heroine' and 'villainess' exchange rôles. Or is it,
rather, that at a revealing moment Isabel is shown to have the hardness of a Roderick Hudson and Madame Merle, for all her competence, merely the administrative talents of a Rowland Mallet? We
feel momentarily grateful, at any rate, for the memory of the assurance that in Isabel 'the love of knowledge coexisted with the finest
capacity for ignorance'.

When, in London, Madame Merle hears from Mrs. Touchett of
Isabel's legacy, her first impulse is to cry out: 'Ah, the clever creature!' As for Miss Archer herself: 'The acquisition of power made
her serious; she scrutinized her power with a kind of tender ferocity,
but was not eager to exercise it'. Her widowed aunt takes her off to
Paris, where the young woman is contemptuous of the 'inane'
American colony and may be presumed to share the author's viewpoint of Ned Rosier, a young effeminate American *déraciné*, who
'had some charming rooms . . . decorated with old Spanish altar-
lace, the envy of his female friends, who declared that his chimney-
piece was better draped than the shoulders of many a duchess'.
Even the disapproving Henrietta Stackpole accuses Isabel, at this
stage, of being 'too fastidious'. She continues to brood over her
nature and her destiny, until cousin Ralph, visited at his invalid's
retreat at San Remo, accuses her in turn: 'Don't try so much to
form your character—it's like trying to pull open a tight, tender
young rose.' We are, by these reiterated but subtly variegated monologues and conversations, gradually made apprehensive for the
fortunate young woman's oft-rehearsed fate.

The scene changes to Florence, to the hill-top house of Gilbert
Osmond. The master of the house, aged forty, is receiving back his
daughter, Pansy, from her convent. His friend Madame Merle
wishes to put Isabel 'in your way'—and 'I want you of course to
marry her'. This sudden directness between a pair who are so very
oblique in company speaks of an intimacy taken for granted, of
'knowing each other well and each on the whole willing to accept
the satisfaction of knowing as a compensation for the inconvenience
—whatever it might be—of being known'. Osmond is presented as
a self-centred vaguely discontented connoisseur who, when in low
spirits, behaves like 'a demoralized prince in exile'—or, as Ralph

puts it, 'a prince who has abdicated in a fit of fastidiousness and has been in a state of disgust ever since'.

It is in front of this professional widower's lack-lustre eyes that Madame Merle dangles the bait of Isabel's seventy thousand pounds. She brings him to the Touchett palazzo ('to live in such a place was, for Isabel, to hold to her ear all day a shell of the sea of the past'). Ralph tries gently to open his cousin's eyes to the character of Madame Merle ('She's too complete, in a word'), for he knows her to fall into that dangerous category of persons who had achieved 'perfect training, but had won none of the prizes'. She was 'almost as universally "liked" as some new volume of smooth twaddle'—and here we certainly detect in Ralph's tone, always trustworthy when moral discriminations are in the air, the personal authentic note of his creator.

Ignoring Ralph's hint, Isabel visits Gilbert in company with his married sister, the sensible but over-experienced Countess Gemini, and begins to feel his strange fascination. He is an unashamed dilettante, but it is his elegant non-competitiveness that seems to attract her: ' "I've a few good things", Mr. Osmond allowed; "indeed I've nothing very bad. But I've not what I should have liked." ' Moreover:

> It was not so much what he said and did, but rather what he withheld, that marked him for her as by one of those signs of the highly curious that he was showing her on the underside of old plates and in the corner of sixteenth-century drawings: he indulged in no striking deflection from common usage, he was an original without being an eccentric.

When Osmond speaks of 'my studied, my wilful renunciation', the reader is alerted at the danger: with her new confidence, her new fortune, her new consciousness of having turned down two splendid *offers*, Isabel now feels the attraction of a *claim*. One is strangely reminded of Portia's Belmont, with Caspar Goodwood and Lord Warburton figuring as the Princes of Morocco and Aragon, and Osmond as an unworthy Bassanio linked with the attractions—for an heiress—of the leaden casket. The minor characters strike their poses while the lady's hand hovers over the fatal choice. Countess Gemini, who openly distrusts the 'chemical combination' of her brother in league with Madame Merle, is anxious to save Isabel from the trap; Mrs. Touchett simply writes off Osmond as 'an obscure American dilettante, a middle-aged widower with an uncanny child and an ambiguous income'; Ralph, who 'had a kind of loose-fitting urbanity that wrapped him about like an ill-made overcoat, but of which he never divested himself', is too distressed, at first, to speak out of turn. Perversely, Isabel-Portia carries away an image of her Osmond-Bassanio as of 'a quiet, clever, sensitive, distinguished man ... holding by the hand a little girl whose bell-like clearness gave a new grace to childhood'.

As if to stress the Belmont memory, Isabel has two more chances of revising her decisions between the suitors. In Rome, she runs into Lord Warburton, who declares that he is still in love with her. The fact that Isabel had turned down such a prize naturally increases her value, in Osmond's eyes, as a collector's item. 'He had never forgiven his star for not appointing him to an English dukedom', and to succeed where the great Lord Warburton failed is a special delight to him. Of course, the radical peer with a park-fence thirty miles in circumference cannot fail to suggest hypocrisy; but the freshness of presentation is such that he does not himself appear as a hypocrite, but rather in an attractive light:

... with his pleasant steady eyes, his bronzed complexion, fresh beneath its seasoning, his manly figure, his minimizing manner and his general air of being a gentleman and an explorer, he was such a representative of the British race as need not in any clime have been disavowed by those who have a kindness for it.

Indeed, the manner in which one's pleasure in the company of Ralph and Warburton is revived just before the chilly Osmond's proposal of marriage is a skilful weighting of the scales. When *he* detects the feel of success—'the most agreeable emotion of the human heart'— the reader shudders. Even the charming image of modest worth disclosed (an image added in the revised text of the New York Edition) has, in his immediate context, a self-satisfied smugness about it:

If an anonymous drawing on a museum wall had been conscious and watchful it might have known this peculiar pleasure of being at last and all of a sudden identified—as from the hand of a great master—by the so high and so unnoticed fact of style. His 'style' was what the girl had discovered with a little help; and now, beside herself enjoying it, she should publish it to the world without his having any of the trouble. She should do the thing *for* him, and he would not have waited in vain.

This is the man who urges Isabel to 'be triumphant', and who arouses her feelings.

Six more chapters unfold before the choice is made irrevocable. Before giving Osmond her answer, Isabel absents herself (in one of those abrupt Jamesian foreshortenings of time: another long journey taken, so to say, within a parenthesis) for a year of Near Eastern travel. On returning, she receives in Florence a last appeal from Caspar Goodwood. He, too, is sent about his business: Isabel had written to him about her engagement, but his instant rocketing to her side flatters her power without changing her course. Mrs. Touchett is angered by the engagement and blames Madame Merle. Ralph, now perilously ill, is grieved deeply enough to say outright 'I think he's narrow, selfish': and from Isabel comes, during a conversation of great restraint and beauty on both sides, the surprising claim that life with Osmond will represent, for her, the 'one ambition—to be free to follow a good feeling'. We suddenly recognize that Isabel, who has been steadily diminishing the store of regard a reader has built up for her earlier in the novel, is falling for the one allowable temptation for a person in her position—the temptation to give. She, who won our interest in the selfish days of her education for life, when all her judgement was consecrated to what she might *want* from life, comes parlously near losing it at the very point when she decides on a course of sacrifice. Ralph, cousinly antennae more sensitive than ever, grasps the high tragic nature of her mistake: 'She was wrong, but she believed; she was deluded, but she was dismally consistent'. She loved Osmond 'for his very poverties dressed out as honours'. It is to this that her vaunted imagination has led her. It remains only to take the measure of the now doubly self-engrossed pair as they prepare to pool their resources, to the consternation of all Isabel's friends—including Osmond's discredited sister. Isabel's superior amusement at her imagination of her own unenlightened sisters' disapproval 'at her not having chosen a consort who was the hero of a richer accumulation of anecdote' is matched by Osmond's icy jubilation: 'Contentment, on his part, took no vulgar form; excitement, in the most self-conscious of men, was a kind of ecstasy of self-control.' He has the conceit to inform his bride-to-be: 'You're remarkably fresh, and I'm remarkably well-seasoned.' For him, the capture is that of a living soul. There is a horrible knell—so far, so wonderfully have we been worked upon—in the notion of this impotent life-sucking mannikin teasing his captured prey: 'he could tap her imagination with his knuckle and make it ring.'

The last twenty chapters of the fifty-five-chapter novel set forth, with a variation of pace and a wealth of creative power that raise James from the level of virtuoso to that of serene master of fiction, the consequences of Isabel's blunder, the full payment exacted for that tragic flaw which had been displayed (and, at that time, justly dismissed) earlier in the book: 'the love of knowledge coexisted in her mind with the finest capacity for ignorance'. The Osmonds are discovered in their Roman palazzo after an interval of nearly three years, during which we are told that they had, and lost, a baby. Pansy, now nineteen, is being sought in marriage by—of all people— Ned Rosier. He applies for aid in his suit to Madame Merle, and it is from her hints that we first gather that Gilbert and Isabel Osmond are barely on speaking terms. Osmond desires a far better *parti* for Pansy than Rosier, who may see her as the perfect American *jeune fille* but can offer her and her father no wordly distinction; it is in his odious rudeness to the sincere young swain that we first see the full nastiness of which Osmond is capable. When Lord Warburton turns up again in Rome, Osmond masters his jealousy of his wife's former suitor and his envy of the Warburton prestige and welcomes him to the palazzo parties, hoping that the noble lord will fall for Pansy. Isabel loyally refrains from exposing Osmond's mental and verbal cruelty to herself, but in such comments (to Warburton) as 'He has a genius for upholstery' she makes her disillusion clear enough. There is built up, in the Palazzo Roccanera, an atmosphere of female unhappiness in a grand setting which is hauntingly akin to that of poor Milly Theale's Venetian palazzo in *The Wings of the Dove*—the presence of a loathsome husband having reduced Isabel Archer to the brave pitiable plight reproduced in Milly by the absence of a compromised lover. As usual, it is cousin Ralph, now mortally sick in Rome, who has the sensibility to crystallize and elucidate, as he ponders with his friend Warburton the awful domestic situation of the girl he himself had freed for great flights: 'The free, keen girl had become quite another person; what he saw was the fine lady who was supposed to represent something . . . she represented Gilbert Osmond. "Good heavens, what a function!" '

Again relying on Ralph's litmus-like judgement, the reader is brought to see that Osmond's vice is not only gross egotism, but an egotism morbidly concerned with the world's opinion, which he takes such pains to appear to despise. Ralph, who hardly ever sees him (for Osmond returns his detestation), senses that 'under the guise of caring only for intrinsic values Osmond lived exclusively for the world', his highest delight being 'to please himself by exciting the world's curiosity and then declining to satisfy it'. It is certainly profoundly significant, not only of the deeply autobiographical sensibility with which James endowed Ralph Touchett, but of the permanent moral-aesthetic tone of James's later development as man and writer far beyond 1880 and *The Portrait of a Lady*, that Ralph's ethical judgement of Osmond is couched in terms of artistic taste: 'He always had an eye to effect, and his effects were deeply calculated. They were produced by no vulgar means, but the motive was as vulgar as the art was great.' This last sentence could stand as epigraph to many a late James story. It should certainly be adduced whenever Henry James is accused by the ignorant and the superficial reader of being, either in life or in art, a snob!

During the first three years of Isabel's marriage, years missing from *The Portrait*, she has seen little of Madame Merle. When they meet to discuss, obliquely, the policy to be pursued in the matter of Ned Rosier's play for Pansy and the superior attractions of Lord Warburton, Isabel feels at first the old admiration. Contrasted with the 'revulsions and disgusts' to which she had become the domestic victim, 'it was a pleasure to see a character so completely armed for the social battle'. As for herself, 'there were days when she asked herself with some sharpness what it was that she was pretending to live for', but Madame Merle was arrayed in her customary purposeful 'corselet of silver'. She agrees, at any rate, to support any bid Lord Warburton may make for Pansy. When the same topic is raised by Osmond, he makes the offensive suggestion that Isabel still has it in her power to influence her old suitor's selection of her step-daughter as the future Lady Warburton. Osmond's lust for the Warburton connexion is nakedly exposed. Its effect is to plunge Isabel into fresh agonies of introspection, peeling away layer after layer of her own folly and her husband's duplicity as she sees how irretrievably she has thrown away her life. Even to *know*, let alone suffer, the atrocities of his snobbish sterility, 'his faculty for making everything wither that he touched', is painful; still more painful is the realization that he, too, loathes *her* because she has not brought him the self-fulfilment, the self-advertisement he had desired of her: 'he despised her; she had no traditions and the moral horizon of a Unitarian minister.' His disappointment is as sharp as her own, and hers is complete: 'She had taken all the first steps in the purest confidence, and then she had suddenly found the infinite vista of a multiplied life to be a dark, narrow alley with a dead wall at the end.' How different from her first view of him as a vocation rather than a cul-de-sac! 'He was like a sceptical voyager strolling on the beach while he waited for the tide, looking seaward yet not putting to sea. It was in all this she had found her occasion. She would launch his boat for him . . .' He thought of himself, she now sees, as 'the first gentleman in Europe', but 'under all his culture, his cleverness, his amenity, under his good-nature, his facility, his knowledge of life, his egotism lay hidden like a serpent in a bank of flowers'. Isabel Archer, the innocently amusing little egotist of the early chapters, is seeing the full blossoming of that quality.

In musing over the steadfast loyalty to her image shown by that great man of the world Lord Warburton, Isabel had at one point envied 'the happier lot of men, who are always free to plunge into the healing waters of action'. She herself is denied the outlet of action. She would willingly abet Rosier's honest love for Pansy, but fear of her husband's rage stifles her good intentions. What she does manage to divine is that Warburton's bid for Pansy is probably a feint aimed at bringing Isabel at last into his family. Meanwhile, two more active ladies are brought back into focus and survey the situation of the Osmonds from their customary viewpoints: the Countess Gemini who delights in the pretended belief that Isabel is betraying her brother with Lord Warburton, while Henrietta Stackpole, advised of her friend's unhappiness, prepares to propel Caspar

Goodwood yet again from the wings to the stage. While these off-stage diversions take place, poor little Pansy resigns herself to a long siege, knowing perfectly well that Lord Warburton is not in love with her, and determined to preserve herself, against her father's wishes, for Ned Rosier. The amiable nobleman, having failed in his last sidelong rescue attempt, takes leave of the Osmonds and returns to England, to the furious bitterness of Gilbert who accuses his wife, in vile words, of having plotted against his plans for Pansy. Standing before his venomous self-pity, 'she might have represented the angel of disdain, first cousin to that of pity. "Oh, Gilbert, for a man who was so fine—!" ' Osmond's verbal sadism, indeed, is as destructive to the notion of married happiness as anything—to snatch at a contemporary instance—in Albee's *Who's Afraid of Virginia Woolf?* And one is reminded, yet again, that although in *The Portrait of a Lady* one's sympathies are enlisted on a full tragic scale, yet the old hackneyed Jamesian theme that marriage is an avoidable disaster still abides as the kernel of the plot.

Henrietta's American cavalry, so to say, swoops to make a fruitless gesture of rescue: Caspar calls on the Osmonds, makes yet another protestation of love to Isabel, finds himself patronizingly 'taken up' by a malicious Osmond who delights in making fun of his wife's friends, and used by Mrs. Osmond (who has conceded that though he may not love, he is now permitted to 'pity' her) to act as fellow-courier with Henrietta for Ralph's safe conduct back to Gardencourt and death. The unsubtle ironclad Henrietta herself becomes, momentarily, a minor irritant to make visible the Osmonds' friction; and nothing is more effective, among all the varied descriptions of and surmises about the Osmonds' domestic hell, than Gilbert's vain attempt to parade a masochistic patience in enduring Miss Stackpole's presence (so that Isabel's loyalty to her friend gains 'a spice of heroism'), an attempt countered by Isabel's restraint in keeping her friend away from her husband: 'Her immediate acceptance of his objections put him too much in the wrong—it being in effect one of the disadvantages of expressing contempt that you cannot enjoy at the same time the credit of expressing sympathy.' The withering touch of Osmond is almost visibly demonstrated at such comparatively unimportant moments, or in passing references such as that to the formal parties which he 'still held for the sake not so much of inviting people as of not inviting them'. His vileness, we are made in various ways to see, lies not in what he does but in what he is.

So far, although our attention has been riveted upon the chief characters in the drama, the pace and tone of the novel have not greatly varied: the slow development of the 'ado' over Isabel's destiny is matched by the slow revelation of her appalling miscalculation. But the last seven chapters of the novel show a remarkable quickening. Brooding monologues give place to confrontations which verge on the melodramatic. Pretences vanish; secrets are revealed; sudden wilful decisions are taken. Yet it is to be noted that none of these occurrences take place until the slow development and the partial dénouement have already placed the reader in an assenting frame of mind and in possession of almost all the facts of the case. Of the three important facts that are yet to be revealed to Isabel, one has been known to readers from the time of its commission, the second has been taken for granted, and the third has probably been guessed. It is all but laid bare when Madame Merle comes to discover, in her own unsentimental way, how far the wretched scheme for Pansy and Lord Warburton had miscarried, and whether Isabel herself had set the noble suitor against it. As the strained dialogue continues, 'a strange truth was filtering into her soul. Madame Merle's interest was identical with Osmond's: that was enough'. Only as the confrontation proceeds, obliquely and obscurely, does Isabel grasp the first simple truth that it was Madame Merle who had arranged her marriage and that Gilbert had married her for her money. We then watch a brief scene between Madame Merle and Osmond himself (it is significant that one slips into the language of the theatre at this point) in which their long complicity is taken for granted and his present disdain for her made manifest. There is a passing reference to a 'cracked cup' motif which briefly pre-figures the controlling image of *The Golden Bowl*; there is, too, her direct accusation to an unfeeling Osmond: 'You have made me as bad as yourself.' This scene is followed by one of Osmond's rare brutalities of action (as opposed to brutalities of thought or speech): after his sister the Countess adds her voice in support of romance in the person of Ned Rosier, he banishes Pansy to a convent retreat.

News comes that Ralph is dying and Osmond, on grounds of propriety, forbids his wife to travel to England to be at her cousin's deathbed. In face of such malignity she hesitates—and it is at this crucial point that the Countess Gemini, eager to encourage her sister-in-law in one act of defiance, reveals to her the second truth that Madame Merle and Osmond had been lovers, some time ago, for a period of six or seven years, and that Pansy is their daughter. This 'aid to innocent ignorance' from so unexpected a quarter knocks out of Isabel's sails, so to say, whatever breath of wind the generosity of Ralph had originally put behind them. Suddenly the astounding if perverse grandeur of Madame Merle's own rôle is laid bare, and for an instant it almost seems that it is she whose stature is worthy of a 'portrait'. For paragraphs at a time, the writing glows with a kind of muted excitement. Isabel, of course, will now travel to England in defiance of Gilbert's ban. Madame Merle, arch-priestess of competence, stands revealed as a pathetically unsuccessful loser in life's battle. There had been no question of Gilbert's marrying his devoted mistress: she had no money for him. The chattering Countess pats Madame Merle back again into non-heroic dimensions:

She hoped she might marry a great man; that has always been her idea . . . The only tangible result she has ever achieved—except, of course, getting to know everyone and staying with them free of expense—has been her bringing you and Osmond together.

Worst of all, the Countess insists that Madame Merle, like Osmond, is a slave to convention: 'Her great idea has been to be tremendously irreproachable—a kind of full-blown lily—the incarnation of propriety.' So far, after all, from being tragic, she has been pathetically cheated of meagre hopes: 'She has worked for him, plotted for him, suffered for him; she has even more than once found money for him; and the end of it is that he's tired of her.'

In the four remaining chapters the novelist has not so much stepped up the pace as changed gear altogether. They throb, these final resolutions of character already revealed, with all the accumulated life of a brilliantly sustained and always witty control of the patiently achieved narrative of the main novel. We know now, readily enough, what will *happen*. Yet, curiously, the desire to see just *how* the main characters will be true to the natures we now so completely know, is vividly insistent. When Isabel meets Madame Merle at Pansy's convent, just before she leaves for England, it is as if the reader, along with Isabel Archer, had 'been thinking all day of her falsity, her audacity, her ability, her probable suffering . . .' The contrast between the imprisoned Pansy, who seems to have succumbed to her father's orders that she should renounce Ned Rosier for a finer match, and her two visitors, her unknown mother who is about to depart for America and her known step-mother who promises to return to her in Rome—all this is almost too much to be handled. The temptation to melodrama, as the two women meet to part for ever, is brilliantly avoided, is replaced by a moment of psychological truth so categorically right that only a major novelist in full control could have identified it and then had the art to bring it off. Isabel, being a James heroine, keeps silent about her new knowledge. Madame Merle, plunging on, suddenly feels, suddenly knows that her long secret has been laid bare:

She had not proceeded far before Isabel noticed a sudden break in her voice, a lapse in her continuity, which was in itself a complete drama. This subtle modulation marked a momentous discovery—the perception of an entirely new attitude on the part of her listener. Madame Merle had guessed in the space of an instant that everything was at an end between them, and in the space of another instant she had guessed the reason why. The person who stood there was not the same one she had seen hitherto, but was a very different person—a person who knew her secret. This discovery was tremendous, and from the moment she made it the most accomplished of women faltered and lost her courage. But only for that moment. Then the conscious stream of her perfect manner gathered itself again and flowed on as smoothly as might be to the end. . . .

She has after all, if only by her own worldly standards, her moment of tragic stature. For Isabel, the shock of complete truth is curiously deflating:

. . . the dry staring fact that she had been an applied handled hung-up tool, as senseless and convenient as mere shaped wood and iron. All the bitterness of this knowledge surged into her soul again; it was as if she felt on her lips the taste of dishonour. There was a moment during which, if she had turned and spoken, she would have said something that would hiss like a lash. But she closed her eyes, and then the hideous vision dropped. What remained was the cleverest woman in the world standing there within a few feet of her and knowing as little what to think as the meanest. Isabel's only revenge was to be silent still—to leave Madame Merle in this unprecedented situation.

There is one last twist of the knife before Madame Merle disappears. She tells Isabel that it was Ralph who induced old Mr. Touchett to make her an heiress. This is the third missing truth, for Isabel. And her only revenge is to reply: 'I believed it was you I had to thank!'

> Madame Merle dropped her eyes; she stood there in a kind of proud penance. 'You're very unhappy, I know. But I'm more so.'
> 'Yes; I can believe that. I think I should like never to see you again.'

Hastening to Gardencourt, Isabel is so overcome by 'the truth of things, their mutual relations, their meaning, and for the most part their horror', that she 'envied Ralph his dying, for if one were thinking of rest that was the most perfect of all'. She soon recovers her still youthful feeling that 'she was too valuable, too capable', not to go on to make something of her life. She is met in London by Henrietta Stackpole and *her* English beau, whose prattle serves to relax—or rather to *isolate*—Isabel's tension, much as the Porter Scene in *Macbeth*, by showing how unconcerned the rest of the world can be, concentrates rather than dissipates the gloom upon certain cursed heads. Her leave-taking of Ralph is the most affecting deathbed scene I have come across in fiction: so brief, so completely true to the best side of the characters both cousins have already displayed in life, so unsentimental, so deeply moving, and, specifically, so witty. 'You were ground in the very mill of the conventional,' says the dying epitome of unconventional good manners. His benediction is as tender as it is honest: 'I don't believe that such a generous mistake as yours can hurt for more than a little.' He has loved her more steadfastly than any of her three suitors.

Last scene of all, a final confrontation with Caspar Goodwood. He embraces her passionately and calls her husband, not unjustly, 'the deadliest of fiends'. But Isabel knows what she must do, what promises she must honour; and she returns to Rome.

The reader curious to assess how much the portrait of Isabel Archer owes to James's close study of George Eliot's novels, and how much to family emotions, is recommended to consult Dr. Cargill's admirable summary of the evidence in his *The Novels of Henry James*—but only after another glance at my own warning on this habit (Introduction, p. 21). Dr. Cargill's own conclusion seems just enough: 'All in all, the characters of *The Portrait of a Lady* are composite figures, as one might expect them to be in a novel which is in a way a summary of all the novelist had learned in his apprenticeship.' Certainly, with *The Portrait of a Lady* the apprenticeship is over. The mechanics, the structure (about which James was so self-congratulatory in the later Preface), are adequate to theme and treatment; one is not irritated by architectonic airs called in to give significance to trivial matter. For all the gentleness of the prose, for all the small examples demonstrated, for all the light social comedy and the well controlled, well disguised personal grief, what we are called upon to experience in this 'probably matchless' novel (the words are Dr. Cargill's) is no less than the fatal miscalculation which can lead a young woman endowed with intelligence and a fortune to throw herself away into a marriage which offers no apparent alternative to lifelong unhappiness. Mr. Graham Greene, who is something of an expert in these matters, has stated (in his Introduction to the World's Classics edition of the novel): 'There is no possibility of a happy ending: this is surely what James always tells us, not with the despairing larger-than-life gesture of a romantic novelist but with a kind of bitter precision.' I do not quarrel with that interpretation: it seems to me better than any of the various 'solutions' less stern critics have offered Isabel Archer. Through all the surface tenderness, through all the pastel delicacy of style, through all the jolly scenes of cultivated leisure, through even the swathing inhumanities of nineteenth-century clothing, we have shared an exposure of human vulnerability as raw as anything in the paintings of Francis Bacon. Mr. Greene adds that the destiny affronting Isabel Archer is simply this: 'you must betray or, more fortunately, perhaps, you must be betrayed'.

One has certainly to remind oneself constantly of the *youth* of the major characters. At the time of their meeting, Osmond is forty and Isabel, twenty-three. Looking round at today's American twenty-three-year-olds, cannot imagine one of them in Isabel Archer's shoes. Acts are no longer irrevocable; morality is no longer a matter of sanctions; and nowadays we can hardly be expected to 'keep up' appearances which neither exist nor are expected to exist. For this reason, it is an effort to grasp the full significance of James's 1880 'ado'. It is all the more remarkable that his portraits, not only of the lady but also of the other personages, remain so lifelike. (Speaking of Mrs. Touchett, Dr. Cargill makes a point which is applicable to all the rest: 'it should be noted that the description is in terms of her mind and conduct and not in those of her appearance'.) The most obvious difference between the young women of then and now lies not so much in sexual emancipation (for one assumes that Caspar Goodwood had kissed Miss Archer at Albany long before embracing the wife and mother of Rome), as in the freedom to select a career other than that of wife or 'companion'. In some ways, indeed, it is the laughable Henrietta Stackpole who has 'affronted her destiny' in the most modern fashion. She may lack the attractions of Isabel, but she will at least avoid the plight of an intelligent woman like Madame Merle who, with all her vivid cleverness, is forced to base her economy on staying with people 'free of expense'. One has a feeling that Lord Warburton might have made a hash of his life as disastrous as Isabel's, had he not, as landed proprietor and hereditary legislator, been 'free to plunge into the healing waters of action'. James's next two major novels, at any rate, were to deal in their different ways with attempts to modify the hurts and boredoms of private life by involvement with public affairs.

Except on the very general basis that it is difficult to imagine any human behaviour of which one could not be oneself *capable*, I cannot bring myself to share in so many words Dr. Edel's uncomfortable thesis (III, 429) that: 'Strange as it may seem, Osmond clearly expresses one side of Henry James—the hidden side—not as malignant as that of his creation, but nevertheless that of the individual who abjures power by clothing it in meekness and deceptive docility.' The view that Isabel and Osmond are 'for all their differences, two sides of the same coin, two studies in egotism—and a kind of egotism which belonged to their author'—puts the point in a more acceptable form. When Isabel contemplates with 'tender ferocity' the power of her money, she is not far from the 'ecstasy of self-control' with which Gilbert Osmond will celebrate the capture of a moneyed wife. One need not seriously think of Henry James as a potential Gilbert Osmond in order to accept quite willingly the notion that there is a love-hate feeling for all his competent 'super-subtle fry'. Beneath all the open admiration for his self-conscious and serene characters (for whom Madame Merle may stand as prime representative) and, one assumes, for himself as their self-conscious and serene creator, there seems to lurk a deep hatred—and not only of the 'villains'. The chill light investing Gilbert Osmond may indeed change, at the end of the novel, into a lurid livid putrescence as he himself changes from a stagey Sir Willoughby Patterne to a stagey but non-melodramatic psychological villain, of the kind to make any warm-hearted young woman long to scratch his eyes out. At the same time it must be recalled that Isabel Archer's non-villainous calculations can be almost equally distasteful. Sometimes, from deep underground sources, one simply detects in James a straight—almost passionate—dislike of his own characters; and to the extent that there is a 'there-but-for-the-grace-of-God-go-I' quality in every human censoriousness, one may accept Dr. Edel's main argument. What I myself find fascinating is the search—usually vain—for any trace of the *direct* Roderick Hudson 'creative' make-up in Henry James, alongside the much more visible Rowland Mallet 'creative commentary' constituent. It is to be found in the occasional poetic glee of his prose, at moments when he is unpre-occupied with function or proportion.

For it does not do to overlook the obvious. The sheer beauty of the writing in *The Portrait of a Lady* may lull a psychologically interested reader into ingratitude, into forgetfulness of the normal stock-in-trade not only of James's contemporary novelists, but also of his own earlier *oeuvre*. The prostitution of Noémie Nioche, the murder of the old Marquis de Bellegarde, the retirement to a nunnery of Madame de Cintré, the death of Valentin in a duel (all these from *The American*): what has happened to *this* kind of writing? Interest is now focused entirely on the minds and feelings of his characters, best expressed in a loving welling-up of fluent precision, rather than on their actions, violent or otherwise; so that the parent-age of Pansy Osmond, for example, comes almost wearily as the confirmation of a corruption already thoroughly grasped from an observance of how Gilbert Osmond misuses his *objets d'art* or merely stands before his chimneypiece. If it is noteworthy now, it was doubly so in 1880, that attention is so concentrated on delicate strokes of delineation as to make the reader not so much unaware of 'what happens next' as actually *impatient* when exigencies of plot interrupt for a moment the fascination of the author's psychological analysis. Although we know from his other writings that James *was* always intensely interested in the working-out of a preconceived plot, the development by thesis and antithesis of his main themes, yet it needs to be recognized, too, that from *The Portrait of a Lady* onwards the plot would never be merely an exciting sequence of violent episodes, but always, however murky, as inward as his steady sardonic discriminations within the universe of human character.

VI

'Slashing Out in the Bewilderment'

The public life and the private life: *The Bostonians;
The Princess Casamassima; The Reverberator*

> It seems probable that if we were never be-
> wildered there would never be a story to tell
> about us . . . 'Give us plenty of bewilder-
> ment . . . so long as there is plenty of
> slashing out in the bewilderment too.'
> *Preface to 'The Princess Casamassima'*

IT IS fair to begin any discussion of *The Bostonians* and *The Princess Casamassima* by admitting that my own high estimation of both novels has not been shared by all critics. Henry James himself, who had devoted immense labour to these long and detailed studies of current social themes in his native and his adopted countries, expressed a pained incredulous disappointment at their failure to make any impression on critics or general readers. 'I am still staggering a good deal', he wrote to W. D. Howells in 1888, 'under the mysterious and (to me) inexplicable injury wrought—apparently— upon my situation by my last two novels, the *Bostonians* and the *Princess*, from which I expected so much and derived so little. They have reduced the desire, and the demand, for my productions to zero. . . .' Twenty years later the disappointment was still fresh and still inexplicable; writing to Howells in 1908, he mentions his desire to revise and re-issue *The Bostonians* in the New York Edition, referring to the book as 'tolerably full and good', and admits that it had never, 'even to my much-disciplined patience, received any sort of justice'. The cool reception afforded to his twin offerings in 1886 hurt but did not daunt him. In the first of the letters to Howells quoted above, he continues:

> However, I don't despair, for I think I am now really in better form than I have ever been in my life, and I propose yet to do many things. Very likely too, some day, all my buried prose will kick off its various tombstones at once. Therefore don't betray me till I myself have given up. That won't be for a long time yet.

He held manfully to his own view of these two novels. Of *The Bostonians* he wrote to his brother William in 1885: 'the story is, I think, the best fiction I have written.' As for *The Princess Casamassima*, it is included in the first of two 'short lists' of his novels, provided as late as 1913 for the benefit of a young aspirant: its companions in the list 'not to be missed' being *Roderick Hudson*, *The Portrait of a Lady*, *The Wings of the Dove*, and *The Golden Bowl*.

Many modern critics have taken up the cudgels against what they consider to be (in the phrasing of Dame Rebecca West's 1916 judgement, which may stand as a pithy sample of this attitude) 'a nagging hostility to political effort'. Some have been so worked upon by these two novels as to utter apparently contradictory judgements. In 1937, Dr. F. R. Leavis recognized in *The Bostonians* and two other early novels 'the abundant, full-blooded life of well-nourished organisms', and in *The Princess Casamassima* he saluted an 'earthy and sappy vitality' (*Scrutiny* V, 4); yet over twenty-five years later he considered *'The Princess Casamassima*, one of James's most embarrassing failures, is so feeble a work that it couldn't have begotten anything . . .'*—a judgement which strangely echoes the view of Mr. Frank Swinnerton that it is 'one of the worst books by a good writer that I have ever read'.† The prince of Jamesians, Dr. Leon Edel (III, 116), allows *The Princess Casamassima* to be 'a large and human work' describing 'the plight of the London working class and its nascent revolutionary impulse', but although he calls *The Bostonians* 'the most considerable American novel of its decade' he nevertheless accounts it (III, 76) 'a failure by comparison with Henry's best work—even though its place in American literature is significant'.

In the year 1882, Henry James lost both his parents; and in the following year, his younger brother Wilky. His two return visits to America in 1882 were sad funereal ones, but he was alive enough to record several revised impressions of his homeland, of which the story *The Point of View*, already noted in Chapter I, was the immediate repository. A more ambitious task in reappraisal of *his* America was the composition of *The Bostonians*, which occupied much of his time in 1884 and early 1885. *The Princess Casamassima*, in some senses a parallel effort to do for *his* London what he had just done for *his* Boston, followed without a break. It was an astonishingly productive period for him, unflagging (indeed, both novels have been criticized for being too exuberantly long rather than too wearily short) and at the same time stern, dedicated. After the customary serialization, both novels appeared in book form in 1886, in the order of composition. If, in linking them, I choose to deal first with *The Princess Casamassima*, it is because I wish first to stress the qualities embodied in little Hyacinth Robinson, that novel's

* In *The Spectator*, 2 August 1963.
† *The Georgian Literary Scene* (1935).

hero, as he is shown 'slashing out in the bewilderment' of an attempt to adjust his private sensibilities to a public life. They are qualities reviving those aspects of Henry James's own personality which to my mind show direct contact with what I have called his 'Roderick Hudson side'; qualities perhaps laid bare during those months of sadness and devotion to work, when the well-springs of his creative genius were not channelled into formal irrigation or decorative-screening fountains, but were surely lapped up, Gideon-like, by parched and grateful lips.

The Princess Casamassima has, as a skeletal plot, a tale of metro-politan revolutionaries and the struggle to right the wrongs of the downtrodden. Dr. Leavis observes that the novel brings 'little comfort to those who would like to justify James by his interest in the class-war', and suggests that it derives, significantly, from a literary source—Dickens. There is ample evidence of James's habit of seeing the 'real' world through the derived world of art, and he has himself told us in *A Small Boy and Others* that as a child he would creep to a corner of the room, hidden behind a screen or table-cloth, to drink in enjoyment as a cousin read aloud to his mother the first instalments of *David Copperfield*. It is true, too, that on his first childhood view of London he found it 'extraordinarily the picture and the scene of Dickens, now so changed and super-seded', and later recalls his horrified fascination when, from the safe interior of an early Victorian four-wheeler, he watched 'swarm-ing crowds . . . of figures reminding me of George Cruikshank's Artful Dodger and his Bill Sykes and his Nancy', figures looming suddenly in 'gas-lit patches . . . culminating, somewhere far to the west, in the vivid picture, framed by the cab-window, of a woman reeling backward as a man felled her to the ground with a blow in the face'. The childhood Dickensian memories we may well accept but James's mature view of London was entirely his own. This is made conveniently explicit in one of his generous letters to the young H. G. Wells. Praising that author's *Kipps* in 1905, he writes:

You have for the very first time treated the English 'lower middle' class, etc., without the picturesque, the grotesque, the fantastic and romantic interference of which Dickens, e.g. is so misleadingly, of which even George Eliot is so deviatingly, full.

'For the very first time' is a phrase generous indeed, from the man who had written *The Princess Casamassima* twenty years before.

Why disbelieve James's own account, in the later Preface, of the origin of the novel? He tells us, *tout court:*

> The simplest account of the origin of *The Princess Casamassima* is, I think, that this fiction proceeded quite directly, during the first year of a long residence in London, from the habit and interest of walking the streets ... the prime idea was unmistakably the ripe round fruit of perambulation.

So it was that little Hyacinth Robinson 'sprang up for me out of the London pavement'—not from Dickens, and still less from any narrow notion of society dominated by political indignation. 'At his elbow', in Dr. Edel's phrase, there certainly 'stood Balzac, Dickens, Turgenev, Zola . . .' At his elbow, precisely; but living London, by his own testimony, was at his feet, at his finger-tips.

It is, indeed, precisely on the ground that James's young hero was *not* Dickensian enough that some critics seem to have been annoyed. Van Wyck Brooks quoted with vexation the lad's habit of 'letting his imagination wander among the haunts of the aristocracy', a habit which he attributed to James's own superstitious reverence for the 'noble blood' he had caused to flow in the poor young book-binder's illegitimate veins. 'In real life', cried this outraged critic from the realistic side of the Atlantic (he cannot forgive James for leaving it), 'the last thing that would have occurred to a young man in Hyacinth's position would have been to "roam and wander and yearn" about the gates of that lost paradise: he would have gone to Australia, or vanished into the slums, or continued with the utmost indifference at his trade of binding books.' That may be indeed what he *should* have done, according to the set social tenets of Boston. Henry James knew better. He knew that the imagination of a child is not bounded by a nice sense of social status or republican zeal. He had only to recall his own childhood dreams, in far-off New York, over 'the full entrancing folios of Nash's lithographed *Mansions of England in the Olden Times*'—another habit frowned upon by the incorruptible Mr. Brooks. Mr.

Stephen Spender* went one better in high-minded indignation and suggested that Hyacinth Robinson 'might today have become a socialist Prime Minister: a Ramsay MacDonald, who, at the height of his power, would dismay his followers by going over to the other side and becoming the most frequent of visitors at large country houses and of diners at Buckingham Palace'.

How wilfully irrelevant are these black-and-white political judgements in the face of Hyacinth's bewilderment between private dreams and public sympathies! For Hyacinth, as Dr. Edel more cogently points out, 'is another version of the artist *manqué*', Roderick Hudson. It is the bewilderment, to quote the Preface again, that supplies the very germ of the novel; to read it as a political tract is to miss the whole meaning. As James admits, with that rueful cynicism which colours so many of the Prefaces,

. . . the wary reader for the most part warns the novelist against making his characters too *interpretative* of the muddle of fate, or in other words too divinely, too priggishly clever. 'Give us plenty of bewilderment', this monitor seems to say, 'so long as there is plenty of slashing out in the bewilderment too. But don't, we beseech you, give us too much intelligence; for intelligence—well, *endangers*; endangers not perhaps the slasher himself, but the very slashing, the subject-matter of any self-respecting story. It opens up too many considerations, possibilities, issues; it *may* lead the slasher into dreary realms where slashing somehow fails and falls to the ground.'

One does not wish to fall into Dame Rebecca's trap, so to say, by identifying those 'dreary realms' too readily with the *milieux* of readers who see in James 'a nagging hostility to political effort'; but it does seem curiously significant that the public loyalty of a fictional lad like Hyacinth who is prepared to kill himself rather than betray political principles he has come personally to distrust, should have been so ignored by self-righteously 'political' critics.

When Hyacinth 'wanted to drive in every carriage, to mount on every horse, to feel on his arm the hand of every pretty woman in the place', and felt bitter when 'these familiar phenomena became symbolic, insolent, defiant, took upon themselves to make him smart with the sense that *he* was out of it', it may be objected by unfriendly critics that the young man is suffering from delusions of grandeur. To

* In the Henry James number of *Hound and Horn*, April–June, 1934.

which the answer is, of course, that some young men *do* suffer from delusions of grandeur (I have seen no pious outcry against *The Bulpington of Blup*, in which H. G. Wells gave us a full-scale study of the disease), and that it is the novelist's job to describe people as they are. A reader's indignation against social injustice is more poignantly aroused by young Robinson's hurtful dreams than by his more overt ('Dickensian', if you like) references:

> . . . but a breath of popular passion had passed over him, and he seemed to see, immensely magnified, the monstrosity of the great ulcers and sores of London—the sick, eternal misery crying, in the darkness, in vain, confronted with granaries and treasure-houses and palaces of delight where shameless satiety kept guard.

The novel is unashamedly 'political' in plot and background, and when Dame Rebecca complained that James 'produced a picture-gallery when he had intended a grave study of social differences', she made a good point but with—I feel—the wrong emphasis. Let a man be never so deeply involved in political theory (and Hyacinth Robinson was not *deeply* involved), he will nevertheless see most clearly—if he has any eyes at all—the people among whom he lives and works; for political conscience is something added to the normal human equipment and not something substituted in its place. It is indeed an additional merit in the novel that James has defined for his chief character, mainly by that very 'picture-gallery' of various types of revolutionary zealot of the 1880's, a highly complex attitude towards politics. But this 'political' interest is subordinated to the overall portrait of the whole humanity of his hero. No one can complain that Henry James, in the early novels at least, was not helpful in supplying guides for the reader; even if we had missed in the pervasive tone of the book his point of stress, there are signposts in plenty. Here is one:

> For this unfortunate but remarkably organized youth, every displeasure or gratification of the visual scene coloured his whole mind, and though he lived in Pentonville and worked in Soho, though he was poor and obscure and cramped and full of unattainable desires, it may be said of him that what was most important in life for him was simply his impressions.

The opening chapters put us at once in possession, with rich and beautiful economy, of the private and public impressions of the boy. He is being brought up by Miss Pynsent, his dear 'Pinnie', a little dressmaker of modest means who lives with simple decorum in a decayed neighbourhood. She is as ' "lower middle" class, etc.' as H. G. Wells could have wished, but James is hardly so insensitive as to set that particular placard over her devoted head. Instead, by a hundred kindly touches her portrait is built up, each touch adding something to the mixture of love and a squeamish sense of the sordid which grew up side by side in the mind of her sensitive young *protégé*. Three illustrative snippets must suffice:

Miss Pynsent could not embrace the state of mind of people who didn't apologize, though she vaguely envied and admired it, she herself spending much of her time in making excuses for obnoxious acts she had not committed.

Miss Pynsent esteemed people in proportion to their success in constituting a family circle—in cases, that is, where the materials were under their hand. This success, among the various members of the house of Henning, had been of the scantiest, and the domestic broils in the establishment adjacent to her own, whose vicissitudes she was able to follow, as she sat at her window at work, by simply inclining an ear to the thin partition behind her—these scenes, amid which the crash of crockery and the imprecations of the wounded were frequently audible, had long been the scandal of a humble but harmonious neighbourhood.

Though it was already November there was no fire in the neatly-kept grate beneath the chimney-piece, on which a design, partly architectural, partly botanical, executed in the hair of Miss Pynsent's parents, was flanked by a pair of vases, under glass, containing muslin flowers.

This last passage reminds me forcibly of T. S. Eliot's *A Cooking Egg*, and I wonder how it is that the indulgent-sardonic inflation has been so rightly appreciated in the one American-born English author, and so signally missed in the other. Listen to the echo of Miss Pynsent in the more austere notes of Eliot on Pipit:

> Pipit sate upright in her chair
>   Some distance from where I was sitting;
> *Views of the Oxford Colleges*
>   Lay on the table, with the knitting.

Daguerreotypes and silhouettes,
  Her grandfather and great great aunts,
Supported on the mantelpiece
  An *Invitation to the Dance*.

.   .   .   .   .

But where is the penny world I bought
  To eat with Pipit behind the screen?
The red-eyed scavengers are creeping
  From Kentish Town and Golders Green;
Where are the eagles and the trumpets?

'Where are the eagles and the trumpets?' is precisely what Hyacinth asked of his own Pipit, and asked in vain. He, too, turned to the 'weeping, weeping multitudes' drooping in the Victorian equivalents of 'a hundred A.B.C.'s', found among them first his fellow outcasts, came to share their political attitudes, and finally died in obedience to their desire to overthrow, in the interests of the weeping multitudes, the eagles and trumpets he so pathetically craved for himself.

The little boy's first view of social injustice (other than the undeserved straitness of poor Pinnie's circumstances) is described in a harrowing melodramatic scene; he is conducted to the prison where his mother lies dying. He is unaware that the gaunt foreign slattern is his mother, a French girl who had served a life-sentence for the murder of her lover (Hyacinth's unknown father), a mysterious 'Lord Frederick'. The scene is grim, ghoulish; dramatic ironies are piled as thick as one could wish, as when a fearful Mrs. Bowerbank, embodying Victorian morality, asks:

'Is there nothing the little gentleman would like to say, now, to the unfortunate? Hasn't he any pleasant remark to make to her about his coming so far to see her when she's so sunk? It isn't often that children are shown over the place (as the little man has been) and there's many that'd think themselves lucky if they could see what he has seen.'

'Mon pauvre joujou, mon pauvre chéri,' the prisoner went on in her tender tragic whisper. . . .

The scene may indeed be Dickensian in treatment, but I think we can trace its germ not to any bookish memory, but to that grim passage in *A Small Boy and Others* (Chapter XIII) describing the impressions crowding in on the young Henry James when he himself was taken on a childhood visit to Sing-Sing—a scene which, we now know from the invaluable Edel biography (III, 86), James deliberately re-enacted late in 1884, when he made a special visit to Millbank Prison. He was 'collecting notes for a fiction scene', as he informs a correspondent, rather callously: 'Look out for the same—a year hence.' But his denunciation is surely as keen as any his politically-minded critics may have expressed: 'Millbank Prison is a worse act of violence than any it was erected to punish.'

The development of Hyacinth's political attitude (it is one of James's better jokes, by the way, that the lad had no objection to his name, considering it to be quite masculine so long as it was not pronounced in the French fashion!) is illustrated almost entirely by means of the 'portrait gallery'. To indicate something of the functional significance of these portraits, it will be necessary to offer a fair number of quotations. It may be useful, first, to enumerate these characters as functional 'types' surrounding and vitalizing the figure of Hyacinth, before noting in how much more lively a form than 'types' they are in fact created. Millicent Henning, a warm-hearted vulgar girl, Miss Pynsent's nearest neighbour, who feels her excluded social status not at all, but glows with the life of her own rampageous London and runs after the nobs, beaming with health and strength, for all she is worth—and for all *they* are worth; Anastasius Vetch, a gentle old fiddler equally content to espouse an old-fashioned Radical philosophy or to take tea with Miss Pynsent, and ever prompt to aid the young man whose genius he recognizes more clearly than do any of the more 'intellectual' characters; Eustache Poupin who reflects in an equally sedentary fashion the fire of the Paris Commune and who longs somewhat passively for the brotherhood of man; Paul Muniment, Hyacinth's contemporary, a young London Socialist of clear sight and hard head and a vivid incorruptibility which is in the event far more corruptible than Hyacinth's own second-hand resolves; his sister Rose Muniment, a bed-ridden cripple nauseatingly *au fait* with the affairs of the titled folk whom she affects to patronize; Lady Aurora Langrish, a self-conscious and wondrously sympathetic Lady Bountiful figuring as the distressed conscience of her gilded class; Captain Sholto, a hanger-on of that class who makes a much more effective alliance with the common

folk via Millicent Henning; Diedrich Hoffendahl, the genuine article
behind real revolution and unliterary assassination; and most
seductive of all, the Princess Casamassima herself, who shares to a
generous extent the hero's sensibility and who dramatizes both him
and herself in her own bored efforts to 'climb down' as he, poor
distracted fellow, is at once trying to climb up and, as it were, to
blow up. A portrait gallery? Yes—and *what* a portrait gallery! Even
if Dame Rebecca were right, in supposing that they do not in sum
help forward the 'grave study of social differences', she was certainly
right in praising them as portraits.

If we look at them a little more closely we shall discover not only
their liveliness but also their constructional effect, as each in turn
illustrates one facet of the hero's 'bewilderment'. First, of more
importance perhaps than any member of the above list, is the en-
dearing figure of Pinnie, from whom, rather than from a shadowy
melodramatic Lord Frederick, we may trace something of the quality
of Hyacinth's Pentonville delicacy (a point, incidentally, which would
have been perceived by Van Wyck Brooks if he had known his
English social types half as well as Henry James knew *his*):

His attention, however, was mainly given to Pinnie: he watched her
jealously, to see whether, on this important occasion, she would not put
forth a certain stiff, quaint, polished politeness, of which she possessed
the secret and which made her resemble a pair of old-fashioned sugar-
tongs.

As the plot unfolds itself, Hyacinth is called upon to invest emotional
capital in very many contrasting human beings, but there is in his
life no more genuine understanding than that existing between the
prim dressmaker and her little waif. One slight passing comment
pierces to the heart of this relationship in that felicitous manner
which seems indeed for so many readers to function not as a revelation but as an over-successful camouflage:

One of the things she loved him for, however, was that he gave you
touching surprises in this line, had sudden inconsistencies of temper that
were all for your advantage. He was by no means always mild when he
ought to have been, but he was sometimes so when there was no
obligation. At such moments Pinnie wanted to kiss him . . .

Hyacinth's upbringing unfits him for a genuine companionship with Millicent Henning, who played with him as a child and would gladly prolong their games beyond adolescence:

There were things in his heart and a hidden passion in his life which he should be glad enough to lay open to some woman. . . . The answer was not in this loud, fresh laughing creature, whose sympathy couldn't have the fineness he was looking for, since her curiosity was vulgar. Hyacinth objected to the vulgar as much as Miss Pynsent herself; in this respect she had long since discovered that he was after her own heart.

But he was grateful for Millicent's warmth of heart, and esteemed that quality even while acknowledging, with a wry twist, its physical basis:

She was bold, and free, and generous, and if she was coarse she was neither false nor cruel. She laughed with the laugh of the people, and if you hit her hard enough she would cry with its tears.

If she had been ugly he couldn't have listened to her; but her beauty glorified even her accent, intensified her cockney genius with prismatic hues, gave her a large and constant impunity.

'No one but a capital girl could give herself such airs', Hyacinth remarks in a later generous mood; it is refreshing to see how deeply his creator could appreciate common vitality, and the following paragraph should be of interest to those who still maintain that Henry James did not like or understand ordinary common folk:

An inner sense told him that her mingled beauty and grossness, her vulgar vitality, the spirit of contradiction yet at the same time of attachment that was in her, had ended by making her indispensable to him. She bored him as much as she irritated him; but if she was full of execrable taste she was also full of life, and her rustlings and chatterings, her wonderful stories, her bad grammar and good health, her insatiable thirst, her shrewd perceptions and grotesque opinions, her mistakes and her felicities, were now all part of the familiar human sound of his little world.

Millicent, clearly, was hardly likely to encourage a young man to desperate deeds against society: she would always, in Spenderian analysis, vote solid Tory. The thoughtful reserve of Mr. Vetch made him, too, a congenial member of the forces of discontent. He is prepared to play his fiddle in the capitalist theatre so long as he can think his private thoughts and indulge, in Pinnie's 'dismal, forsaken bower', in 'so many sociable droppings-in and hot tumblers'. He voices very clearly one aspect of Hyacinth's inherent resistance to the revolutionary creed: 'The way certain classes arrogate to themselves the title of the people has never pleased me.' As for the gallant Monsieur Poupin, he is a retired and exiled member of the Old Guard who has already shot his bolt; his portrait is indeed a luxury, and a splendid example of the novelist's high spirits:

> M. Poupin was a socialist, which Anastasius Vetch was not, and a constructive democrat (instead of being a mere scoffer at effete things), and a theorist and an optimist and a visionary; he believed that the day was to come when all the nations of the earth would abolish their frontiers and armies and customs-houses, and embrace on both cheeks, and cover the globe with boulevards, radiating from Paris, where the human family would sit, in groups, at little tables, according to affinities, drinking coffee (not tea, *par exemple!*) and listening to the music of the spheres. Mr. Vetch neither prefigured nor desired this organized felicity; he was fond of his cup of tea, and only wanted to see the British constitution a good deal simplified . . .

In Paul Muniment the straightforward political theorist is shown to best advantage; Hyacinth falls quickly under the spell of this young man who reminds a reader of the simplified intellectual life enjoyed by those of his modern brothers who echo his opinion that 'one must be narrow to penetrate'. After a time, however, the negative austerities of his creed give Hyacinth pause:

> . . . he moved in a dry statistical and scientific air in which it cost Hyacinth an effort of respiration to accompany him . . . he sometimes emitted a short satiric gleam which showed that his esteem for the poor was small and that if he had no illusions about the people who had got everything into their hands he had as few about those who had egregiously failed to do so.

This sort of perception has far more effect on the reader's understanding of Hyacinth's character than any later chink in the young revolutionary's armour required by the exigencies of the plot. Sister

Rose, presented on her sick-bed as an object of pity, succeeds in filling the reader with a reluctant shamefaced distaste, so that it is a positive relief to discover, in a chance tone of irony, that the author is of the same way of thinking:

'Well, I have told you often enough that I don't go with you at all,' said Rose Muniment, whose recumbency appeared not in the least to interfere with her sense of responsibility.

Long before the appearance of the Princess Casamassima, Hyacinth is perplexed by the conflict between the views of his friends, who all for different reasons desire the collapse of capitalist society, and his own excluded response to the finer fruits of that society. There, of course, lies his formal tragedy in the plot—that it should be Hyacinth who has to become a political assassin and who kills himself rather than go through with it. The deeper tragedy of character (so exhausting the reader's emotional response that the melodramatic ending somewhat misses fire) lies in the boy's aspirations. To these, even the sympathetic interest of the Princess is no more than a fortunate following wind—and this in spite of her own desire to play at liberty, equality and fraternity. She is, of course, that same Christina Light who was the downfall of Roderick Hudson, but that fact is of no special significance other than as an instance of an author's weakness for a created figure; though Professor Cargill does ask, and not without insight, the question: 'Is it not credible that she has drawn a parallel between the finer sensibility of Hyacinth and the talent of Roderick Hudson, to both of which she may seem to herself to have been destructive, or if not, is she not to draw it after covering the body of the poor suicide with her own?' Another parallel is to *The Portrait of a Lady*, for the Princess 'puts a little wind' into Hyacinth's sails, just as Ralph Touchett did for Isabel Archer—and just as disastrously. But it is of the other conspirators, without any guidance from this condescending love-hunting lady, that he first grows tired:

He wondered at their zeal, their continuity, their vivacity, their incorruptibility; at the abundant supply of conviction and prophecy which they always had on hand. He believed that at bottom he was sorer than they, yet he had deviations and lapses, moments when the social question bored him and he forgot not only his own wrongs, which would have been pardonable, but those of the people at large, of his brothers and sisters in misery.

When he is enabled to take a short holiday on the Continent, his own Pentonville imagination has prepared him for a response quicker and more piercing than that of a dozen Princesses.

... as he lingered, before crossing the Seine, a sudden sense overtook him, making his heart sink with a kind of desolation—a sense of everything that might hold one to the world, of the sweetness of not dying, the fascination of great cities, the charm of travel and discovery, the generosity of admiration ...

and he slashes out, in his bewilderment, at Paul Muniment who 'would cut up the ceilings of Veronese into strips, so that every one might have a little piece'.

It is significant that, in attempting the briefest *précis* of this novel, it is to the portraits that one turns and not to the melodramatic plot, full of surprises and coincidences and other unnecessary devices to keep alive an interest already and otherwise fully quickened. What Hyacinth had precisely to *do* soon slips from our memory; we recall him as a prim unhappy little book-binder and forget his embroilment in underground machinations while remembering his endowment with an eye for character and a soul stirred by any manifestation of the beautiful or the moving. If he has a 'split personality' it is only the ambiguity of full sanity, of a grimly reconciled Benvolio, of

the rather helpless sense that, whatever he saw, he saw (and this was always the case) so many other things beside. He saw the immeasurable misery of the people, and yet he saw all that had been, as it were, rescued and redeemed from it: the treasures, the felicities, the splendours, the successes, of the world.

He can grasp on the instant that sense of injustice towards which his fellow-conspirators had laboured long, but at a crisis in their plotting he can cry out with exasperated impatience: 'Isn't it enough, now, to give my life to the beastly cause ... without giving my sympathy?' His ambivalence is his tragedy; for it is precisely his sympathy that he *does* give, as well as his life: as Dr. Cargill puts it, 'he does not windily debate his situation—because he only *feels* it'. The same bewilderment is also his inner strength of private glory amid public woe, as his creator progressively reveals, as in a recreation of his own youth, 'the torment of his present life, the perpetual laceration of the rebound'.

The vivid evocative quality of Hyacinth Robinson's impressions are illustrated by his sense of the *characters* of his associates, to which he gives his whole mind and heart, rather than to their overt political attitudes, to which he gives half his mind and as much of his heart as he can spare. The liveliness of Hyacinth himself and the authenticity of his claim to be (as a created character) alive in the real world and therefore *available* to all these impressions, are established primarily through his creator's ability to recreate the sights and sounds and smells of Hyacinth's London, and (still more important) the manner in which an adolescent of unusual sensibility might react to those sights and sounds and smells. We have Henry James's word for it (almost, indeed, his last word) that 'the mid-Victorian London was sincere—that was a vast virtue and a vast appeal'. In those same mellow autobiographical pages of *The Middle Years* he has told us how in a certain eating-house of the very old English tradition 'I said to myself under every shock and at the hint of every savour that this was what it was for an exhibition to reek with local colour, and one could dispense with a napkin, with a crusty roll, with room for one's elbows or one's feet, with an immunity from intermittence of the "plain boiled", much better than one could dispense with that'; he has gone still further and admitted again (as plainly as in the Preface to *The Princess*) his determination to *do* something with this acute receptivity of atmosphere:

If the commonest street-vista was a fairly heart-shaking contributive image, if the incidents of the thick renascent light anywhere, and the perpetual excitement of never knowing, between it and the historic and determined gloom, which was which and which one could most 'back' for the general outcome and picture, so the great sought-out compositions, the Hampton Courts and the Windsors, the Richmonds, the Dulwiches, even the very Hampstead Heaths and Putney Commons, to say nothing of the Towers, the Temples, the Cathedrals and the strange penetrabilities of the City, ranged themselves like the rows of great figures in a sum, an amount immeasurably huge, that one would draw on if not quite as long as one lived, yet as soon as ever one should seriously get to work.

It is to this kind of sensibility, rather than to sour notions of what a young revolutionary should or should not think or dream, that a wise reader will relate Hyacinth's longings for the world represented in his untutored mind by the figure and setting of the Princess Casamassima; it is in this divided sympathy, and not in any technical deviation from the views of a Paul Muniment or a Diedrich Hoffendahl, that lies the tragic weakness—and thus the human kinship—of the Pentonville book-binder. At the same time, Professor Trilling (among others) has pointed out* that although the politics of his friends had nothing in common with modern revolutionary Communism, Hyacinth was in fact placed in a 'classic Anarchist situation' in keeping with the political assassinations and other acts of terrorism prevalent in the 1880's, and that The Princess Casamassima shows James to have been capable of producing 'a first-class rendering of literal social reality'. Moreover, as the works to be studied in Chapters VIII and IX will amply demonstrate, Henry James was by no means unmoved by the revolting selfishness he saw in the behaviour of the London rich. His personal attack on that ignorant corruption could not be made in terms of overt politics. He was, after all, an American citizen, and could properly show his political colours in no more active fashion than, say, his membership of the Reform Club—in which comfortable non-revolutionary Liberal nest he presumably met, among other political types, the kind of reforming aristocrat exemplified by Lord Warburton of The Portrait of a Lady. His attack was to be launched on the front where he was at once strongest and most sensitive: the moral-aesthetic front. For all his Pentonville background, little Hyacinth Robinson was too much the 'passionate pilgrim' to see, before his still youthful suicide, that other side of the life of stately homes which his creator would mercilessly expose in such works as The Spoils of Poynton. The evidence of his private letters, no less than of the whole body of his later fiction, suggests that those critics who consider Henry James to have been a temperamental Tory are very far indeed from the truth.

If in The Princess Casamassima there are pain, pathos, evocative twinges of childhood and adolescence, flashes of intuition in the private and public impressions of a sensitive youth, in The Bostonians

* In Horizon, Vol. XVII, No. 100.

there are all these things plus passion pure and simple, passion of the kind we mean when we talk about (usually without having re-read) *Wuthering Heights*. *The Bostonians* bears a striking resemblance to *The Princess Casamassima* in certain matters of tone and in the evocation of that strained human anguish between the conception of a political ideal and its execution in the face of contrary private impulses. The impression of both books that remains most vividly in the reader's mind is just this strained grey quality of the prose—relieved by some amazing set-pieces of character-drawing. Nowhere in the later novels did Henry James so demonstrate his power to introduce into the very texture of his writing all the tension of his characters as they 'slash out in the bewilderment' of the contrast between life as a conscious political effort towards an attitude, and life as a more complex and aching system of personal desires and denials which may run, if not in direct opposition to the conscious will, in a direction oblique enough to cause a harsh grating of responses.

In both novels, the subtler tension in the central character is made more easy to appreciate by the placing, as an immediate background, of some more overt but not quite crude instance of a similar unsteadiness of purpose. To set off the social perplexities of Hyacinth Robinson, striving to rise from poverty to the *haut monde* against his conviction that the *haut monde* should be destroyed, there is the less complicated social urge of the Princess Casamassima, striving to climb down in the other direction to satisfy a passing whim; there is also the more active revolutionary zeal of Paul Muniment and his friends, itself somewhat tangled with personal implications and thrown into relief by the more mature (if less precise) commentary of Anastasius Vetch and Pinnie. So here, in *The Bostonians*, the conflict in the mind of Olive Chancellor is thrown against the background of a much less complicated instance in the person of Miss Birdseye, the true Bostonian reformer.

It is worth noting the extraordinary tenderness of the portrait of Miss Birdseye, from the very beginning. We are guided to see courage and honest value in the dim drapery of a foolish old woman fumbling in a muddle-headed way with causes beyond her scope. Her detailed portrait, that great set-piece framed in a description of her apartments all prepared for yet another meeting in aid of some good cause, overflows with adjectives, but there is no straining after effect: the adjectives tumble out as though the author is quite saturated with his appreciation of her:

> She was a little old lady, with an enormous head; that was the first thing Ransom noticed—the vast, fair, protuberant, candid, ungarnished brow, surmounting a pair of weak, kind, tired-looking eyes, and ineffectually balanced in the rear by a cap which had the air of falling backwards, and which Miss Birdseye suddenly felt for while she talked, with unsuccessful irrelevant movements. She had a sad, soft, pale face, which (and it was the effect of her whole head) looked as if it had been soaked, blurred, and made vague by exposure to some slow dissolvent. The long practice of philanthropy had not given accent to her features; it had rubbed out their transitions, their meanings. The waves of sympathy, of enthusiasm, had wrought upon them in the same way in which the waves of time finally modify the surface of old marble busts, gradually washing away their sharpness, their details. In her large countenence her dim, little smile scarcely showed. It was a mere sketch of a smile, a kind of instalment, or payment on account; it seemed to say that she would smile more if she had time, but that you could see, without this, that she was gentle and easy to beguile.

Henry James, struck 'deadly sick' when his brother William wrote a letter accusing him of painting in Miss Birdseye a recognizable portrait of the respected Bostonian philanthropist Miss Peabody, categorically stated that 'Miss Birdseye was evolved entirely from my moral consciousness, like every other person I have ever drawn'. He goes on to claim that 'though subordinate, she is, I think, the best figure in the book', and—which is more to our present purpose—'she is represented as the embodiment of pure, the purest philanthropy'.

But tender though the portrait is, it is important to recognize in Miss Birdseye a kindly example of those professional reformers who, deep in magnanimous schemes for foreigners and others with whom they have no valid individual contact, fail entirely to establish for themselves any true personal relationship with the world and with their fellows: a judgement summed up in the observation that the legend of an *affaire* between Miss Birdseye and a Hungarian refugee must have been apocryphal because 'it was open to grave doubt that she could have entertained a sentiment so personal'. This manner of life, however kindly displayed in the person of Miss Birdseye, clearly represents to the author a fatal error in the investment of emotional capital—and this manner of life is what Olive Chancellor wished to persuade herself was admirable. Her tragedy is greater than that of Miss Birdseye, not because her sense of values was any less mistaken, but simply because she was unable to pursue her mistaken course with anything like success. Temperament and history alike had aided Miss Birdseye, so that her eccentricity took on, at the last, an aura of honesty and integrity, and made her possibly as happy as she could ever have been in any other mode of life. But with Olive, the personal heresy which she strove to damp down by denying herself any relations with men (an unsympathetic tribe represented by her cousin Basil Ransom) and devoting herself single-mindedly to Women's Rights, flared up again with a terrible intensity in her love for Verena Tarrant, flared up inside and destroyed the very holy sanctuary of their mutual and vowed devotion to an impersonal cause.

Another instance of James's detached sympathy in the delineation of minor figures, introduced in *The Bostonians* (as so often elsewhere) in a series of sketches, to the splendid *economy* of which his long sentences and inflated periphrasis so oddly and actively contribute, is the gentle ironical humour of the portraits of Selah Tarrant the mesmeric healer and his wife, daughter of Abraham Greenstreet the Abolitionist. It comes out in a kind of amused outrage at their pathetic poverty of taste, their shoddy system of pretences and makeshifts. One doesn't in the least resent the narrator's tone of superiority: one *has* to feel superior to such fry, if one is to make anything of them at all, and there is a caressing humour about it all which never declines into a snigger. Underneath, one is always conscious of a deep human sympathy, a beautiful apprehension of the tortured twists and quirks producing all this corrugation of personality. The portrait of Verena Tarrant's mother, admirable in itself, has much functional significance. It helps to explain the girl's willingness to leave home in order to live as Olive Chancellor's guest; it certainly provides her with an incentive for her final desertion of public life for a private career as Mrs. Basil Ransom; and it offers another clear indication of the author's disapproval of those who allow amateur and ineffective gestures towards the political life to diminish whatever chance they may have of developing a rich private integrity.

She was a queer, indeed ... a flaccid, unhealthy, whimsical woman, who still had a capacity to cling. What she clung to was 'society' and a position in the world which a secret whisper told her she had never had and a voice more audible reminded her she was in danger of losing. ... Verena was born not only to lead their common sex out of bondage, but to re-model a visiting-list which bulged and contracted in the wrong places, like a country-made garment. As the daughter of Abraham Greenstreet, Mrs. Tarrant had passed her youth in the first Abolitionist circles, and she was aware how much such a prospect was clouded by her union with a young man who had begun life as an itinerant vendor of lead-pencils (he had called at Mr. Greenstreet's door in the exercise of this function), had afterwards been for a while a member of the celebrated Cayuga community, where there were no wives, or no husbands, or something of that sort (Mrs. Tarrant could never remember), and had still later (though before the development of the healing faculty) achieved distinction in the spiritualistic world.

We can read this sort of sketch with an indulgent smile, confident that Henry James will never be so crude as to betray our mood and suddenly turn on us with sermons about motives or compensations or wish-fulfilments. The humour and the sympathy coexist without embarrassment. It is largely the inflation that brings the smile, and there is not cruelty about *that*. As an 'itinerant vendor of lead pencils', Selah is both funnier and more dignified than as a 'pedlar', for instance. If the Greenstreets objected to mesmeric healing as 'manual activity', there is rich comedy in the inflation, and yet the term suits both their own and Selah's view of his exercises. The tattered garments of pretence are held up to ridicule, but they are not still further rent; James restores them to their wearers for whatever warmth they may still afford, and does not (like a Swift) leave his models entirely naked and comfortless.

Selah Tarrant himself is a medium for a double assault on the less rooted forms of public life: he is not only, like his wife, a camp-follower of the irregular skirmishers among the intellectual forces, but also a fascinated devotee of the power of the American Press, that lusty organ of collective vulgarity which Henry James viewed with peculiar aversion:

The newspapers were his world, the richest expression, in his eyes, of human life; and for him, if a diviner day was to come upon earth, it would be brought about by copious advertisement in the daily prints. ...

... the places that knew him best were the offices of the newspapers and the vestibules of the hotels—the big marble-paved chambers of informal reunion which offer to the streets, through high-glass plates, the sight of the American citizen suspended by his heels. Here, amid the piled-up luggage, the convenient spittoons, the elbowing loungers, the disconsolate 'guests', the truculent Irish porters, the rows of shaggy-backed men in strange hats, writing letters at a table inlaid with advertisements, Selah Tarrant made innumerable contemplative stations.

The consistency of tone which characterizes all the items in the richly stocked 'portrait galleries' of *The Bostonians* and *The Princess Casamassima* is perhaps more significant, in any consideration of James's prose style, than the admittedly fascinating game of tracking down literary models for them. Mr. Marius Bewley, for example, has matched Selah Tarrant against Westervelt in Hawthorne's *The Blithedale Romance*;* but there is a Jamesian prototype, too, in the major figure of that strangely indicative tale *Professor Fargo* (see Chapter I). With Fargo and *his* shady chicaneries in mind from a decade back, as well as the less villainous Tarrant and his daughter Verena, 'schooled', in Dr. Edel's phrase, 'in primitive American grandiloquence', there emerges an expression of Henry James's own strong desire—more familiarly documented in his letters, essays in autobiography, and in the long series of novels and tales devoted to his international obsession—to escape from all this sort of thing to a more civilized sphere. A wincing appreciation of every last scrap of vulgarity in nineteenth-century American domestic conversation, whether exemplified in Matthias Pardon the slick reporter or Mrs. Tarrant the addle-pated explainer-away of social awkwardnesses, is set down with tormented accuracy. No wonder, the reader cannot help but feel, no wonder Henry James was so much in love with the European style of conversation recorded by the European novelists; no wonder he was determined to find it and in the end make his own characters speak always with point, always in the spirit of 'revised wisdom', and not merely, like Mrs. Tarrant, making an ado about offering a piece of apple-fritter, or 'taking a gossip's view of great tendencies' like Matthias Pardon.

* In *The Complex Fate* (1952); his findings are usefully summarized by Cargill.

Much has been written about the exclusion of *The Bostonians*, at the publishers' instance, from the New York Edition. We lack, for this reason, an elaborate late-style Preface which might have drenched us again in the atmosphere of reformist Boston; but it is scarcely likely (to judge by the obliquities of other Prefaces) that it would have thrown any direct light on the tragic plight of Olive Chancellor, even though the revision of the text itself might have given James the chance, which he regretted as late as 1915, of 'making it a much truer and more curious thing—it was meant to be curious from the first'. There is certainly no reason to suppose that James would at any time have been more likely to utter frankly physical descriptions of a situation potentially Lesbian than he ever did in situations openly heterosexual. We are never told exactly what 'happened' between, say, Merton Densher and Kate Croy in *The Wings of the Dove*, any more than we are told what, if anything, 'happened' during those long studious evenings spent together by Olive and Verena Tarrant. It is Olive's tragically unrequited *love*, whether or not it sought or even recognized a full physical outlet, that fills the novel with the tensions of possessive jealousy. As for James's interest in feminism in general, what have *all* his important heroines been to date, from Daisy Miller to Isabel Archer, but women whose intellects, senses, plans, hopes, are all frustrated simply because they are women? Although he showed impatience with some of their less attractive expositors, Henry James was consistently sympathetic to the basic claims of nineteenth-century feminist movements; he is, indeed, one of their unsung heroes.

Olive's tragedy is fairly simply that of self-delusion, but the self-delusion itself is anything but simple. It is soon clear that love and jealousy prompt all her actions with regard to Verena: the stresses and strains are pitiable to recognize. But it is altogether too easy a matter to point a finger at the raw spot and to say: 'She was in love with Verena and was ashamed of it, or perhaps did not really admit it to herself, but covered it up with all sorts of rationalizations which in turn were directed against man, the natural and favoured enemy of her unnatural passion.' James himself certainly stoops to no such crude analysis. Her consequent morbidity of temperament is not, even for Basil Ransom, a matter for superior comment—'any sufficient account of her must lie very much to the rear of that'. James returns here, with more ambitious mastery, to the theme he had so brilliantly sketched in *Roderick Hudson*: the relationship between a conscientious thoughtful moralist and a creature of grace and personal fascination whose lack of those same qualities of moral high-seriousness alternately infatuate and disgust the pursuer. The essential lack of balance in the human situation was clear enough in *Roderick Hudson*, but it was not there developed on the plane of tragedy. Here, it indubitably *is*.

It adds to the complexity of the situation that Olive Chancellor does honestly believe in her public cause. We see her deeply devoted to it before ever Verena Tarrant steps on to the stage. We see her instinctive fear of Basil Ransom, that bright-eyed exponent of personal arrangements and the anti-progressive enemy of causes, long before that fear becomes a dread that he will steal Verena away from her. Indeed, if his intrusion were the only fear, Olive would, even in the face of the successful conclusion of his outrage to her happiness, lose tragic stature. It is so much more than that. We are shown that Verena herself was bound in the end to disappoint her protectress, with or without assistance from that lady's cousin. If Olive had her own tragic flaw, so—from Olive's point of view—had Verena. It was the flaw most likely to strike against Olive's own, and wound her at her weakest point.

In her previous shy attempts to nourish her sad courage on something more tangible than causes, Olive had found the young women whom she approached all 'odiously mixed up with Charlie', and had retired conscious of defeat. With Verena there was no 'Charlie'. She was not just another 'pale shop-maiden' who 'couldn't make out what she wanted them to do'. Verena, who had 'sat on the knees of somnambulists, and had been passed from hand to hand by trance-speakers', had been hitherto defended from the danger of 'Charlie' by the accident of her eccentric upbringing. It soon becomes evident that it *was* only an accident, and Olive's first major self-delusion was in setting any store by it. Olive's sister Mrs. Luna, that bedizened arch-priestess of *la vie intime*, was not wholly prejudiced when she announced that Verena was 'an artful little minx and cared as much for the rights of women as she did for the Panama Canal', and added: 'She will give Olive the greatest cut she has ever had in her life. She will run off with some lion-tamer; she will marry a circus-man!'

Coming quite early in the novel there is a significance—sinister for Olive—in one brief sentence about Verena, a sentence gaining point from its position at the end of a chapter: 'Her ideas of enjoyment were very simple; she enjoyed putting on her new hat, with its redundancy of feather, and twenty cents appeared to her a very large sum.' The redundancy of feather, that gay straw in the wind of Verena's freshness, implies a potential 'Charlie', that figure appearing to Miss Chancellor's distressed imagination as 'a young man in a white overcoat and a paper collar'.

The recurring theme, in James's novels, of the relationship between two contrasted and mutually attractive types (the integrated moralist and the wavering child of genius or intuition) had already been worked out between man and man in *Roderick Hudson*, between man and woman in *The Portrait of a Lady* and is now worked out in *The Bostonians* between woman and woman. Whether or not we are justified in suspecting that the 'ambiguity' of Henry James is progressively revealed as a tormented uncertainty of purpose, of wish, in himself, we may guess that no novelist has ever described the state so often or so well, with all those vague gradations of mood somehow absorbed into the very texture of his prose and never forced—to their inevitable destruction—into a harsh code of pros and cons. Here, it is Verena who is ambiguous. Her aims are, at first, truly mixed, for her *capacities* are, at first, truly mixed. With Olive herself the intuitive free personal life could never have succeeded, and it was her tragic delusion to make that attempt. The person Olive fell in love with was the brilliant accidental personification of her own left-handed craving for a personal life. That she could never honestly allow for the flowering of the free personal life in Verena herself was not only fatal to the false relationship of compromise between them (a relationship based, for a time steadily enough, on mutual admiration); it also proclaimed her own inability to love freely, free from her morals, free from her programme, free from her other self. Courage she had in plenty, but not that saving disgrace of moral slovenliness that would bid her follow the moment's whim. When she has achieved her aim and has quite literally bought Verena from her parents (a curious relapse into bondage for a granddaughter of Abraham Greenstreet the Abolitionist), she still shows every sign of resisting her personal motives— for it is not until the very end that Olive's passion breaks through her own defensive positions. Meanwhile, with the impressionable girl her prisoner, with this Bohemian wayward unorthodox object of her affection living as her friend and *protégée*, Olive manages to convince herself (and, for a long time, Verena too) of the high morality of her programme:

'We will work at it together—we will study everything.' Olive almost panted; and while she spoke the peaceful picture hung before her of still winter evenings under the lamp, with falling snow outside, and tea on a little table, and successful renderings, with a chosen companion, of Goethe; almost the only foreign writer she cared about; for she hated the writing of the French, in spite of the importance they had given to women.

Olive's loss of Verena to Basil Ransom reaches the plane of stark tragedy in those harrowing closing chapters of the novel where the strain breaks at last in shrill hysteria like the shriek of an unlubricated engine. Henry James, with that customary embarrassment which overwhelmed him always on such occasions, calls in the aid of rhetoric, even of melodrama. It is all competently done, but on what a disappointing level, after the sustained critical poise of the rest of the novel:

The expression on her face was a thing to remain with him for ever; it was impossible to imagine a more vivid presentment of blighted hope and wounded pride. Dry, desperate, rigid, she yet wavered and seemed uncertain; her pale, glittering eyes strained forward, as if they were looking for death. Ransom had a vision, even at that crowded moment, that if she could have met it there and then, bristling with steel or lurid with fire, she could have rushed on it without a tremor, like the heroine that she was.

With Verena, for a time, there had been a balance, a poise of warring elements. Like a needle between two magnets she could swing freely, now to Olive, now to Basil Ransom. It is not too much to say that in the end she swung home to that magnet whose forces were constant, undivided: she could with her personal life love Basil on his own terms and find in the end her 'Charlie': she could possibly with her public self have loved Olive on Olive's public terms. It was the essence of Olive's tragedy that when she in turn attempted to put out a personal attraction, the needle flickered awhile and then finally came to rest where that particular pull was strongest and simplest—not in Olive against whom no needle sensitive to manifold impulsions and repulsions could ever quietly nestle, but in Basil whose powers were concentrated in a single attraction.

Van Wyck Brooks, by no means an over-sympathetic critic, asks: 'Who that recalls *The Bostonians*, that picture of a world which seems to consist of nothing but hands, reproving, pushing, pulling, exploiting hands, can doubt that, in all this, James was inspired by the sacred terror of his own individuality?'

Here, I think, we have the germ of the matter. The Leon Edel biography has uncovered in Henry James's day-to-day life much that would support the evidence of all the novels and stories so far discussed: no man who saw so keenly and felt so intuitively could possibly have preserved in his own private heart an imperturbable insensitivity to—to whatever point one may wish to select in the whole range of human love, from simple companionship to hopeless infatuation. Whatever he may have enjoyed of a 'private life' was kept, inviolably, private; or it may never have existed, in terms recognizable to non-psychiatrist readers. But the 'sacred terror of his own individuality' was transferred, time and time again, to his best developed characters and also to the puppets of tales about withdrawals and renunciations. Only occasionally does he dip down to his own subjective blood-springs for material directly pumped, so to say, into a created character. If we are right in detecting this element in Roderick Hudson, in Hyacinth Robinson and at times in Isabel Archer, then I think we may risk a second leap across the sex barrier (never very high, in this lifelong portraitist of womankind) and find it, too, in Olive Chancellor.

In *The Bostonians*, of course, as in the other novels I have just grouped with it, this germ, this element, is largely hidden by conditions which are, for the reader, all gain. I agree with Dame Rebecca that there are passages in the novel 'that one would like to learn by heart'. There is observable in this book and in *The Princess Casamassima* an exuberance only superficially at variance with the strained strenuous themes. Minor characters are endowed with a quality of life far in excess of anything required by purely structural considerations, peppering both novels with wholly gratuitous felicities. Miss Birdseye may be claimed as essential to the pattern, but what are we to say of that superb first presentation of Mrs. Farrinder, except that although unnecessary she is wonderfully welcome, and would have served, together with other free marginal sketches, to make the reputation of a lesser novelist? She, if anyone, provides a passage 'that one would like to learn by heart':

She was a copious, handsome woman, in whom angularity had been corrected by the air of success: she had a rustling dress (it was evident what *she* thought about taste), abundant hair of a glossy blackness, a pair of folded arms, the expression of which seemed to say that rest, in such a career as hers, was as sweet as it was brief, and a terrible regularity of feature . . . You could contest neither the measurements nor the nobleness, and had to feel that Mrs. Farrinder imposed herself. There was a lithographic smoothness about her, and a mixture of the American matron and the public character. There was something public in her eye, which was large, cold, and quiet: it had acquired a sort of exposed reticence from the habit of looking down from a lecture-desk, over a sea of heads, while its distinguished owner was eulogized by a leading citizen. Mrs. Farrinder, at almost any time, had the air of being introduced by a few remarks . . . If, in conversation with her, you attempted to take anything for granted, or to jump two or three steps at a time, she paused, looking at you with a cold patience, as if she knew that trick, and then went on at her own measured pace. She lectured on temperance and the rights of women: the ends she laboured for were to give the ballot to every woman in the country and to take the flowing bowl from every man. She was held to have a very fine manner, and to embody the domestic virtues and the graces of the drawing-room: to be a shining proof, in short, that the forum, for ladies, is not necessarily hostile to the fireside. She had a husband, and his name was Amariah.

Is there not in all this wealth of personal observation an object-lesson by James himself in the precept, so largely smothered by his own enthusiastic practice, that until man is at home in his immediate social life he cannot hope to derive sufficient inner nourishment to be strong enough to face, let alone think of contributing towards the solution of the problems of his larger political setting? If there is a message in *The Princess Casamassima* and *The Bostonians*, it is surely: 'Put your own house in order.' We need not be unfriendly to political progress in order to understand Basil Ransom's view: 'He, too, had a private vision of reform, but the first principle of it was to reform the reformers.' And just as Hyacinth Robinson's plight is in effect a far more damning indictment of the Victorian social system than any speech from the lips of Paul Muniment, so even Basil Ransom himself, constitutionally averse to schemes of amelioration, gives us a personal wince at the unfairness of things as he looks about him in the rich home of his reforming cousin:

He ground his teeth a little as he thought of the contrasts of the human lot; this cushioned feminine nest made him feel unhoused and underfed. Such a mood, however, could only be momentary, for he was conscious at bottom of a bigger stomach than all of the culture of Charles Street could fill.

The author's sympathy goes out, of course, to his chief figures, bewildered in their public world—to Hyacinth and to Olive. But he cannot conceal his sidelong admiration for those happier mortals who have come to terms with their environment—for Pinnie in *The Princess Casamassima*, and in *The Bostonians* for such a person as Doctor Prance, that trim little female physician who wins the esteem even of Basil Ransom, a Southerner through and through and the bitter masculine enemy of Women's Rights:

She stood there an instant, turning over the whole assembly a glance like the flash of a watchman's bull's-eye, and then quickly passed out. Ransom could see that she was impatient of the general question and bored with being reminded, even for the sake of her rights, that she was a woman—a detail that she was in the habit of forgetting, having as many rights as she had time for. It was certain that whatever might become of the movement at large, Doctor Prance's own little revolution was a success.

This sneaking sympathy for people who are competent in small matters is matched in innumerable instances by a cynical irritation aroused by people who are incompetent in larger affairs. Mrs. Luna laughs at sister Olive's 'thoughtfulness': 'That's what they call in Boston being very "thoughtful", ... giving you the Back Bay (don't you hate the name?) to look at, and then taking the credit for it.' Olive herself winces at vulgarity and is virtuously ashamed of her every wince ('in a career in which she was constantly exposing herself to offence and laceration, her most poignant suffering came from the injury of her taste'), whereas her adored Miss Birdseye, for whom 'there was a genius in every bush', 'was always trying to obtain employment, lessons in drawing, orders for portraits, for poor foreign artists, as to the greatness of whose talent she pledged herself without reserve; but in point of fact she had not the faintest sense of the scenic or plastic side of life'. Selah Tarrant, for all his pretensions, 'couldn't hold the attention of an audience; he was not acceptable as a lecturer', and as for his wife, 'she knew that he was an awful humbug', and she herself was not worthy of Verena's gifts: 'the commonness of her own surface was a non-conductor of the girl's quality'. Matthias Pardon, representative of the Great American Press, 'regarded the mission of mankind upon earth as a perpetual evolution of telegrams', and it was only the 'newest thing' that 'came nearest exciting in his mind the sentiment of respect'. The whole caricature of Mrs. Farrinder is etched with enjoyable malice, and even Mrs. Burrage, the female Anti-Feminist rampant, represents the domestic hearth at its most complacent but does not escape the barb of James's satire, directed in *The Bostonians* against all those who adopt a rigid attitude to life based on insufficient personal grounds: 'she could fancy how Mrs. Burrage would be affected by the knowledge that her son had been refused by the daughter of a mesmeric healer. She would be almost as angry as if she had learnt that he had been accepted.' Finally, the gaunt tragic figure of Olive Chancellor is sometimes shown in a light not so much unsympathetic as critical in the somewhat academic sense of the word. In the first introductory sketch we are told that 'it was the usual things of life that filled her with silent rage; which was natural enough, inasmuch as, to her vision, everything that was usual was iniquitous'. She and Verena, congratulating themselves on 'the wonderful insight they had obtained into the history of feminine anguish', nevertheless plan their future activities with unbruised will, and there is some savagery in the comment: 'A person who might have overheard some of the talk of this possibly infatuated pair would have been touched by their extreme familiarity with the idea of earthly glory.' There is even at times a direct charge against Olive's intellectual integrity: 'I have said that it was Miss Chancellor's plan of life not to lie, but such a plan was compatible with a kind of consideration for the truth which led her to shrink from producing it on poor occasions.'

These instances of narrative comment lend plausibility to the view that Henry James was speaking his own mind (or part of it) when he puts tart observations into the mouth of Basil Ransom. This thoughtful Southerner disliked 'mediums, communists, vegetarians', was sensitive to the wrongs suffered by the defeated Confederate States, but refrained from 'prating in the market place'. Yet we are explicitly informed that 'he had always had a desire for public life; to cause one's ideas to be embodied in national conduct appeared to him the highest form of human enjoyment'. At the same time (and here the personal views of his creator are surely apparent?) 'he thought [his age] talkative, querulous, hysterical, maudlin, full of false ideas, of unhealthy germs, of extravagant, dissipated habits, for which a great reckoning was in store', and we are made to feel that it was from this caricature of the public life, the 'windy, wordy reiteration of inanities', as well as from the personal clutches of Olive Chancellor, that he wished to rescue Verena.

Yet there is ample evidence of James's complementary sympathy for his band of suffragettes. Basil Ransom immediately sensed his cousin's intense gravity: 'the simplest division it is possible to make of the human race is into the people who take things hard and the people who take things easy. He perceived very quickly that Miss Chancellor belonged to the former class.' And a little later: 'she gave him an uneasy feeling—the sense that you could never be safe with a person who took things so hard'. We are left in no doubt as to her private psychology: she complains to Verena that 'you don't dislike men as a class' and yet it is carefully pointed out that 'it was a curious incident of her zeal for the regeneration of her sex that manly things were, perhaps on the whole, what she understood best'. But far more evocative of the reader's sympathy than any clumsy indication of her half recognized motives is the slow cumulative weight of Olive's conscious braveries and a certain undeniable *quality*. She is credited with 'a gentle dignity, a serenity of wisdom', and 'the detachment from error, of a woman whose self scrutiny had been as sharp as her deflexions'. Verena speaks for the reader when she tells her friend 'you have a fearful power of suffering'—and suffering of such intensity would, we feel, be neither humanly possible nor artistically effective in a character of less than Olive's stature. She is, no less than the 'battered, unpensioned' Miss Birdseye herself, a representative of the 'heroic age of New England'.

The scattered quotations in these notes on *The Bostonians* and *The Princess Casamassima* will have given small notion of the fluent rich elegance of the style of James's early maturity; there are whole chapters in which subtlety and dignity combine to form a medium of quite astonishing self-sufficiency. I would invite attention to a single aspect of this prose of James's early maturity, mainly for the explanatory light it may throw on his later more difficult mode of communication. I have already suggested that the inflation in the portraits of the Tarrant family has a function as well as (for readers who enjoy stylistic jokes) a gratuitous delight. We may smile at Verena's 'perpendicular journeys' strap-hanging in a tramcar, and even more when, on boarding a similar vehicle, Miss Birdseye was 'insert[ed] . . . into the oblong receptacle'. Mrs. Tarrant doesn't merely enjoy the paper—'from this publication she derived inscrutable solace'; Ransom's Southern relations exist on a 'farinaceous diet' and Olive's conscience is indicated as 'that attentive organ'; in a poor quarter of a town little children become 'the infant population'; and the grass 'thin herbage'; the erratic violence of Verena's education is deemed to show 'a want of continuity', and Matthias Pardon's gossip columns are devoted 'to the great end of preventing the American citizen from attempting clandestine journeys'. Sarcasm is altogether too simple a label for these apparent verbal absurdities; there is a very real sense in which each one of them is *true*, more true than the simpler paraphrase, because in smiling at them we remember that from the *inside* of the mind of the character concerned there is nothing funny in the tone. Mrs. Tarrant may never have used the words, but she did somehow see herself as 'deriving inscrutable solace' rather than just reading the paper—as anyone will agree who has been irritated by the complacent smirk of some clubman behind his copy of *The Times*.

In the second volume of *The Princess Casamassima* there is a subtler instance rather more indicative of the controlled conscious inflation of the later style, still ahead. The Prince and Madame Grandoni are sitting in Hyde Park, watching the riders jogging up and down. The state of mind of these self-conscious observers, meeting to debate in solemn ceremony some matter which in our less stately age would be disposed of in a few words of psycho-analytical slang, is indicated with beautiful *economy* (there is the signal point) in the half-amused half-serious tone of the narrator: they sat 'amid a wilderness of empty chairs and with nothing to distract their attention from an equestrian or two left over from the cavalcades of a fortnight before, and whose vain agitation in the saddle the desolate scene seemed to throw into high relief'. For those particular characters and at that particular period, jogging riders could appear accurately and vividly as agitated equestrians, and the phrase tells us as much about *them* as it does about their creator's limitless joy in words.

As a pendant to a consideration of two major examples of Henry James's efforts to treat in fiction some of the problems bound up with the adjustment of private lives to public lives, we may briefly dispose of one simple social evil against which he was for ever on guard—the intrusion into private affairs not of genuine public concerns but the slick professionalism of publicity. This he detested. One could readily compile from James's works an anthology of hatred against the intrusions of the press, as he knew it: Henrietta Stackpole and the ineffable Matthias Pardon have already contributed to the rich harvest. Even to contemplate the range of James's probable vituperation against more up-to-date methods of 'market research' and 'public relations' should send a shudder down the spines of those who nowadays commit such practices, for the 'deluge of the lowest insult' which engulfed the Franco-American family in *The Reverberator* would surely be out-deluged by today's version of what the Preface stigmatized as the 'recording, slobbering sheet'.

The Reverberator (1888) is an awkwardly sized and stylistically contradictory *nouvelle*, included as a 'tale' in the Martin Secker series of 1915–20 (though not in Dr. Edel's edition of the Complete Tales) but normally classed as a short novel. Based on James's disgust at an actual case of grossly tactless reporting by an American female correspondent in Venice, it consists of the treatment of an anecdote concerning an engagement between a Daisy-Miller-type American girl and the scion of a stuffy American family rooted in, and much married among, the French aristocracy and *haute bourgeoisie*. Their boy-meets-girl affair is threatened and all but broken by just such another case of journalistic insensibility. The anecdote, spun out with James's customary amplitude, offers yet another version of the old American 'innocent abroad' theme, merging (as in so many of the 'international' tales) with normal nineteenth-century class-consciousness, plus a moral-aesthetic swing at what struck the author as the crudest contemporary expression of American vulgarity, namely 'the press, the great institution of our time'.

At the Hôtel de l'Univers et de Cheltenham, Mr. Dosson and his two daughters are sampling Paris. Old Dosson is a lighter semi-comic version of Isabel Archer's uncle Touchett, providing another economically yet indulgently observed sketch of the mild American paterfamilias: 'Whatever he did he ever seemed to wander: he had an impermanent transitory air, an aspect of weary yet patient non-arrival ...' His younger daughter Francie is friendly with Mr. Flack, an American journalist:

> She was pretty without emphasis and as might almost have been said without point, and your fancy that a little stiffness would have improved her was at once qualified by the question of what her softness would have made of it. There was nothing in her, however, to confirm the implication that she had rushed about the deck of a Cunarder with a newspaper-man.

Flack's conscious ambition for his paper, *The Reverberator*, is 'to make it bigger; the most universal society-paper the world has seen. That's where the future lies ...' Like Matthias Pardon, he sees himself not as a scavenger but as a democratic hero: 'it ain't going to continue to be possible to keep out anywhere the light of the Press ... but I'll make the touchy folks crowd in *themselves* with their information ...' He is cynical enough to notice (and this is a note that will occur more and more forcibly in James's 'social' stories as he himself grew progressively disenchanted with the ways of the gilded world) that there was a betraying ambiguity about the boasted exclusiveness of the sort of families about whom he was paid to prattle; they wanted, so to say, their exclusiveness to be publicly recognized. One is reminded of Gilbert Osmond's deeply vulgar desire to arouse curiosity and then decline to satisfy it. As the social comedy of *The Reverberator* develops, one ends by feeling that the outraged aristos are in essence as vulgar as their traducer.

It is only half-way through the book that Flack's plan to use Francie Dosson's engagement to Gaston Probert as a source of high-class gossip sharpens the existing social contrast between the engaged pair. Up to that point, James's 'international' and 'social' debating points have been made in an over-diffuse and dawdling introduction, marred by some stale obliquities of manner as if the old theme, not unnaturally, was beginning to be something of a bore. The return of Flack and his breath of raw air quickens the pace. To Francie, whom he too would like to marry, Flack turns for information, about the Probert sisters and their French husbands: 'I should like to hear you talk right out about their ways.' He wants 'first-rate, first-hand information, straight from the tap', and he is convinced that 'people just yearn to come in; they make love to me for it all over the place; there's the biggest crowd at the door'. For to Flack, 'it's all literature... it's the press, the great institution of our time . . . It's the history of the age'. Francie innocently prattles away; Flack gives the Probert family secrets the right glossy processing for *The Reverberator*; the scandals are printed in America and read by the horrified Proberts in Paris; the fat is in the fire.

From the ensuing conflagration, no character emerges with much credit. The appalling prudery of French manners, their exaggerated protection of affianced maidens and their cynical betrayal of married wives, has already astonished the innocent Dossons and alerted the reader. The Probert code, *if* it had been strictly followed, might admittedly have offered some moral-aesthetic sanctions; there is just a germ of sympathy with the viewpoint of one of Gaston's sisters who asks, about the Dossons, 'But how can you possibly know, with such people . . . what you've got hold of? . . . It's simply impossible for us to live with vulgar people. It's a defect, no doubt . . .' The sympathy dries up at once when the code is *not* followed, as when the class-conscious sister proceeds nevertheless to ask how much money Francie is likely to inherit, whereupon the somewhat spineless Gaston is nerved to reply: 'That's a question *she* would never ask!' (The American shrinking from the murky business of marriage settlements is as marked here as it was in *Lady Barberina*.) Indeed, the Probert refinements have throughout been presented in an ambiguous light, as though they were as a family all strenuously acting out a part:

. . . they were all social creatures. That was doubtless part of the reason why the family had acclimatized itself in France. They had affinities with a society of conversation; they liked general talk and old high salons, slightly tarnished and dim, containing precious relics, where winged words flew about through a circle round the fire and some clever person, before the chimney-piece, held or challenged the others.

The ambiguity disappears entirely when Probert *père*, so unsympathetic a type of American paterfamilias by the side of shambling good-natured old Dosson, is mercilessly pinned down in two sentences: 'He read a great deal, and very serious books; works about the origin of things—of man, of institutions, of speech, of religion. This habit he had taken up more particularly since the circle of his social life had contracted.'

So far, much of the dialogue and surmise-ridden narrative has been—compared, say, with *The Europeans*—faintly fusty, as if James had moved beyond the stage of comic economy but had not yet reached that later style which, with all its difficulties, *rewards* disentanglement.

There are, of course, gleams of pure social entertainment, as in the quick sketch of a Probert sister (whose husband 'carried his umbrella . . . with something of a sceptral air'), who

viewed people solely in the light projected upon them by others; that is not as good or wicked, ugly or handsome, wise or foolish, but as grandsons, nephews, uncles and aunts, brothers and sisters-in-law, cousins and second cousins. You might have supposed, to listen to her, that human beings were susceptible of no attribute but that of a dwindling or thickening consanguinity.

But it is the vivid particularity of the new theme, the monstrous journalistic indiscretion, that dramatizes the Probert–Dosson confrontation and gives the last third of the story a theatrical verve far superior to anything James had managed to bring off in the somewhat similar confrontations in *The American*. The assembled Proberts, American wives and French husbands, struck down from a clear sky by Flack's dreadful thunderbolt, are alternately pathetic and ludicrous; there is wonderful social tension in their tragi-comic denunciation of poor Francie's unwitting treachery.

On the one hand, as Gaston points out, 'it's they who are buried beneath the filthy rubbish'. In a solemn moment, even flighty

Francie 'thought of the lively and chatty letters they had seen in the papers and wondered if they *all* meant a violation of sanctities, a convulsion of homes, a burning of smitten faces, a rupture of girls' engagements'. On the other hand, the basically *bourgeois* Proberts seem to protest too much and can hardly oppose the pure white of style to the pure black of detraction, so that Flack is no doubt right in considering their indignation 'a bigger pose than ever ... It's *thin*—that's what it is ... They pretend to be shocked because it looks exclusive, but in point of fact they like it first rate'. For a moment, indeed, it almost looks as if Flack, as ardent a representative of the American cavalry as Caspar Goodwood, would swoop down and rescue Francie from all these unsavoury European social complexities.

The Reverberator nevertheless ends happily, with a fairly stirring performance by a hitherto unassertive Gaston. Urged by an American friend to 'marry her tomorrow ... and come out of this—into the air', he claims his erring sweetheart and leaves his outraged family who had been 'doing their best to kill you morally—to render you incapable of individual life'. The words remind us that the moral issues aroused by this anecdote, the particular version of the private-public dichotomy disclosed by it, were insufficient for more than a highly entertaining, positively stagey treatment. One closes the book with a 'Good for Gaston!'—and that is that. And yet there are very serious matters just under the surface, which James would deal with more thoroughly elsewhere. For one example, a more shaming instance of 'invasion of privacy, the failure to enter into human feeling' (the phrase is Dr. Edel's) appeared the same year in *The Aspern Papers*—more shaming simply because the injured parties in that story confront the reader as real people, rather than as gesticulating comedians like the Probert clan. For another example, namely James's abiding distaste for newspaper indelicacies, a much more extreme fable would be presented a dozen years later in *Flicker-bridge* (see Chapter II), where the hero breaks his engagement to a female newspaper correspondent merely on his supposition that she *might* vulgarly miss the quality of a particular stately home and its owner! But the essential message of this *jeu d'esprit* (as James called *The Reverberator* in the Preface), the betraying tone which points ahead to other more substantial treatments of society, is that the classes or nations (for at this stage of his life, 'international' and 'social' often coincided) which had hitherto claimed privilege were beginning to retreat, not because their enemies were strong but because they themselves were fatally weakened. This is, in a sense, the final effect of all three novels here grouped together. *The Princess Casamassima*, *The Bostonians*, *The Reverberator*, all in their several ways proclaim the moral that the real struggle in men's minds is not between their public and their private interests, but rather between integrity, both public and private, on the one hand, and shoddiness, whether private or public, on the other.

VII

'Something About Art'

The Tragic Muse and tales of the artistic life

To 'do something about art'—art, that is, as a human complication and a social stumbling-block—must have been for me early a good deal of a nursed intention, the conflict between art and 'the world' striking me thus betimes as one of the half-dozen great primary motives.

Preface to 'The Tragic Muse'

Nature had dedicated him to intellectual, not personal passion.

The Lesson of the Master

IN REVIEWING his novels and tales in roughly chronological succession, we have seen how Henry James the American, conscious of opposing natures within himself, endowed many of his characters with geminian or cousinly contradictions; how Henry James the 'passionate pilgrim' consciously allowed his interest in people to be channelled for long periods to a study of one aspect of human intercourse, the international, to which as an American in Europe his attention was quite naturally drawn; and how, in nerving himself to devote his own powers to the lonely business of literary creation, he became fascinated by the conflicting claims of the public and the private life. There are other aspects of his literary personality, other choices among 'great primary motives', reflected in novels and tales of his immensely productive maturity, which may conveniently be discussed with a broadly thematic emphasis. His interest in the conscious behaviour of civilized people would lead him on to devote to the *minutiae* of social conduct an attention (at times inordinate in the opinion of many readers) which is matched only by that displayed by Marcel Proust; and at the same time his interest in the enrichment of life by art—an interest, after all, even more natural to a conscious artist than either the international or the social themes—caused him, by an analogous and deliberate shuffling of ends and means, to concentrate on art as a *subject* for art.

However natural that desire to 'do something about art', and however well the implied 'conflict between art and "the world"' would chime in with his other literary interests in conflicting personalities and conflicting national cultures, there is little doubt that when James set about to deal with artistic and literary themes *in his fiction*, he was treading on dangerous ground. The limitations of this present study do not permit a consideration of Henry James's admirable and at times superlative gifts as essayist and literary critic. Yet however much one may take for granted those gifts, one may still question the wisdom of incorporating them into novels and stories. Some of these works may even help to account for James's comparative unpopularity among 'ordinary lovers of fiction' who may have happened to discover them before reading any of his other work. If this is indeed true, it is an irony worthy of his own subtlest style that his steadfast devotion to his art should sometimes have screened from public admiration a novelist of such superb ability to present 'a character in a nutshell', as novel-readers say, and to penetrate to the deepest and *least* 'literary' recesses of the heart. Henry James's avowed belief that 'the conflict between art and "the world" ' is a 'great primary motive' must, in short, be accepted; but we can understand his thesis without necessarily agreeing that it is a good or sympathetic point of view for a novelist to adopt. To the popular objection that James indulged a tendency to turn his back on 'real life' (shades of Hyacinth Robinson!), the one convincing answer must be that to him art *was* as real as, if not more real than, 'the world'. Many people would agree with him—and none more so, curiously enough, than those who 'love to lose themselves in a good novel'. But they, alas for James, are usually the last people ever to recognize their own demonstrable interest in art, and certainly the very last to wish to read about other people's interest in the subject.

It was rash indeed to challenge comparison with Tolstoy. One would quite happily have said that James's novels made no attempt to cover Tolstoy's ground, that they were wilfully restricted, that he was aware of the sacrifices and took them in good part. But no; we are asked to believe that all this was not rueful austerity but a satisfied abstention from the indelicate profusion of life. For in the later Preface to the New York Edition volume containing *The Tragic Muse*, James castigates Tolstoy's *Peace and War* [*sic*] as one of a class of 'large loose baggy monsters', and the reader is invited to wonder what such books artistically 'mean'. The audacity of such a charge is indeed daunting. One would as soon tweak a tiger's whiskers and complain of its lack of fearful symmetry. The apparent primness is chilling. It is out of line with that zest for life which is so essential a quality of James's work. It calls for some explanation. Indeed, the further away James grows from the roots of his creative genius, the more we are advised to remind ourselves of the strength of those roots, recalling that the driest and most twisted twigs have ultimately owed their life to the same living sap.

The Tragic Muse (1889–90) was the first full-scale novel in which James attempted to treat his new 'great primary motive' (for although

Roderick Hudson poses the art-life problem, much of the reader's attention is diverted, as we have seen, to other issues). In line with my foregoing argument, and before discussing the life-art diagram of the plot, I propose to use the text of this novel itself as a source for a brief recapitulation of four stages in James's writing. I attempt this elementary demonstration in a spirit of frank propaganda—for a case for the defence of James's method will rest largely on the contention that his attainment of the fourth stage, however uncomfortable we may feel when we see him there, does not at any time invalidate his progress through the other three.

First, then—and always first—the creator's intuitive observations, the serene clarity of his apprehension of human states. In *The Tragic Muse* there is reassuring and ample evidence of these qualities in every sort of context; in the recreation of the atmosphere of summer mornings in Paris:

Miriam liked the Paris of the summer mornings, the clever freshness of all the little trades and the open-air life, the cries, the talk from door to door.... The greatest amusement perhaps was to recognize the pretty sentiment of earliness, the particular congruity with the hour, in the studied, selected dress of the little tripping women who were taking the day, for important advantages, while it was tender.

—or in Nick Dormer's historical rhapsody at Beauclere, a recognizable glow of the pilgrim's authentic passion:

You saw the great church from the doorstep, beyond gardens of course, and in the stillness you could hear the flutter of the birds that circled round its huge short towers. The towers had been finished only as time finishes things, by lending assurances to their lapses. There is something right in old monuments that have been wrong for centuries: some such moral as that was usually in Nick's mind when he saw the grand line of the roof ride the sky and draw out its length.

—or in one of several 'straight' early views of Julia Dallow:

It was one of the things in her that Nick mentally pronounced ungraceful, the perversity of pride or shyness that always made her disappoint you a little if she saw you expected a thing. She snubbed effusiveness in a way that yet gave no interesting hint of any wish to keep it herself in reserve.

The second stage is the conscious effort to exhibit, to articulate, these apprehensions—here is the impelling drive behind James's developing style, here is the pressure that forces his curiosity into remote crevices, so that at times his living substance seems drawn out too fine, squandered or distracted in grotesque antennae or tendrils. Much of the attitude to life voiced by Gabriel Nash, that oddly likeable Bohemian connoisseur, falls into this category—particularly his sincere belief that what one contributes to life, in one's individual experiments, is just *style*. Gabriel's profession of faith reads remarkably like James's own effort to convince us—and himself—that this second stage is as human and lively as the first:

'It's the simplest thing in the world; just take for granted our right to be happy and brave. What's essentially kinder and more helpful than that, what's more beneficent? But the tradition of dreariness, of stodginess, of dull, dense, literal prose, has so sealed people's eyes that they've ended by thinking the most natural of all things the most perverse.'

The argument fascinates him—it will help us if we listen a moment longer to Gabriel's apologia:

'Life consists of the personal experiments of each of us, and the point of an experiment is that it shall succeed. What we contribute is our treatment of the material, our rendering of the text, our style. A sense of the qualities of a style is so rare that many persons should doubtless be forgiven for not being able to read, or at all events to enjoy, us; but is that a reason for giving it up—for not being, in this other sphere, if one possibly can, an Addison, a Ruskin, a Renan. . .?

'People may not read you at sight, may not like you, but there's a chance they'll come round; and the only way to court the chance is to keep it up—always keep it up. . . .'

'Don't you think your style's a trifle affected?' Nick asked for further amusement.

'That's always the charge against a personal manner: if you've any at all people think you've too much. Perhaps, perhaps—who can say? The lurking unexpressed is infinite, and affectation must have begun, long ago, with the first act of reflective expression—the substitute of the few placed articulate words for the cry or the thump or the hug.'

All this could hardly be bettered as a brief exposition of the second stage in the progress towards the selection of art as subject matter—for what is more proper in a novelist than a feeling for the superiority of articulation over cries or thumps or hugs?*

So, naturally, as a third stage there follows James's interest in the *products* of that effort of articulation, and in all efforts of art, as subject matter. Again, these are interests no one could deny a great artist, but already we find him at two removes from the mainspring. Colour and shape, form and quantity, light and shadow, texture and rhythm, thesis and antithesis, contrast and repetition—all the plastic and visual and musical terms seem fitting, as James meditates on his articulation of his intuitions, and, taking the elementary feelings now for granted, and the facility of expression for granted, strains to find the perfect mould and shape to show off that expression. The language of literary criticism is not enough; we shall find him, in the Prefaces, constantly invoking images of the studio or the orchestra. Of this stage, the slightest illustration will serve. The *economy* of art in the prodigality of life, and the joy of the artist in created form; these things are positively singing in the air when Nick and Gabriel are looking at Notre Dame:

'How it straightens things out and blows away one's vapours—anything that's *done*!' said Nick; while his companion exclaimed blandly and affectionately: 'The dear old thing!'

While still adhering to the view that all these things are better saved for criticism than for fiction (and here I hail in passing Dr. Edel's remark that *The Tragic Muse* 'has a hard dry essay-like quality'), it is when contemplating this third stage of James's progress that I turn to the magisterial support of Coleridge's *Biographia Literaria:*

One man's consciousness extends only to the pleasant or unpleasant sensations caused in him by external impressions; another enlarges his inner sense to a consciousness of forms and quantity; a third in addition to the image is conscious of the conception or notion of the thing; a fourth attains to a notion of his notions—he reflects on his own reflections; and

* It should be noted that the 'articulate words' passage was added in James's revision for the New York Edition.

thus we may say, without impropriety, that the one possesses more or less inner sense than the other.

The same exhilaration of appreciation, when a novelist 'reflects on his own reflections', may of course be applied as readily to people as to things; and the text of *The Tragic Muse* produces plenty of ruminative comments such as: 'If she was genuine it was with the genuineness of doing it well.'

The fourth stage is reached when James begins to display an interest in other similar critics of life, other connoisseurs of human beings or artifacts, and treats *them* in turn as fit material for fiction, refining on refinement by making a life study of the sort of people who make life-study a life study. Here is the dangerous stage (dangerous to James the novelist: not, of course, to James the critic) exemplified in *The Tragic Muse* and even more so in several of the stories to be considered in this chapter. All James's superb apparatus of criticism and appreciation will now, for uncomfortably long periods, be focused on characters chosen not for their representative *life*, but for some correspondence with his own immediate artistic problems, for some aptness as mouthpieces for literary theses, or simply as mannikins denoting the corners of some geometrical life-art riddle-me-ree. When this happens he is no longer, himself, an artist painting a picture 'from the life'. His method of presenting Miriam Rooth and her admirers, in *The Tragic Muse*, is not even that of an artist painting another artist—which would at least entail an excellent portrait. It is, rather, as though we were watching an artist expending his technique on sketches of other artists' backs as they in turn paint other artists; or even on sketches of the easel and brushes and palettes with which they work. It is true, of course, that much even of the 'artistic' material of *The Tragic Muse* (the opening scene in the Paris Salon, the conversation arising from that setting, and a good deal of vivid aesthetic argument by the main characters throughout) is 'lifelike' enough in treatment. As I have tried to claim, James's three earlier stages remain valid. Yet in general the limitation of scope cannot but flatten the characters, most of the time, into diagrammatic figures who illustrate an attitude to life rather than a way of living; and *The Tragic Muse* suffers accordingly—as a *novel*.

In *The Tragic Muse*, too, one is made fully aware, perhaps for the first time, of the limitations imposed by James's determination to dot every 'i' and cross every 't'. A comparatively slight character like Miriam Rooth has to be explained and examined from all sides by indirect approach through other people. He explains in the Preface that he, the author, 'goes behind' Peter Sherringham and Nick Dormer as they, the first 'a great deal' and the second 'a little', 'go behind' Miriam. Why the author does not consider it sufficient that he himself should 'go behind' Miriam is never made convincingly clear. That all this should be necessary for Miriam when Natasha in *War and Peace* is presented *as* herself and requires no special apprehension by peeping over somebody's shoulder who is looking at her when she isn't looking—this is, after all the offered explanations, even less clear. There is indeed, to quote the Preface again, 'an awkwardness in having thus belatedly to point such features out'; in view of the slightness of the folk in *The Tragic Muse* about whom such an ado is organized, an adverse reader may well ask why it is necessary to 'point such features out' at all, whether belatedly or in the texture of the novel itself. And however much one may be persuaded to take the characters as symbols, it does seem a fundamental weakness, in so complex a study of so small a circle, that with all the presentation of the many facets of each character as in some symmetrical Hall of Mirrors, the reader doesn't really care in the end whether Miriam should marry Peter or Nick or neither. In the face of that paralysing indifference, all the piling-up of subtle reasons why we *should* care seems pitifully beside the point.

In the foregoing paragraph, I am myself looking over the shoulder of a hypothetical adverse critic. The problem of the indirect approach may be put aside for later consideration: it bulks larger in later novels. In acknowledging the first considerable appearance of the method, together with a narrowing of interest on an 'artistic' subject, it must be sufficient for the moment to claim that the very richness of James's permanent primary qualities—comprehensive interest in life and people and artistic creation, felt in a tenderness of response at times approaching the agonizing—may have made it necessary for him, at times, to limit each particular field if he were to retain sanity as a man and comprehensibility as an author. Just as at one time one is conscious of the narrowness of the 'artistic' field, so at another time one is conscious of the richness, the masterly organization by which such a wealth of observation and comment is marshalled and held in check; of the generalship over such an army of attitudes, such a potential rabble of notions.

There is an apparent effort by James himself to justify what one might call the misplaced focus of the characters of *The Tragic Muse* —their interest as samples of the 'artistic' life. This explicit plea falsifies the end of the novel, where Peter Sherringham is rejected entirely because he is unwilling to renounce a worldly career for the sake of art—for art personified by Miriam as an actress-wife. This is so lame a conclusion in view of what James has previously invited us to know or care about the parties concerned, as to sacrifice the novel to the thesis. The 'precious waistband or girdle', to quote his Prefatory reference to the 'middle' of a novel, has indeed fallen down 'perilously near the knees' when the novelist trips to such an ungainly dénouement, so timid a piece of melodrama. Of greater *novelistic* value are the typically Jamesian comments on the affront of any form of slick spry cleverness: 'Wasn't it better to be perfectly stupid than to have only one eye open and wear for ever in the great face of the world the expression of a knowing wink?' Similarly, although the best views of Nick do not add up to a living portrait, they do display brilliant aspects of unlocalized character:

He had none of that wish to appear deep which is at the bottom of most forms of fatuity; he was perfectly willing to pass for decently superficial; he only aspired to be decently continuous. When you were not suitably shallow this presented difficulties; but he would have assented to the proposition that you must be as subtle as you can and that a high use of subtlety is in consuming the smoke of your inner fire. The fire was the great thing, not the chimney. He had no view of life that counted out the need of learning; it was teaching rather as to which he was conscious of no particular mission. He enjoyed life, enjoyed it immensely, and was ready to pursue it with patience through as many channels as possible. He was on his guard, however, against making an ass of himself, that is against not thinking out his experiments before trying them in public.

Even the comments on the 'artistic' life are best when they are dissociated from the diagram: 'It was all very Bohemian and dis-

hevelled and delightful, very supposedly droll and enviable to out-
siders. . . .'

From the point of view of novel-readers, the diagrammatic characters will be remembered not because of their function in the plot
and certainly not because they embody different attitudes towards
art (and what indecisive attitudes, after all), but because by this
time Henry James, not unlike Shakespeare, can hardly avoid endowing even his expository characters with at least that vitality which
comes from the sympathetic accuracy of incidental and external
touches. It is, however, this knack of infusing life by quiet wit and
deft touches that disconcertingly galvanizes such minor figures as
Mrs. Lendon or Mrs. Gresham, while Miriam, whose quota of verisimilitude is merely one ingredient of a more ambitious portrait,
remains for the most part a carbon-copy of other people's opinions.
She never attains this particularity of Mrs. Lendon:

... a large, mild, healthy woman with a heavy tread, a person who
preferred early breakfasts, uncomfortable chairs and the advertisement
sheets of the *Times*. . . . She was extremely fond of an herbaceous garden—
her main consciousness was of herbaceous possibilities. . . . She went out
of the room always as if it were after some one else; and on the gentlemen
'joining' her later—the junction was not very close—she received them
with an air of gratified surprise.

—or Mrs. Gresham:

Mrs. Gresham was a married woman who was usually taken for a
widow, mainly because she was perpetually 'sent for' by her friends, who
in no event sent for Mr. Gresham. . . . She slipped in and out, accompanied at the piano, talked to the neglected visitors, walked in the rain,
and after the arrival of the post usually had conferences with her hostess,
during which she stroked her chin and looked familiarly responsible. It
was her peculiarity that people were always saying things to her in a
lowered voice. . . . No one had ever discovered whether any one else
paid her. People only knew that *they* did.

Mrs. Gresham lived so much in the world that being left now and
then to one's own company had become her idea of true sociability.

In much the same way, the figure of old Mr. Carteret will come
quickly to mind when one may try in vain to distinguish in memory

between the various facets which go to make up Peter Sherringham
and Nick Dormer:

> It often made him say to himself that Mr. Carteret must have had many
> odd parts to have been able to achieve with his means so many things
> requiring cleverness. It was as if experience, though coming to him in
> abundance, had dealt with him so clean-handedly as to leave no stain,
> and had moreover never provoked him to any general reflexion. He had
> never proceeded in any ironic way from the particular to the general;
> certainly he had never made a reflexion upon anything so unparliamentary
> as Life.

The diagrammatic theme which, to my mind, so sadly diminishes
the total impact of *The Tragic Muse* as a novel, is satisfactorily
handled in itself. Nick Dormer is destined for a high political career,
but is presented as a dedicated painter. Peter Sherringham, diplomat
brother of the widowed Julia Dallow who is expected to ally herself
to Nick in his political career, becomes infatuated in Paris with the
actress Miriam Rooth. There develop two tugs-of-war. In the first
Julia tries to pluck Nick, so to say, from his studio into the Cabinet;
tugging behind Julia is the wealthy old politician Mr. Carteret who
sees Nick as an adopted political son, and tugging behind Nick is
his friend Gabriel Nash, a 'greenery-yallery Grosvenor-Gallery'
epigrammatic spokesman of the artistic view of life (aptly labelled
by Professor Cargill 'a wandering breviary of aestheticism'). In the
second, lesser, tug-of-war, Peter wavers between his diplomatic
career and Miriam. Nick appears to be winning *his* tug-of-war, for
he turns down Carteret's offer of a handsome legacy, and his Julia
shows signs of jealousy of Miriam, whose portrait Nick is painting.
She 'gives him his freedom'. By this time, of course, we are all
keyed up to expect that the two strong creative personalities, Nick
and Miriam, will come together. (Their lines are cleared, for Peter
has chosen diplomacy and has been posted abroad.) But, alas, this
is not the diagram. For although Nick represents devotion to his
art just as Miriam does to hers, his is of the private self-communing
variety just as hers is of the social interpretative kind. In the Preface,
James points out that 'all we then—in his triumph—see of the
charm-compeller is the back he turns to us as he bends over his
work ... the better part of him is locked too much away from us'.

This may indeed be a true (and certainly autobiographically true) description of the creative artist as James saw him, but it is a pretty poor posture for a major character in a novel. So Miriam is allowed to marry a suitable actor and Nick paints Julia's portrait ... We are almost persuaded that Nick has taken literally the *poseur*'s view twittered by Gabriel Nash: 'Merely to be is such a *métier*; to live is such an art; to feel is such a career!'

Alas (once more), James has not really succeeded in making us feel that Nick is much more substantially an artist than his friend Peter was a genuine theatre-lover—poor Peter, who is described in his author's Preface as being of the type of upper-class British Philistine who has 'unappeasable curiosity for things of the theatre; for every one of them, that is, except the drama itself'. There is no space here for an examination of Henry James's own private insensitivity to the significant movements in visual art taking place around him in Paris and London; he was always deeply interested in the plastic arts, but the material collected in *The Painter's Eye* shows him to have been, in both the best and worst senses of the word, a 'literary' interpreter of art. Nor is the point of crucial importance in aiding an assessment of *The Tragic Muse* and the associated tales now to be discussed. Even if one grants that Nick Dormer is incompetent to figure as a dedicated painter, no one could deny that James himself was eminently competent to discuss *literature*—and yet his choice of writers as 'heroes' of his tales is equally unrewarding to those stories *as fiction*, however much they may have given him opportunities to express critical or autobiographical truths. And so it comes about, ironically enough, that when one turns back to *The Tragic Muse* to sample James's immensely accomplished commentaries on art, one turns not to Nick Dormer for an insight into the mind of a painter, nor even to Miriam Rooth for an insight into the world of the theatre, but rather to the semi-comic figure of Gabriel Nash, who chatters away at such a rate that, in Dr. Edel's phrase, 'we are almost surfeited with sophistication and epigrams'.

To Mr. Michael Ramsbotham I am indebted for the illuminating comment that the difference between such a work as *The Tragic Muse* and those 'loose baggy monsters' of Tolstoy and other writers mentioned in James's Preface, is essentially the same as the difference, in music, between variations on a theme and a symphony, in that the very cleverness of the one somehow places it in a lower category than the full profundity and range of the other.

The Tragic Muse is a cue for a note on Henry James's own hopeful but in the end disastrous flirtation with the theatre—but the cue must go unregarded in this guide to his fiction. We know from his letters and notebooks and from the testimony of a host of contemporaries that he nourished a wild dream of public success, if not notoriety. We know, with the benefit of hindsight, that his own true glory *was* to act like those hapless heroes of his literary and artistic tales, who turned on the public their bowed backs as they produced, in solitude, works destined to intrigue a public yet unborn.

The Tragic Muse was by no means James's first attempt to 'do something about art'. Roderick Hudson, his first considerable character, was an artist, lived among artists, talked about art, listened to other people talking about art—but it is as a young man that we remember him, not as a young artist. One of the earliest attempts to make a *plot* out of art itself is the story *The Madonna of the Future* (1873), and it is significant that this plot turns on an artistic failure. No failure, indeed, could be more complete: the wretched Theobald has lived for years with his idea of the perfect Madonna, but the model has grown old and plump and when he dies his work is still undone; he has dawdled away his time, and life and art have leagued together to avenge themselves on him. It is a sad little tale, scarcely marred by a slight stiffness in its original prose, and capable of sustaining the stylistic elaborations of the revised version in the New York Edition. The lengthy disquisitions on art and sensibility lead to nothing more than this: '. . . at last, sickened by the vacant misery of the spot,* I passed behind Theobald, eagerly and tenderly. I can hardly say that I was surprised at what I found—a canvas that was a mere dead blank, cracked and discoloured by time. This was his immortal work!' The bitterness of the disparity between high aims and wretched performance is exaggerated by the introduction into the tale of a 'jaunty Juvenal', a hateful man who 'combines sculpture and satire' and produces

---

* The revised version substitutes 'my impression of vacant misery' for 'the vacant misery of the spot'—an instance of James's change of focus in his later notion of 'the conflict between art and "the world" '.

grotesque little figures of cats and monkeys, which sell like hot cakes: 'For a week afterwards, whenever I was seized among the ruins of triumphant Rome with some peculiarly poignant memory of Theobald's transcendent illusions and deplorable failure, I seemed to hear a fantastic, impertinent murmur, "Cats and monkeys, monkeys and cats; all human life is there!"' Every drop of extra bitterness is squeezed from this addition to the fable: the disillusioned Juvenal is successful and very productive; he is as pleased with the technical quality of his 'peculiar plastic compound' as with the models themselves; 'their imitative felicity was revolting', says the narrator, echoing James's absurd scorn for the 'life-like'; and —most unkindest cut!—his beastly caricatures are 'especially admired by Americans'.

You can't be dogmatic about an artist's view of his own life and work. It seems ridiculous that an author who wrote with such rich fluency and was able to find publishers (if not readers) for all his immense output should have brooded so much on artistic and commercial failure as to devote to this theme a considerable number of his own best *nouvelles*. And yet that is just what Henry James did, over a period of some twenty years—years which saw the production of his own masterpieces. A rapid survey of some of these by-products of his obsession with art will assemble a group of disillusioned—almost masochistic—commentaries which add up to a sizeable distrust of the public to which his own art, like all other art however personal, is dedicated.

The Author of 'Beltraffio' (1884) mixes an 'art' theme with that curious sadistic interest (as in *My Friend Bingham*, *The Turn of the Screw* and *The Other House*) in the torture or murder of children. Mark Ambient, a great artist in the novel, is visited by the narrator, a young American devotee. The young man also meets Mrs. Ambient, who 'shone with a certain coldness and practised in intercourse a certain bland detachment, but she was muffled in gentleness as in one of those vaporous redundant scarves that muffle the heroines of Gainsborough and Romney. She also had a vague air of race, justified by my afterwards learning that she was "connected with the aristocracy".' This thin priggish woman disapproves of her husband's work, is blind to its beauty and fears it will have an immoral influence on their young angelic son Dolcino. The narrator, single-minded in his admiration of Mark Ambient, is so enraptured with the proofs of the latest novel that he persuades the wife, against her recent custom, to read them. She does so, and her prudery is so shocked that when Dolcino falls ill she allows him to die (by refusing to admit the doctor) rather than risk the peril to his soul latent in his father's prose. The bare story is incredible. Mark Ambient's confession of his aims and methods is the only real substance, and the reader's pity is canvassed less by Dolcino's death than by the public's rejection of Ambient's novels: 'he had an air of thinking it quite natural that he should leave many simple folk, tasting of him, as simple as ever he found them . . .' Ambient is very much a per-sonification of an important facet of James's own view of himself as creator, with the watchword 'firm and bright, firm and bright', and a feeling for the printed word so acute that he 'indulged the luxury, so dear to writers of deliberation', of having each chapter printed as he wrote it. But what a waste of effort it all is! All the business of argument and analysis, unenlivened even by the melo-drama, is not worth that one passage of creative writing in which James presents us with another of his incomparable caricatures—Miss Ambient, a lady unnecessary to plot or atmosphere, who is thrown in to relieve us by a reminder of the developing quality of James's power when he is not writing stories about the prose of fictitious story-tellers:

Her laugh was modern—by which I mean that it consisted of the vocal agitation serving between people who meet in drawing-rooms as the solvent of social disparities, the medium of transitions; but her appear-ance was—what shall I call it?—medieval. She was pale and angular, her long thin face was inhabited by sad dark eyes and her black hair inter-twined with golden fillets and curious clasps. She wore a faded velvet robe which clung to her when she moved and was 'cut', as to the neck and sleeves, like the garments of old Italians. She suggested a symbolic picture, something akin even to Dürer's Melancholia, and was so perfect an image of a type which I, in my ignorance, supposed to be extinct, that while she rose before me I was almost as much startled as if I had seen a ghost.

Miss Ambient was a restless romantic disappointed spinster, consumed with the love of Michael-Angelesque attitudes and mystical robes; but I'm now convinced she hadn't in her nature those depths of unutterable thought which, when you first knew her, seemed to look out from her eyes and to prompt her complicated gestures. Those features in especial had a misleading eloquence; they lingered on you with a far-off dimness, an air of obstructed sympathy, which was certainly not always a key to the spirit of their owner; so that, of a truth, a young lady could scarce have been so dejected and disillusioned without having committed a crime for which she was consumed with remorse, or having parted with a hope that she couldn't sanely have entertained.

This is so much the fluent Henry James of those good moments when he forgets his unnecessarily defensive pretence that 'imitative felicity was revolting', that one greets it as almost a judgement on him that his own chief stylistic blunder in this story should occur not in his lively picture of Miss Ambient but in Ambient's own precious account of his own precious prose:

'This new affair must be a golden vessel, filled with the purest distillation of the actual; and oh how it worries me, the shaping of the vase, the hammering of the metal! I've to hammer it so fine, so smooth; I don't do more than an inch or two a day. And all the while I have to be careful not to let a drop of the liquor escape!'

After all, the reader is forced to exclaim, nobody but a fool would attempt to hammer a *full* vessel! And one is compelled to observe that since this sort of thing was to be done admirably—and without howlers—in the Prefaces and critical essays, there is no need for it in the stories.

It is, indeed, the singularly *un*imitative *in*felicity of such a theme for a 'master of the *nouvelle*' that turns *The Author of 'Beltraffio'* and many other tales 'about art' into awkward mixtures of creative observation on the one hand and an inappropriate aesthetic theory on the other. The effect can, at times, be deplorable. One vivid example must serve:

'Such a very odd time to be reading an author whom she never could abide!' In her agitation Miss Ambient was guilty of this vulgarism of speech, and I was so impressed by her narrative that only in recalling her words later did I notice the lapse.

What *is* extraordinary in this scene, of course, is not that Miss Ambient used a rum word, but that the narrator should have noticed it at all, under circumstances as harrowing as little Dolcino's mortal illness.

Again, the kind of moral problem posed is much less competently handled than some of the incidental wit which brings sporadic life to the dialogue:

'... my wife would tell you it's the difference between Christian and Pagan. ... It's the difference between making the most of life and making the least, so that you'll get another better one in some other time and place. Will it be a sin to make the most of that one too, I wonder ...?'

Such a remark is of less questionable quality than the 'problem' itself, which can be summed up by Mr. Quentin Anderson (*Scrutiny*, XIV, 249) as: 'Between them they kill the child who represents their "marriage", and James indicates in this way their moral death—they have sought to make a possession of the divinity.' Mr. Leon Edel, in an introductory remark to this tale, notes that 'the piping voice of childhood is smothered by a righteousness more evil than the evil it imagines and seeks to defy'. We are reminded that James's *donnée* for the plot was the report that the wife of John Addington Symonds 'abhorred her husband's work and never read his books'. Recent revelations about the private life of Symonds do provide Mrs. Symonds, retrospectively, with a more credible motive: and one feels, somehow, that the essential falseness of the given facts in James's cautious version of the affair has somehow blurred the whole grisly fable.

But before he turned to face, in increasingly self-pitying mood, his own relationships with the reading public, Henry James first embodied in a short story the struggle within himself—whether or not he was prepared to sacrifice the time-absorbing business of 'living' in order to concentrate on his art. It was the mock-battle he had pretended to fight in some of the early short stories; it crops up again and again in his working notebooks; it peppers his more intimate letters of the late 1870's and early 1880's, when he was approaching the watershed of his fortieth bachelor year; and he reverts to it when, his personal decision having been made, if only by default, he set out a guarded yet at times radiant version of the victory, and its cost, in his three autobiographical volumes. As Mr.

Laurence Holland comments,—quoting a phrase from one of James's letters: 'I believe almost as much in matrimony for other people as I believe in it little for myself'—he envisaged in 'the form of matrimony an image of commitments to life itself'.* Such commitments he was temperamentally unwilling to make; and the long list of his 'art' stories is in effect a history of the various excuses he made, decade after decade, for his deliberate withdrawal.

In *The Lesson of the Master* (1888), the choice between matrimony and literary dedication is posed in simple diagrammatic terms, if the concept of matrimony be allowed to stand symbol for the demands of an active social life in general. It is a restatement, fifteen years later, of the dilemma of *Benvolio;* another dozen years would pass before the same nagging riddle was quietened, for a moment, in the escapist fantasy of *The Great Good Place*. In 1888, the problem and the prose were alike fresh: the dilemma *was* a dilemma in the sense that an alternative solution was still valid. By the turn of the century, the long-rehearsed private struggle had become a dispirited exercise in shadow-boxing; and the stories in which James dramatized his self-indulgent abstinence would show, in their style no less than in their question-begging special pleading, a disquieting loss of vitality.

The ambiguity of *The Lesson of the Master* is a simple ambiguity of plot. The elderly novelist who warns his young disciple against marriage, ends up by marrying the young woman from whom his young convert had fled. This is merely the technical 'let-down' of a trick ending; it has nothing to do with the dilemma as stated. As 'head of the profession', Henry St. George knows that his famous novels, still selling well and increasing his fame, have in fact declined in quality. He urges young Paul Overt, whose first novels have an integrity St. George once cherished in his own work, not to compromise—while admitting 'that's the devil of the whole thing, keeping it up'. St. George is in no doubt as to the identity of the artist's enemy, the temptation to compromise: 'The idols of the market; money and luxury and "the world"; placing one's children and dressing one's wife; everything that drives one to the short and easy way'. The world is too much with us: this is the burden of his comfortable complaint. And if one's wife is the enemy's fifth column within the gates, there is no compensating ally outside the citadel.

* *The Expense of Vision*, Princeton, 1964.

In an implied attack on the feebleness of contemporary literary criticism, the Master admits that 'not more than two or three people will notice you don't go straight. The others—*all* the rest, every blest soul in England, will think you do—will think you *are* keeping it up ...' Trapped by his social success, St. George has sacrificed 'the sense which is the real life of the artist and the absence of which is his death, of having drawn from his intellectual instrument the finest music that nature had hidden in it, of playing it as it should be played'. All else is vanity: he had refused the price of dedication and as a result 'I've had everything. In other words I've missed everything'.

The solemn young Overt is predisposed to believe the Master's dictum that an artist marries only 'at his peril'. Like his creator, he runs off to Switzerland and Italy, returning after two years with a presumed masterpiece for his publisher and in time to celebrate his mentor's marriage, *en secondes noces*, to his own adored but sacrificed Marian. We are left with the impression that 'Nature had dedicated him to intellectual, not personal passion'—Nature, and not merely Henry St. George. When the young novelist had asked his Master if there were no women who would 'really understand—who can take part in a sacrifice', we feel that he knew in advance the answer he would receive: 'How can they take part? They themselves are the sacrifice. They're the idol and the altar and the flame.' You may say that the Master, in so swiftly replacing his own hampering wife, acted better than he spoke; that this action was, in effect, his real 'lesson'. But St. George's own 'radiance' in his new happiness shows Overt quite conclusively that he had 'now definitely ceased to count—ceased to count as a writer'. He had become 'almost banal, was almost smug'. From *that* kind of happiness, at any rate, Overt—or Benvolio, or James himself—found it easy to walk away into the inner room of dedication. The temptation to add the phrase 'where no other human being could interrupt his self-esteem', is difficult to resist. In terms of Henry James's biography, such a solution was probably in true consonance with his own temperament and therefore justified. In terms of the very art in whose name (quite deceptively, I believe) the supposed sacrifice was made, the result was deplorable, as James's later worryings at this 'artistic' bone themselves prove only too clearly.

The best known of all James's stories about writers and their world is *The Aspern Papers* (1888), which shared with *The Turn of the Screw*, long before its successful adaptation for the modern stage, the distinction of being selected to represent the author in the Everyman Library and in many other selections and anthologies. The reason for its popularity is obvious enough: it is itself a gripping character-study, with its haunting evocation of the 'domestic desolation' of a dilapidated Venetian palazzo housing old Miss Bordereau, guardian of the 'papers' of the long-dead poet Jeffrey Aspern (as it were a Shelley), and her tremulous niece Miss Tina. The theme is a problem of literary or scholarly morals: how far is one justified in offending the sensibilities of the living in order to disinter and publish surviving manuscripts of the illustrious dead? The charm of the story lies elsewhere. The writing has the flowing competence of James at his narrative best; clear, finely allusive but always organically alive. The struggle between elderly privacy and a rapacious agent of enlightenment is tense because both forces are part-justified and part-corrupt in their several ways; and there is a sureness of touch in the witty yet sympathetic delineation of the small cast of characters which excludes all that is mawkish and self-deluding in some of the other stories of this group. Confronted by the doggedness of the Bordereau ladies, the treasure-seeker felt that 'hypocrisy, duplicity are my only chance'. He can spare pity for poor imprisoned Miss Tina when she murmurs: 'We are terribly quiet. I don't know how the days pass. We have no life.' He can spare a superior speculation about 'what mystic rites of ennui the Misses Bordereau celebrated in their darkened rooms'. But when the cat-and-mouse game of the old lady begins to exhaust his patience, when he suspects that he is being held to ransom for a large sum of money for Miss Tina's *dot*, and when finally it dawns that he himself has been earmarked as both financial and matrimonial emancipator, then a sourness of motive begins to corrode the atmosphere of friendly companionship in which poor Miss Tina had begun, late in life, to put forward timid blossoms of trust: 'From the moment you were kind to her she depended on you absolutely; her self-consciousness dropped from her and she took the greatest intimacy, the innocent intimacy which was the only thing she could conceive, for granted.' The final tense embarrassment of Miss Tina's near-proposal to the letter-hunter is wonderfully conveyed. (When Dame Flora Robson played the rôle in the dramatized version, one hid one's face for very shame as she, too, lowered her eyes at the lack of response from the visiting scholar, who was prepared to lose the papers rather than take them with Miss Tina 'thrown in' on terms of conditional sale). The crisis passes. 'I could not, for a bundle of tattered papers, marry a ridiculous, pathetic, provincial old woman.' For the elder Miss Bordereau has died after accusing the narrator of being a 'publishing scoundrel' (here is the link with *The Reverberator* of the same year) and Miss Tina now possesses the papers. Rejected, she burns them.

Of the stories still to be considered, several were written during the years when James, distressed by the public's indifference to his novels, courted a wider audience with stage plays and set himself to ration his prose fiction. One aspect of the life-art antithesis pre-occupying him at this time is illustrated in *The Real Thing* (1892), an engaging and entertaining little sermon on 'the perverse and cruel law in virtue of which the real thing could be so much less precious than the unreal'. The narrator this time is a painter; to his studio come Major and Mrs. Monarch, a couple who have 'an indefinable air of prosperous thrift—they evidently got a good deal of luxury for their money'. The Monarchs seek, with the utmost diffidence, to sell their services as models for illustrations to high-society fiction: they will, in spite of their present straitness of circumstances, be 'the real thing' and so help his illustrator to the production of authentic work. The painter, for the part, quickly estimates their social status:

I could imagine their leggings and waterproofs, their knowing tweeds and rugs, their rolls of sticks and cases of tackle and neat umbrellas; and I could evoke the exact appearance of their servants and the compact variety of their luggage on country stations.

He hadn't a stray sixpence of an idea to fumble for, so we didn't spin it very fine; we confined ourselves to questions of leather and even of liquor—saddlers and breeches-makers and how to get excellent claret cheap—and matters like 'good trains' and the habits of small game.

It is just because they *are* 'the real thing', however, that the artist cannot in the end use them; it is not only that 'such people as that, all convention and patent-leather, with ejaculations that stopped conversation, had no business in a studio'; their very authenticity inhibits them when he requires them to *look* authentic. Instead, he finds in the acted postures of a drab professional model and jaunty Italian free-lance 'the real thing' he misses in the hall-marked Monarchs.

This little parable succeeds, though, where *The Author of 'Beltraffio'* fails, because although the point is clear enough, the figures who make it are given a tender independent life, and they are not made to appear conscious of their expository rôle. (One might even draw the conclusion that Mark Ambient ruined the other tale because he was 'the real thing' in art as the Monarchs were in society.) The amused affectionate tone of James's 'placing' of the Monarchs, as illustrated in the quotations above, brings into question Mrs. Leavis's view (*Scrutiny*, XIV, 227) that in *The Real Thing* he was 'expressing his contempt as an artist for the English country-house culture and its social values'—a judgement more fitting, surely, for *The Death of the Lion*.

Collaboration (1892) is another success. Here, art wins a victory over 'the world'. In order to collaborate in writing an opera with a German composer, a young French writer is willing to renounce his fiancée, whose mother will not countenance an alliance with the hated enemy—the Franco-Prussian War had not unnaturally scarred her pride: 'she made me think of a priestess or mourner, of revolutions and sieges, detested treaties and ugly public things', even though her very narrowness of outlook also suggested 'encircling and fortifying things' to the American narrator. There is a hint, too, that the young Frenchman is not exactly heart-broken by his sacrifice of the girl's love for his collaborator's company (' "what do you mean by being deliberately perverse?" He fixed me so with his intensely living French eye that I became almost blushingly conscious of a certain insincerity and, instead of telling him what I meant, tried to get off with the deplorable remark that the prejudices of Mesdames de Brindes were after all respectable')—but the interesting thing about the reader's suspicion is that on this occasion at least one is not obliged to regard the character merely as the spokesman for or personification of James's view of the supranationality of art. By his very liveliness and possible ambivalence he is, of course, made a more effective exponent of that viewpoint. Lively beyond the needs of a debating puppet, too, is his German friend, who made the narrator feel 'thin and empirical, conscious that *he* was one of the higher kind whom the future has looked in the face'. In these two stories, in other words, there is art in James's method as well as in his subject-matter.

Perhaps the slightest and most gimmicky of the series is *Nona Vincent* (1892), a direct product of James's current interest in the theatre. The author of a play, 'Nona Vincent', is encouraged in his career by a married woman who acts as his 'angel'; he is also intrigued by the young actress who plays his name part, although at first her professional skill is only moderate: 'She was like a knife without an edge—good steel that had never been sharpened; she hacked away at her hard dramatic loaf, she couldn't cut it smooth.' Each lady tells the dramatist that the other is in love with him. He broods over his Galatea, Nona Vincent, who comes to him in a dream, murmuring 'I live—I live—I live'. His older female friend teaches the younger just *how* to act the sacred part of Nona Vincent, with the result that the dramatist, in a hasty scamped ending, marries the pupil. There are echoes here of *The Real Thing*, the puzzling contrast between verisimilitude on the stage or in art and integrity in real life; but the tale must be classed among the fantasies of a writer tired and over-anxious about professional problems.

Two other stories of the same period dwelt significantly on the theme of best-sellers and unregarded masterpieces. In *The Middle Years* (1893), James, in his fiftieth year, sees himself in the self-subsiding figure of a disappointed stylist 'discovered', just before his death, by a young devotee: Dencombe, ageing and ailing at Bournemouth, meets a young doctor who admires his work as a novelist and who, to show his devotion, is prepared to wait at the master's death bed while a chance of personal fortune passes him by. It is a beautifully concentrated *morceau* or 'concise anecdote' (to quote the Preface), but even here James has to pay the price for shifting his emphasis to satisfactions too smug and remote. As in Mark Ambient's faulty image, so in this careful tale any awkwardness of construction is thrown into unfortunate relief by the author's insistence, through the mouth of his chief characters, on finish and balance. Dencombe and his young admirer meet accidentally on a

Bournemouth cliff-path, and each is reading an advance copy of Dencombe's new unpublished novel; the staginess of this opening is, we feel, just the kind of thing the James-like Dencombe would abhor. And again, as with Ambient, the lapse may strike the reader as almost a judgement. Self-pity, in this tale, is made explicit: 'The tears filled his mild eyes; something precious had passed away. . . . He read his own prose, he turned his own leaves, and had as he sat there with the spring sunshine on the page an emotion peculiar and intense. His career was over, no doubt, but it was over, when all was said, with *that*.' Self-gratification is no less openly averred: 'Dencombe was a passionate corrector, a fingerer of style; the last thing he ever arrived at was a form final to himself. His ideal would have been to publish secretly, and then, on the published text, treat himself to the terrified revise, sacrificing always a first edition and beginning for posterity and even for the collectors, poor dears, with a second.' (This, the least attractive side of Henry James's complex nature, has at least the merit of an apparent shamelessness. The reader who winces at this mawkishness will wince more violently, but with less embarrassment, at the author's own bland preoccupation with his own words: 'it consists, in fact,' he later announced in the Preface to the volume of the New York Edition containing this story, 'should the curious care to know, of some 5550 [words]'.) The reader is likely to stir uncomfortably, to seize with relief on any substantial offering of the outward-looking objective 'comical' James:

> The humble dependent, discouraged by his remoteness, wandered with a martyred droop of the head in another direction, and the exorbitant lady, watching the waves, offered a confused resemblance to a flying-machine that had broken down.

Dencombe dies in a pale melancholy, fingering his sickly fame: 'It *is* glory—to have been tested, to have had our little quality and cast our little spell. The thing is to have made somebody care.' The more obvious success of the popular novelist is flayed in *Greville Fane* ('a minor miracle of foreshortening', James notes agreeably in the same Preface). *Greville Fane* (1892) tells the story of a writer of best-sellers, vulgar and tasteless but of a kind heart, who writes herself to death to support a lazy ingrate son and a snobbish daughter.

The plot is cruel, arousing indignation rather than pity. Identification of the model for the lady who writes under the pen-name Greville Fane would doubtless be simple, and pointless. What is of interest is the sour charity bestowed upon her by James in his most Dencombe-like mood:

> She thought the English novel deplorably lacking in that element [passion], and the task she had cut out for herself had been to supply the deficiency. . . . She adored in truth the aristocracy, and they constituted for her the romance of the world or, what is more to the point, the prime material of fiction. . . . She was not a belated producer of the old fashionable novel, but, with a cleverness and a modernness of her own, had freshened up the fly-blown tinsel.

Greville Fane had never known 'the torment of form', but we are invited to see her suffer in other ways. She had 'kept throughout all her riot of absurdity a witless confidence that should have been as safe from criticism as a stutter or a squint', but witless confidence in her children was less than wise. Her daughter, etched maliciously with a Jamesian near-image plus a Jamesian simile proper, 'was long-necked and near-sighted and striking, and I thought I had never seen sweet seventeen in a form so hard and high and dry. . . . I felt as if she were surrounded with a spiked iron railing'. As for her son, the poor novelist had 'wrung her own flaccid little sponge into the torrent' of his 'flood of life'. More significant even than these cruel inventions is the tell-tale tone of James's direct commentary; even when he seems to be sympathetic towards the personification of the prostitution of the novelist's art, he cannot avoid the perspective of that aloof prim distance which brought about the inflation of the 'comic' characters in The Bostonians. If he wished to invoke a genuine sympathy for the cheated hack, drained of her swelling royalties by ungrateful children, this was hardly the tone to adopt: 'she favoured cheap places and set up her desk in the smaller capitals'. It suggests rather the high level from which we are invited to view such a figure as Mrs. Tarrant. And since by his fiftieth year it can hardly be maintained that Henry James was unable to achieve precisely the tone he required, one can only accept the implication that in such a story as Greville Fane there is first-hand acrimony behind the second-hand sympathy.

In 1894, two long stories were printed in 'The Yellow Book': *The Death of the Lion,* and *The Coxon Fund;* both reprinted in 1895 in the volume *Terminations.* The first concerns the scurvy treatment of a real genius by an allegedly cultivated aristocracy; the second inverts the theme, presenting a sedulously nurtured humbug. Neil Paraday, the 'Lion', is, like his creator, a fifty-year-old novelist. His working notes sound not unlike those of James's later phase: 'loose, liberal, confident, it might have passed for a great gossiping eloquent letter—the overflow into talk of an artist's amorous plan.' The narrator, consciously prim, attempts to screen Paraday from the attentions of people whose interest in his work is at best meretricious and at worst frivolous, snobbish like Mr. Rumble the fashionable artist, 'reporter on canvas', 'whose little game ... was to be the first to perch on the shoulders of renown', or the devastating 'Mrs. Weeks Wimbush, wife of the boundless brewer and proprietress of the universal menagerie', in whose establishment, 'on occasions when the crush is great, the animals rub shoulders freely with the spectators and the lions sit for whole evenings with the lambs'. In the crush of such undiscriminating connoisseurs, the narrator 'could do nothing for him but exchange with him over people's heads looks of intense but futile intelligence'. Among such fry, Paraday 'circulated in person in a manner that the libraries might well have envied'. The narrator, holding that 'the artist's life is his work, and this is the place to observe him', drives away the one sightseer who genuinely reveres the master's prose, but is powerless to keep the Lion from a week-end visit to a horribly gilded cage. Here he is first accorded insensitive honours, then pushed aside on the advent of two more popular novelists—creators of pseudonymous best-sellers who are bitterly caricatured by the long-suffering narrator: the novelist who signs her books Guy Walsingham is 'a pretty little girl who wore her hair in what used to be called a crop'; her colleague who is known to the libraries as Dora Forbes is 'florid and bald; he had a big red moustache and wore showy knickerbockers'. The setting aside of Paraday is made grotesquely complete. His precious last manuscript is lost—Lady Augusta's maid gave it to Lord Dorimont's valet, and these elegant *cognoscenti* muddle it into oblivion. The same fate awaits Paraday himself. Unnerved by the cultivated hubbub, he suffers a relapse and dies, to the great inconvenience of the household, in his forgotten bedroom. As guest and author alike, he had sadly overstayed his welcome by the English upper class.

The tone in which our sympathy is canvassed is uncertain in its effects. By present-day standards the Lion is moderately well-to-do: 'Paraday lived at no great cost, and the frisk of petticoats, with a timorous "Sherry, sir?" was about his modest mahogany.' We can pity his comparative failure as a novelist as much or as little as we can pity that comparative poverty: it is, after all, the eternal Jamesian narrator who makes all the fuss, and not Paraday himself. We are, in short, made half aware that although his hero is no humbug, the narrator *is*, and we are not shocked by the discovery. Frank Saltram, on the other hand, beneficiary of *The Coxon Fund*, is the author-humbug, and gains the reader's sympathy not by reason of his intellectual probity but insidiously by reason of his very spineless-ness. He is so much more human than the Jamesian busybodies who flock, sanctimoniously, to his assistance. The man is a superb talker; he brings into prim suburban lives 'the sight of a great suspended, swaying crystal, huge, lucid, lustrous, a block of light, flashing back every impression of life and every possibility of thought'. His protectors are willing dupes—they insist, indeed, on being deceived. The relationship is sketched in James's most assured style:

I remember that at dinner that evening he wore slippers, new and predominatingly purple, of some queer carpet-stuff; but the Mulvilles were still in the stage of supposing that he might be snatched from them by higher bidders. At a later time they grew, poor dears, to fear no snatch-ing; but theirs was a fidelity which needed no help from competition to make them proud. Wonderful indeed as, when all was said, you inevitably pronounced Frank Saltram, it was not to be overlooked that the Kent Mulvilles were in their way still more extraordinary: as striking an instance as could easily be encountered of the familiar truth that remark-able men find remarkable conveniences.

Saltram, an inferior Coleridge, plays truant from the platform when his sponsors arrange neat lectures for him. 'If he had loved us for our dinners we could have paid with our dinners, and it would have been a great economy of finer matter.' The finer matter, one comes to see, was a stupid attempt to canalize the sluggish flow of Saltram's creative genius. 'Middle-aged, fat, featureless save for his great eyes', he neither asks for nor rejects their patronage: 'He took whatever came, but he never plotted for it, and no man who was so much of an absorbent can ever have been so little of a parasite.' Into this backwater swims a young heiress who, 'flattening her nose against the clear, hard pane of an eternal question—that of the relative importance of virtue', makes over to Saltram the funds which would otherwise have bought her the hand of a rising politician. As for Saltram, 'there was majesty in his mere unconsciousness of our little conferences and puzzlements over his maintenance and his reward', and only the egregious folly of his benefactors is responsible for the obvious result that 'the very day he found himself able to publish he wholly ceased to produce'. The success of this second parable is due largely to the careful provision of an independent life for the minor figures. We see the defrauded Miss Amory at her aunt's house, far away from Saltram's influence, and yet his presence is felt the more keenly because their life is valid without him, and even so he manages to obtrude. Just as the narrator 'lighted my little taper at his smoky lamp, and lo, it continued to twinkle', so the Mulvilles and the rest are happy to pay for the presence of real life in the form of a fat fraud. 'Nature herself had brought him out in voluminous form, and the money was simply a deposit on borrowing the work.' Their official disapproval melts away whenever Saltram absents himself: 'Oh you see', cries his last victim, 'one forgets so wonderfully how one dislikes him!'

The diptych represented by these tales is the clearest and at the same time subtlest version, among his many attempts to 'do something about art', of Henry James's growing dissatisfaction with the intellectual temper of his British hosts. True, the exaggerated shelving of Paraday by tuft-hunters is made so extreme as to smack of a certain hysterical indulgence of self-pity—but here we must judge with caution, for it is never wise to identify James too closely with the tone of his narrator. But of his genuine scorn for their prurient half-hearted interest in 'the larger latitude' as represented in the novels of Guy Walsingham, there is no reasonable doubt. And James and his narrator surely speak at one in such a passage as this:

The Princess is a massive lady with the organization of an athlete and the confusion of tongues of a *valet de place*. She contrives to commit herself very little in a great many languages, and is entertained and conversed with in detachments and relays, like an institution which goes on from generation to generation or a big building contracted for under a forfeit.... She has been told everything in the world and has never perceived anything, and the echoes of her education respond awfully to the rash footfall—I mean the casual remark—in the cold Valhalla of her memory.

Throughout both tales the old wit is reinforced by solidity; orthodox intellectual superiority is shown to be as lively as any bear-baiting irreverence. There is a sly dignity combined with felicity of phrase, as if Oscar Wilde had stepped into Dr. Johnson's shoes or Samuel Richardson passed judgement in flippant Restoration terms. The severity of social and artistic standards is nowhere more apparent than on the occasions when, in such tales, they come into conflict. In *The Coxon Fund* the narrator's intellectual values are no whit more elevated than the social tone of his friend Gravener, who on the vexed subject of Frank Saltram could retort, from his own unyielding assumptions, 'that there was no cad like your cultivated cad and that I might depend upon discovering ... that my shining light proceeded, a generation back, from a Methodist cheesemonger'. So far have both sets of standards come tumbling down that it is odd to be reminded, by a passing reference to the District Railway, that we are reading of an age only a year or two away from the twentieth century, in which cads circulate as freely as *kitsch*. And it is from the stiff-necked unintellectual Gravener, and not the busy narrator, that the really penetrating judgement is delivered upon the self-styled artistic initiates, the Mulvilles: 'They were born to be duped, they like it, they cry for it, *they don't know anything from anything....*'

The Next Time (1895), another appropriate contribution to 'The Yellow Book', presents a literary rendering of the theme 'you can't make a sow's ear out of a silk purse'. Ralph Limbert is a faultless writer who tries desperately to compose a best-seller, but each time produces instead 'an unscrupulous, an unsparing, a shameless, merciless masterpiece'. The poor man can only, like the narrator whose own enthusiastic reviews have helped to kill his works stone dead, construct 'exquisite failures'. If the pitiable plight of this delicate artist reminds one of the member of a B.B.C. Brains Trust who is said to have remarked that his colleagues on the panel made him feel 'like china in a bull-shop', the narrator's sturdy attack on devotees who will not *buy* the books they admire could come straight from the mouth of one of Mr. William Gerhardi's characters (Mr. Baldridge, say, of *My Wife's the Least of It*):

> Several persons admired his books—nothing was less contestable; but they appeared to have a mortal objection to acquiring them by subscription or by purchase: they begged or borrowed or stole, they delegated one of the party perhaps to commit the volumes to memory and repeat them, like the bards of old, to listening multitudes.

This vigorous ironic fun is a good deal less mawkish than his attempt to define the *dilettanti*, which uncomfortably suggests an affinity with O'Shaughnessy's 'We are the music-makers,/And we are the dreamers of dreams . . .':

> We are a numerous band, partakers of the same repose, who sit together in the shade of the tree, by the splash of the fountain, with the glare of the desert around us and no great vice that I know of but the habit perhaps of estimating people a little too much by what they think of a certain style.

The narrator, like his idol, finds it impossible to tone himself down to the level of the magazines; and when it is reported to him that 'it isn't your price—he says you're dear at any price; you do so much to sink the ship', one is conscious of a middle-aged Henry James not only indulging a little passing self-pity in the rôle of the novelist Limbert but also in the rôle of the narrator, taking another belated swipe at Whitelaw Reid of the New York *Tribune*, some twenty years after he had written to that editor, of his contributions from Paris, that 'they are the poorest I can do, especially for the money'.

But once again, although the idea of this tale is pleasantly slight, its treatment—minor characters, long stage-like dialogue and all—is far too elaborate, too Limbert-like, indeed, for the frail structure. As so often, the penalty for this sort of thing had already been recognized and read out by James himself, when he rightly promulgated the law, when praising Turgenev for writing stories which are 'not the result of a preconceived action, but a consequence of the

232

qualities of the actors', that this method is to be preferred to the admittedly beguiling alternative of constructing a tale as if it were a dance, 'a series of steps the more complicated and lively the better, of course, determined from without and forming a figure'.* In *The Next Time* and almost all the other contrived attempts to 'do something about art' in the form of stories, James is in fact infringing his own sensible rule, even while 'treating' literary matters of equal delicacy of appreciation. There is, one feels, room for a *very* late James story in which he would have shown himself, *à la façon de* Limbert, writing about Limbert and making his point only at the expense of blunting his own ill-chosen tool. From the full rigour of such harsh judgements, however, this and many other of the 'arty' tales are saved precisely by their incidental wit, a by-product of that *other* side of James's equipment which at the time of writing he seems to have undervalued. One forgives much of the awkwardness of *The Next Time*, for example, for the delightful exchange:

'The book has extraordinary beauty.'
'Poor duck—after trying so hard!'

A similar fate attends the even more inbred, almost auto-erotic parable *The Figure in the Carpet* (1896), which treats of the 'secret' informing the published works of Hugh Vereker, which his friends the narrator and another critic seek in vain to unravel. The rival critic at last 'gets' it—but dies before he can publish his fine critical scoop. Whereupon the narrator tries in vain to 'pump' his friend's widow, and even, in turn, *her* widower. For all his pains, he never discovers the secret, the figure in the carpet, whatever it is.

Now, although all this is in its way beautifully done, the unwisdom of doing it at all is equally great. Not only does the notion of major art concealing some vital 'secret' contradict all that a reader is likely to have experienced in his own direct dealings with creative art of the highest order; the endless hesitating nosings of the two defeated sleuths of this story can hardly avoid, in an atmosphere dangerously near that of pure farce, presenting them as unusually dim-witted. One can only revert to the freshness of James's *own* critical judgement at

* The essay is reprinted in *The Art of Fiction*, ed. Morris Roberts, New York, 1948.

the time of his Turgenev essay (1884) and suggest that the frustrations of literary critics are likely to form a 'figure' of very little interest to lovers of stories constructed 'from without', and of still less interest to lovers of stories constructed on the superior plan of 'a consequence of the qualities of the actors'.

Yet another literary critic narrator worships at the shrine of yet another novelist (whose hinted qualities are again those of James himself) who gives his name to the story *John Delavoy* (1898). This critic is luckier than the bemused pair in *The Figure in the Carpet*. His essay, written soon after Delavoy's death, is admired by the novelist's daughter as the one really understanding tribute to her late father's work. Alas, the editor of the influential review to which the essay is submitted, prefers something 'chatty' and accepts instead her own portrait of her father. She, faithful to the quality of the true critical essay, stands by it and marries the essayist. If *The Figure in the Carpet* is the day-dream of an 'unrecognized' novelist, *John Delavoy* should comfort the hallucinations of sensitive unappreciated literary critics. From such a tale it is indeed a relief to be able to pluck one small proof that even in his most tedious self-communings, James never wrote anything quite unredeemed by some occasional flash of fresh amused observation:

He was in love, moreover, or thought he was; that flushed with a general glow the large surface he presented. This surface, from my quiet corner, struck me as a huge tract, a sort of particoloured map, a great spotted social chart. He abounded in the names of things, and his mind was like a great staircase at a party—you heard them bawled at the top.

One would prefer to hurry, too, past a couple of tales first published in 1900, which clothe in fictional form two unremarkable parables of visual art. In *The Tone of Time*, painter Mary Tredick produces 'from memory' a portrait of a distinguished man for her rich client, Mrs. Bridgenorth, who is anxious to give herself the respectability that will accrue from 'the portrait of her late husband'. Mary paints a striking likeness, composed in hatred, of a man who had deceived her. Lo, it is also the man who had deceived Mrs. Bridgenorth. Mary takes the picture back again and will not part with it for any sum; for, as she informs the narrator in words which wickedly parody the U - echo form of dialogue fashionable in the early years of this century (noted more fully in Chapter XI on *The Ambassadors*) and which may be offered as a free sample to Mr. Maxwell Geismar and other collectors of the 'gamey' James style at its most exasperating:

> 'He's taken from me, and for all those years he's kept. Then she herself, by a prodigy—'
> She lost herself again in the wonder of it.
> 'Unwittingly gives him back?'
> She gaily, for an instant over the marvel, closed her eyes. 'Gives him back.'

The Tree of Knowledge, curtly dismissed by Mrs. Leavis as 'a bore' (*Scrutiny*, XIV, 223), reveals that the poverty of the bogus works of a rich *dilettante* sculptor, who thinks himself to be a great artist, is secretly recognized not only by his wife and his friend, but also by his son when he in turn goes to Paris to be trained as an artist. All three, independently, keep up the fiction of the artist's renown. One feels that neither desert nor renown, in this situation, would have deceived anyone less dense than the Master. His own vanity and his wife's loyalty were adjudged to be of a quality 'of which success, depriving these things of innocence, would have diminished the merit and the grace'. The usual narrator is given an external appearance which might have served to clothe a minoi character in a better tale: 'he was massive but mild . . . large and loose and ruddy and curly, with deep tones, deep eyes, deep pockets, to say nothing of the habit of long pipes, soft hats and brownish greyish weather-faded clothes apparently always the same.' It is an identity label one instinctively prefers to the initial presentation of him as a person perilously like an unfriendly description of Henry James himself at this period of his life: 'a man who had reached fifty, who had escaped marriage, who had lived within his means, who had been in love with Mrs. Mallow for years without breathing it, and who, last not least, had judged himself once for all.'

More brooding about the caprices of posthumous fame produced the fable *The Abasement of the Northmores* (1900). After the death of the well-known public figure Lord Northmore, the newspapers and the world find 'almost nothing but the fine monotony of his success to mention'. Of Northmore's old but equally *un*successful friend Warren

Hope, the bitter Mrs. Hope remarks: 'He never recognized you, but he never let you go. You kept him up, and he kept you down.' All Hope has left is 'his wasted genius, his ruined health and his paltry pension'. But he insists on braving the elements to attend Northmore's funeral, and there catches the chill that soon sends him following his dishonest old colleague to the grave. Northmore's widow collects the illustrious statesman's letters for a memorial edition, and the widow Hope resentfully sends her a packet of correspondence her own husband had kept. When she in turn tries to collect Hope's papers, she finds nothing publishable, for all their being 'rich confused relics' like 'loose blocks of marble'. Perhaps *his* letters could be collected? Those she herself has kept, of course, show 'his easy power'. But she discovers, when circulating Hope's friends, that they, not recognizing his powers, had destroyed all his letters. While the insipid Northmore is immortalized, Hope is dead beyond recall. 'All sense, all measure of anything, could only leave one—leave one indifferent and dumb.' The wretched widow contemplates publishing, in revenge, the love-letters Northmore had sent to *her*, long ago, before she married Warren. But a more insidious fate has already overtaken the Northmore family: the public man's published letters, deferentially received in the press, have revealed themselves as 'an abyss of inanity' and the Northmores are sufficiently abased already. The last drop is wrung from this self-pitying parable when widow Hope has one copy printed of Hope's own marvellous letters to herself, and then awaits merciful and justifying death to right all wrongs and restore the literary balance. (It would be interesting to know if it was about this time that Henry James resolved to destroy, before death, his own personal papers. As *The Aspern Papers* indicate, he had mixed feelings about the availability of an author's private relics. In the end, a passion for privacy tipped the scales towards destruction, in his own case. Fortunately, the wealth of his own surviving letters show him to have been as considerate and charming a friend as he assumed Warren Hope to be.)

Personal disillusionments and professional disappointments were combining, at this time, to concentrate James's attention on the moral beauties of failure and the crudity of wordly success. His motivation may be as suspect now as it was when, incapacitated during the Civil War, he made a virtue of his misfortune and pretended that his temperamental rôle as observer had been a matter of choice rather than a psychological retreat. But however self-exculpating his attitude, his actual criticism of society—especially of society as tasteless undiscriminating patron of the arts—is now sharp and intelligent. In *Broken Wings* (1900) we are confronted with the cruel tricks played on the artist who, at first accepted for his 'success' when real success (financial as well as artistic) is in fact eluding him, is quietly dropped when his failure becomes publicly apparent. In this little geometrical parable a female novelist and a male painter, kept apart each by a mistaken notion of the other's 'success', meet again and come together as confessed failures. As in so many of these geometrical 'situations', the people are too real for the diagram. The creative pair grow bitter about their treatment by the careless rich:

'We can't afford to be opulent. But it isn't only the money they take.'
'It's the imagination,' said Mrs. Harvey. 'As they have none themselves—'
'It's an article we have to supply?'

But it is only in social defeat that they embrace together, *faute de mieux*, a self-abnegating devotion to their own real life—their art.

The Beldonald Holbein (1901) and *The Velvet Glove* (1909) could equally well be bracketed with James's half-disgusted half-fascinated vignettes of the cruel pretences of social life in a self-satisfied self-absorbed group (to be discussed in the next two chapters); except that their samples of insincerity are in each case seen through the eyes of artists (a painter and a novelist). There is the usual Jamesian implication that when art and life collide, the adamantine integrity of the one must always expose and shatter the pathetic friable texture of the other.

The heartless theme of *The Beldonald Holbein* is that Lady Beldonald makes a habit of engaging, in that peculiarly brutal Victorian-Edwardian subservient rôle as 'companion', a series of excessively plain women whose ugliness acts as foil to her own beauty. The painter narrator notices that her current victim, Mrs. Brash, has—in spite of her lack of easy beauty—the striking attraction of a Holbein portrait. He communicates this discovery to the restricted social circle in which he and the ladies revolve, and Mrs. Brash becomes 'famous'. Lady Beldonald is consumed with jealousy; Mrs. Brash withdraws to America and dies—we are to suppose—of grief; whereupon the *grande dame*, whom vanity has preserved as 'absolutely proper and prim', profits by her mistake and enslaves a new and 'pretty' successor who will not, like the discarded Holbein lady, break 'the law of her ugliness and [turn] beautiful on the hands of her employer'.

In *The Velvet Glove* it is the inflexible standard of literature which touches and exposes the pretensions of another gracious lady. Unhappily, the particular piece of literature in which the moral is conveyed is contrived and artificial enough to leave the lady's own disingenuousness far behind. The James-like novelist of this new day-dream is John Berridge, who meets at a Parisian salon a Princess who herself writes books under a pseudonym. Enslaved, in her presence, by Proustian feelings of the romance of aristocracy, Berridge takes the lady home, only to learn that all *she* requires from him is an adulatory preface to her own forthcoming 'romance'. He refuses: she *is* romance, and should not demean herself by dabbling in literary make-belief. It is difficult enough to credit the standards of Berridge when we are informed, apropos the elegant young gentleman who first introduces him to the literate Princess, that 'perhaps the very brightest and most diamond-like twinkle he had yet seen the star of his renown emit was just the light brought into this young Lord's eyes by this so easy consent to oblige'. He reveals himself, later, as a megalomaniac if fumbling snob, like a low-grade Baron de Charlus whistling to keep his courage up, and vulgarly impressed (for so delicate a writer) by social 'Olympians':

He should have consented to know but the grand personal adventure on the grand personal basis: nothing short of this, no poor cognizance of confusable, pettifogging things, the sphere of earth-grubbing questions and twopenny issues would begin to be, on any side, Olympian enough. . . . Ah, Olympians were unconventional indeed—that was a part of their high bravery and privilege; but what it also appeared to attest in this wondrous manner was that they could communicate to their chosen in three minutes, by the mere light of their eyes, the same shining cynicism.

It is a direct consequence of this phoney-ness of Berridge as a social being that his protective gesture towards the inviolability of art falls so dismally flat. We are likely to remember him, rather, as the ludicrous hero of perhaps the most inanely awkward act of hand-kissing in the whole of polite literature:

The motor had slackened and in a moment would stop; and meanwhile even after lowering his hand again she hadn't let it go. This enabled it, while he after a further moment roused himself to a more confessed consciousness, to form with his friend's a more active relation, to possess himself of hers, in turn, and with an intention the straighter that her glove had by this time somehow come off. Bending over it without hindrance, he returned as firmly and fully as the application of all his recovered wholeness of feeling, under his moustache, might express, the consecration the bareness of his own knuckles had received; only after which it was that, still thus drawing out his grasp of her, and having let down their front glass by his free hand, he signified to the footman his view of their stopping short.

Poor, immortal, Berridge! No conscious parody of the late James style would dare go as far as this. The reason for full quotation here is simply to concede the point that in all these *later* parables of 'art', the ageing James could strike obese and maudlin postures thoroughly unworthy of the views debated in *The Tragic Muse* or, say, *The Lesson of the Master*; and postures conveyed, moreover, in a flatulent unconvincing prose thoroughly inferior to the fresh vitality of those works.

VIII

Marriage and Society (i)

*The Spoils of Poynton, What
Maisie Knew, The Awkward Age,
The Sacred Fount, The Outcry*

'In *his* time ... the best manners had
been the best kindness ...'
                              Crapy Cornelia

HERE and there, dotted about the expensive suburbs of England's industrial cities or affronting some well chosen countryside, an awed traveller may still happen upon large sturdily constructed houses which testify, inside and out, to a riotous effort to capture in stone and/or brick the expansive imaginations of rich men whose energy had goaded them into wanting 'a little of everything' in their domestic setting.

There was nothing particularly new, of course, about Victorian residential extravagances. The Sir Epicure Mammons of Ben Jonson's day who could cry out

> I will have all my beds blown up, not stuft:
> Down is too hard . . .
> My mists
> I'll have of perfume, vapour'd 'bout the room,
> To lose ourselves in; and my baths, like pits
> To fall into . . .

were responsible for several surviving monstrosities to which time has lent quaintness but hardly decorum. Andrew Marvell pictured the Lord General Fairfax domestically suited at Appleton House:

> Yet thus the laden House does sweat
> And scarce indures the *Master* great:
> But where he comes the swelling Hall
> Stirs, and the *Square* grows *Sphericall* . . .

Pope's Timon, in the full English Augustan Age itself, indulged a Brobdingnagian hunger:

> To compass this, his building is a Town,
> His pond an Ocean, his parterre a Down:
> Who but must laugh, the Master when he sees,
> A puny insect, shiv'ring at a breeze!
> Lo! what huge heaps of littleness around!
> The whole, a labour'd Quarry above ground.

And even William Collins, pastel pastoralist *par excellence*, could imagine a gorgeous feast of mixed goodies for a most unclassical architectural appetite.

> Ev'n now before his favour'd Eyes,
> In Gothick Pride it seems to rise!
> But Graecia's graceful Orders join,
> Majestick thro' the mix'd Design.

Yet it was pre-eminently the period from the 1870's up to the taste for *art nouveau* (only recently exhumed as an amusing aberration) that produced a bumper crop of examples, many of which may still be examined before they are demolished, made over into public institutions, or sliced up into flats. I myself have been privileged to witness, in an Edwardian structure vaguely suggestive of a Moorish mahogany railway-station, a dining-room mainly puce in colour, over the vast central table of which was suspended, on pulleys which enabled it to be lowered almost into the soup-plates, an outsize gilt wire pagoda with celluloid birds. There was, and is, something disarming about such bloated prodigalities, such disastrous breakdowns in the race to overtake material with aesthetic satisfactions.

Disarming, that is, in an easy-going mood. But by no means disarming—arming, even!—to a 'passionate pilgrim' with moral-aesthetic tastes based firmly on the expectation that great riches carried an obligation for greatness of conception, that opportunity should breed consideration, that a faulty transmission of inherited beauty was a near-criminal social lapse, at best fraudulent and at worst morally loathsome. We have seen how, when he came to assert as a critical principle (in his study of Nathaniel Hawthorne, 1879) the 'passionate pilgrim' viewpoint he had adopted in so many early novels and tales, James announced that 'the flower of art blooms only where the soil is deep, that it takes a great deal of history to produce a little literature, that it needs a complex social machinery to set a writer in motion'. Alas, it was not long before a disillusioned James was preparing, in *The Spoils of Poynton* (1897), a devastating exposure of the cultural claims of an England possessing 'a great deal of history' and still creaking with the workings of 'a complex social machinery'. After his pincer-movement against the moral and aesthetic flanks of such a society had laid bare the basis of much stately living, it was no longer the gracious Poynton that seemed to figure as the representative blossoming of our deep-soiled culture, but equally the monstrous ineptitudes of Waterbath:

The house was bad in all conscience, but it might have passed if they had only let it alone. This saving mercy was beyond them; they had smothered it with trumpery ornament and scrap-book art, with strange excrescences and bunchy draperies, with gimcracks that might have been keepsakes for maidservants and nondescript conveniences that might have been prizes for the blind. . . . The house was perversely full of souvenirs of places even more ugly than itself and of things it would have been a pious duty to forget. The worst horror was the acres of varnish, something advertised and smelly, with which everything was smeared: it was Fleda Vetch's conviction that the application of it, by their own hands and hilariously shoving each other, was the amusement of the Brigstocks on rainy days.

In the novels grouped in the present chapter, together with the long series of tales considered in the succeeding chapter. James offered in effect a sustained commentary on the society of the nation in which he had chosen to live and of which he became a naturalized subject shortly before his death. By the side of *The Princess Casamassima* and *The Bostonians*, the range of society here exmained may be thought meagre. But it is as if James, in dissecting the rotting head of the smelly fish of late Victorian and Edwardian England, takes for granted the proverbial assumption that the rest of the body is hardly likely to be notable for its freshness. There is, of course, a danger that in concentrating on the social content of these works as it presents itself in alternating moods—sometimes admiration, sometimes witty satire, sometimes plain flat disgust—one will be less than just to James's developing regard for the individual human conscience, the unique human sensibility. When Conrad* called James 'the historian of fine consciences' he was hardly praising him for professional zeal in social history. When Ralph Barton Perry* remarked that 'Henry let William do his philosophizing for him', we may willingly concede the addition that he let William and others do his sociologizing, too. The complementary point is that William, for his part,

*Both quoted in Edward Stone's *The Battle and the Books*, 1964.

let Henry write his novels for *him*—and however much the cumulative effect of the novels and tales under discussion may be to display Henry James as a progressively disenchanted critic of the moral and aesthetic values upon which his own chosen and richly enjoyed social *milieu* was based, yet it was always as a novelist, and never as a cultural anthropologist or political statistician, that he made his damaging assessments and treasured, like a more compendious caravan in the train of Lot, what could be salvaged from the doomed cities.

Thus, when Ford Madox Ford, discussing *The Spoils of Poynton* in 1913, jeered at 'the passion of an English family, with their solicitors and the paraphernalia of the law at their back, to stick a small Crystal Palace on to the back of a Jacobean house like Poynton', he also recalled that in the whole sordid story of 'whether a mother or a daughter-in-law is to grab the beautiful contents of one of the most beautiful houses in England', there is no direct allusion to the processes of law. For Ford, *Poynton* was James's 'greatest book', and yet in bracketing it with *What Maisie Knew* he asserts that 'he couldn't by any possibility be the great writer that he is if he had any public aims'.

For the widowed Mrs. Gereth, condemned to the dower-house while her son and his coarse tasteless *fiancée* Mona Brigstock (heiress of the unspeakable Waterbath) inhabit the matchless beauties of Poynton, the reader feels first sympathy and then distaste: distaste for a discrimination so self-consciously shaped by a moral as well as an aesthetic narrowness of vision. Mrs. Gereth, who 'would rather have perished than have looked *endimanchée*' like a grocer's wife, also 'had the finest views' on the subject of doors—but if 'the thing in the world she most despised was the meanness of the undivided opening', we are reminded in the next sentence that 'from end to end of Poynton there swung high double leaves', and it is clear that James is pointing out that the *possession* as well as the appreciation of such matters owes more to accidents of birth or money than to acquired taste. But instead of a socialist tract demanding that Poyntons be allocated to those who have gained a First Class in an aesthetic examination, we draw from James the novelist a wonderful sense that the basic coarseness of Mrs. Gereth's refinement must debase her as a person no less than as an interior decorator. 'Mrs. Gereth had really no perception of anybody's nature—she had only one question about persons: were they clever or stupid? To be clever meant to know the "marks".' She is, for all her poise and judgement, an English version of Madame Merle of *The Portrait of a Lady*. And since it is largely through Mrs. Gereth's eyes that the other characters are viewed, we come to be uncertain in our judgement of her *protegée* Fleda Vetch, who sincerely loves Mrs. Gereth's son Owen but who is made ambiguous by being the girl with whom his mother hopes to save him from the hearty hockey-mistressy Mona Brigstock of his own choice; and the girl who, as Owen's wife, would surely be more amenable than the grasping Mona to Mrs. Gereth's intention to hold fast to the most precious *objets d'art* of Poynton, which she could not bear to lose when her son succeeded to the house, and had had transferred to her dower-house. For Fleda, too, was prized because she knew the 'marks' by 'direct inspiration'; she, too, was the sort of girl who could be kept awake by an unfortunate wall-paper.

Fleda, however, has an independent moral sense also by 'direct inspiration'. Sensing not only that Owen is attracted to her but also that if she encouraged his mother to keep her 'spoils', Mona would probably break off her engagement to him, she nevertheless refuses to play any of the cards placed in her hands. A direct avowal of Owen's love is not sufficient—the spoils must also be returned to Poynton *before* the Brigstocks are sacrificed. Mona, of course, gets her final lawful possession of both Owen and the restocked Poynton. The selfless (if rather consciously so) Fleda is begged by the honey-mooning Owen to select a keepsake from the loot she has helped to save for him. She reaches Poynton too late—it is a smouldering ruin. It is certainly no surprise to a James reader that James himself offers no clue to the cause of the fire which destroys everything that mother and son have wrangled about; but I find it strange that none of the critics of the novel mentioned in Professor Cargill's handbook, nor any other to the best of my knowledge, has seriously questioned the cause of the 'accident'. Am I betraying a further sign of coarseness among English materialists when I confess that I myself stir uneasily at the thought that Mrs. Gereth, quite literally, could not bear to think of a Brigstock thumbing 'her' treasures?

This novel is without doubt a triumph of James's mature style. Professor Holland claims that 'its drama is created within the strained gestures, and the taut structures, of a manneristic style which is inherently dramatic and compatible with the deepest impulsions and compressions of expressionistic art'. There is a high-spirited competence, a richly comic confidence in the author's own superiority of judgement (of which the description of Waterbath, quoted above, is but one outstanding example) which is shown in his 'placing' of people, rather than of objects of art. Dr. Holland may go on to acknowledge that 'at stake in the novel's acts of expression are the creation and appreciation of art—indeed the very definition of art which is characteristic of a manneristic style'; but it is surely not without significance that one remembers no single passage describing, with anything recognizable as vivid architectural or plastic sensibility, Poynton itself! No; it is the 'creation and appreciation' of *people*, not of art, that makes *Poynton* so beautifully shaped a product of *its* art, the art of fiction. That is why *Poynton* is incomparably fresher, for all its vindictive and avaricious theme, than the stories in which James deliberately sought to 'do something about art'. James's Preface, in oft-quoted words, speaks of 'life being all inclusion and confusion, and art being all discrimination and selection'. The vitality of James's own art is betrayed, rather, in the exuberance of such comic detail as the description of Mrs. Gereth and Fleda drawing 'refreshment from the great tranquil sky, whence no cheap blue plates depended', or the observation that 'Miss Brigstock had been laughing and even romping, but the circumstance hadn't contributed the ghost of an expression to her countenance'. It is a novel to be placed with confidence in the hands of almost any reader who can appreciate decorum and proportion in the use of the English language—and that, for all their other qualities, can hardly be said of all the other 'social' novels and tales now to be considered.

It may be convenient to treat briefly here the long *nouvelle Covering End* (1898) as a pendant to *Poynton*, if only to produce another of James's mature 'passionate pilgrim' studies of the late Victorian economics of stately homes; a story, this time, with a happy ending. At Covering End converge, as in a one-act play (which was in fact its first form), Captain Yule the impoverished and politically-minded owner, Mr. Prodmore a vulgar business man who holds the mortgages, Cora his daughter, and Mrs. Gracedew an indomitable American tourist. Prodmore has a plan for Yule to marry his daughter and keep, with her, the property. Cora doesn't want him; Mrs. Gracedew, at first sight, *does*. She glories in the old house and buys it at an inflated price from Prodmore, 'buying' Yule with it—who, during their one meeting, has in turn fallen in love with her appreciation for his neglected embarrassed home. The theme thus baldly outlined is never so bald in the telling. But for the brooding Poynton-like presence of the house Covering End, the tale might be classified among those dealing with the marriage market; but it is one of the few of this group with a kindly fairy-Godmother ending. For although the continuities of Covering End are more responsibly embodied in the butler Chivers than in his master, it is the unexpected American visitor (like Clement Searle of *A Passionate Pilgrim*, Frank Granger of *Flickerbridge*, or even Ralph Pendrel of *The Sense of the Past*) who gives articulation to the magic exuded by a house 'for which the ages have been tender and the generations wise: letting it change so slowly that there's always more left than taken—living their lives in it, but letting it shape their lives!' Yule himself, a politician with 'pure, passionate, pledged Radical' views, eager to fight 'misery and ignorance and vice—injustice and privilege and wrong', feels guiltily that there is 'something else in the world than the beauty of old show-houses and the glory of old show-families. There are thousands of people in England who can show no houses at all . . .' (It is a reaction quite foreign to the Gereths, still more to the Brigstocks.) It is left to the American passionate pilgrim to persuade Yule that he has it all 'in trust', and that 'heaven only knows what will become of it' if he cedes it to the Prodmores of this world: 'Parties and programmes come and go, but a duty like this abides.' It is a restatement, in an innocent C-major key, of the discordant faith of a Mrs. Gereth.

The reader of *What Maisie Knew* (1897) is advised to render himself plot-perfect by reference to Professor Gale's checklist of James's plots and characters (see Bibliographical Note). Before the turn of the present century, so elaborate a quadrille of *divorcés* as make up the human setting of the child Maisie was evidently not so well rehearsed as in contemporary society. Maisie's parents, Beale and Ida Farange, are divorced, and each remarries: 'they were now prepared . . . to enjoy the distinction that waits upon vulgarity sufficiently attested.

Their rupture had resounded, and after being perfectly insignificant together they would be decidedly striking apart.' Maisie's newly acquired substitute parents, both of whom seem to be better fitted to bring up a child than her original set, begin to feel a mutual attraction and Maisie is offered a chance—after a second set of divorces—to compound with a fresh domestic equipment made up of her father's second divorced wife and her mother's second divorced husband. By this time, the child seems to have grasped that her catalytic agency has done its work, and like all good catalysts she remains unattached and unaffected. She has earned a pause, in the temporary and less stimulating company of Mrs. Wix. So much for the *donnée*. The actual Jamesian theme is well summarized by Dr. Leavis (*Scrutiny*, V, 399–400) as 'the incorruptible innocence of Maisie; innocence that not merely preserves itself in what might have seemed to be irresistibly corrupting circumstances, but can even generate decency out of the egotistic squalors of adult personal relations'.

In spite of the geometrical boxing-in of these squalid arrangements (a system which James, in his Preface, longs to complicate still further, like a Restoration dramatist supplying extra characters to turn Shakespeare's parallels into quadrilaterals: 'The second step-parent would have but to be correspondingly incommoded by obligations to the offspring of a hated predecessor for the misfortune of the little victim to become altogether exemplary'), a first reading of *What Maisie Knew* is likely to convey the impression of a study uncertain of its main emphasis, the most striking impact of which is not the plot but the Jamesian envelope. This is singularly unfortunate when what that envelope contains is supposed to be the fresh impressions of a young girl bewildered among dubious moral surroundings. As a novel's theme it is admirable: how such a child would slowly make out the motives and behaviour of addicted adulterers, in much the same way as another child would slowly make out the springs and effects of ordinary married domestic life. What, after all, is Maisie's mental age? This is never very clear. She certainly has no child*ish* traits, so that for long spells one thinks of her as yet another Jamesian 'young person'. So far from eliciting agreement with James's Prefatory self-congratulations, a first reading may well produce the judgement that *What Maisie Knew* is yet another example of this novelist's natural gifts overcoming, by sheer wasteful profusion, the unnecessarily straitened task he had set himself. One is tempted to adopt not James's own account of the book but rather Ford's view that it 'would certainly not have been a passionless masterpiece if Mr. James had thought that it was his business, as a writer, passionately to uphold on the one hand the claims of marriage to be a sacrament, or on the other passionately to deny the claim of the marriage law to have any existence whatever. Indeed ... the figure of Mr. James, the writer, is that of a philosophic anarchist.' Is it a sign of that anarchy that his occasional thumbnail sketches, even here, reveal the less laboured and more successful outcome of his inventive capacity?

A closer reading substantiates James's claim that if it is true that Beale and Ida and their deplorable friends have value only in Maisie's consciousness, the comparative paltriness of the adults helps to stress, rather than call in question, the distinct quality of the child's recording instrument. One sentence from the Preface puts the basic case in terms that every reader can accept: 'Small children have many more perceptions than they have terms to translate them; their vision is at any moment much richer, their apprehension even constantly stronger, than their prompt, their at all producible, vocabulary.' The novelist's own *use* of such a human instrument, undervalued by those who are none the less profoundly if unwittingly affected by her, is put with characteristic care for overt discriminatory judgement: Maisie's function is to change the lives of her pack of parents and pseudo-parents 'by drawing some stray fragrance of an ideal across the scent of selfishness, by sowing on barren strands, through the mere fact of presence, the seed of the moral life'. That fact once grasped, one may return to the incidental felicities with a fresh understanding that they are not merely wittily accurate, but morally accurate, too.

This extra dimension, so to say, may be most simply demonstrated in the case of the one character in the whole shifting cast of defaulters and experimenters who seems to stand for the permanent unimaginative ignorant qualities of the peasant—Mrs. Wix, the governess. To little Maisie, the first charm of Mrs. Wix was that 'somehow, in her ugliness and her poverty, she was peculiarly and soothingly safe, safer than anyone in the world, than papa, than mamma, than the lady with the arched eyebrows ...' This safeness is exemplified in external

descriptions which, if they make use of words far indeed from a
child's 'at all producible vocabulary', do capture a child's habit of
basing important judgements on immediate material particulars:

> She wore glasses which, in humble reference to a divergent obliquity
> of vision, she called her straighteners, and a little ugly snuff-coloured
> dress trimmed with satin bands in the form of scallops and glazed with
> antiquity. The straighteners, she explained to Maisie, were put on for
> the sake of others, whom, as she believed, they helped to recognize the
> bearing, otherwise doubtful, of her regard; the rest of the melancholy
> garb could only have been put on for herself.

Soon, we feel that the personally neglected child's compassion for the
professionally neglected Mrs. Wix is based on perceptions that go
beyond the safeness of straighteners and a snuff-coloured dress.
When Sir Claude, Maisie's stepfather, drops in from time to time on
the child and her governess ('his patient friends' is James's savage
phrase for them in this context), he brings presents including 'ever
so many games in boxes, with printed directions'. They were, said
Sir Claude, intended 'to while away the evening hour'. In one brilliant
stroke, characteristic of scores of similar unstressed accuracies
embedded in the dense prose of James's maturity, we are made to see
that within their shared forlorn sense of being deserted, the child has
an extra quality of quick wit quite beyond her companion's range;
for it is noted, as if with the sardonic affectionate cleverness of the
child herself, that 'the evening hour indeed often passed in futile
attempts on Mrs. Wix's part to master what "it said" on the papers'.
We are reminded of such earlier hapless figures as Hyacinth Robinson's Pinnie or Verena Tarrant's mother. Like that of Mrs. Wix, the
real pathos of their dimness is that they are utterly unaware of it.
Hyacinth and Verena were more clever than Pinnie and Mrs. Tarrant,
and noted these things. But in this novel, the perception is that of a
little girl—and a quite extraordinary warmth of pity for both Maisie
and Mrs. Wix wells up through the thick texture of paragraphs steeped
in ironic and devastating exposures of adult falsenesses. It is through
such training that Maisie herself learns, with regard to her parents
and step-parents, 'to recognize how at last, sometimes, patient little
silences and intelligent little looks could be rewarded by delightful
little glimpses'. One's hatred of the Beale-Ida 'fast set' glows far

fiercer for these lashes of Ford's 'philosophic anarchist' than from any conceivable sociological sermonizing.

Of course, it cannot be denied that the dense prose in which such *aperçus* are embedded can at other times be so viscous, so glutinous as to weary the reader when no particular purpose is served by it. That obliquity of reference which sometimes accurately reflects a character's view of other people, or even the author's own fastidious distance from his distasteful crew, can too often be squandered on sheer old-maidish periphrasis. Nothing is gained, for example, from a sentence like this: 'Our young lady's consciousness was indeed mainly filled for several days by the too slow subsidence of her attendant's sense of wrong.' Nor is it always easy to see what benefit accrues from James's increasingly frequent habit of raising matters from the particular to the general and then lowering the general—but in another and far distant place—to the particular again, in the form of some far-fetched and non-poetic image. A tense little scene between Maisie and Ida is quite difficult enough to follow, without the added mystification of this sort of writing: 'she draped herself in the tatters of her impudence, postured to her utmost before the last little triangle of cracked glass to which so many fractures had reduced the polished plate of filial superstition.' It is a relief to turn from this hothouse atmosphere to such gulps of fresh air as may be enjoyed, for instance, when Maisie is taken to Boulogne, as if on approval, by her second set of 'parents'. There is, curiously enough, a similar freshness in several passages in which Mrs. Wix conducts herself with absurdly melodramatic phrase and gesture—for it is in precisely such second-hand terms, one feels, that the poor lady managed her emotional life. When she and her 'little unfortunate' engage in dreadful surmise about the goings-on of the adults, it is entirely proper that Mrs. Wix, like Mrs. Grose the housekeeper of *The Turn of the Screw*, should throw herself 'for the millionth time on Maisie's neck'. *Here*, at any rate, inflation of language accurately represents the wild exaggerations of ignorance.

For Mr. Tony Tanner is right to point out, in his admirable discussion of this novel, that 'there is of course one thing which determines Maisie's groping ignorance, one missing clue without which the whole tangled web of adult involvements will remain forever incomprehensible—sex. She has picked up all the terms, but she does not understand the matching substance'. Ida betrays, for her string of lovers, not only her own daughter but also herself. The comings and goings that outrage Mrs. Wix's simple moral tenets and bounce Maisie herself to and fro between adults to whom she is obviously beginning to feel superior in all other areas of human understanding —these oscillations represent to the adult reader (as not to the staid governess or the clever child) the vibrations of off-stage passion far beyond anything revealed or guessed at in the novel itself. For all we know (or even care, with our heads clamped by the author so firmly upon Maisie alone as our source of enlightenment), Ida may possess the temperament of an Anna Karenina. In other later novels, Henry James comes to closer terms with the ravages of sexual infatuation. Here, it is his deliberate technical triumph that after all the obliquities and evasions, all the graspings and exculpations, we are content to remain within the willing blinkers of Maisie's direct experience of life. As Mr. Tanner remarks, 'she is the recipient of innumerable impressions: but she lacks any co-ordinating key'. Yet in the final melodramatic scene when her two step-parents, Sir Claude and the second ex-Mrs. Beale, beg her to stay and live with them, while Mrs. Wix, virtue militant, shrilly demands her release from the contagion of shameless impropriety, it is a combination of both innocence and experience that prompt Maisie to leave the stepfather she has come to love. Without knowing *why*, she knows that he is happy with his newly freed lover. Experience of a kind, Mrs. Wix's kind, tells her that this latest marital conjunction somehow offends against her new-found 'moral sense'. Innocence tells her that in any case they and she will be happier apart.

Dr. Cargill's survey assembles impressive evidence suggesting that Maisie was anything but innocent, making much play with the phrase used by Maisie to Sir Claude at Boulogne when she begs him to leave the second Mrs. Beale: 'I'll sit on that old bench where you can see the gold Virgin.' But even if the symbol is deliberate, it is surely more likely that Maisie, in those pre-Lolita days, was offering her virginity in appealing *contrast* to the sexual depravity of the elders, and not inviting Sir Claude to violate it. Curiously enough, I suspect Mrs. Gereth of burning down Poynton far more than I do Maisie of juvenile delinquency, if only because in James's novels the Devil seems to find greed and jealousy more effective temptations than sex.

At various points in this book I have felt obliged, in order to invite attention to what I myself consider to be the major virtues of James as a novelist, to set up in contrast an almost disparaging reassessment of the technical tricks of plot and 'dramatic scenes' which the novelist himself and most of his admirers seem to have overvalued. It is all the more pleasant to be able to claim that any novelist who can toss off with such superlative economy the opening chapter of *The Awkward Age* (1898–99) may still serve as a pattern for disciplined energy and atmospheric exactitude. The character of Mr. Longdon, who will later act as a *deus ex machina* to remove Nanda Brookenham, at her 'awkward age', from the over-sophisticated *milieu* of her parents, is never more deftly revealed than on the occasion of his first appearance:

He ... seemed to carry in the flicker of his quick brown eyes and the positive sun-play of his smile even more than the equivalent of what might, superficially or stupidly, elsewhere be missed in him; which was mass, substance, presence—what is vulgarly called importance. He had indeed no presence, but he had somehow an effect. He might almost have been a priest, if priests ... were ever such dandies.

It may be said that *The Awkward Age* has obvious parallels with *What Maisie Knew* as a study of the unsuitability of a sophisticated and complacently selfish metropolitan *clique* as a nursery for unspotted young ladies. Yet Maisie's elders were for the most part a cheap and raffish crew; whereas Nanda Brookenham's parents and friends, for all their self-centred concern for social trivialities, showed a certain bravery in their efforts to maintain the manners and standards of a *salon*. Judged harshly, the *fin-de-siècle* London society presented by James may properly be dismissed as fraudulent, falling far short of even its own worldly standards and certainly making no attempt to maintain any other-worldly ones. Thus, Dr. Leavis can hold that the novel, 'though it exhibits James's genius for social comedy at its most brilliant, is a tragedy; a tragedy conceived in an imagination that was robustly, delicately and clairvoyantly moral' (*Scrutiny*, V., 414). At the same time, James allows the Brookenhams and their set the virtues of their chosen rôle: the witty 'Mrs. Brook', for example, is as unashamed of her lack of money as her rich contemporaries were unashamed of their lack of wit. The technical triumph of *The Awkward Age* is rightly acclaimed as a mastery of the novel in dialogue form; but if it is true that the talk is often like that of a Wilde play, it is talk interleaved with elaborate and exact social commentary more suggestive of Proust—so that 'Mrs. Brook' emerges with something of the absurd valour of Madame Verdurin herself. It is natural, too, that in James's special case the sustained dialogue should sometimes suggest a hankering after stagey qualities, as in that expository orgy when Mr. Longdon and others sit down and discuss whom they like and whom they don't or the scene at Mertle where Mr. Longdon and Van wander round and round the billiard-table as their financial arrangement is being discussed (the old gentleman's offer to endow Nanda if Van will marry her).

Dr. Leavis's further comment that the novel, 'brilliant success as it is, represents a disproportionate amount of "doing", a disproportionate interest in technique', is true only if a reader allows his admiration for the technique to divert him from the book's main theme, which is the social attractions and the incidental infelicities of a *salon*:

'We're simply a collection of natural affinities', Mitchy explained, 'meeting perhaps principally in Mrs. Brook's drawing-room ... and governed at any rate everywhere by Mrs. Brook, in our mysterious ebbs and flows, very much as the tides are governed by the moon.'

The amiable but weak Vanderbank ('Old Van') grows to prefer the easy irresponsible 'intellectual' discussion of life at Mrs. Brook's tea-table to the effort of living a life of his own with Mrs. Brook's daughter. Naturally enough, the older visitors, like Mr. Langdon or the Duchess, deplore the change of manners represented by so self-consciously emancipated a group—a distaste expressed most forcibly in their horror at the freedom of society and talk allowed to the young daughter Nanda. Even so, the samples of a wickedly emancipated life, such as Carrie Donner, appear as a comparatively common-place lot, so that in a sense the lowering standards of sinning in one half of the tattered turn-of-the-century *beau monde* is a parallel to the lowering standards of intellectual distinction in the other half.

One may argue about the degree to which Nanda's exposure to such a world, or her loss of the attractive Vanderbank, may be 'tragic'. There is hardly room for argument about the brilliance of the social comedy. The lesser figures—the Duchess and her sheltered daughter 'Little Aggie', foil to Nanda; Mr. Mitcham ('Mitchy') and his inseparable Lord Petherton; the chattering flock of *demi-mondaines*; Nanda's complaisant father—all deserve the applause reserved for unexpected star-turns among the supporting cast, while the major figures—Nanda herself; Mrs. Brook; the never-quite-compromised Vanderbank; the flawless *eminence grise* Mr. Longdon —insinuate themselves into our consciousness like the really great actors whose gaining of our credulity inhibits applause until they are safely off-stage. Together, they compose an unforgettable picture of an amusing, tolerant, unprincipled, money-motivated and essentially weary group of worldlings. Erect upon his own unexamined basis of inheritance, Mr. Longdon views it all with the kind of bruised hauteur nowadays mainly exhibited (as if in revenge for Henry James's perceptions) by elderly British critics of America:

'Now this sudden invasion of somebody's—heaven knows whose— house, and our dropping down on it like a swarm of locusts . . . what are people made of that they consent, just for money, to the violation of their homes? . . . the more one seems to see that society—for we're *in* society, aren't we, and that's our horizon?—can never have been anything but increasingly vulgar. The point is that in the twilight of time—and I belong, you see, to the twilight—it had made out much less how vulgar it *could* be.'

It is part of the attraction of Vanderbank that he, so committed to the Brookenham circle, could from his first meeting with Mr. Longdon be in sympathy with the old gentleman's values:

'But beauty, in London . . . staring, glaring, obvious, knock-down beauty, as plain as a poster on a wall, an advertisement of soap or whisky, something that speaks to the crowd and crosses the footlights, fetches such a price in the markets that the absence of it, for a woman with a girl to marry, inspires endless terrors and constitutes for the wretched pair— to speak of mother and daughter alone—a sort of social bankruptcy. London . . . wants cash over the counter and letters ten feet high.'

The surface standards, at any rate, are maintained by the *salonnière* of this increasingly brassy society. She could not hope to emulate the unearned increments of a Longdon, whose house, allowed by James to keep its full nostalgic 'passionate pilgrim' romance, was 'suggestive of panelled rooms' housing 'those impressions of a particular period that it takes two centuries to produce'. But she could fly her *own* flag as high in Buckingham Crescent, for 'the votaries of that temple of analysis', as any Longdon could at Beccles: 'Good talk; you know—no one, dear Van, should know better—what part for me that plays.' Even the Duchess has to admit that 'the men, the young and the clever ones, find it a house. ... with intellectual elbow-room, with freedom of talk. Most English talk is a quadrille in a sentry-box'. As for the other missing qualities, the Duchess is honest enough to admit, when talking to Mr. Longdon of the incomparable 'thing we speak of' that had distinguished Nanda's grandmother (Mr. Longdon's adored Lady Julia of the old days), that they were based, fundamentally, on moneyed privilege: 'But that dear sweet blessed thing is very much the same lost secret as that dear sweet blessed *other* thing that went away with it—the decent leisure that, for the most part, we've also seen the last of.' Moreover, there are several occasions when Van himself shows an ironic detachment from the world of Buckingham Crescent, indicating a possibility that he, too, in turn, may grow into a Mr. Longdon who will doubtless in time romanticize the brave charade he now half joins, half disowns: 'We hate and we love—the latter especially—but to tell each other why is to break that little tacit rule of finding out for ourselves which is the delight of our lives and the source of our triumphs.'

However clever the chatter at Buckingham Crescent, the underlying values are mercenary enough: money and the marriage-market. Arguments about female education (the 'pure' Aggie versus the 'knowing' Nanda) are merely differences of opinion as to the baiting of hooks:

Both the girls struck him as lambs with the great shambles of life in their future; but while one, with its neck in a pink ribbon, had no consciousness but that of being fed from the hand with the small sweet biscuit of unobjectionable knowledge, the other struggled with instincts and forebodings, with the suspicion of its doom and the far-borne scent, in the flowery fields, of blood.

It is a wonderful example of James's *real* technical skill that the reader, having become as bemused as the Brookenham set by all the elaborations of matchings and pairings, cynicisms and advantageous moves, avoidances of unpalatable truths and honest enjoyment of verbal play, does almost come to forget that in Nanda there is an awakening human heart likely to suffer sharp hurt in all the shuffling for position. Although in one sense we are prepared for it throughout the whole novel, yet it takes us by surprise when we are made conscious of the girl's tragic dignity in 'letting down lightly' a Van who cannot summon up sufficient feeling to return her love. One may grow weary of James's endless propensity for scenes of renunciation, but sometimes his handling of the theme is faultlessly, tenderly true. One such occasion is the rejection of Miss Tina in *The Aspern Papers*. Another is Nanda's relinquishment of Van to her mother's shallower world:

... what that she could ever do for him would really be so beautiful as this present chance to smooth his confusion and add as much as possible to that refined satisfaction with himself which would proceed from his having dealt with a difficult hour in a gallant and delicate way? To force upon him an awkwardness was like forcing a disfigurement or a hurt, so that at the end of a minute, during which the expression on her face became a kind of uplifted view of her opportunity, she arrived at the appearance of having changed places with him and of their being together precisely that he—not she—should be let down easily.

Such penetration is all the more startling, when we have had our surface minds—like the minds of almost everyone else in the novel—diverted and satisfied by observations of merely social brilliance, such as the identification, in Lord Petheton, of 'a nature reclaimed, super-civilized, adjusted to the perpetual "chaff" that kept him smiling in a way that would have been a mistake, and indeed an impossibility, if he had really been witty'. The *real* suffering, a mere incident in the world of marriage-markets and *salons*, raises moral problems as profound as those that troubled, some twenty years earlier, the drawing-rooms of *Washington Square*. There, a marriage was prevented (by Catherine's father) for good reasons: but was Catherine the happier for it? Here, a marriage is arranged (by Mr. Longdon) and brings sorrow when it fails because of the resistance of Van to the set-up. Yet, most important, the reader of both novels is left with the conclusion that it is the character of the two girls that will remain the same, whatever happens to them. We are faced, once again, by one of Henry James's categorical imperatives: the folly, uselessness and danger of trying to interfere, even for their good, in other people's lives. Chance, accident, desert, design—all are levelled, James once again seems to be saying, quietly, from the wings of his brilliantly witty social scene, before the inescapable lot of human vulnerability—and the finer the consciousness, as in Nanda's case among the better-protected chatterers, the more vulnerable it will be. Yet James is open to the lesser claims of the other world, too. As indestructible as human needs, are social needs. It is Mitchy who sums up *that* theme: 'The generations will come and go, and the *personnel*, as the newspapers say, of the saloon will shift and change, but the institution itself, as resting on a deep human need, has a long course yet to run and a good work yet to do. *We* shan't last, but your mother will . . .'

The Sacred Fount (1901) is the very last novel one would wish to see placed in the hands of a newcomer to James's fiction. Its attractions (and it has some) are all acquired tastes; they show James as a skilful player, so to say, of a game which looks meaningless, or even revolting, until the difficult rules are explained. Its unpalatable qualities, on the other hand—preciosity, snobbery, the self-hugging lubricity of a Peeping Tom—are only too obvious to the casual reader. One may seek to account for its mood by hunting for clues in Henry James's private life—but a writer must be judged by what he chooses to publish and not by his supposed mood at the time. *The Sacred Fount* is a nettle to be grasped.

From the first, the novel seemed to beg for special indulgences. Writing to Howells just after completing the manuscript, James described it as 'a fine flight (of eighty thousand words) into the high fantastic, which has rather depleted me . . .' To the same friend, later, he confessed that this novel (like so many of his others) had outgrown its original plan: like *Poynton, What Maisie Knew, The Turn of the Screw*, it had been conceived as a *short* story. 'I remember,' James wrote, 'how I would have "chucked" *The Sacred Fount* at the 15th thousand word, if in the first place I could have afforded to "waste" 15,000 . . .' He fears that Howells will have found the finished product 'chaff in the mouth'. It is a sadly vivid description of how the book *has* struck many readers. Another of James's old friends,

John Hay, greeted the triumph of *The Wings of the Dove* with the words: 'He did *The Sacred Fount* just to scare us. This is the old manner again.'* The sales had been poor and the novel was not included by James in the New York Edition (one gasps to imagine the tortuosities of *its* unwritten Preface!).

Perhaps the best starting-point for an understanding of *The Sacred Fount* is an acknowledgement that the idea of emotional cannibalism had always fascinated James. The basic theme of this ultra-sophisticated novel had been stated, in such stories as *Poor Richard* and *De Grey: A Romance*, over thirty years earlier by a young man in his twenties, so that those who wish for autobiographical models must go back far beyond the dedicated professional novelist of Lamb House, Rye. It could be said, in this context, that what had happened during the intervening years was a lifetime's observation of the complicated depredations of greedy and leisured emotional cannibals at loose among the fatstock of high society, so that what had begun as an interest in the imbalance of one loving couple (a character in *The Sacred Fount* puts it simply enough: 'One of them—you know the saying—gives the lips, the other gives the cheek') had ended as a general suspicion of wholesale orgies of blood-sucking. Having arrived at such a point of hysterical curiosity, the narrator of *The Sacred Fount*, at any rate, feels a compulsive mania for geometrical exactitude. Every happy rejuvenated person implies the existence of a complementary ravaged and depleted partner—who *is* it? Every shrivelled life correspondingly implies the recent attack of a sexual vampire—who *is* it? When such investigations as these are conducted in the atmosphere of free-for-all Edwardian house-parties where adulterous licence coexists with gossip, curiosity and a penchant for sublimation in psychological theorizing, it is no wonder that one's first reaction to the novel is plain abhorrence. Curiously enough, several recent exposures of the substantial truth behind so many Edwardian scandals have at least had the effect of lending credence to the fleshly background of a work like *The Sacred Fount*, so that only James's actual handling of the subject is now in question.

The complicated pattern itself is brilliantly sustained and would have held much promise as a theme for the short story James had originally intended. The narrator first noticed that Mrs. Brissenden

*Quoted in George Monteiro's *Henry James and John Hay*, 1965.

('Mrs. Briss'), though some ten years older than her husband, seems astonishingly to have drained him of his vitality so that she appears radiantly youthful while he declines daily into premature middle age. His wife, in the close intimacy, is sucking him dry. Do they recognize it? Next, the eager inquisitor notes an equally astonishing change in another guest, Gilbert Long, a stupid affable oaf who now shows such signs of wit and intellectual confidence that the narrator looks about him for somebody *he* must have drained. In this search, he takes Mrs. Briss into his confidence, which is itself—given her own assumed experience—a rather stagey irony in the design. He lights upon May Server as a candidate for the missing rôle of Long's supply-fount, but becomes so touched and moved by her obvious unhappiness and emptiness, according exactly to his theory, that he takes pity on her and, protecting her from his own busy rumours, denies the imputations of his too-successful analogy and now pretends to Mrs. Briss that May is not Long's victim. From this point onwards, the pace of peeping and speculation grows more frenetic, and one's interest wanes in inverse proportion to the mounting fever of prurient guesswork. Mrs. Briss tries to fight shy of the whole thing, but another half of the book is still to run, with repressed motion and confused double references and a host of more or less interchangeable suspects. The narrator loses our sympathy and that means that we lose sympathy with the novel, since he, rather than any of the active parties, is its central figure.

For the one character in the whole pack of guests at Newmarch who seems to grow and change before our eyes—even if only into an obsessive maniac—is the narrator himself. After collecting a lot of earlier critical impressions, Dr. Cargill bursts out: 'It is the most extraordinary misinterpretation which associates his morbid constructions with the creations of artistic fancy.' Whether or not one holds the narrator to be a creator of artistic fancy, it will be conceded by admirers and detractors alike that he is emotionally more interested in himself than in his fellow guests: they are merely pieces in his diagram, without life save as they figure in the pattern. It is this self-hugging quality of the narrator, more than anything else, that arouses a reader's hostility. It is of interest that even in the most Nosey Parker passages of *Remembrance of Things Past*, the reader's sympathy is not so alienated. The reason is a technical one. Although Proust, as Marcel, is his own narrator, he is never so much 'inside the story', as a character like all the others, as James's narrator is. It is difficult for a reader to accept unremitting theorizing from people *in* the story, although he may be willing to do so from the author, speaking as such. Even the button-holing asides of a Thackeray can be tolerated for a few moments at a time. A reader's assent is normally more readily granted when psychological commentary or speculation comes naturally in the course of straight narrative. James's narrator in *The Sacred Fount*, simply because he roams the corridors and lawns of Newmarch just like his (at first) unsuspecting victims, is externalized as a character, and we resent him as an outrageous Paul Pry of a house-guest rather than crediting him with the acknowledged omniscience granted by all readers to the ultimate narrator, the author himself. (It is significant that in the briefest commentary on this novel, antagonistic nursery types like Peeping Tom, Nosey Parker, Paul Pry, come so readily, unbidden, to mind.)

Once one has identified, and tried to allow for, this special reason for a dislike of the unnamed narrator, it is easier to see the point of those critics who, disagreeing with Dr. Cargill, find with Mr. Edmund Wilson (also quoted by Cargill) that James 'has intended some sort of fable about the imagination and the material with which it works'. The most forthright defender of James's intentions in *The Sacred Fount* is Mr. Tony Tanner, who maintains that 'he was probing and exploring a profound aesthetic issue and that his notion of non-participatory speculation is related to the ancient and persistent idea of the artist as a man who creates forms which might be truer than the truth—the truth, that is, as apprehended by those immersed in the "destructive element" seeking only to satisfy their "provoked senses".'* Mr. Tanner produces an ingenious parallel with the philosophical tenets of Shaftesbury, two hundred years earlier, that 'the beauty of an object is only really felt ... when all thoughts of possessing, enjoying, or controlling it are absent'. If Mr. Tanner is right, then James's tendency to fob us off, in fiction, with the kind of aesthetic speculations more proper to the essay, must be deplored in *The Sacred Fount* no less than in those tales

*In *Essays and Studies* (English Association), 1963; the version of this essay in Mr. Tanner's *The Reign of Wonder* (1965) omits the Shaftesbury references.

which more overtly seek to 'do something about art'. Shaftesbury or no Shaftesbury, the reader of *fiction* is left with an impression that the narrator of *The Sacred Fount* and his temporary accomplices are merely toying with life.

'I had theorized with Mrs. Brissenden', muses the narrator on the subject of May Server, 'on her suppositious inanity, but the explanation of such cynicism in us could only be a sensibility to the truth that attractions so great might float her even a long time after intelligence pure and simple should have collapsed.' Interesting enough, perhaps; but a far cry, from a *novelist's* viewpoint, from such direct presentations of May Server as this:

I saw as I had never seen before what consuming passion can make of the marked mortal on whom, with fixed beak and claws, it has settled as on a prey. She reminded me of a sponge wrung dry and with fine pores agape. Voided and scraped of everything, her shell was merely crushable.

It is true that even such straight descriptions are introduced by the quasi-omnipotent narrator with the observation that 'it was exactly as if she had been there by the operation of my intelligence, or even by that—in a still happier way—of my feeling'. But here, the means and the end are in harmony, for the reader's benefit. Here one experiences, in short, the flash of communication a novel-reader may decently expect. Elsewhere, the narrator's communication is often with himself alone, and we are as oddly perturbed as when, in real life, we pass in the street a man who is busily talking to himself.

The Outcry (1911), the last novel published in James's lifetime, after the great flowering of 'the major phase' in the first four years of the new century, reverts somewhat wearily to the form of another melodrama of money. In structure, its original drafting as a play is very apparent; the narrative reads at times like expanded stage-directions; the dialogue is heavy, charged with ponderous 'meaning' as from across the footlights. There is a main plot about the public outcry over the possibility of a famous painting being sold from an English collection to a heavily caricatured American millionaire vulgarian—but it fails to stir the reader, as it would certainly fail to stir a theatre audience. The sub-plot of the attribution of another valuable painting to one of two possible Italian artists is too tedious to retail. Whether Lord Theign's family Reynolds shall be sold to repay his daughter's huge gambling debts (with an odious husband thrown in) is a question of little urgency in itself; nor is one sufficiently relieved to cheer the final curtain when Lord Theign and Lady Sandgate (who had, of course, been tempted to sell *her* family Lawrence) decide to marry, after declaring that instead of selling their portraits they will both present them to the National Gallery, which with superb Philistine snobbery they refer to as 'the Thingumbob'.

The lifeless parallelism of plotting shows James at his most exhausted (his health was failing); what vigour there is in the book lies in James's disgust at the rapacity of the English aristocracy, out to make money from their inheritance. It is a late disillusioned growl from the old 'passionate pilgrim' who can still feel the charm of a Dedborough Place with its 'thick solicitation of the eye' and its 'old portraits in more or less deserved salience [which] hung over the happy scene as the sworn members of a great guild might have sat, on a beautiful April day, at one of their annual feasts', but is now also aware that among these gracious relics 'people are trafficking all round'—and trafficking in daughters no less than in art. Had James been in better health, one guesses that a more richly satiric portrait would have been drawn of the complacent peer who can exclaim, when his loyalty is questioned: 'And pray who in the world's "England" . . . unless *I* am?'

IX

Marriage and Society (ii)

Tales of the Marriage Market

... we may speculate that having ruled out marriage for himself he found it genuinely difficult to offer it to those of his heroes with whom he was in some way identified. Leon Edel: *'Henry James: The Conquest of London'*

The intimate connexion between comprehensiveness of vision and renunciation of participation is discernible in James's work almost from the first.

Tony Tanner: *'The Reign of Wonder'*

So MANY of James's stories are based on the theme of unhappy or uncompleted marriages—marriages avoided, abortive marriages, misalliances, marriages cursed by vague supernatural agencies, the love of the living conveniently shelved in favour of love for the dead —that it seems almost arbitrary to select for commentary here even the wide range of forty-odd tales which supplement the primarily social-matrimonial novels just discussed. As early as 1876, the year which saw the publication of Christopher Newman's elaborate attempt but actual failure to bring off, in *The American*, one of the author's long series of international unions, James printed a story, *Crawford's Consistency*, recording the hideous self-sacrifice of a man to a ghastly wife whom he had married in pique because his first love had jilted him at the instance of her social-climbing money-grubbing mother. Crawford is pictured as a personification of 'intelligent innocence', with 'the look of an absent-minded seraph', who at first causes his narrator-friend to reflect, in words which have the ring of the author's assent, that 'a desire to lead a single life is not necessarily a proof of a morose disposition'. All is set for this mild paragon to marry his choice, for it was 'a bad year in the matrimonial market' and no better offer had presented itself to the rapacious mother of his intended. Then comes the push-off—Crawford vengefully marries a vulgarian who has some traces of the robustness of Hyacinth Robinson's neighbour, Millicent Henning. 'There is nothing like the bad manners of society', muses the narrator, detailing the scandalized avidity with which Crawford's brassy wife is both devoured and spurned by his friends. Crawford's 'consistency' is merely to be faithful to this slattern who maims him in a drunken brawl—much as poor Isabel's consistency in *The Portrait of a Lady* would be to endure being Mrs. Gilbert Osmond. But Crawford's real escape, we are made more significantly to feel, is from his first love: for her original beauty is blasted by smallpox and she, in turn, is jilted by Crawford's preferred rival. It is all incredible nonsense, interesting only for the occasional examples of those inescapable amusing observations which partially redeem even the worst of James's potboilers, and also for his hysterically vindictive portraits of the two women in poor Crawford's life. The bachelor author seems hard to please, in this slight but suggestive tale: a horrible vengeance overtakes the girl who *doesn't* marry the hero, and the girl who *does* is a vixen who dies of *delirium tremens*.

There is even more meat for the suspicious reader of day dreams in the absurd semi-farcical story *Rose-Agathe* (1878), in which the non-marrier is a young collector of gimcracks—not unlike Ned Rosier of *Portrait of a Lady* or the more frivolous bric-à-brac side of Gabriel Nash of *The Tragic Muse*—who is in the narrator's opinion 'such a pure-minded mortal, sitting there in his innocent company of Dresden shepherdesses. . . . He was the perfect authority on pretty things'. When this trim self-satisfied dilettante gazes amorously into a Parisian hairdresser's window, the narrator thinks that he has designs on the hairdresser's wife; but the prize, carried off to his bedizened nest 'lined from ceiling to floor with the "pretty things" of the occupant', turns out to be merely a female dummy, the effigy from the coiffeur's window! 'It is a pity she creaks', as the young aesthete remarks of his substitute bride. He might have been commenting on the story itself. But a desire to find a non-living substitute for marriage could hardly, even in farcical fantasy, go further than this.

Yet more morbid is *Longstaff's Marriage* (also 1878), the maudlin parable of a love-sick young man who is rejected on his supposed death-bed by a proud Diana, who later herself falls sick of love for him; whereupon *he*, restored by 'the miracle of wounded pride', marries her to demonstrate his superior forbearance. Not to be outdone, she herself, even more considerately and forbearingly, promptly dies, in order, as the lady's friend carefully explains to Longstaff, 'to leave you at liberty'. Here, in a parable which is as crudely a pattern for *The Sacred Fount* as *Benvolio* was for *Roderick Hudson* and a tribe of geminian heroes, is the love-cannibal theme laid bare in a peculiarly unpleasant atmosphere, where self-abnegation is exposed as the most chilling demonstration of possessiveness. James had a sharp nose for that kind of superior suffering which is inseparable from moral blackmail. It is a quality which has misled high-minded critics of, say, *The Golden Bowl*. A remembrance of the nastiness of competitive sacrifice as displayed in *Longstaff's Marriage* would be salutary to sentimentally-minded readers of James's most morally ambitious late work.

In *The Diary of a Man of Fifty* (1879), the narrator attempts to save a young man from entanglement with a fascinating young Italian countess, daughter of the woman from whose dangerous charm he himself, many years before, had simply run away. But the young man, so like himself at the same age, has more courage. He marries the coquette and seems to be happy. The narrator begins to wonder if his own intemperate flight had killed, in the mother, a genuine love for him. 'If I marred her happiness, I certainly didn't make my own. And I might have made it—eh? That's a charming discovery for a man of my age!' It was to be, at immense length, the discovery of poor Strether of *The Ambassadors*. With this sort of direct self-fantasy, at any rate, James was considerably more successful than with the irritatingly symmetrical patterns he so often set up. Here, the early premonition of remorse for moral or emotional cowardice is the result of balanced judgement, the weighing of probabilities, and not of mere mawkishness. As Mrs. Leavis has pointed out (*Scrutiny* XIV, 226), this tale 'allows an exploration of certain possibilities of life to be presented dramatically, with the tensions, the contrasts and the psychological surprises that make a work of art instead of a narrative'. The narrator himself, in short, is no puppet; he is recognizably James in one of his Benvolio moods: 'Everything reminds me of something else, and yet of itself at the same time; my imagination makes a great circuit and comes back to the starting-point.'

If it were not for the absurdities of its plot, *The Impressions of a Cousin* (1883) would be a remarkable *tour de force* for a male author, consisting as it does of the diary entries of the female cousin and companion, a water-colourist, of a New York heiress who is being diddled out for a fortune by her trustee, the flamboyant Mr. Caliph with whom she is secretly in love. Meanwhile Caliph's half-brother (the geminian theme again) is calling officially to woo the heiress Eunice whom he doesn't love, but is falling under the spell of the intellectually dominating diarist. All this is done with great skill and subtlety; the reader feels an increasing and almost illicit interest in the narrator's own character, which was originally fairly colourless as befitted the official spectator of her cousin's drama. This gained interest is squandered in the last quarter of the story by another of James's unbelievable marriage-bargains: the narrator begs her own suitor to marry Eunice in order to make up her financial loss. He manages, via his rascally half-brother, to return her fortune, but refrains from marriage, making off instead to live in Italy on his now reduced means. Meanwhile Caliph himself has lost his hold over the masochistic Eunice, who, no longer diddled by him, does not after all marry him. So the strong-minded diarist now refuses to marry her lover until Eunice does decide to marry the villainous Caliph. This absurd end to the story comes with the affront of trickery and all the long-prepared plausibility and subtle building-up of character are wasted. The bandying of emotional bargains is a ludicrous excuse and alibi for a more complete use of the realistic narrative and its quite charming social and architectural commentary. Mr. Leon Edel (II, 501) considers that this tale 'is but half-heartedly written, a throwing together of miscellaneous observations' made during James's recent visit to America at the time of his father's death—a judgement which, though true as regards the half-heartedness, hardly does justice to the quite unusual skill of James's ability to capture one's interest in his fictional diarist, before losing it again in the deliberate let-down of yet another version of escape from matrimony.

An even more elaborate writhing keeps the miserable hero of *Georgina's Reasons* (1884) from a full participation in the married state: his wife, the 'imperial' Georgina, insists that their marriage be kept an absolute secret, to which the craven wretch (though a naval officer!) agrees. Georgina, foreshadowing the bold Kate Croy of *The Wings of the Dove* in that 'her whole person seemed to exhale a tranquil, happy consciousness of having broken a law', makes off to Italy to bear her baby, of whom she quickly rids herself, displaying a 'blooming hardness' which strikes her female companion as being 'like a kind of Medusa-mask', and then proceeds to contract a second bigamous marriage. Georgina's husband, the seafaring permanent grass-widower, meets and falls in love with an attractive American girl, who is attending in Italy her dying sister who promises a legacy for the robuster lover of the fascinating sea-captain (as if, with the appearance of a Milly Theale to balance a Kate Croy, the plot of *The Wings of the Dove* were already forming). But Georgina, though she brazenly introduces him to her second husband, is nevertheless still his legal wife. Her legal existence (for it is no more than that) gives him a protective alibi, and the new couple settle down patiently 'to wait'. It is as thorough a protection as any of the Jamesian non-marriers enjoys: to keep faith with a legal fiction of a wife who has long since foresworn all wifely claims, and thus to fend off his true love. 'What would become of this precious little force?' muses the captain, of his second love. It would take the full scope of *The Portrait of a Lady* to answer such a question. In the tale, we only know what does *not* happen—which we must learn to accept, from early on, as one typical Jamesian solution. For it *is* a solution, of a kind; and we cannot justly turn to special pleading to excuse the author. If such a story is unsatisfactory, it is he, the professional author, who deliberately makes it so. A potboiler? Perhaps. But the potboiling story-teller can also toss off such confident asperities as the description of a minor female character who considered clothes 'with a complacency which might have led you to suppose that she had invented the custom of draping the human form'; he can compress into two sardonic sentences the sort of social observation that enlivens pages of *The Bostonians*: 'She used to read to the blind, and, more onerously, to the deaf. She looked after other people's children while the parents attended anti-slavery conventions.' Such a writer is in need of no exculpation on the grounds of fatigue or incapacity. No; it is perhaps even more saddening that the least attractive of James's fictions always, *somewhere*, remind the reader of the writer's mastery of his craft. If, on occasion, he seems perverse in aim and direction, we must always pay him the credit, or discredit, of having known precisely what he *was* doing.

A New England Winter (1884) is a long aimless rigmarole readable only as an example of the acuteness of observation with which James had rediscovered his native land. (It is amusing, for instance, to spot in the midst of a ruthless description of Boston under its muddy winter snow, that 'oblong receptacle' of a streetcar in which Miss Birdseye of *The Bostonians* was wont to insert herself.) For all its cosy matter-of-fact 'period' atmospheric accuracy, which gives it some value as a document of social history, the story is threaded on the tenuous string of the reactions of young Florimond, who has returned for a few months from the artistic pleasures of Paris, and who first jibs at the young woman predestined for him by his mother, then shows an inconvenient interest in her old married friend, and is finally content to be bundled back to *la vie de Bohème* unshackled and fancy-free. He escapes more lightly than most of the non-marriers—as befits, perhaps, a Bostonian named Florimond.

Utterly different in tone is a tale of the same year, *The Path of Duty*. It is an uncomfortable study in refined sadism by a morally irreproachable pair whose virtue is, to an *un*wronged wife, a torture worse than plain betrayal. The characters sound like Victorian dummies (Sir Ambrose Tester, Joscelind Bernardstone, Lady Vandaleur), but their situation is real enough. Tester, deeply in love with Lady Vandaleur, nevertheless marries his fiancée Joscelind even after the unexpected death of Lord Vandaleur has left the lovers, to that extent at least, 'free'. They take immense satisfaction in parading before their disappointed social set the fact that they are *not* having an affair; that Tester has neither jilted nor wronged the girl to whom he had become engaged, *faute de mieux*, while his real choice was technically beyond his reach. The cheers for this nobility, forced from the ranks of Tuscany, are bitter indeed to poor Lady Tester, who has not the vestige of a reason for complaint. It is as if James, in his conscientious catalogue of the horrors of married life, is determined to show that blameless rectitude is also, in wedlock, painful to all concerned. As Mr. Marius Bewley points out (*Scrutiny* XVII, 93), the noble pair 'have sinned by being virtuous, and lied by adhering to their conception of the truth'.

Middle-aged readers who have tenacious memories and were brought up in polite provincial backwaters may recall that even after the Great War it was possible to meet stately mothers who walked abroad with marriageable daughters chained to their will like bibles to old-fashioned lecterns or iron cups to the lingering Victorian public fountains. It is difficult, no doubt, for modern readers to imagine the universality of assent for such authority: neither the conscientious mothers, playing their daughters like a hand of cards, nor the girls themselves, nor polite society at large, questioned the admirable restraint of these widowed rulers (they were usually widowed). It had been from a similar system that a previous generation had gleaned its stock of expendable daughters, 'left over' from the play like undiscarded redundancies in the hand of an unsuccessful player of rummy, who would serve out their lives as servant-companions to their parents and servant-aunts to the broods of their own more successful sisters. And to complete the historical sketch of this so recent and yet to our minds so ante-diluvian a class of maiden lady, one must also make an effort to recreate the appalling domestic boredom, the utter lack of alternative entertainment, offered to those females who had failed to find an opportunity to busy themselves in the elaborate administration of late-nineteenth-century domestic life (lingering, in pockets, into our own century). Henry James seems to have had an instinctive sympathy for such ladies: they usually escape, as a class, the sardonic asides which even his pampered heroines suffer from their creator from time to time. When Mrs. Touchett in *The Portrait of a Lady*, reminds Isabel that if she so wishes she can now command the services of 'a companion—some decayed gentlewoman with a darned cashmere and dyed hair, who paints on velvet', she is not portrayed as being herself, in her station, unusually cruel, but is merely a sounding board for an unusually compassionate observation by her creator. There are dozens of such decayed gentlewomen scattered among the 'social-matrimonial' group of novels and tales, as if James wishes to remind the reader that such is likely to be the fate of his female creations who do *not* succeed on the marriage-market. (Is it any wonder that the male prey are permitted to take such elaborate evasive action, when their huntresses are spurred on, among other things, by the knowledge of what dreadful fate awaits them if they return from the chase empty-handed?)

Some such recollection is helpful, perhaps, when one turns to such tales as *Mrs. Temperly* (1887) and *Louisa Pallant* (1888), in which a mother's command over the disposal of her daughters' affections is held to be absolute. The first of these stories is light indeed: a suitor for one of Mrs. Temperley's daughters is simply compelled to wait until that lady has made an advantageous match for his sweetheart's sister—and since *that* particular offering on the marriage-booth happens to be an undersized piece of flawed merchandise named Tishy, the docile pair must take their place in the queue and wait, presumably for ever. What social *ennui* must meanwhile be endured is exemplified by the narrator's rapid sketch of such appalling Victorian middle-class jocosities as 'a large ring of people who had drawn up their chairs in the public room of an hotel: some one was sure to undertake to be funny'. In *Louisa Pallant*, a hard-boiled widow reverses the normal rôle, and drives an innocent lad away from her even more hard-boiled daughter—who appears to the narrator as 'the result of a process of calculation; a process patiently educative in order that she should reach a high point'. In the case of daughter Linda, one such high point had been achieved when, reviewing her amiable and eligible young suitor, she was aware that 'a woman's cleverness most shines in contrast with a man's stupidity when she pretends to take that stupidity for wisdom'. But this time the angler relents and throws back the fish: Linda's mother, remorseful for her own past ill-treatment of the narrator, exposes her daughter's character to his infatuated young nephew, and the young man escapes. Yet another non-marrying victory—this time a present, so to say, from the enemy. The surrender is complete: it is Louisa Pallant herself who disarms both her daughter and herself:

'To climb to the top and be splendid and envied there,' she went on—'to do that at any cost or by any meanness and cruelty is the only thing she had a heart for. She'd lie for it, she'd steal for it, she'd kill for it! ... God in his mercy has let me see it in time, but his ways are strange and he has let me see it in my daughter. It's myself he has let me see—myself as I was for years ...'

The kind of moral blackmail practised by the Tester-Vandaleur pair in *The Path of Duty* is treated again in *The Liar* (1888), which opens with a rapturous account of a country house party (at the first dinner, it is noticed approvingly that a lady turns from one table-neighbour to another 'with a methodical air, as a good cook lifts the cover of the next sauce-pan') at which a portrait painter re-encounters a happily married woman who had once rejected him. He discovers with unholy satisfaction that her husband is a socially entertaining vulgarian, with 'good manners and bad taste', whose tall stories are simply downright lies. With odious rectitude, the artist Lyon paints a portrait of the yarn-spinning Colonel Capadose in which he displays, to the wife, his ability to expose the man as a fraud. When she loyally destroys the tell-tale portrait it is as if, as Mr. Bewley points out (*Scrutiny* XVII, 95), she 'knows that it is not her husband but Lyon who is the liar', who cannot see the truth that married love recognizes and overcomes such shortcomings.

Many of James's stories of the late nineteenth-century marriage market are put in the mouths of narrators or told from the viewpoint of participants who seem themselves to move familiarly enough in the stale compromised air. Some of the tales already briefly discussed have expressed so disillusioned a cynicism that the solutions proffered by the 'good' characters are as distasteful as the problems. The reader is at a loss, at the end, to know where his sympathies lie, or even where they are supposed to lie. In the long story *A London Life* (1888), we are for long periods permitted to breathe again the fresher air of illusion, of the 'passionate pilgrim' days. This not only restores to James's prose a tonic vivacity which has been increasingly toned down to a wry destructive off-level awkwardness, but also retrieves that earlier skill in presenting a sense of human, of family, tension. Once a reader can 'take sides', even if it turns out to be the 'wrong' side, the fusty social-moral Victorian problems flicker into life. *A London Life* comes as a salutary reminder that James was still capable of voicing simple indignation and innocent gratification. When bleary bloodshot situations are viewed, as it were, by bleary bloodshot eyes, the whole affair can become so compromised as to leave only a sour distaste. The young American girl, Laura Wing, who gapes at first wide-eyed and then half hysterically at the indulgent personal lives of the London well-to-do, may prove to be a ninny; but while we are pretending, for the story's sake, to borrow for a moment her point of view, we are rewarded with a series of wonderfully fresh vignettes and surprised by a sequence of first-class dialogue.

Through Laura Wing's eyes we first get a partly appraising and partly disapproving view of the ideally comfortable English wealthy world into which her sister has married. We can guess that, when in the country, she will disapprove of the harshness of dower-houses (even though 'the iniquity did not as a general thing prevent these retreats from being occupied by old ladies with wonderful reminiscences and rare voices, whose reverses had not deprived them of a great deal of becoming hereditary lace') and the martyrdom of governesses ('You know they are always crying, governesses— whatever line you take', as one of her confidantes tries to enlighten her). She approves of the schoolroom and the peacocks, but she is anything but a gullible pilgrim and can marvel 'at the waste involved in some institutions (the English country gentry for instance) when she perceived that it had taken so much to produce so little'. She is, in fact, as socially perceptive as her creator had now become, noting 'that perfection of machinery which can still at certain times make English life go on of itself with a stately rhythm long after there is corruption within it'. Even while sorrowing over the way in which her sister neglects her little sons, Aunt Laura tartly predicts that 'Geordie would grow up to be a master-hand at polo . . . and Ferdy perhaps would develop into "the best shot in England".' She takes at first, too, a canny 'outside' view of the sort of muffled whirligig of flashy life indulged in by her sister, much as if she were describing at a great distance the practical background for such later close-ups as *The Sacred Fount*: 'she had so many friends, who were always rushing about like herself and making appointments and putting them off and wanting to know if she were going to certain places or whether she would go if they did . . .'—a sort of innocent recipe for house-party adultery. She accuses her brother-in-law, no less than her sister, of neglecting their 'so sacred and so beautiful' house, another such treasure as Poynton, for a hectic life of 'vulgar pleasure'. It is only when she can no longer be blind to the fact that her sister, *à la* Becky Sharp, is carrying on a shameless affair—involving dashes to the Continent—with a fashionable cad, that Laura takes things to heart and loses her balance of judgement.

In her sister's London house, Laura 'had a distinct sense of interfering with the free interchange of anecdote and pleasantry' among all the gentlemen callers; she recognized that 'nature had dedicated her more to the relief of old women than to that of young men'. But she does see something of another devoted 'passionate pilgrim' of the innocent type, the American Mr. Wendover, in whose company, on a visit to the Soane Museum, she 'surprises' her sister and the philandering Captain Crispin. After this brief preview of a *Wings of the Dove* scene, we are treated to a preview from *The Ambassadors*, where all kinds of shady social comings and goings take place in an opera-house box. The wicked sister leaves her there deliberately 'exposed' to the public gaze with her innocent Mr. Wendover (though it is clear to him, at least, that the rest of the audience are too busy applauding the singers), to whom in desperation she turns for assurances that *his* intentions are honourable: the poor hysterical girl wishes, by marriage to Wendover, to be dissociated from her sinful sister—as if anyone would think of associating so very different a pair. She dashes to Brussels to try to 'save' her sister, but we are left, in a hasty fudged-up ending, to suppose that Laura's brother-in-law will claim his divorce and that she herself, in the pure air of America, may one day become Mrs. Wendover. Laura has made frenzied scenes, but the gay wicked world goes its own way and one has a residual sense that of all the discreditable characters in *A London Life*, Laura herself is perhaps the least charitable. Her headlong purity is not, after all, quite free of family likeness to her sister's headlong wordliness. She strikes, at any rate, what Dr. Leavis calls (*Scrutiny* XVII, 119) 'the note of moral horror' as she watches her sister pursuing 'a career resembling Maisie's mama's'. That note of horror, however unsympathetic its medium, has forced us to take an *outside* view of the fast set, as valuable in its way as Laura's earlier outsider's 'passionate pilgrim' view. There is real tension, and *A London Life* is proportionately successful, not only as a *nouvelle* but also as a social commentary.

One remembers *The Patagonia* (1888) for its excellent sketches of life on board a Victorian Cunarder, long after the muted melodrama —including, this time, a female non-marrying suicide—has grown dim. The young American heroine, travelling to Europe to marry a dull worthy American architect to whom she has been engaged for many years, falls in love with Jasper Nettlepoint, a selfish young man, son of the lady in whose care she is travelling. She cannot bear to meet her dim respectable fiancé after the stimulation of knowing Jasper, and throws herself overboard before the *Patagonia* docks. Writing at the top of his 'social' form, James presents his small cast of characters with light brilliantly economical strokes and sets them moving in bursts of brief pointed dialogue. Jasper, unwitting cause of a suicide, 'looked intelligent but also slightly brutal, though not in a morose way. His brutality, if he had any, was bright and finished'. This is the physical mnemonic. The moral one is briefer still: 'He was of the type of those whom other people worry about, not of those who worry about other people.' Hardly surprising, perhaps, that such a person should quickly find himself 'ensconced behind the lifeboat with Miss Mavis'. The admirably civilized conversation, the relaxed atmosphere of the liner, are not markedly different from those of a similar passage today, given the good luck of intelligent table-companions:

... repetition at sea is somehow not repetition; monotony is in the air, the mind is flat and everything recurs—the bells, the meals, the stewards' faces, the romp of children, the walk, the clothes, the very shoes and buttons of passengers taking their exercise. These things finally grow at once so circumstantial and so arid that, in comparison, lights on the personal history of one's companions become a substitute for the friendly flicker of the lost fireside.

For the Jamesian narrator, indeed, the sea voyage acts as a kind of preliminary sketch for poor George Dane's *Great Good Place*: 'When it doesn't confer trouble it takes trouble away—takes away letters and telegrams and newspapers and visits and duties and efforts, all the complications, all the superfluities and superstitions that we have stuffed into our terrene life.' But what *is* different, in the late 1880's, is the vulnerability of an engaged girl to the malicious gossip of other hucksters in the marriage-market. For her mild mid-Atlantic flirtation, Miss Mavis is literally gossiped to death. Upon the narrator himself, as upon the narrator of *The Sacred Fount*, hovers the ambiguous label of benevolent busybody.

A similar tale, based on the grotesque imputations to which Mrs. Grundy-like innuendoes had reduced Victorian maidens, could be treated in a quite different manner—swift of pace, lightweight, even farcical. In *The Solution* (1889), a priggish young American diplomat who is 'innocent without being stupid' and 'unworldly without being underbred', is teased by his friends because he has taken a short stroll with an unchaperoned girl. Mortified, he feels obliged to propose to her. A worldly-wise widow who had been cultivated by the narrator (himself a party to the practical joke that went too far), manages to extricate the poor dupe, and in so doing falls for his naïveté and marries him herself. These two stories are parallel in several ways. Both have a vividly accurate local setting: *The Solution* has a backdrop of old Papal Rome to match *The Patagonia*'s liner. A similar economy of 'placing' is exemplified by such a remark as:

'It is a mistake to suppose it is only the people who would like to be what they are not who are snobs. That class includes equally many of those who are what the others would like to be.' Both have a vigorous confident narrative pace rather more competent than the plots warrant. Most strikingly, both stories, the melodramatic-tragic and the melodramatic-farcical, are based on the premise, itself a by-product of Victorian marriage-market ethics, that a young woman observed in the company of a young man for even half an hour or so in 'polite' society is thereby fatally 'compromised'. Needless to say, both James's 'compromised' characters escape, the one by suicide and the other by an alternative marriage.

Two stories of 1891, *The Marriages* and *Brooksmith*, offer splendid examples of the mocking asperity of James's mature style as a critic of society, though they are wholly unlike in construction—the one being held together by a hectic anti-marriage plot that goes wrong, and the other, an elaborate character-sketch, having no plot at all. The intricate plotting of *The Marriages* is built on assumptions no longer universally valid. The main plot exposes the passionate reluctance of a girl to let her widower father marry again: a motivation any modern reader will spot as 'Freudian' and therefore, presumably, so general as to be admitted and somehow coped with. (Indeed, even while this present chapter was being written, a happy wife and mother who had married a husband very much older than herself was heard to say at a dinner-party, perfectly seriously and openly: 'Of course, I had always been looking round for a father-substitute.') Adela tells a lie about her father and thinks she has prevented the companionable widow Mrs. Churchley from accepting him. She is full of remorse when her father, 'jilted', is obviously miserable. But we discover that it was not her wicked fib but only Mrs. Churchley's intense dislike of *her*, and her father's unwillingness to 'give up' his daughter, that had wrecked the marriage. The sub-plot, concerning Adela's brother's foolish secret marriage to a hag whom he hopes Mrs. Churchley will help to 'buy off' after she has married his father, is based on the assumptions first that social inequality in marriage is an unnameable horror, and secondly on the lack of any simple ready-made escape via divorce.

This preternatural meddling of a young girl in adult affairs has something of the smack of *What Maisie Knew*. Treated at greater length and with a steadier seriousness, Adela's case could have been developed as an instance of 'slashing out in . . . bewilderment'. As it is, James leaves one assenting in the view of her as an interfering blockhead. The 'social' value of the tale is all in its asides. Adela may be a jealous ninny so far as her father is concerned, but she is made the medium of such amusing yet sensitive observations as: 'She was conscious of the queerness, the shyness, in London, of the gregarious flight of guests after a dinner, the general *sauve qui peut* and panic fear of being left with the host and hostess.' She is bitter but perceptive, too, on the score of the fading memories of her own dead mother: 'The patient dead were sacrificed; they had no shrines, for people were literally ashamed of mourning. When they had hustled all sensibility out of their lives they invented the fiction that they felt too much to utter.' Having ruined her father's second chance for companionship, she is nevertheless quite inadequate to supply that need herself, and the author's sidelong summary convicts them both of a pitiful lack of inner resource: 'She watched his attempts to wind himself up on the subject of shorthorns and drainage, and she favoured to the utmost of her ability his intermittent disposition to make a figure in orchids.' In such sentences as these one grasps how very far the novelist has travelled beyond the 'passionate pilgrim' stage.

Brooksmith preserves something of the original 'passionate pilgrim' reverence for the old order, but presents it in a violently ironical fashion. The 'hero' who represents all that is best in that old transmitted order is discerned not in the ranks of its fortunate inheritors but in the ranks of their own neglected servants. The residuary legatee of consideration and graciousness is Brooksmith, the butler. This sensitive retainer fades away when his master dies, for he cannot bring himself to minister in richer, vulgar, houses where the conversation is less remarkably educative than that in his former master's 'salon'. Snobbish? Far from it! James is merciless, in this footnote-tale, to the normal objects of snobbish adulation. The reader is incidentally vexed equally by the meanness of Brooksmith's former employer in leaving him only £80, and by the false delicacy of the narrator which makes him too 'gentlemanly' to help him. The slight sketch shows a wonderful power to dramatize a neglected social type. The style is perfectly fitting: its gentle ironies and detached wit are deliberately subdued to render merely the sympathetic if ineffectual attitude of the narrator, because anything more pointed would have been offensive, would have burst the thin bubble of Brooksmith's own imputed sensibility. But there is acid social criticism, below the surface, of the perfunctory interest of the well-to-do in the private lives of their devoted servants who, when their patron's sun sets, just creep away to die. So far from branding Henry James as a Tory, *Brooksmith* is a wonderful advertisement for Social Security!

A London Life presented a proud little Puritan horrified by her sister's adulteries; the complementary pattern is treated in *The Chaperon* (1891) which treats of a girl volunteering to share the social ostracism suffered by her errant mother. Nowhere is James's indignation against the hypocritical harshness of late-Victorian London society more overtly displayed than here: the self-righteous vindictiveness of the heroine's family towards her divorced mother is intolerable mainly because the moral basis of these prudes is itself so capricious. London decides to 'cut' Mrs. Tramore: 'Apparently she had not the qualities for which London compounds; though in the cases in which it does compound you may often wonder what those qualities are.' One can see, too, why daughter Rose had so little sympathy with her 'deceived' father, who is pinned in one tart sentence as the kind of husband from whom any high-spirited wife might well have absconded: 'Fortune, which but for that one stroke had been generous to him, had provided him with deputies and trouble-takers, as well as with whimsical opinions, and a reputation for excellent taste, and whist at his club, and perpetual cigars on morocco sofas, and a beautiful absence of purpose.' Where the novelist's power rises superior to his diagrammatic plot, however, is in his perception that the courageous young lady has equally little tenderness for her 'wronged' mother. Her 'purpose was a pious game, but it was still essentially a game'. Rose was still essentially, in fact, the child of her parents. For Mrs. Tramore, on whose behalf the reader's sympathies have been at least negatively canvassed (for one's dislike of her persecutors is real enough), has by no means been ennobled by her social suffering. When Rose joins her, leaving behind an outraged grandmother who will disinherit her and an outraged suitor who will presumably (like most of James's suitors) abandon the chase if she *is* disinherited, the frivolous Mrs. Tramore looks upon her not so much as 'a high-strung and clever daughter' as 'a new, charming, clever, useful friend'. What the poor lady yearns for, in short, is not filial affection but simply a chance to be refloated on the social tide. 'She had drunk deep of every dishonour, but the bitter cup had left her with a taste for candles, for squeezing up staircases and hooking herself to the human elbow.'

The social irony of *The Chaperon* is thorough indeed: nobody emerges from the lively tale with much credit. 'Society' begins to accept the disgraced Mrs. Tramore again the moment it recognizes in her daughter's sacrifice not a noble gesture but an amusing rarity of behaviour akin to that of professional entertainers—fiddlers, perhaps, or tumblers. Because they are such an odd pair, so much talked about, they are received back into the herd almost as a pair of licensed jesters, the blameless daughter in this case acting as chaperon to her own mother. Poor Rose can no longer, of course, be *seriously* treated by London society: when it is clear that she has lost her share of her adamant grandmother's fortune, the naked cupidity of the marriage-market dictates that she shall be passed over in favour of her teenage sister. The final twist—of wry comedy, this time, instead of wry disgust—is that by the time Rose marries her straight-laced suitor, her mother has been so successfully refloated that she now has no time to spare for her heroic stay-at-home daughter and son-in-law. In this social scramble, the weakest goes to the wall—pushed there, in this instance, by the rescued stricken deer.

It is all brilliantly done; the sentences are (for James) short, the dialogue steely and vivid, the narrative pace spanking, the social knowingness beautifully put across, the social scorn devastating, the moral assessments merciless. When, as here, James is in full command both as social critic and as 'master of the *nouvelle*', his penetration into both social and human motivation can be relentless—a point reinforced by reference to less successful tales of this group in which either the given social predicament, or the human figure confronting it, can be merely a diagrammatic bore. In savouring a tale like *The Chaperon* I am reminded of Dr. Leavis's contrast between the irony of a Gibbon, which the reader may share in perfect safety so long as he shares the assumptions of the writer, and the irony of a Swift, which so often whips round to 'catch' the reader who thinks, mistakenly, that Swift is 'on his side'. So here. We feel reasonably safe in enjoying the set-piece satirical portrait of the appalling prig Bertram Jay, Rose's suitor (almost worthy to be placed beside that of Mrs. Farrinder of *The Bostonians*): 'He had a passion for instance for open-air speaking, but was not thought on the whole to excel in it unless he could help himself out with a hymn.' We feel safe in sharing Rose's view that he was more alarmed lest 'her mother should contaminate her' than that she should fail to be a merciful daughter. We cheer her indignation that 'a gentleman could see so much in mere vulgarities of opinion . . .' And then, when the heroic bereaved daughter goes out to meet her shunned mother and is greeted with the words 'Heavens, dear, where did you get your mourning?' we suddenly realize that Mrs. Tramore, too, is just as shabby morally as her persecutors. When she, in turn, clambers over her daughter as upon a convenient social ladder, we lose our moral bearings—which is precisely, I maintain, what James intended us to do. In such a society as this, where *is* the authority? Pharisees and publicans are alike untrustworthy in this particular Vanity Fair. Of course it was wrong for her moral equals to cold-shoulder the sinning Mrs. Tramore; but, equally, 'the mother, a person of gross insensibility, evidently wouldn't die of cold-shouldering'. *The Chaperon*, more simply and clearly than *What Maisie Knew* or *The Awkward Age*, presents late-Victorian London society as one great cynical *sauve qui peut*.

It is worth belabouring these points because the best of James's 'marriage and society' stories are only saved from tedium for the present-day reader precisely when some at least of his distinctive gifts—wit, irony, moral sense—or all of them combined, are brought into play. Deprived of them, the marriage-market tales can be as chillingly unreal as *Lord Beaupré* (1892). This tells the story of how Mary Gosselin allows herself to become fictitiously 'engaged' to Lord Beaupré, an old family friend, merely in order to protect him, for a spell, from the savage attentions of female fortune-hunters and their vulture-like mothers. The complacent peer is one of James's cosiest non-marriers. But Mary is one of his quiet young women, and it is inevitable that during the course of the engagement *de convenance* the young people shall independently fall in love; equally inevitable that Mary's pride compels her to break off the fake 'engagement' in order to accept the hand of an American who genuinely loves her. In contrast with the lively yet basically stern context of *The Chaperon*, this tale is no more than a pointless piece of ingenuity, enlivened only by occasional felicities of phrase such as 'never was a man more conscientiously superficial' or 'his happiness would have been offensive if people generally hadn't liked him, for it consisted of a kind of monstrous candid comfort'.

As Dr. Edel tells us in his introduction to Volume 8 of the Collected Tales, James was writing a steady stream of stories in 1891–92 'in conformity with his decision to confine himself to short fiction while he was writing plays'. It is hardly surprising that some of them show a dispirited lapse of creativity and could be grouped under several possible thematic headings. Such a potboiler is *Sir Dominick Ferrand* (1892), which has vague touches of the supernatural or uncanny, but is in essence yet another minor melodramatic comment on Victorian social morality. A struggling young writer buys a davenport in which he discovers private papers revealing the secret scandals of a late public figure, Sir Dominick Ferrand. His editor offers him a large sum for them and even (a bigger bribe still, to the professional Henry James in a self-pitying mood!) a promise to print his own normally unsaleable fiction unaltered; but the high-minded young man burns the incriminating papers—and lo! the fair widow in the same lodging-house reveals herself as Sir Dominick's bastard daughter, whom he marries. With its ludicrous coincidences and its mawkish suppression of truth, I cannot find in this tale even the 'mere echo' of *The Aspern Papers* allowed it by Dr. Edel. All *Sir Dominick Ferrand* has to tell us about life, or art, or even the occult, is of less value than the passing remark, in Victorian London, that 'there is nobody so bereft of joy as not to be able to command for twopence the services of somebody less joyous'. James sometimes flagged with his bourgeois puppets. He never lost sympathy with *their* slaves, the companions and governesses who suffered in professional silence.

In studying the marriage-market, James has hitherto mainly adopted the viewpoint of the sellers, the mothers and daughters (or, for that matter, fathers and sons) looking for the largest fortune. In two tales which squeamish readers will find unpleasant, he turns to the buyers' viewpoint and with a callousness bred of the marketplace his men finger the goods on display, examining teeth, eyes and muscles as a purchaser might have done in the less hypocritical slave-markets of other cultures. *The Wheel of Time* (1892) and *Glasses* (1896) both treat unashamedly of physical defects which reduce, if detected, the social value of females offered for sale. The first is another diagrammatic (almost algebraic) arrangement of personifications of beauty and ugliness. Young Maurice Glanvil rushed away from a prearranged marriage to Fanny Knocker because she was repellently ugly. He meets her twenty years later, a strangely beautiful widow. His own daughter, ugly in turn, falls in love with Fanny's handsome son, who in turn flies from her in repugnance and breaks her heart. This type of 'trick' story, as we have been forced to acknowledge with too many of James's pot-boilers, is unappetizing at the best of times, but is doubly so when the author manages to get us involved in the lives of his figurines. The uneasy reader feels like asking for either a trick story played out with disposable dummies, or else a treatment of real people motivated by something other than clockwork. There is, in fact, too much life in the quartet making up *The Wheel of Time* to make the plot tolerable. They run away from plainness in spite of hankering after the attendant dowries, discovering too late the other superior qualities of the rejected goods. One's squeamishness is increased by Dr. Edel's plausible theory (III, 253–7) that poor Fanny Knocker is based on James's own ambiguous friend, the 'elderly, plain, deaf, devoted' Constance Fenimore Woolson, since 'however much Henry might appreciate and admire Fenimore's devotion to him, there was nothing he could give in return save a certain tenderness and consideration, and the pledge of a yearly visit'. When Maurice Glanvil, meeting again the transformed Fanny, surmises that she has been beautified specifically by 'a miracle of heroic docilities and accepted pangs and vanquished egotisms', one does indeed stir uneasily when one connects her with the tragic end of James's own faithful female friend.

Glasses (1896) is a more extended essay on this gruesome business of physical factors in the marriage-market. It is no less than a full-length treatment of the truism most neatly phrased by (I believe) Dorothy Parker: 'Men seldom make passes/At girls who wear glasses.' Flora Saunt, a beautiful girl with nothing but her looks to commend her, seeks desperately to become engaged to Lord Iffield before her failing eyesight, now dangerously neglected, compels her to wear hideous spectacles—the 'great vitreous badge' of ugliness as worn by an old family friend, Mrs. Meldrum. She misses her peer by inches, but a softer-hearted suitor marries her. She is enabled, by his generous sympathy for her ninny-headed predicament, to shine in public places as a beauty while her husband conceals from others the fact, and attempts to shield Flora from the dreaded social consequences, that she is going blind. It is a tale equally disquieting whether one takes it at Flora's own valuation or at the valuation of the fascinated narrator: if social rules are *so* false and the cowed obedience of its devotees *so* abject, then one cares little whether the victims fail or succeed in their hapless devices. The reader's sympathy rests, if anywhere, upon the ugly old Mrs. Meldrum, whose appearance was 'enhanced by the wild braveries of dress, reckless charges of colour and stubborn resistances of cut, wondrous encounters in which the art of the toilet seemed to lay down its life'. Even the man who marries Flora is jeered at for his appearance, which is presented as almost as much his own fault as his acquired manner:

He bore in its most indelible pressure the postmark, as it were, of Oxford, and as soon as he opened his mouth I perceived, in addition to a remarkable revelation of gums, that the text of the queer communication matched the registered envelope. He was full of refinements and angles, of dreary and distinguished knowledge. Of his unconscious drollery his dress freely partook . . . There were moments when his over-done urbanity, all suggestive stammers and interrogative quavers, made him scarcely intelligible; but I felt him to be a gentleman . . .

In such a company observed by such a recorder, it is hardly surprising that the narrator is quite genuinely moved by the discovery 'that there is, strangely, in very deep misfortune a dignity finer even than in the most inveterate habit of being all right'. It is all as distasteful as an earlier tale, *The Visits* (1892), the brusque account of a girl who literally dies of shame after indicating to a strange young man that she loves him. It is all the more horrible that this ultimate sacrifice to the double standards of late-Victorian sexual morality should have taken place in her 'sleepy, silvery old home . . . where you could have confidence in your leisure: it would be as genuine as the butter and the claret'. In such a one-sided paradise, one longs to hear the accents of Mrs. Farrinder's Boston, or the coming boot-falls of the Feminist Movement in James's adopted England.

Henry James was not only a voluminous correspondent but also a devoted user of the British telegraph system. (The phrase 'for I shrink from the brutality of a telegram', from one of his social notes, is a mere pleasantry.) In the Preface to Volume VIII of the New York Edition, which contains the long story *In the Cage* (1898), he confesses of his local telegraph office 'that any momentary wait there seemed to take place in a strong social draught, the stiffest possible breeze of the human comedy'. (One gasps at the thought of Henry James spinning a tale based on the operations of some central telephone exchange!) The germ of *In the Cage* is simply the notion of a sensitive and intelligent girl at the telegram counter taking an inordinate interest in messages passed to and fro between members of the gentry with whom, in *fin-de-siècle* London, she herself could hope for no kind of social intercourse. James wondered what precisely it would mean (to quote the Preface again) 'for confined and cramped and yet considerably tutored young officials of either sex to be made so free, intellectually, of a range of experience otherwise quite closed to them'. One can see at once the attractions such a theme held for him: the mild flavour of the *voyeur*, 'the girl's "subjective" adventure', the mordant scorn for upper-class Londoners and the no less mordant pity for their uncomplaining slaves. The background of the nameless telegraphist is etched (in the portrait of one of her neighbours) not only with a social satirist's venom but also with something of a revolutionary's impatience:

... the bereaved lady, without a penny of provision, and with stop-gaps like their own, all gone, had, across the sordid landing on which the opposite doors of the pair of scared miseries opened and to which they were bewilderingly bolted, borrowed coals and umbrellas that were repaid in potatoes and postage-stamps. It had been a questionable help, at that time, to ladies submerged, floundering, panting, swimming for their lives, that they *were* ladies; but such an advantage could come up again in proportion as others vanished, and it had grown very great by the time it was the only ghost of one they possessed.

The impatience is even more explicit in the Preface: 'You may starve in London, it is clear, without discovering a use for any theory of the more equal division of victuals—which is moreover exactly what it would appear that thousands of the non-speculative annually do.' How strange to find Henry James, of all people, putting his finger, like a Marxist agitator, on the supine acceptance of the dispossessed? He is merciless in his exposure of the meek subservience of the telegraphist's fiancé, Mr. Mudge, to 'the charm of the existence of a class that Providence had raised up to be the blessing of grocers'. For him and his craven fellows, 'the exuberance of the aristocracy was the advantage of trade'. 'The more flirtatious, as he might roughly express it, the more cheese and pickles.' Strange? Well, no; not to those who recall little Hyacinth Robinson and his foster-mother Miss Pynsent. What does seem to have happened, in the years since *The Princess Casamassima*, is that Henry James's tart sympathy for the under-dog had remained constant, while his contempt for their feckless unconscious oppressors had grown.

The girl in the telegraphist's cage, living vicariously through the telegrams of Lady Bradeen and Captain Everard, prefers to stay there (until the very end) rather than marry her petit-bourgeois Mudge. She has saved the pair of toffs from a scandal by emending and remembering their raffish if incompetent telegrams sent in the course of the kind of high-class adulterous tangle James had treated at greater length elsewhere. As a result, the Captain is under an obligation to the compromised Lady Bradeen, and marries her. Her dream ended, the girl in the cage at last consents to become Mrs. Mudge. It is a curious and powerful essay in remote affinities; it is akin to *What Maisie Knew* in its treatment of the unexpected perceptions of children or underlings; but its real power lies not in the tricky subtlety of its plot (though this is very much neater and less forced than in some of James's similar 'situations') but in the acute analysis of social disparities in late-Victorian London. After giving them so many idylls in country houses, James shows his readers that he is not ignorant (he never *was!*) of the real, the economic, basis of class distinctions. The girl in the cage may be like Maisie as a person, but she is like Hyacinth Robinson as a social type. The pathos of undeserved exclusion is greater, in this story, than the pathos of the girl's individual sacrifice of a real life with Mr. Mudge to an illusory life as a distant adorer of Captain Everard. There is a great warmth of heart behind James's entirely unsentimental treatment. Even Mr. Mudge is a sorry figure in more than one sense of the word. One is reminded, yet again, of the humanity illuminating James's satire in, say, the world of the faith-healers of *The Bostonians*. There is no more poignant—or withering —moment in the whole marvellously sustained *nouvelle* than when the Captain, grateful to the girl for her intelligent interventions on his behalf, chats with her after office hours in Hyde Park. She admits that she has yet to eat her supper. 'Then you haven't eaten——?' asks the Captain, so unaware of the daily habits of clerks that she has to reassure him: 'Yes, we do feed once.' She knows that he, for all the services she has done him, could never possibly say 'Then sup with *me!*' She fibs: 'I'm not a bit hungry.' To which the irresistible Captain, in words which revive memories of the bomb-throwing co-conspirators of little Hyacinth, replies with the utmost amiability: 'Ah, you *must* be, awfully!'

Before the turn of the century, James threw off three more tales of the marriage-market, all more or less unsavoury; but the un-pleasantness attaches to the prying prigs and not to the imputed sinners. *The Given Case* (1898) is a tedious inconclusive sketch of crossed affections, as artificial as the lovers' quartet in *A Midsummer Night's Dream* but without the excuse of fairies and love-philtres. Two couples in 'high society' are in love: but one of the ladies is already married to a bounder and the other is engaged to a negligent absentee, so the importunate suitors are alike lured on by the females' fickleness but thwarted by their 'safety' in abiding by the con-ventional rules. One of the love-sick gentlemen complains: 'There's only one thing for *any* woman to do ... when she has drawn a man on to believe there's nothing she's not ready for ... It's simply to do everything!' But the ardour on the male side is as unconvincing as the virtue on the female side; the marriage-vow of the one holds, and the plighted troth of the other is broken, but in each case the guilty wooing has been so tepidly conducted through third parties that the outcome is of no moment.

The Great Condition (1899) is slightly less ludicrous in construction, being based upon a version of trust rather than upon a vexation of second-best solutions wrested from prior entanglements. Again

James reveals the seamy side of Victorian pruderies about female virtue: what dreadful licence are these frail ladies imagined by the virtuous to be indulging, the moment the eye of society is *not* fixed on their every waking movement? In *The Great Condition*, two shipboard philanderers make a play for the fascinating Mrs. Damerel, who gives herself finally to the one who is *not* prying into the presumed secrets of her 'past'. The first man, Bertram Braddle, knows so little of her 'past' that he feels she must have a secret. His rival remarks: 'You seem to me to see her as a column of figures each in itself highly satisfactory, but which, when you add them up, make only a total of doubt.' 'That's exactly it!' replied the other— 'She really hasn't *any* references.' He cannot bring himself to marry her in ignorance, but her own 'great condition' is that she will only reveal whatever her 'secret' is, six months after her marriage. As he confides to his rival, Henry Chilver: 'Where did you ever discover that being in love makes a searching light, makes anything but a most damnable and demoralizing darkness? One has been in love with creatures such that one's condition has lighted nothing in the world but one's asininity.' He will not accept Mrs. Damerel's condition, but sets off to ferret things out for himself. During his absence, Chilver, who is prepared to shelve his own suspicions and take the lady on trust, marries her. Bertram returns empty-handed but still desperately curious. Although it is now fifteen months since her marriage, Chilver has not asked for his wife's 'secret'. Bertram learns from his rival's wife that there never *had* been a secret. He himself had failed the test she prescribed when his own lack of trust became apparent to her. She forbids him to reveal the truth of her 'innocence' to her husband, whose own married happiness so largely rests on a sense of his trust and generosity in not asking her about an imputed 'past' which he, no less than Bertram himself, did undoubtedly suspect. As the triumphant lady remarks to Bertram: 'His sacrifice is his idea. And his idea...is his happiness.' James's amused contempt for these high- and dirty-minded gentlemen would place him, yet again, in the undeclared ranks of Feminist supporters.

Most unsavoury of all is *Paste* (1899, in which prurience is conquered only by greed. Mrs. Leavis (*Scrutiny* XIV, 223) considered it 'an adaptation of one of Maupassant's slickest stories, and ... hardly less shallow than its model'; but it out-Maupassants

Maupassant by exposing the squalid-moral truth that when the chips are down, a naked cupidity is stronger even than self-protective hypocrisy. The plot is swiftly set in motion: on the death of his step-mother, an ex-actress, Arthur Prime allows his female cousin to select one item from the load of stage-jewellery she had accumulated in her earlier career. The girl picks out some 'paste' pearls so lifelike that she judges them, and later knows them, to be the genuine article. Honourably, she returns them to Arthur. The pious stepson, wondering how an ex-actress could ever have acquired real pearls, jumps to the conclusion that the revelation could only tarnish the dead woman's (and hence his own) reputation—how *did* actresses of no great merit acquire real pearls? But this same prudish stepson, having regained what he considers to be the incriminating evidence, is greedy enough to sell the pearls, while swearing to the cheated cousin that he has merely destroyed the paste ones he still swears them to be. As so often in these tales, the professionally virtuous are exposed as utterly fraudulent and the 'decent' people (in this case, the girl cousin) as selfless ninnies. Only the older woman who counsels the girl to keep the pearls for herself, one of James's innumerable versions of the Madame Merle-type competent wordly woman with 'the face of a baby and the authority of a commodore', manages for a brief instant to win the reader's assent. In a world of moral liars, the accomplished teller of fibs is king.

The first year of a new century had found James in anything but a forward-looking mood. He was prolific but regretful. His 'art' stories of this period, already noted, are gloomily defeatist, as in *Broken Wings* or *The Abasement of the Northmores*. Of the social tales first printed in 1900, the best that can be said is that they demonstrate the depth of the trough from which he was to climb, so triumphantly, with the three great masterpieces of 1902–4. A possible regret for past emotional cowardice combined with a certain revulsion from the present heaviness of middle age to produce, in *Maud-Evelyn* and *The Special Type* (1900), two peculiarly mawkish variations on the theme of avoiding wedlock. In the first, a young man is 'adopted' by an old couple who are brooding over their dead daughter, Maud-Evelyn. He falls into their emotional clutches and in return for their material protection he is accepted as their 'son-in-law', pretending to be the spouse of a still-living Maud-Evelyn who had in fact died in childhood. As he himself complacently puts it, 'they couldn't like me so much ... without wanting me to have been the man'. For this safe marriage of necrophilic fantasy, he neglects the young woman who is in love with him and shares his incredible secret. Even the living figures in this stuffy fantasy of escape from life's obligations seem half-dead: the girl's parents, so sentimentally greedy, are a 'plain, shy couple, who were sensitive to the wrong things and whose sincerity and fidelity, as well as their tameness and twaddle, were of a rigid, antique pattern'. Their make-believe son-in-law grows 'fat' on their bounty until, dying not long after them, he in turn passes on their inheritance as a consolation prize to the living girl he had failed to marry. Beside this make-believe union with a dead child, the poor lady in *The Special Type* who is fobbed off with a mere portrait instead of a living husband seems comparatively sane. A new note in this latter tale is the increasing tolerance of divorce among the turn-of-the-century devotees of the high life: the sad semi-professional 'friend' of the wealthy Frank Brivet desired his portrait as a keepsake because she had 'never seen him alone', although she had pretended in public to be his mistress, thus giving him the technical freedom to shed his wife (who had a candidate in the wings) in order to marry a third lady, also married. With the new century, at least, marriage was no longer quite so frighteningly irrevocable.

The Two Faces (1900) is a small anecdote of jealous revenge on the part of a lady who had hoped to ensnare Lord Gwyther for herself but instead is asked by him, as a favour, to steer through 'the great labyrinth' of social London the little innocent wife he has brought home with him from Germany. Swallowing her pride, the jilted lady offers to befriend the new Lady Gwyther, selecting her outfit of clothes for her first grand appearance in English society at a house-party at Burbeck. Burbeck is one of those vast houses where afternoon tea is 'almost an incident of grand opera. One of the beautiful women might quite have been expected to rise with a gold cup and a celebrated song'. Its high-born guests seem, at any rate, to have discarded the old maxim that servants talk about people while gentlefolk discuss things, for they are all agog to appraise little Lady Gwyther. Her clothes, selected with loving hate by her official protectress, damn her—we are to suppose—for ever in their eyes: she appears, pathetically, 'overloaded like a monkey in a show'. Her pretty little face shows 'scared or sick' among the feathers and excrescences; the face of her rival glows with sadistic triumph. It is a quick sketch of the vile fury of envy. The implication that the crowd at Burbeck are universally deceived by superficial trappings is, however, an even nastier comment on social life: but in this particular trifle it merely falsifies the story without being developed into substantial satiric purpose. Far more successful as a savage mockery of the hypocritical double standards of the social set is *Mrs. Medwin* (1902), a well constructed four-part morality farce. Mamie Cutter is an American who keeps herself by 'introducing' tarnished ladies into society, in which she has preserved an impregnable little niche. Mrs. Medwin buys, for a fee, a place at a tea-party graced by the formidable Lady Wantridge, whose word is social law. But the official forgiveness of Mrs. Medwin's social lapses comes about only because Miss Cutter's disreputable half-brother happens to have intrigued Lady Wantridge, and the presence there of Mrs. Medwin is Mamie Cutter's price for steering down to Catchmore, for the amusements of Lady Wantridge's blasé guests, a bounder who is entertaining as an American and also, it is hinted, as a gigolo. As the young man remarks: 'The bigger bugs they are the more they're on the look-out ... for anything that will help them to live ... They're dead, don't you see? And we're alive.' He will provide, in short, the sexual excitement which is a counterpart to the artistic creativity provided, in *Broken Wings*, by society's other fee-taking mountebanks, the artists. As for Lady Wantridge herself, the self-appointed St. Peter at the gates of polite society: 'she was no younger, no fresher, no stronger, really, than any of them; she was only, with a kind of haggard fineness, a sharpened taste for life, and with all sorts of things behind and beneath her, more abysmal and more immoral, more secure and more impertinent'. James objected not so much to rigid moral and social standards as to the pretence of them when they did not exist. One is reminded of Proust, of the comment (in *Cities of the Plain*) that 'there is no vice that does not find ready support in the best society, and one has seen a country house turned upside down in order that'—and there follows the report of an accommodation of Lesbian incest that makes the arrangements of James's Edwardian house-parties seem positively squeamish. As Proust again remarked, in a sentence quoted by Mr. Milton Hindus,* 'for the distinguishing characteristic of this social set was its prodigious aptitude at wiping out social classifications'. The context is the great reception of the Princesse de Guermantes—herself, of all people, the former Madame Verdurin. It is not so far off, in time or place, from the corrupt hypocrisies of a late-Roman-Empire Catchmore, where a Mrs. Medwin can be reinstated for the price of a new gladiator.

If in his tales of the marriage-market James grew more maudlin in his search for alternatives to direct passion, and more wearily sated with the false values of a second-rate social set aping first-rate standards, there remained some factors in the general social scene which continued to stimulate him to full-blooded active engagement. Chief among them was his long-sustained dislike of the popular press and even more of those who lowered themselves to seek its publicity. It is a relief to turn, for a moment, from stories of negative emotions and social cheatings to another of James's direct onslaughts on the world of publicity as an identifiable, tangible evil—an onslaught in which negative impulses are released, for a change, in tones of positive rather than merely passive disgust. Thus, although of the three stories dated 1903, *The Birthplace* and *The Beast in the Jungle* are better known and more frequently quoted, it is the vigorous crusading ardour of the story *The Papers* that revives James's prose and reminds the reader of such far-off freshness as the satirical portrait of Mathias Pardon of *The Bostonians* or the funniest excesses of *The Reverberator*. The involved and contrived plot concerns the manoeuvres of Sir A. B. C. Beadel-Muffet, K.C.B., M.P., who is always publicized as being 'distinguished' although he has accomplished absolutely nothing, and the dramatist Mortimer Marshal who pines away for lack of publicity and makes pathetic attempts to attract it. Of far greater interest is James's considerate and sympathetic portrait of two young professional journalists, male and female. He catches to perfection their professionalism, their poverty, their youth, their sense of superiority to their bread-and-butter job; they are as lively, in their Edwardian Fleet Street dive, as a couple of young television producers relaxing in a coffee-bar after a bad

*A Reader's Guide to Marcel Proust, 1962.

bout with publicity-hounds. Their bright young integrity, the reader is made to feel, deserves a better reward than the 'small table, swabbed like the deck of a steam-packet, nose-to-nose with a mustard-pot and a price-list', where they meet to comfort one another that they are, somehow, better than their squalid trade allows. On the business side of the press there are the bright young professional slaves climbing their ladder:

... their novitiate seemed to them interminable and the steps of their ladder fearfully far apart. It rested—the ladder—against the great stony wall of the public attention—a sustaining mass which apparently wore somewhere, in the upper air, a big, thankless, expressionless face, a countenance equipped with eyes, ears, an uplifted nose and a gaping mouth—all convenient if they could only be reached. The ladder groaned meanwhile, swayed and shook with the weight of the close-pressed climbers, tier upon tier, occupying the upper, the middle, the nethermost rounds and quite preventing, for young persons placed as our young friends were placed, any view of the summit.

On the parasitic side are such puffed-up frauds as Beadel-Muffet:

He was universal and ubiquitous, commemorated, under some rank rubric, on every page of every public print every day in every year, and as inveterate a feature of each issue of any self-respecting sheet as the name, the date, the tariffed advertisements. He had always done some-thing, or was about to do something, round which the honours of announcement clustered, and indeed, as he had inevitably thus become a subject of fallacious report, one half of his chronicle appeared to consist of official contradiction of the other half.

Serving both groups, the submerged anonymous drudges of London who had no hope of climbing any professional ladder:

These talks over greasy white slabs, repeatedly mopped with moist grey cloths by young women in black uniforms, with inexorable braided 'buns' in the nape of weak necks, these sessions, sometimes prolonged in halls of oilcloth, among penal-looking tariffs and pyramids of scones, enabled them to rest on their oars; the more that they were on terms with the whole families, chartered companies, of food-stations, each a race of innumerable and indistinguishable members, and had mastered those hours of comparative elegance, the earlier and the later, when the little weary ministrants were limply sitting down and the occupants of the red benches bleakly interspaced.

It is in passages such as these that a tale like *The Papers* glows with life. At times, even the old extravagance of physical exaggeration is revived, as when Beadel-Muffet's daughters, ready and ripe for a new generation of publicity, are caricatured by the long-suffering reporters as 'hurtling through the air, clubbed by the paternal hand, like golf-balls in a suburb'. Once again James emerges, from behind the creaking machinery of his plot, as a first-class essayist in social commentary. And *how* his own memories of his brief journalistic excursions in Paris must have rankled! We find him repeating, yet again, after nearly thirty years, the injured joke with which he had sought to make his own New York editor blush: his young male journalist is made to say to his girl-friend 'we do the worst we can for the money'. The girl herself, type of the new 'emancipated' career-woman, partakes of the sympathy James always nourished for competent underpaid female professionals.

Better rounded, no doubt, as a *nouvelle*, but much inferior to *The Papers* in vigour, is the literary parable *The Birthplace*. A dim, failed but infinitely refined pair, Mr. and Mrs. Morris Gedge, are promoted from a 'grey town-library . . . all granite, fog and female fiction', to become the custodians of the shrine of the National Poet, as it were at Stratford-on-Avon. Disgusted by the commercial phoneyness of the place itself and of the insensitive tourists who gawp at it while leaving the Poet unread, Gedge perseveres with his flowery guide's patter and is suitably rewarded by a committee of high-minded sponsors who are as insensitive as the mobs to whom he prostitutes his own love of the Poet. Another of the vaguely 'artistic' tales that may best be grouped among James's social parables is *The Story in It* (1902). 'A picture of life founded on the mere reserves and omissions and suppressions of life, what sort of performance—for beauty, for interest, for tone—could *that* hope to be?'—this is the question James asked himself, rhetorically, when he came to comment on this tale in his Prefaces; and although he himself found an answer, most readers will merely echo the question. For the parable seeks to embody in a short story the truth that a reticent lady who nourishes a silent passion for an extrovert gentleman is likely to gain 'a small scared starved subjective satisfaction, that could do her no harm and nobody else any good'. The extrovert gentleman and the literate but more enterprising widow who satisfies him both agree that although the passive lady may be their moral superior, she is poor meat for fiction. James, of all people, must have known that this superficial conclusion was absurdly untrue! But it was in the great novels of 1902-4, of course, and not in this marginal and dispirited contemporaneous diagram, that he was to prove it.

Passivity, as an evil almost as absolute as accidie, forms the basis of *The Beast in the Jungle* (1903), with which is linked one of James's last tales, *The Bench of Desolation* (1910). There is something inescapably personal about James's confession, in *The Beast in the Jungle*, that the ravaging maiming anguish in a man's life consists not in what a man does, but in what he has failed to do; not in his sins of commission, but his sins of omission. On the surface, it is an unpleasant parable in which the abominable mental selfishness of a man is matched with the almost equally abominable mental docility of a woman. John Marcher is haunted by an unknown fear that something dreadful will happen to him. spring out at him like a beast in the jungle. His female friend May Bartram learns and shares this obsession, and for years her solicitude forms the basis of their close intimacy, allowing him to enjoy her comforting interest without any obligation on his part. After some years, she tells him that *she* has divined the awful thing that is to happen to him, but that he doesn't—and, moreover, that 'it' has already happened. She dies. Marcher wanders forlorn, and returning later to her grave, he realizes that his 'beast' was simply the lack of the power to love. She had loved him, but he was incapable of returning her love. That was his curse; the great positive hurt was, after all, the essence of the negative: he was corroded, not by acid, but by alkaline quicklime. It was all, *au fond*, a matter of Marcher's recognition—like James's own—that marriage was out of the question for him. After all the dodges and tricks of the earlier tales, this one simply admits, with safe graveyard sobbings after the death of the un-accepted wife, the woe of loneliness. In *The Bench of Desolation*, the weakness, timidity and frustration of the pale and passive hero are more wretched still, for instead of collapsing on a tombstone, he is disinflated, with even less credit, upon a long-rejected female bosom. The legend is even simpler. Kate Cookham threatens to bring a breach of promise action against Herbert Dodd, a poor effete bookseller. He pays over money to her and she absconds. He marries another woman, who dies. Years later, Kate returns with a larger sum of money: she has 'made it' for him—that is all she ever wanted it for. She comes back, *dea ex machina*, to take care of him. In both tales, James was writing with a hypnotic skill that could turn an essentially selfish *cri de coeur* into a cry of the doom of humanity itself. But they are morbid masturbatory minor achievements which might have bolstered the reputation of a lesser Edwardian effeteness, but add nothing to the stature of a novelist who, in *The Wings of the Dove* and *The Ambassadors* and *The Golden Bowl*, could strike a tragic, and not merely a pathetic, chord from the minor keys of withdrawal and abnegation.

Abnegation and rejection, together with a deepening disgust for the social world upon which he had squandered so much time and talent, are the keynotes of James's remaining tales. Some of them, like *The Jolly Corner* already noted in Chapter I, would draw for their background on Henry James's refreshed impressions of America, revisited in 1904–5 and reported in the last of his substantial travel books, *The American Scene* (1907); but the selfishness of the social heart would seem to him as complete in New York as in London or Paris. *Fordham Castle* (1904) reduces the inane frenzies of social climbing to the proportions of sheer farce, with characters of almost subhuman lack of integrity willing to obliterate their own and their families' personality, in the wild scramble after appearances at the right houses. Abel Taker's wife, seeking a social success quite unattainable to the bearer of *that* name, leaves her husband in a Swiss pension while she seeks to scale the social ladder of London. He, acting 'dead', meets at his pension a Mrs. Vanderplank (whose real name is Mrs. Magaw) who is lying doggo in a similar attempt to aid her daughter's advance up the same greasy pole of social acceptance. The Magaw daughter and Mrs. Taker, under their assumed names of Miss Vanderplank and Mrs. Sherrington Reeves, meet at the top of the pile at Fordham Castle. Mattie Magaw gets engaged to her young peer and is now so safe that Mrs. Magaw may be summoned to join her. Abel Taker remains, now genuinely extinct at the departure of his sympathetic friend. There is absurdity in the coincidental meeting of two people who have both sacrificed themselves in the semi-suicide of non-entity; but the life of the tale, as so often, is confined to James's marginal expressions of loathing for his tasteless frauds. There is, for instance, a world of emotional distance between the 'design, partly architectural, partly botanical, executed in the hair of Miss Pynsent's parents', decorating that dear lady's bower in *The Princess Casamassima*, and the 'mathematical hair' of poor Mrs. Magaw, which reminded Abel Taker of 'the old-fashioned "work", the weeping willows and mortuary urns represented by the little glazed-over flaxen or sable or silvered convolutions and tendrils, the capillary flowers, that he had admired in the days of his innocence . . .' Abel Taker is as abjectly masochistic a failure as James ever drew:

It kept coming back to him, naturally, that he hadn't the breadth of fancy, that he knew himself as he knew the taste of ill-made coffee, that he was the same old Abel Taker he had ever been, in whose aggregation of items it was as vain to feel about for latent heroisms as it was useless to rummage one's trunk for presentable clothes that one didn't possess.

His one last pleasure is a wry glee at the completeness of his sacrifice to his awful wife: when she sails into Fordham Castle under her new assumed name, he reflects that as mere Mrs. Taker 'she had to die to go—as it would be for her like going to heaven'. But for him there is no social resurrection. His last curiously contented comment is: 'Why certainly I'm dead'. The prose and setting of such a tale may be 'late Henry James', but we are perilously near the brink of the world of raw cannibalism exposed by Tennessee Williams's story *Desire and the Black Masseur*.

By 1908, the date of *Julia Bride*, the relative ease of divorce—in America, at least—had opened up, for writers of James's temperament, fictional possibilities as squalid as the earlier horrors of irrevocable union. In the Preface to this tale, he jeers outright at the slackening of his countrymen's conventions, not only in marriage but also in pre-marital experimentation: 'the large juvenile licence as to getting "engaged", disengaged and re-engaged . . .' It is an unpleasant tale, wrapping up radically novelette-ish motives in extravagantly oblique language. Poor Julia's life is made almost impossible, in strait-laced society, by 'her own six engagements and her mother's three nullified marriages—nine nice distinct little horrors in all'. She wants Mr. Pitman, second in the sequence of her mother's ex-husbands, to tell a lie about her mother's marital innocence, in order to remove from the mind of Mr. French, her own seventh and richest and most respectable fiancé, any fear of marrying the daughter of so notorious a divorcée. ' "So if I could hear from you that you just made her life a hell—why,' Julia concluded, "it would be too lovely".' But Mr. Pitman, in turn, is waiting to get engaged to a millionaire widow, and requires that Julia should paint *him* in innocent colours and stress her mother's flightiness. Julia obligingly throws the mud in the required direction. Still further coils of selfishness wind about Julia when one of her own ex-fiancés, now engaged to another girl, proposes to her that *they* will clear her own compromised reputation to Mr. French, her seventh and current swain, and she grasps that all they really want from this offer is the chance to be introduced to the Frenches, who represent the ultimate summit of the whole Babbit-like social pyramid. These odious proliferations of suspicions and treacheries are conveyed in language at times almost incomprehensible. It is, to take a thoroughly representative sentence, difficult to summon up much interest in a heroine so miz mazed by the 'plot' and so obliquely presented: 'She was so far from doubtful that she was but too appalled at it and at the officious mass in which it loomed, and this instinct of dread, before their walk was over, before she had guided him round to one of the smaller gates, there to slip off again by herself, was positively to find on the bosom of her flood a plank under aid of which she kept in a manner and for the time afloat'. It is as if James's distaste, by this time, is almost physically inhibiting his faculty of communication.

If poor Julia was overwhelmed with relationships and glutted with courtships, the girl who gives her name to *Mora Montravers* (1909) seems to point the moral that the kindest thing one can do for one's relations and dependents is to leave them severely alone. For when she runs off to live with an artist, her aunt and uncle seek to save her skin by offering the presumed lovers an annuity if only they will become conventionally married. Having thus secured her painter an income, Mora thereupon quits him. Uncle Traffle had presumably been right, after all, when he assured his rigid wife that whereas they themselves enjoyed 'the sense of decency', it was the outrageous Mora who 'has tremendously the sense of life'. Guessing that Mora's desire to share a roof with her painter is in fact purely platonic, Traffle makes to his wife, in their respectable Wimbledon home, the point that in their own respectability 'only one kind of irregularity is possible', simply because they lack the imagination to offend against convention in any other way. The fancy they *do* adopt, however, is quite incredible: namely, to go on paying the painter his comfortable income even after Mora has deserted him for another man. The bemused, trance-like behaviour of the Traffles is unfolded in prose of such viscosity that the reader has to struggle through sentences that no parodist of James would dare invent, and no guide, however conscientious, wish to quote.

It was convenient to treat *The Jolly Corner* as a pendant to the introductory survey of James as a young novelist writing in America. The second work of art arising directly from that return visit of 1904–5 was the beautifully controlled tale *Crapy Cornelia* (1909). Here, the accent is so much on the quality of the *present* James's sixty-six-year-old assessment of his boyhood city of New York that it may more usefully be displayed as a prime example of how, at its best, his mastery of 'the art of the *nouvelle*' was made complete by— so to say—external correlatives, by the distancing and discriminations of an essayist in fiction. The contrast with *Mora Montravers* is extreme, and instructive. There, a wholly contrived 'plot' did nothing to save the story from a mawkish and glutinous tone of querulous fumbling, made manifest in a prose style deadened by the conditional mood and by the sad emotional sheaths which the real organic feelings of the characters had, somehow, sloughed off in their escape from the whole atmosphere and *milieu* of their own story. Here, in *Crapy Cornelia*, the sad hero's equally sardonic view of life and of himself is made vivid because of the freshness of his observations on life *outside* himself. The difference between the self-loathing abnegatory urges of a Traffle (*Mora Montravers*) or an Abel Taker (*Fordham Castle*) and the no less unattractive figure of

White-Mason of *Crapy Cornelia* is simply the difference between sickness and health in the mind of their creator. Henry James *was*, in these declining years of his life, subject to moods of physical and mental depression. It was when his jaundiced observation was switched from himself to the world in which he moved, that the old flame was rekindled; one returns to a re-reading of *Crapy Cornelia* not in order to subside into the emotional cowardice of White-Mason, but to share the vigorously intelligent appraisal of the world around him which even such a maimed character—and this is the real point of the tale—can still legitimately make. His, for all his Traffle-like or Taker-like unattractiveness as a personality, is a quality of sharp observation like that of Strether in *The Ambassadors*. His 'story' may reflect the gloomy regrets of a Henry James plagued by the sour loneliness of a man who has rejected first-hand living; but his plight is presented within a credible objective healthy competence of judgement created by James the intelligent artist and the still amazingly energetic social critic.

The stew-in-one's-own-juice plot may be stated in a sentence: selfish dilettante New Yorker White-Mason decides to propose to rich, bright modern Mrs. Worthingham, but meeting at her house Cornelia Rasch, an old dim female friend, he prefers to sit with the latter discussing old and better New York days; and being assured of a permanent echo for his memories, is content to marry neither lady. The reasons for the rejection of Mrs. Worthingham and the selection of 'crapy' Cornelia as a confidante are presented as being entirely aesthetic—aesthetic, that is, with the normal Jamesian connotation of the richest flowering of the moral sense. This naturally has the effect, since the presumed emotions of the two ladies are also involved, of making White-Mason himself seem a callous cold-blooded figure. Indeed, with the real life of the tale confined to White-Mason's social-aesthetic assessments, there seems no real reason why James should have cast the material in fictional form at all: it is a lively essay through which a few half-dead figures loom for purely diagrammatic effect. White-Mason's consciousness is so completely his author's own that its presentation might have come straight from the autobiographical volumes James was now planning: 'The high pitch of interest, to his taste, was the pitch of history, the pitch of acquired and earned suggestion, the pitch of association, in a word; so that he lived by preference, incontestably, if not in a rich gloom, which would have been beyond his means and spirits, at least amid objects and images that confessed to the tone of time.' Utterly Jamesian, too, is the recoil of such a man from 'that gloss of new money' in the vulgar home and affluent world of Mrs. Worthingham, the 'new' New Yorker, with 'every particular expensive object shrieking at him in its artless pride that it had just "come home".' Like Lambert Strether half hypnotized by and half longing to escape from Mrs. Newsome of *The Ambassadors*, White-Mason shrinks from the Worthingham *milieu* which

seemed to reflect as never before the lustre of Mrs. Worthingham's own polished and prosperous little person—to smile, it struck him, with her smile, to twinkle not only with the gleam of her lovely teeth, but with that of all her rings and brooches and bangles and other gew-gaws, to curl and spasmodically cluster as in emulation of her charming complicated yellow tresses, to surround the most animated of pink-and-white, of ruffled and ribboned, of frilled and festooned Dresden china shepherdesses with exactly the right system of curves and convolutions and other flourishes, a perfect bower of painted and gilded and moulded conceits.

His affronted eyes fall restfully upon the figure of her other guest— a person at first ludicrously out of place in so brash an atmosphere of social success ('. . . this oddly unassertive little rotund figure whom one seemed no more obliged to address than if she had been a black satin ottoman "treated" with buttons and gimp; a class of object as to which the policy of blindness was imperative'), but soon to be valued as a living reminder of what seems to him in retrospect to have been the better taste and certainly the more storied and peopled world of his youth. He sums it up in the private judgement that 'Mrs. Worthingham had no data', whereas Cornelia was 'a massive little bundle of data'. Cornelia's modestly framed photographs, in her flat, may at first satisfy him as decently tasteful in contrast with Mrs. Worthingham's 'swaggering reproductions', but what he really values them for is a soothing nostalgia expressed in a phrase that might have come, in all its exactness of emotional shading, from James's autobiographical *A Small Boy and Others*: if these 'faithfully framed but spectrally faded' photographs did not possess 'the tone of time, the secret for warding and easing off the perpetual immanent ache of one's protective scowl, one would verily but have to let the scowl stiffen or take up seriously the question of blue goggles, during what remains of life'. This has the ring of the disillusioned and miraculously revived Proust of the last symphonic passages of *Remembrance of Things Past*—Cornelia's photographs having all the effect of the famous 'little *madeleine*'.

But if White-Mason is battered enough to wish to subside into a storied past (which at the time might well have been viewed, by a person of his present age and spirits, as equally lacking in 'data'), his critical nose for false values in life as in art is as keen as ever it was. It is the inanely ignorant 'knowingness' of Mrs. Worthingham and her set that really offends him: 'She was "up" to everything, aware of everything if one counted from a short enough time back (from the week before last, say, and as if quantities of history had burst upon the world within the fortnight) . . .' And bound up with that vulgar lack of perspective there is—inevitably, for James's perception —its accompanying and more horrible moral flaw, a crack in the gilded-over bowl that brings from him an outburst something like sheer sermonizing: 'In *his* time, when he was young or even when he was only but a little less middle-aged, the best manners had been the best kindness, and the best kindness had mostly been some art of not insisting on one's luxurious differences, of concealing rather, for common humanity, if not for common decency, a part at least of the intensity or the ferocity with which one might be "in the know".' Yet a moral intelligence so keen had cohabited, in White-Mason as in his so clearly autobiographical author, with an emotional cowardice so craven as to be pinned down, by that same keen intelligence, with an image of brutal self-criticism: 'He had hesitated like an ass erect on absurd hind legs between two bundles of hay . . .' For once, one feels positive that in this bloody *and* bowed posture the writer, in the still unassailed bravery of his art, is speaking direct from his own heart. 'You are not Cornelia, but I am very much White-Mason', wrote Henry James to an old female friend who had grasped the essence of the story. The full scale of James's own titanic weariness, the degree to which he had been worn down by (in Percy Lubbock's fine phrase) 'the wear and tear of discrimination', may be grasped by those readers who recall that it was at this precise period that the proud ageing Master began to embark upon a flirtatious correspondence and relationship with, of all people in the world, the young Hugh Walpole.*

The last of all James's tales, *A Round of Visits* (1910), points the jaded social moral that nobody is really interested in anybody else. The skeleton of the plot, dealing with the crudest possible form of human duplicity, namely the confidence tricks practised by financial cheats, merely articulates and animates a story which in its full flesh is a distressed recognition of vulgar self-interest as the main or only spring of human activity in human society. Mark Monteith revisits New York to rescue what can be saved from the financial speculation of his trusted friend Phil Bloodgood. He visits several other friends for comfort, but they all have their own worries, especially Newton Winch, who keeps his visitor talking until the police arrive, and then commits suicide as Monteith admits them to his room: for Winch has also, it seems, been involved in scandals which are but modern society's organized professionalization of greed and theft. As Ford Madox Ford remarked, Monteith 'had penetrated into a world so corrupted by money that the only escape seemed to be by violence'. But the cheated trusting Monteith is hurt less by robbery than by his new consciousness of a coarseness of grain inhibiting human sympathy: 'so decidedly, by the morning's end, and that of his scattered sombre stations, had he been sated with meaningless contacts, with the sense of people all about him intensely, though harmlessly animated, yet at the same time raspingly indifferent'. 'Your nerves have needed company', Mark bursts out to Newton Winch in deep understanding, just before that wretched man blows his brains out. Yet it is Winch, and not Monteith, who cannot stand the strain. And at the very end of the long cycle of social tales one is left with the one minimal certainty that remains, the one nugget of truth that has resisted and survived, in Henry James's vicarious exposure to the social world in which he himself had figured to the superficial as a bland success, every disappointment and every disillusion—the truth that for ever and in all circumstances, it is more blessed to be deceived than to deceive.

*See Rupert Hart-Davis's *Hugh Walpole* (1952).

X

The Wings of the Dove

(with a note on *The Other House*)

> Her voice was ever soft,
> Gentle and low, an excellent thing in
> woman.
>
> *King Lear*

I HAPPEN, personally, to feel that if *The Wings of the Dove* (1902) is not James's masterpiece (though it seems to me to demonstrate his powers and his weaknesses on the grandest scale), it does undoubtedly contain passages, such as Milly Theale's solitary musing in Regent's Park after she has been in effect condemned to death by her doctor, which combine verbal beauty and psychological penetration to a degree not surpassed by this novelist—or, to my mind, by any other. This finest single flowering of James's genius must be esteemed as a novel of character rather than of situation, and yet its construction is so elaborate and so highly regarded by the author that it demands very careful attention. To comfort those readers who do not share my view, I recall that in *The Georgian Literary Scene* Mr. Frank Swinnerton found in this novel 'no redeeming features', while Mr. Maxwell Geismar denies its greatness on the grounds that 'all our major novels do bear on human destiny, while this one concerns itself with human day-dreams of a very special order'.

My view that the novel shows a triumph of living character over a successful construction may be illustrated by a preliminary glance at one of the novels of the 'social' group (it was published between *The Spoils of Poynton* and *What Maisie Knew*), in which a very similar situation overshadows the characters and points the useful moral that a good *dramatic* construction is not necessarily a good basis for a novel. Indeed, to select *The Other House* (1896) for complementary reference is almost to invite the charge of cheating, for as Dr. Edel pointed out in his introduction to the 1948 reprint, it was 'first written as a play-scenario under the title of *The Promise*, turned into a novel and then, after the lapse of more than a decade, reconverted into a play'. James found the work of dramatization 'ferociously difficult', but he makes it plain (in a letter of 1909 which contains some admirable good sense on plays in general) that the problem is not a matter of dramatic form but of human credibility: 'If I can go on *believing in* my subject I can go on treating it; but sometimes I have a mortal chill and wonder if I ain't damnably deluded.' In the event, *The Other House* is a disappointing novel of the middle period, a stage play sketchily cast in novel form by plentiful admixture of the James 'style'—and by no means his best. His old propensity to melodrama had returned in full force, and a bare outline of the plot will indicate the full domination of situation over character in a manner miraculously overcome by the author of *The Wings of the Dove:*

Tony Bream gave his wife Julia a deathbed promise that he would not marry again during the lifetime of their little daughter, Effie. The sudden death of Julia was entirely unexpected, but it is assumed throughout that Tony's promise, given in a spirit of an almost lighthearted humouring of the whim of an invalid, is morally binding. (This, more than any subsequent extravagance, is the real weakness in the motivation of the plot; in *The Wings of the Dove* a somewhat similar treatment of an invalid's desires is made credible by the credibility of the characters themselves.) Rose Armiger, Julia's friend, is staying with the Breams at the time of the exacted promise, and just before Julia's death Rose rejects the proposal of Dennis Vidal, who has been seeking her hand for a long while. The widower is now the object of the veiled attentions of Rose, and also of Jean Martle, the young friend of his neighbour, Mrs. Beever. Jean Martle rejects the hand of Paul, Mrs. Beever's son, who has proposed to her at the instance of his domineering mother, but who is in fact in love with Rose.

An interval elapses (it is significant that in writing a précis of the narrative, the conventions of the stage come so easily to mind), and we find the main characters assembled in Mrs. Beever's garden at Eastmead, divided from Tony's house by a bridge over a stream. Rose hints to Tony that Jean might do an injury to little Effie in order to remove the obstacle to her marrying him. Unseen by the others, Rose takes Effie across the bridge. The child is found drowned. Rose meanwhile has told the others that Jean was last seen with the child. Tony, distraught, thinks Jean has been guilty, and publicly confesses that he himself was responsible for the child's death. Dennis Vidal, home from China whither he repaired after his dismissal by Rose, has secretly seen Rose and Effie on the bridge together. In a scene of some obliquity, Rose shares with him her guilty secret. Still loving her, although appalled by her callousness, he promises to protect her. He will take her away, and announce that they are to be married.

A family council, played out in twos and threes on the stage with the assistance of the family doctor, tacitly agrees that the whole affair be hushed up. The murderess, in failing to implicate Jean, has in fact made it possible for Jean to marry Tony. A parting interview reveals that Paul, too, would have shielded the guilty woman, if asked. She leaves with Dennis. The curtain descends on a rueful admission by Tony that the tragedy has been due to the unfortunate fact that people 'like him too much':

'I mean you'll have such a pull. You'll meet nothing but sympathy.'
Tony looked indifferent and uncertain; but his optimism finally assented. 'I daresay I shall get on. People perhaps won't challenge me.'
'They like you too much.'
Tony, with his hand on the door, appeared struck with this; but it embittered again the taste of his tragedy. He remembered with all his vividness to what tune he had been 'liked', and he wearily bowed his head. 'Oh, too much, Paul!' he sighed as he went out.

All this would have made a passable *drama*, but it fails as a novel. In *The Wings of the Dove*, a contrived and potentially melodramatic theme is made credible because James concentrates on personality, near-perfect though the careful elaboration of plot may be. In *The Other House*, where the accent is on situation, the whole thing is a sham—or if considered seriously, then distinctly unpleasant.

There are, of course, as in everything James wrote, flashes of the novelist in the sketches of minor characters. Mrs. Beever, 'like an odd volume, "sensibly" bound, of some old magazine', is one of a long series of self-possessed matrons with a store of worldly wisdom and astringent valuations: 'Mrs. Beever had once said with regard to sending for [Dr. Ramage]: "It isn't to take his medicine, it's to take *him*. I take him twice a week in a cup of tea".' But the hero himself comes to life only at rare moments when he loses his galvanic stagey property and becomes the subject of commentary, as when it is noted that he had 'a certain quality of passive excess which was the note of the whole man and which, for an attentive eye, began with his neckties and ended with his intonations'. The other chief character, Rose Armiger, 'a person constitutionally averse to making unmeasured displays', has in her cold self-sufficiency many sisters in the earlier novels; only dimly does she adumbrate Kate Croy in *The Wings of the Dove*. Her effect on poor Dennis Vidal is not unlike that of Kate Croy on Merton Densher—a repellent fascination; but Vidal's 'sense that in a single hour she had so altered as to be ugly' is a bleak statement beside that slow change of attitude towards Kate which Densher will share only step by step with the reader, in an unfolding of character unsurpassed elsewhere by this master of the gradual revelation.

To attempt a synopsis of a major James novel, where by his own confession there is ever 'an inch of canvas to an acre of embroidery', is always difficult. From *The Wings of the Dove* one could extract something like this as the theme:

Merton Densher and Kate Croy are secretly engaged to be married, secretly because she is living with her rich and domineering Aunt Maud who has in view more distinguished game in general and a certain Lord Mark in particular. The lovers, with harmonious common sense, are content to wait until something shall turn up to render their union less inapt. One could hardly put it less indefinitely than that: Kate is prepared to jog along with an occasional meeting in the Park until they can 'square' Aunt Maud. For Densher, a poor journalist, cannot hope by his own efforts to attain to the required financial standards of Lancaster Gate.

Upon this grey but fallow scene enter two new characters: Mrs. Susie Stringham, an American, being an old school-friend of Aunt Maud's, and her younger friend Milly Theale. During a journalistic tour in the United States, Densher had met Milly in New York, where, as a notoriously rich young hostess, she had given him passing hospitality.

Sponsored by an enthusiastic Aunt Maud, Milly (a 'princess' to her devoted Mrs. Stringham, a 'dove' to her new friend Kate) becomes the success of the London season. Densher, more by his ability to 'talk America' than his relationship with Kate (for that is still their guarded secret), sees something of these ladies during their modest conquest of London. But Milly's triumph is more arranged for her by other people than enjoyed by herself.

Her health is very low and she nourishes a private melancholy. A visit to Sir Luke Strett, a distinguished and sympathetic physician, brings her some hope: she must be off at once to Venice for a change of climate and surroundings—and she must bestir herself to face life. Sir Luke perceives that she is in love, and may soon die. We, by this time, know her to be in love with Merton Densher.

So the ailing 'princess' sets up her household in the Venetian Palazzo Leporelli, the stricken 'dove' retires to balance her will to live against her destiny to die. Aunt Maud and Kate go with the party: the two younger ladies have become 'inseparable'. Merton Densher also appears in Venice, and his visits to the palace provide Milly with her only real pleasure in the gathering gloom of her unspoken malaise. Insidiously at first, and then explicitly, we have become aware that Kate is directing Densher to woo and marry the slowly dying Milly, from whom, as from everyone else, their private engagement is still concealed. Kate is prepared to wait, in fine, until the poor journalist has become a rich widower —it is thus that Aunt Maud shall be 'squared'.

We are left slightly puzzled as to the precise degree of Densher's compliance in this morbid scheme until the point when Kate has demanded from him complete trust and obedience, and in surrendering his will to hers he claims her bodily surrender. Kate and her aunt return to England, leaving Densher to provide in his loved presence Milly's last relaxing grip on life. He feels abject in his ambiguous rôle, but the beautiful reticence of Milly's behaviour supports him, and he stays.

Lord Mark, who has danced attendance on all the ladies during the London season, now appears in Venice and brings the uneasy calm to an end. He proposes to Milly, and, when not accepted (for 'rejected' would be too harsh a term for their little scene), reveals to her the true relationship between Kate and Densher. (This is done behind the scenes: the reader is made aware of the consequences, but is not made privy to the fatal part of their interview.) Apprised that he is no longer welcome—but feeling technically innocent of any mortal hurt—Densher returns to London. Left alone with her faithful Susie, Milly dies in Venice.

On Christmas Eve, Densher receives from Venice a letter in Milly's handwriting. On the same day, Kate and her aunt receive news of her death. Guessing only too clearly the contents of his own letter, realizing with shame that the dying 'dove' has made him rich so that he can marry Kate, he confronts his betrothed. There are unspoken—and spoken—recriminations. How, asks Densher, was Lord Mark, just after he had been refused by Kate, in a position to rush to Venice and, with a revealing word, end Milly's happiness and her life? He will not touch the money; the letter is burned unread. Later, legal documents from New York put the matter beyond all doubt. But for Merton Densher, now, with the memory of Milly ever before him, the fruit is too bitter. He would still marry Kate, but he will have none of the money. She will not have him without it. They part.

Doubly disconcerting, such a *résumé*. In the first place, the bare plot is indubitably nasty. It is shocking, thus baldly told, as it is never shocking in the novel itself. In the second place, the whole tone and art of the book are nowhere apparent. What one really remembers of *The Wings of the Dove* is not the plot, nor even specifically the 'parts' played by the characters, but the delicacy with which so fragile a web of human entanglement has been constructed. As a work of art, *The Wings of the Dove* is elaborately wrought, but the author's aim is the same as ever: to show the individual consciousness in its most secret development, to repeat yet again, behind a new veil of obscurity and indirectness, his impression of the hunted yet defiant spirit 'slashing out in bewilderment'. Mr. Edmund Wilson* describes the intention and achievement: 'Milly Theale, for example, is one of the best pictures of a rich New Yorker in fiction: when we have forgotten the cloudy integument through which we have been obliged to divine her we find that she remains in our mind as a personality independent of the novel, the kind of personality, deeply felt, invested with poetic beauty and unmistakably individualized, which only the creators of the first rank can give life to.'

That is partly true. But there is an error of judgement, a misplaced emphasis, rare indeed in Mr. Wilson's criticism. For it is through the medium of, and not in spite of, that cloudy integument that the character of Milly and the whole effect of the novel are

Hound and Horn, April–June, 1934. (Henry James number.)

achieved, and remembered. Once 'forgotten', the spell has vanished and the shape behind the opacity is meagre indeed. One may go further: the shape would be not only meagre but false. Henry James was not so artless as not to make proper allowances for his own apparatus of perspective and divination. The cloudy integument may indeed be between the reader and the subject, but he knew about it, and the integument is in truth a very important part of the subject. One could as reasonably complain of the bloom on a peach.

With this most important reservation made, it is helpful to go in some detail into the construction of this novel. Two points support the venture in the case of this particular novel as representing James's art at its finest.

First, the very sense of discouragement that attends an effort at paraphrase, that feeling of loss and vandalism when the matter and the form have, as it were, been prised apart—these ineptitudes have their positive contribution to one's appreciation. These first feelings of loss offer to the formal critic or to the fascinated but not quite comprehending reader perhaps the most easily localized illustration in Henry James's fiction of the creative *value* of his 'cloudy integument' (call it what one will—indirectness, opacity, timorousness, craftsmanship, squeamishness, insight, poetry, or guff, according to one's taste and mood). It is a demonstration arithmetically simple. Subtract from the prodigious total of one's impressions of the novel all that sum which may be classed under the heading of plot and narrative skill—no trivial constituent. Then the *remainder*—still ampler—falls into some other category flowering from a mature but still passionate scholarship in the field of human experience and behaviour. It is this remainder that provides a wealth of matter for appreciation. For in *The Wings of the Dove*, as Mr. Wilson has pointed out in a somewhat back-handed way, the separation indicated above is a relatively simple affair. Perhaps because of the very 'ripeness' of the novel, the two constituent elements fall apart at the least tap. Putting it quite bluntly, Mr. Wilson's admirably concise sketch of the main character—'the pathetic Milly Theale ... who wastes away in Venice and whose doctor recommends a lover'—is so central and yet so loose a part of the mechanism of the whole that one may slide it in and out without any fear of abrasion.

Secondly, and more immediately to the purpose, Henry James has himself provided in the Preface to *The Wings of the Dove* his own considered version of the novel's theme and his own inimitable account of its development. This Preface is closer to its novel than most of the others: it is possibly the only example of a James Preface which could be read with advantage before embarking on the novel itself. The others deal largely with critical theories for which references to the work in hand are used as instances and starting-points: here the relation of the Preface to its own book is more tightly enforced, embarrassing or comforting the reader, according to the degree of confirmation involved, by the deep authoritative tone of James's own auto-criticism. At times he can be hard on himself, and wish a firmer hand than most other critics would care to bring to the task of chastisement. (It is a remarkable thing to watch him, in the ample Preface to an almost over-ample novel, rapping himself over the knuckles for skimpiness of treatment.) And because he so clearly knew what he was doing and so judicially viewed the whole and the parts of the whole, his praise too is more informed and certainly more illuminating than anything an outsider could supply. That quality of ever-wakeful ever-watchful *consciousness* that gives him stature as a man and artist is demonstrated in its least adulterated form in the Prefaces, where his permanent love of insisting, of pointing it out and rubbing it in, appears as an all but perverse self-indulgence of commentary and soliloquy. His familiar yet respectful handling of what in a letter he called 'my poor blest old genius' should preserve any other reader from the fear of spoiling the freshness of an impression by over-attention to detail, even if detailed attention had not been so serenely and explicitly called for as in this passage:

Attention of perusal, I thus confess by the way, is what I at every point, as well as here, absolutely invoke and take for granted.... The enjoyment of a work of art, the acceptance of an irresistible illusion, constituting, to my sense, our highest experience of 'luxury', the luxury is not greatest, by my consequent measure, when the work asks for as little attention as possible. It is greatest, it is delightfully, divinely great, when we feel the surface, like the thick ice of a skater's pond, bear without cracking the strongest pressure we can throw on it. The sound of the crack one may recognize, but never surely to call it a luxury.

A man is pretty sure of his point of view when, having stated it dogmatically, he can thus immediately accept it as an assumption and turn to that use of irony which indicates the rooted security of a private prejudice.

Here, then, is 'The Dove', in the inspired *procédé* of her creator:

The idea, reduced to its essence, is that of a young person conscious of a great capacity for life, but early stricken and doomed, condemned to die under short respite, while also enamoured of the world; aware moreover of the condemnation and passionately desiring to 'put in' before extinction as many of the finer vibrations as possible, and so achieve, however briefly and brokenly, the sense of having lived.

The theme, thus presented, verges on the melodramatic. One can imagine how the James of the early tales would have attacked it. But here, immediately, with one self-confident stroke, we are presented with a clue to that tone which will bulk so much larger in the total impact of the novel than the plot itself; we are introduced, in other words, to the feel and function of the cloudy integument:

It involved, to begin with, the placing in the strongest light a person infirm and ill—a case sure to prove difficult and to require much handling; though giving perhaps, with other matters, one of those chances for good taste, possibly even for the play of the very best in the world, that are not only always to be invoked and cultivated, but that are absolutely to be jumped at from the moment they make a sign. . . .

Why should a figure be disqualified for a central position by the particular circumstance that might most quicken, that might crown with a fine intensity, its liability to many accidents, its consciousness of all relations?

But such a figure, the very essence of which is fragility and an indistinctness of outline, is to be apprehended by reference to other more definite characters, whose interrelations with Milly, and with one another, will provide the movements we shall expect to find mirrored in the pool of Milly's consciousness. Kate and Merton Densher, then, are to be the figures of harder outline in relation to whom the configuration of Milly will begin to take shape:

If her impulse to wrest from her shrinking hour still as much of the fruit of life as possible, if this longing can take effect only by the aid of others, their participation (appealed to, entangled and coerced as they find themselves) becomes their drama too—that of their prompting her illusions, under her importunity, for reasons, for interests and advantages, from motives and points of view, of their own.

And because these agents in turn are 'bribed away, it may even be, from more prescribed and natural orbits', then in order to take up our own position in relation to *them*, we must be allowed to see them at some length and grow familiar with them *before* they meet Milly. We are, in short, to have an opportunity to examine the springs and mechanism of that double trap in which our 'Dove' is predestined to be caught.

I had secured my ticket over the tolerably long line laid down for *The Wings of the Dove* from the moment I had noted that there could be no full presentation of Milly Theale as *engaged* with elements amid which she was to draw her breath in such pain, should not the elements have been, with all solicitude, duly prefigured.

But how these very supporters and supernumeraries, when they in turn come up for handling and treatment, are dealt with! Kate and Merton Densher themselves, in the process of being independently 'fixed' before they are confronted with Milly and the possibilities for their life inherent in her state as a 'princess' and her nature as a 'dove', have become prime figures. One can almost feel James straining after new sub-supporters through whose perceptions they too may more fully be apprehended.

... the whole preliminary presentation of Kate Croy ... from the first, I recall, absolutely declined to enact itself save in terms of amplitude. Terms of amplitude, terms of atmosphere, those terms, and those terms only, in which images assert their fullness and roundness, their power to revolve, so that they have sides and backs, parts in the shade as true as parts in the sun—these were plainly to be my conditions, right and left.

For Kate, the amplitude and atmosphere lie ready to hand in her family. Lionel Croy, her discredited father, forms indeed the very covers or endpapers of the novel. We meet him in the first chapter, we are conscious—to the point of embarrassment—of his presence in the last chapter, and throughout all the intervening space we fumble back to him in memory, from time to time, as to a yardstick for Kate. That indeed is how James intended him to be of service. The amount of aid we are able to summon from that shadowy figure as we seek now to excuse the developing hardness and cruelty of Kate and now to discover some alleviating source for her controlling avarice, does vindicate her creator's contention that once one is committed to the roundabout method of presentation, all these references and cross-references are no luxury, but serve an indispensable function. How much wider a function, then, the author would have wished Lionel Croy to serve, had he but secured ample room and verge enough, is made explicit in this illuminating passage:

> The building up of Kate Croy's consciousness to the capacity for the load little by little to be laid on it was . . . to have been a matter of as many hundred close-packed bricks as there are actually poor dozens. The image of her so compromised and so compromising father was all effectively to have pervaded her life, was in a certain particular way to have tampered with her spring . . . But where do we find him, at this time of day, save in a beggarly scene or two which scarce arrives at the dignity of functional reference? He but looks in, poor beautiful dazzling, damning apparition that he was to have been . . .

Should even this 'functional reference' fail of full explanation, there are sister Marian and Aunt Maud ever available to figure, on either side of Kate's strenuous manipulations, like heraldic emblems of poverty at its most crippling and repulsive, and wealth with all its gracious appointments.

For Merton Densher no such apparatus of localization and reference is set up. Indeed, the lack of it is itself effective and noteworthy. We feel to the full the independent and unattached state of the young journalist from the first moment of his appearance, and in that state we can appreciate how it is that Aunt Maud, though she fears him in theory and honestly likes him in practice, can never really come to take him seriously, since for her a person without relations (in both the family and the general sense of the word) is automatically insignificant. Equally we are made to feel that this same state is, in other directions, his strength. It is for this, we feel, that Milly loves him; it is this conscious aimlessness of his that allows him to become so closely attached to Kate that he will give the appearance—and it *is* only an appearance—of having made over his will to her entirely. With these advantages springing from his 'free' state, one does not rate too seriously his creator's later and nostalgic wish, in the Preface, that he too had been embellished with a more elaborate setting:

> The who and the what, the how and the why, the whence and the whither of Merton Densher, these, no less, were qualities and attributes that should have danced about him with the antique grace of nymphs and fauns circling round a bland Hermes and crowning him with flowers.
> ... the pattern of Densher's final position and fullest consciousness was to have been marked in fine stitches, all silk and gold, all pink and silver, that have had to remain, alas, but entwined upon the reel.

The 'attentive' reader of *The Wings of the Dove* will not, I suggest, echo that rueful 'alas!'. Indeed, one may sometimes complain of James that 'the hand of generosity' is too infrequently stayed, or even that it becomes the hand of mistrust, over-anxious to point out *nuances* and transitions which we might safely have been left to descry for ourselves. One moves on safer and freer ground in *Roderick Hudson*, for instance, than when one is being so solicitously guided through the later novels by a veritable cat's-cradle of leading-strings.

Here at any rate we have an instance (and there are others) where James the creator is wiser than James the critic. It is surely well for the structure of this great novel that Densher's pink and silver embroidery remained on the reel, and that James should have turned instead, especially in Book First, to establish 'the associated consciousness of my two prime young persons'.

> They are far from a common couple, Merton Densher and Kate Croy ... but what they have most to tell us is that, all unconsciously and with the best faith in the world, all by mere force of the terms of their superior passion combined with their superior diplomacy, they are laying a trap for the great innocence to come.

But not every piece of adverse self-criticism in the Preface (or in other Prefaces) can thus be dismissed as showing less tactful wisdom than is displayed in the creative writing. In *The Wings of the Dove*, as in so many of the other novels, the reader feels vaguely that the wonderful apparatus of introduction is not fully used in the later sections, that the richness of the atmosphere is somehow thinned away, that the unsurpassed delineation and shading of the major characters fits them for a fuller and more active life than they are afterwards called upon to live out in the comparatively short space allotted to narrative after we have grown intimate with the men and women who are to be involved in that narrative. For although the reader may sometimes indulge a momentary restless complaint that the game is hardly worth the candle—or rather the magnificent candelabra that would in truth make any game seem embarrassingly wasteful—he must face the fact, as James himself fairly faced it (with amusing unconvincing excuses), that the first part of a James novel is almost always better than the second part. Almost without exception, his opening paragraphs set the scene with a richness and economy unrivalled in English or American fiction, almost without exception, the closing chapters seem to trail away or to be cut short as in disappointment or despair of rounding off the whole.

The Wings of the Dove happens to offer perhaps the most striking example I may cite ... of my regular failure to keep the appointed halves of my whole equal ... Nowhere, I seem to recall, had the need of dissimulation been felt so as anguish; nowhere had I condemned a luckless theme to complete its revolution, burdened with the accumulation of its difficulties ... in quarters so cramped.

The latter half, that is the false and deformed half ... bristles with 'dodges' ... for disguising the reduced scale of the exhibition, for foreshortening at any cost, for imparting to patches the value of presences, for dressing objects in an *air* as of the dimensions they can't possibly have.

The most ardent admirer of Henry James's art, then, may willingly concede the faults of construction which he himself not only recognized but for which he was eager on many occasions to perform 'public penance', with most sincerity perhaps in the present Preface, and with wry humour in the Preface to *The Tragic Muse*:

Time after time, then, has the precious waistband or girdle, studded
and buckled and placed for brave outward show, practically worked
itself, and in spite of desperate remonstrance, or in other words essential
counterplotting, to a point perilously near the knees—perilously I mean
for the freedom of those parts.

For in *The Wings of the Dove*, any failure in the 'brave outward
show' is, after all, only a minor foreshortening in a novel so wonderfully constructed as to make most others appear in very truth
like 'large loose baggy monsters'. Indeed, in making the concession,
one is able in a sense to turn the tables on those detractors of
Henry James who hold (as most of his detractors do hold) that he
has undoubted craftmanship to offer and nothing much else. In *The
Wings of the Dove* the slight awkwardness of construction is more
than compensated by the extraordinary warmth and subtlety of the
content—that raw material which a concentration on the obvious
form of the novel usually passes over without comment.

A study of James's Preface, then, brings to light something of
those qualities of literary construction and human insight which
elaborated so rich a work. That second quality is impossible to assess
with any finality, but the first is at least demonstrable. If *The Wings
of the Dove* is one of the most difficult of his novels, it is also one of
the most revealing. No analysis of any other James novel could
provide a better example of his power of making much out of little,
or illustrate how much portentous importance is attributed by the
novelist to every minor encounter and every slight change of position
of the characters whose interrelations make up his tale.

Once again, as in so many of James's novels, the prime interest
lies in the relationship between people of two contrasted types, types
at the same time mutually attractive and mutually inimical and even
destructive. Here, in *The Wings of the Dove*, is yet another study in
opposed ways of living, the hard and the soft, the arranged and the
unarranged life. Here again, for long periods, we are asked to
espouse now one way and now the other. Our sympathies, though
clear in the end, are for long divided.

It is interesting, and unexpected, to notice that by comparison
with the much earlier novel *Roderick Hudson* the cards are less

intricately shuffled. It is fair to suggest that in *Roderick Hudson* the problem was subtler. For there, James confronted us with what may be termed a soft and arranged life in Rowland Mallet, and a hard and unarranged life in Roderick Hudson. The potential mutual attraction and mutual destruction was stronger for that reason. The arranged life of Rowland could yearn nostalgically after what he considered to be the spontaneous genius of Roderick, and at the same time the essential selfish hard core of his hero, while hurting him bitterly, was yet enough akin to his own feeling for order and conscious planning to forbid that simple disgusted reaction which might have severed their relationship and so put an end to his suffering. There were times, indeed, when Rowland sincerely wished that he too *could* become hard, could lose his 'constitutional tendency to magnanimous interpretations' and gain that clarity of selfishness which might have transmuted his talents to something like his friend's genius. Allow that these feelings were in the opposite direction engaging the consciousness of Roderick himself—that he was at once repelled by the complacency and attracted by the security of Rowland's way of life—and we are immediately presented with that quadruple stress which will always remain as the cause of that novel's extraordinary power, and which elevates it to a very high place in the long James canon.

The Wings of the Dove treats with greater elaboration of detail an essentially simpler diagram. The hard and arranged life of Kate comes into contrast and conflict with the soft and unarranged life of Milly: the likelihood of hurt is one-sided. It is not until the very end of the book that we see Kate lose her objective as inevitably as Milly lost hers. If Milly is a dove, then Kate is immediately accepted as a more metallic creature—like the Emperor's clockwork nightingale, perhaps, with springs and bright metal parts suggesting a trap in which a dove could be, and was, caught.

To Henry James the interest lay in the progressive development of these characters side by side in a certain pattern of construction, that 'double or alternating centre' described at some length in the Preface. But the astonishing thing about *The Wings of the Dove* is not the construction (which does at times falter), but the author's renewed demonstration of a familiarity with the mental processes of two opposed human types, his ability to pop from inside one to

inside the other with—in spite of an enormous elaboration of presentation—a minimum of outside commentary. (Indeed, as will be
noted later, a lack of external precision detracts from the final
impact of this and other later novels.) It is the *inwardness* of it all
that makes the novel, that reconciles the reader to so much pother.
Milly's yielding softness and Kate's hard clarity are so inwardly
done that we view the events of the book through their eyes—or,
to change the metaphor and quote a Prefatory remark about Kate:
'we surrender again to our major convenience ... that of drawing
breath through the young woman's lungs.' What we thus gain in
intensity of feeling is only partially offset by the loss of any consistent
picture of these characters (just as in real life we can have no very
true objective picture of ourselves). We see *through* Kate and Milly,
we do not see *them* very clearly.* This is made plain when we consider the bright particularity of the minor figures—Aunt Maud or
Susan Stringham—who are wholly consistent and yet have no more
of the caricature about them than is needed to give stability to
minor characters drawn from the outside.

The 'inward' apprehension of Kate Croy is not however attempted
until we have had an initial introduction from the outside, in the
first two Books: this is no doubt why always throughout the novel
her figure is one degree clearer than Milly's. We see her in relation
to her father, her sister, her aunt. There are, very early in the book,
one or two hints that she has only recently, and by force of pressing
circumstances, decided to take up a firm line in creating an individual life for herself. Other people had clearly until now (until the
novel opens, that is) dominated her. 'It wouldn't be the first time',
we are told in an early soliloquy (Book First, Chapter 2), 'she had
seen herself obliged to accept with smothered irony other people's
interpretation of her conduct. She often ended by giving up to them
—it really seemed the way to live—the version that met their convenience'. Aunt Maud had been from the beginning a repressive
influence: 'The main office of this relative for the young Croys—
apart from giving them their fixed measure of social greatness—

*Dr. Leavis puts the point, trenchantly, in a negative way: 'A vivid, particularly
realized Milly might for him stand in the midst of his indirections, but what for
the reader these skirt round is too much like emptiness; she isn't there ...'
(*Scrutiny* V, 402).

had struck them as being to form them to a conception of what they were not to expect.' As for sister Marian, she had drained her sympathy without giving anything in return:

> [Kate] noticed with profundity that disappointment made people selfish; she marvelled at the serenity—it was the poor woman's only one— of what Marian took for granted: her own state of abasement as the second-born, her life reduced to mere inexhaustible sisterhood. She existed in that view wholly for the small house in Chelsea; the moral of which moreover, of course, was that the more you gave yourself the less of you was left. There were always people to snatch at you, and it would never occur to *them* that they were eating you up. They did that without tasting.

Marian also provides a terrible warning against the penalties incurred by marriage to a poor man:*

> Mr. Condrip's widow ... was little more than a ragged relic, a plain prosaic result of him—as if she had somehow been pulled through him as through an obstinate funnel, only to be left crumpled and useless. (Book First, Chapter 2.)

These are fair indications, and fair excuses. But at first Kate needs no lenience of judgement. Her relationship with Merton Densher, which later seems to deteriorate and harden into that between schemer and agent, is at first presented in a far more attractive light. She sees in his vague but spontaneous qualities something to which she can cling, something to save her from that harsh material outlook which circumstances are forcing upon her.

> She had observed a ladder against a garden-wall and had trusted herself so to climb it as to be able to see over into the probable garden on the other side. On reaching the top she had found herself face to face with a gentleman engaged in a like calculation at the same moment, and the two inquirers had remained confronted on their ladders.

*Mr. Maxwell Geismar, in a comment wildly off the mark when one recalls the tender portrait of Hyacinth Robinson's Pinnie, considers the opening sentences of *The Wings of the Dove* to be 'an illuminating exposition of the genteel poverty which James considered to be the most ignoble human or social existence'.

They had accepted their acquaintance as far too short for an engagement, but they had treated it as long enough for almost anything else, and marriage was somehow before them like a temple without an avenue.

They belonged to the temple and met in the grounds; they were in the stage at which grounds in general offered much scattered refreshment. (Book Second, Chapter 1.)

When we remember that Merton Densher is introduced as looking 'vague without looking weak—idle without looking empty', it is a tribute to Kate that, in her narrow plight, we feel her to be in full sympathy with the tone of the rest of his portrait:

He suggested above all, however, that wondrous state of youth in which the elements, the metals more or less precious, are so in fusion and fermentation that the question of the final stamp, the pressure that fixes the value, must wait for comparative coolness. (Book Second, Chapter 1.)

It is Kate's tragedy, and a tragedy demonstrably to be accounted for by the circumstances which, like her father's corrupting influence, had 'tampered with her spring', that she attempted to stamp on Merton Densher's character an unworthy denomination of value which in the end it was not willing to receive. With Aunt Maud as model and guardian, and with a father and a sister alike persuading her to accept that model, it was the only value she had left to play with. In the end it is Milly who stamps *her* value on Densher, and his acceptance of *her* standards rather than Kate's manages to keep him, still dominated by Kate, in the reader's sympathy.

Ten Books run their course, however, before Kate's scheme is finally shown up and finally defeated. Meanwhile, the better side of her character is as a guide and a beacon to the true heroine, the 'Dove,' who sighs in vain to secure for herself something of its poise. Softness of outline and hesitancy of plan make up Milly's own tone, and we are made to feel its attraction from the first. It is warm and unspoiled and unformulated; it calls for careful guarding, for protection.

She had arts and idiosyncrasies of which no great account could have been given, but which were a daily grace if you lived with them; such as the art of being almost tragically impatient and yet making it as light as air; of being inexplicably sad and yet making it as clear as noon; of being unmistakably gay and yet making it as soft as dusk.* (Book Third, Chapter 1.)

Yet although Milly at no point forfeits our sympathy, we never lose sight of her millions and of her protected state—so protected, indeed, that she hated it herself and felt in her faithful Susie Stringham a positive need to treat her like a princess:

Susan had read history, had read Gibbon and Froude and Saint-Simon; she had high lights as to the special allowances made for the class, and, since she saw them, when young, as effete and over-tutored, inevitably ironic and inevitably refined, one must take it for amusing if she inclined to an indulgence verily Byzantine. If one *could* only be Byzantine!— wasn't that what she insidiously led one on to sigh? (Book Fifth, Chapter 4.)

So that when the two women meet, in that 'compact constructional block' (to quote the Preface again) provided by the dinner-party at Lancaster Gate, 'where all the offered life centres, to intensity, in the disclosure of Milly's single throbbing consciousness', it is Milly who is bowled over by Kate:

She thrilled, she consciously flushed, and all to turn pale again, with the certitude—it had never been so present—that she should find herself completely involved: the very air of the place, the pitch of the occasion, had for her both so sharp a ring and so deep an undertone.

Mrs. Lowder and her niece, however dissimilar, had at least in common that each was a great reality ... yet she none the less felt Mrs. Lowder as a person of whom the mind might in two or three days roughly make the circuit. She would sit there massive at least while one attempted it; whereas Miss Croy, the handsome girl, would indulge in incalculable movements that might interfere with one's tour. (Book Fourth, Chapter 1.)

And again later:

Kate had for her new friend's eyes the extraordinary and attaching property of appearing at a given moment to show as a beautiful stranger,

*It is in this particular passage, I believe, that one may detect a note so affectionate that one feels confident in claiming it as a direct personal expression —presumably of James's affection for his cousin, Minny Temple.

to cut her connexions and lose her identity, letting the imagination for the time make what it would of them—make her merely a person striking from afar, more and more pleasing as one watched, but who was above all a subject for curiosity. (Book Fifth, Chapter 1.)

From that Lancaster Gate dinner-party onwards, as Milly falls more and more under the spell of Kate's apparent firmness of purpose and makes the attempt to stiffen her own failing existence with purposeful splints, the reader finds much 'constructional' support from the first chapter in Book Third where Miss Theale and her *confidante* are first presented. In particular we recall that curiously evocative scene (it does not yield to quotation, for it is thickly shrouded with the cloudy integument and needs its context) where Milly is discovered gazing from an Alpine crest and seems to be facing for a moment alone Life with a capital 'L'. For it is one of James's recurring felicities of touch that he will always present his prime figures *before* they come into contact, in order to correct too easy or exaggerated impression of their later mutual influence or interdependence. Just as in *The Bostonians* we are introduced to an Olive Chancellor whose psychology is already fairly clear *before* her discovery of Verena Tarrant, so here Milly's Alpine meditation gives us a clue to her problem before she meets Kate—and (although we are aware of a previous passage in New York) before, in the pages of the novel at least, she meets Merton Densher. Milly's later head-on encounter with Life and Death as she sits in Regent's Park *after* having met the persons who are most to influence the remaining months of her existence, gains immensely in power thereby.

It is not until after she has come into the orbit of Kate and renewed her acquaintance with Merton Densher that Milly is made conscious in Sir Luke Strett's consulting room—a room 'somewhat sallow with years of celebrity'—of the ironic fact that her new pathetic attempt to order her life has not got under way before that life is condemned.

It would be strange for the firmness to come, after all, from her learning in these agreeable conditions that she was in some way doomed; but above all it would prove how little she had hitherto had to hold her up. If she was now to be held up by the mere process—since that was perhaps on the cards—of being let down, this would only testify in turn to her queer little history. *That* sense of loosely rattling had been no process at all; and it was ridiculously true that her thus sitting there to see her life put into the scales represented her first approach to the taste of orderly living. Such was Milly's romantic version . . . (Book Fourth, Chapter 3.)

The full force of that word 'romantic' is difficult to assess. Her visits to the great specialist, seen through her own eyes, are blurred with a kind of fascinated mystification. She does not seem to listen with much attention to what he has to say (perhaps the very vagueness of his utterances is to be attributed to her own version of them?) but she is swept away by his presence and the comfortable feeling that he will somehow 'help' her. She has not won any clearer notion of her state of health, but—what she seems to need even more urgently—she has in her own soft romantic fashion achieved a new 'relation' with someone:

. . . the relation was the special trophy that, for the hour, she bore off. It was like an absolute possession, a new resource altogether, something done up in the softest silk and tucked away under the arm of memory. She hadn't had it when she went in, and she had it when she came out . . . (Book Fourth, Chapter 3.)

The reader who protests that this is not how a perfectly normal young woman comes away from her doctor will have made a comment of no small value, perhaps, to an understanding of the pathetic nature and character of 'The Dove'. At all events, whether we take these pages at their face value or read something else into them, the next chapter brings us to the heart of Milly's malaise and to that section of the novel where Henry James throws aside the veil and moves from a treatment of peripheral states of consciousness to the very centre of human vulnerability. We are back on familiar ground; this is the creator of Roderick Hudson and of Hyacinth Robinson speaking. The beauty of the revelation demands, at some length, his own words:

No one in the world could have sufficiently entered into her state; no tie could have been close enough to enable a companion to walk beside her without some disparity. She literally felt, in this first flush, that her own company must be the human race at large, present all round her, but inspiringly impersonal, and that her only field must be, then and there, the grey immensity of London.

The beauty of the bloom had gone from the small old sense of safety—that was distinct: she had left it there behind her for ever. But the beauty of the idea of a big adventure, a big dim experiment or struggle in which she might more responsibly than ever before take a hand, had been offered her instead. It was as if she had had to pluck off her breast, to throw away, some friendly ornament, a familiar flower, a little old jewel, that was part of her daily dress; and to take up and shoulder as a substitute some queer defensive weapon, a musket, a spear, a battle-axe—conducive possibly in a higher degree to a startling appearance, but demanding all the effort of a military posture.

Here [in Regents Park] were benches and smutty sheep; here were idle lads at games of ball, with their cries mild in the thick air; here were wanderers anxious and tired like herself; here doubtless were hundreds of others just in the same box. Their box, their great common anxiety, what was it, in this grim breathing-space, but the great practical question of life? They would live if they would; that is, like herself, they had been told so: she saw them all about her, on seats, digesting the information, recognizing it again as something in a slightly different shape familiar enough, the blessed old truth that they would live if they could. All she thus shared with them made her wish to sit in their company; which she so far did that she looked for a bench that was empty, eschewing a still emptier chair that she saw hard by, and for which she would have paid, with superiority, a fee. (Book Fourth, Chapter 4.)

In this passage and that describing Milly's Alpine vigil, James has come as near as he ever did to a statement of the general human predicament—seen not in terms of high drama of decision, but as a sudden void in the heart which can afflict a gentle grey-habited young lady with an irresistible desire to claim for herself, for an instant, some part in human kinship.

Milly's unaided striving for a new sense of order is clearly doomed to failure: she can only look longingly at what she considers to be order in other lives. Her own flinching interest in Merton Densher, the only emotion that had any real chance of shaping a new order for her, can never compete with Kate's. This is so apparent that we feel Kate's wicked plan to be particularly wicked because it was so unnecessary: 'The Dove' could surely have been easily separated from her cash without having her spirit murdered in the process.

Entering the National Gallery to seek composure and stability, Milly turns away even from the pictures as from too rich a diet:

> She really knew before long that what held her was the mere refuge, that something within her was after all too weak for the Turners and the Titians. They joined hands about her in a circle too vast, though a circle that a year before she would only have desired to trace ... She marked absurdly her little stations, blinking, in her shrinkage of curiosity, at the glorious walls. ... (Book Fifth, Chapter 7.)

Instead, she finds a passing envy for the poor circumscribed lives of the lady-copyists there, who simply because they lacked her own embarrassing material and spiritual resources, seemed to be the better able to cope with what little they did have:

> It was immense, outside, the personal question; but she had blissfully left it outside, and the nearest it came, for a quarter of an hour, to glimmering again into view was when she watched for a little one of the more earnest of the lady-copyists. Two or three in particular, spectacled, aproned, absorbed, engaged her sympathy to an absurd extent, seemed to show her for a time the right way to live. She should have been a lady-copyist—it met so the case. The case was the case of escape, of living under water, of being at once impersonal and firm. There it was before one—one had only to stick and stick. (Book Fifth, Chapter 7.)

Remembering that contrasting but mutually attractive types are a very keynote of Henry James's art, it is more than usually dangerous to look for traces of the author's own personality on any one side of the diptych. But is it fanciful to recall the similar impression created in the mind of Christopher Newman of *The American* as he watched Noémie Nioche at work in The Louvre, and to suggest that the creator of both Newman and Milly was himself, in certain moods, peculiarly susceptible to the attractions of the small neat organized life?

It is here, in the National Gallery, when she surprises Kate and Merton Densher together, that Milly enjoys by contrast with her own helplessness a fresh sense of Kate's superb 'management' in the smoothing away of what might have been an awkward situation:

> It was perhaps only afterwards that the girl fully felt the connexion between this touch and her own already established conviction that Kate

was a prodigious person; yet on the spot she none the less, in a degree, knew herself handled and again, as she had been the night before, dealt with—absolutely even dealt with for her greater pleasure. A minute in fine hadn't elapsed before Kate had somehow made her provisionally take everything as natural. (Book Fifth, Chapter 7.)

We feel that it is Milly's neurotic desire to be managed rather than any specific duplicity on Kate's part which allows her so readily to accept Kate's artificial version of their situation *vis-à-vis* the passive Merton Densher:

Little by little indeed, under the vividness of Kate's behaviour the probabilities fell back into their order. Merton Densher was in love and Kate couldn't help it—could only be sorry and kind: wouldn't that, without wild flurries, cover everything? Milly at all events tried it as a cover, tried it hard, for the time; pulled it over her . . . drew it up to her chin with energy. (Book Fifth, Chapter 7.)

Kate is, in short, beginning to manage Milly as she has all along manipulated Merton Densher; there is a malleability in both characters which allows—indeed, asks for—such treatment. We remember that gold is malleable and cast-iron is not, and although there must be from time to time in the reader a genuine annoyance at the softness or weakness of the only two sympathetic figures in a novel full of coarsening lives, it is already beginning to dawn on us that what is fine in Milly and in Densher will draw them together, even while Kate's more powerful will is driving them apart. Book Sixth, which has its strain and its *longueurs*, shows Kate coming more and more into the open with her hard plans, with Milly and Densher alike grudgingly succumbing to *force majeure* and in the process sensing in one another a kinship which neither has the will to acclaim, but which will effectively, in the end, lose them both to Kate. In the very next chapter after the National Gallery episode, where Milly's strength and weakness were revealed in her beautiful yet almost craven behaviour in asking the couple back to luncheon and engaging Merton in tourist gossip about America, we are shown by a well-placed stroke how this new interest in Milly fills him with an increasing resentment against Kate, makes him bitterly conscious at last of every 'irritating mark of her expertness'.

This expertness, under providence, had been great from the first, so far as joining him was concerned; and he was critical only because it had been still greater, even from the first too, in respect of leaving him. (Book Sixth, Chapter 1.)

Let Kate expertly reveal a few more details of her programme, and he is bitter to the point of mutiny:

He walked up the Bayswater Road, but he stopped short, under the murky stars ... He had had his brief stupidity, but now he understood. She had guaranteed to Milly Theale through Mrs. Stringham that Kate didn't care for him ... she had described Kate as merely compassionate, so that Milly might be compassionate too. 'Proper' indeed it was, her lie— the very properest possible and the most deeply, richly diplomatic. So Milly was successfully deceived. (Book Sixth, Chapter 4.)

And when, his will still subject to Kate's, he calls on Milly to play the first strokes of the game laid down for him, his sympathies are already on the side of the intended victim:

Since it was false that he wasn't loved, so his right was quite quenched to figure on that ground as important; and if he didn't look out he should find himself appreciating in a way quite at odds with his straightness the good faith of Milly's benevolence ... If it wasn't proper for him to enjoy consideration on a perfectly false footing, where was the guarantee that, if he kept on, he mightn't soon himself pretend to the grievance in order not to miss the sweet? (Book Sixth, Chapter 5.)

In *The Tragic Muse*, our hope that the like-minded Nick Dormer and Miriam Rooth will come together is disappointed for no very acceptable reason, and the novel itself disappoints accordingly. In *The Wings of the Dove*, our hope that the softer qualities of Milly and Densher will draw them together is disappointed by death: irritated frustration is replaced by human tragedy. (That is why, although he is technically quite correct, Mr. Geismar is, I feel, insensitive in claiming that Densher's final remorse followed 'a still deeper, fixed, and recurrent Jamesian pattern of the impossible love, of always loving the woman you cannot have'. It is true: but that the pathos of Milly's case puts Densher in an altogether different category is even more true.)

In six Books, then, the characters are made ready. The remaining four need little more commentary than has been provided in the foregoing synopsis. The texture of the writing grows ever richer, the serenity of intuition ever clearer, the fastidious avoidance of over-emphasis yet more delicate, as throughout the mounting tension and up to the *dénouement* itself we are invited to concentrate our attention not on scenes of overt recrimination and retribution but rather on the small inward adjustments of sensibility, so faintly perceptible that even in our own lives we can hardly descern them— any more than we are normally able to spot those moments when, in Mr. W. H. Auden's vivid phrase, 'the crack in the tea-cup opens/ A lane to the land of the dead'. Yet it is precisely those adjustments and readjustments that cause the final human cleavages or fusions, and are in themselves of so much more value to a novelist of James's gifts than the actions to which they lead. Brief illustrations of his treatment of two major themes for the novel—the veiled jealousy of Kate for Milly and Milly for Kate, and the final change of heart in Merton Densher—must suffice here to demonstrate that remarkable artistic mastery.

Kate's jealousy is the simpler: it is financial jealousy providing the mainspring of a novel which *in toto* might be considered, from the strictly outside or social point of view, as a morality play on the evils of money. It is this simpler jealousy that shapes the plot. But its subtler effects shape the human tragedy, and in a very different direction. These effects are best shown at the party given by Milly at her Venetian Palazzo Leporelli, a party the significance of which —if we had missed it—the Preface makes unmistakably explicit:

It is in Kate's consciousness that at the stage in question the drama is brought to a head, and the occasion on which, in the splendid saloon of poor Milly's hired palace, she takes the measure of her friends' festal evening, squares itself to the same synthetic firmness as the compact constructional block inserted by the scene at Lancaster Gate.

But even more, it is in Merton Densher's consciousness of Kate's consciousness:

Yet he knew in a moment that Kate was just now, for reasons hidden from him, exceptionally under the impression of that element of wealth

in [Milly] which was a great power, and which was dove-like only so far
as one remembered that doves have wings and wondrous flights, have
them as well as tender tints and soft sounds.

It might have been in her face too that, well as she certainly looked in
pearls, pearls were exactly what Merton Densher would never be able to
give her. Wasn't *that* the great difference that Milly tonight symbolized?
(Book Eighth, Chapter 3.)

And the *effect* on Merton Densher—for that is the true value of the
scene:

So at all events he read the case while he noted that Kate was somehow
—for Kate—lacking in lustre. As a striking young presence she was
practically superseded . . . she might fairly have been dressed to-night in
the little black frock, superficially indistinguishable, that Milly had laid
aside. (Book Eighth, Chapter 3.)

Milly's frailer jealousy of Kate, a self-effacing view bereft of the
animus normally associated with the word, comes out characteris-
tically in the scenes when she is aware of Kate as Kate must appear
to the eyes of Densher, scenes which convey some of the most
quietly brutal touches of pathetic jealousy I have met in any fiction.
In the first scene, Milly is looking through her window at Kate,
who waves to her from the pavement:

What was also, however, determined for her was, again, that the
image presented to her, the splendid young woman who looked so
particularly handsome in impatience, with the fine freedom of her signal,
was the peculiar property of someone else's vision, that this fine freedom
in short was the fine freedom she showed Mr. Densher. Just so was how
she looked to him, and just so was how Milly was held by her—held as
by a strange sense of seeing through that distant person's eyes. (Book
Fifth, Chapter 4.)

In the second, Kate is standing by the window and Milly, watching
her, knows by some unspoken sense that Densher is in London:

. . . [Kate] hovered there with conscious eyes and some added advantage.
Then indeed, with small delay, her friend sufficiently saw. The conscious

eyes, the added advantage were but those she had now always at command—those proper to the person Milly knew as known to Merton Densher. It was for several seconds again as if the *total* of her identity had been that of the person known to him—a determination having for result another sharpness of its own. Kate had positively but to be there just as she was to tell her he had come back. (Book Fifth, Chapter 5.)

Between the claims of innocence and experience where is the author's sympathy? It wavers as in other novels. *The Portrait of a Lady* is especially close to *The Wings of the Dove* in this respect. There, it was Madame Merle who represented to Isabel Archer the advantages of the ordered life but who was never so hide-bound as to be insensitive to the delicate pre-occupations of the heroine. Here, it is Aunt Maud who gains admiration for a prodigious calm and who figures to the elated imagination of Mrs. Stringham from New England as 'a projectile, of great size, loaded and ready for use' or as 'some great sleeping fortress', and yet is no monster of callousness. Even Mrs. Lowder's restrictions are deliberate, political, and not merely poverties of spirit:

It had never been her pride, Maud Manningham* had hinted, that kept *her* from crying when other things made for it; it had only been that these same things, at such times, made still more for business, arrangements, correspondence, the ringing of bells, the marshalling of servants, the taking of decisions. 'I might be crying now,' she said, 'if I weren't writing letters.' (Book Seventh, Chapter 1.)

Merton Densher is the symbol of that wavering sympathy between the two views of life. He is the quiet centre of the storm—a storm, an unfriendly reader might exclaim, in a teacup. He is the *punctum indifferens*, the mere male among all the petticoats ('They were all *such* petticoats!' the poor man wails, at the crisis of his Venetian ordeal). It is curious that the wretched dominated fellow doesn't lose more of our sympathy than he does. In the morality play, at least, he represents a condemnation not so much of riches as of the crippling limitations of poverty, and his feeling of helplessness in the rich vulgarity of the Lancaster Gate drawing-room is less like Kate's envy of Milly's fortune than the frustrations of Hyacinth

* The maiden-name of Mrs. Lowder.

Robinson of *The Princess Casamassima*—a character who never lost our sympathy even in his weakest moments. During the tension of the last scenes with Kate, Densher plays Macbeth to her Lady Macbeth, still feeling the old admiration for her spirit but feeling now too the power of Milly's goodness. Yet it is never so much the horror of their guilt that drives Densher to repudiate his lover, as the less spectacular but infinitely more human growth of his exasperation at her 'Call me a good cab!' moods. Milly does all unconsciously exert 'the shaping spirit of Imagination', while Kate, like Coleridge's Fancy, 'has no other counters to play with but fixities and definites'. The Milly who could—on the Alps or in Regent's Park—experience a poetic mysticism akin to the promptings of his own timorous sensibility, becomes the mistress of his ideals, while Kate holds him to the end a slave to her will.

The quotations embodied in the foregoing notes are too few to indicate with any persuasion Henry James's essentially poetic approach to fiction. They may however suffice to illustrate the strength and weakness of his now steady concentration on peripheral states of consciousness. The whole 'ado' has been organized with a lack of direct exposition or even direct presentation of motive and emotion: to discover what one person is thinking or feeling we are compelled to look through another pair of eyes, to arrive at an appreciation by means of 'reflectors' working 'in arranged alternation'. It is a wilful and at times a fatal limitation. Not to know at first hand, for example, what Milly thought and felt during her last weeks of life at Venice, is a perverse denial for which no amount of peeping and cross-inferences can atone. It is for this reason above all that the later novels lack freshness, lack certainly the evocative powers of *Roderick Hudson* or *The Princess Casamassima* where Henry James was willing to grapple overtly and spontaneously with life instead of moving always by hints and side-steps.

All this raises the question of his 'morbidity': is it true that the early James was a keen observer and the later James something of a *voyeur*? Such an accusation would find more ample substance in the later short stories, but already in *The Wings of the Dove* the deliberate idiosyncrasy is marked enough to give rise to such a comment as this by Mr. Edmund Wilson:

He was squeamish about matters of sex, it is true—and the people he wrote about were squeamish. And it is true that much of his contact with life was effected, not at close quarters, but through long infinitely sensitive antennae. Yet why, in a given story, should he leave us in doubt as to the facts, as to what kind of people we should think the actors?

—a complaint provoked, it is true, by the ambiguity of *The Turn of the Screw*, but entirely relevant.

But if, as another critic* remarks, Henry James 'had lived cloistered too long and had actually forgotten the things people do', he never forgot how people *feel*. The essence, the fugitive perfume of life he never missed: it almost becomes a choice between flowers without scent or scent without flowers. Other novelists without number can present us with scentless accurate drawings or photographs of flowers; if Henry James with enormous industry preferred to offer instead a small phial of scent, we can be confident that the essence is never synthetic, but that to the very last, even in his most self-pitying moments, the uncomfortable odours will have been distilled from real life as we know it. Another metaphor, developed in the Preface, indicates that the author himself was aware how the real quality of his work could not be explained fully as the sum of its carefully joined parts, and that the final unity had a functional strength as well as a beauty not readily to be reduced to its elements. He is speaking of the artist at work:

He places, after an earnest survey, the piers of his bridge—he has at least sounded deep enough, heaven knows, for their brave position; yet the bridge spans the stream, after the fact, in apparently complete independence of these properties, the principal grace of the original design. *They* were the illusion, for their necessary hour; but the span itself, whether of a single arch or of many, seems by the oddest chance in the world to be a reality; since, actually, the rueful builder, passing under it, sees figures and hears sounds above: he makes out, with his heart in his throat, that it bears and is positively being 'used'.

When arguing for a patient recapitulation of the stages through which James passed to concentrate misguided attention on 'art' as subject-matter, I was emboldened to quote Coleridge (p. 207). The

*H. R. Hays, in *Hound and Horn*, April–June, 1934.

point Henry James was trying to make in the above quotation from his Preface seems to me to be made even more clearly in another superb image from the *Biographia Literaria:*

The first range of hills, that encircles the scanty vale of human life, is the horizon for the majority of its inhabitants . . . But in all ages there have been a few, who measuring and sounding the rivers of the vale at the feet of their furthest inaccessible falls, have learned that the sources must be far higher and far inward; a few, who even in the level streams have detected elements, which neither the vale itself nor the surrounding mountains contained or could supply.

It could never be claimed, then, that *The Wings of the Dove* is in any simple sense a moving or stirring novel. It excels rather in the emotional presentation of very quiet and secret states of consciousness, unfamiliar in fiction not because they are unworthy of presentation, but rather because so few novelists have been brave enough to face the exacting and so largely unrewarding task. It has, certainly, its Proustian *longueurs*. ('Proustian' I say advisedly and in the spirit of propaganda, for we should not refuse to the one great artist the tolerant patience we are prepared to extend to the other.) But it does report with unflinching honesty the frightening amount of emotional capital expended on residual or peripheral contacts, and demonstrates (as for instance through the experiences of Kate and Milly at the same dinner-party) how the deep better-known emotions are poured out, only very thinly disguised, in these border areas—'border' indeed, for here people touch, here above all they are, as Henry James so often puts it, 'in relation'. It is against that background of honesty that stand out most vividly—as in the case of the Regent's Park episode—those fearful flashes of reality which afflict us perhaps at moments of grief or exaltation, but even more poignantly as we turn restlessly between sleep and waking.

So that although, in discussing *The Wings of the Dove*, one must at times deplore the distant wandering away from prime sources, yet it seems not so much to throw a shadow over the earlier lucidities as to light up with a wiser autumnal glow from that same stupendous sun of consciousness the still murkier tracts of his creative genius which lie ahead.

XI

The Ambassadors

No! I am not Prince Hamlet, nor was meant
to be . . .
I have heard the mermaids singing, each
to each.

T. S. Eliot

The Ambassadors (1903) and *The Golden Bowl* (1904) require, from any tactful guide, a more gingerly and at the same time more thorough-going treatment than that considered adequate for *The Wings of the Dove*. For one thing, *The Dove* is much easier to read. This is true partly because of the helpful comic relief offered by such minor figures as Aunt Maud, but mainly because plot and tone, situation and character are so sandwiched that the novel's appeal is on a broad front and its rewards are both incidental and cumulative. Its very poetic texture seldom impedes and often helps forward the story, while the story itself is sufficiently tense to keep the attention of less impressionable or speculative readers.

Alas, I see no way of avoiding the admission that to many tastes *The Ambassadors* will seem a terrible fuss about nothing—or about very little. To tackle *The Dove*, one may need a little coaxing. To tackle *The Ambassadors* or *The Golden Bowl*, a reader may welcome an almost physical helping hand, so to say, through the muddier patches: a guide must humble himself to point out submerged stepping-stones, to indicate a few half-concealed dry places, in short to abate his commentary in the effort to hoist the reader somehow across and through the difficult terrain to be traversed. Only then—certainly breathless, possibly bespattered by the morass and perhaps even resentfully fatigued by the journey—only then is it possible for us to see what astonishing discoveries may be made in the wake of the most devoted and dogged explorer of fiction in our language.

So that, whereas in considering *The Dove* it was (I believe) helpful to discuss plot and atmosphere together, taking up Mr. Edmund Wilson's challenge about the 'cloudy integument', I propose in discussing *The Ambassadors* to adopt a different tactic. I shall attempt a brief sketch or synopsis as a guide-rope for readers whose enjoyment of this remarkable book may otherwise be quite wrecked by panic cries of 'Where *are* we? What are we *doing*? Where are we *going*?' When we have reached base-camp, there will be time for a picnic survey of the journey. And before setting out at all, it will be essential to establish trust in the proposition that the air through which we are to stumble is rare but extraordinarily tonic —that, in fact, the journey is worth while.

More intrepid guides than I have uttered words of caution. Dr. Leavis (*Scrutiny*, V, 405) considered 'the energy of the "doing" and the energy demanded for the reading disproportionate to the issues'. Nine years later, the same critic complained that 'James utterly fails to justify the essential imputations of value that are involved in the offered theme of Strether's awakening to Life'. (*Scrutiny*, XIV, 230–1). This is certainly true, if one thinks of the reward of the journey as some kind of crock of gold, some clue, some artistic redemption. Indeed, Dr. Leavis's disappointment on this latter score is pretty explicit. He objects, and with perfect justice, that if the novel's heroine, Mme de Vionnet, is 'to be accepted by us as so miraculously transcending the familiar type and ethos, James would have had to do something more creative and convincing than the transmutation by atmospheric vagueness and Impressionist aestheticizing that he attempts'. Quite so. Down-grade Mme de Vionnet, by all means. Down-grade, too, if you like, the artistic pretensions of that Parisian society in which she and the liberated Chad (liberated, that is to say, from the materialist pretensions of the New England society from which he had fled) moved and even postured. All this, surely, leaves the effects of his embassy on Strether essentially unsmirched—just as the quality of Marcel's responses to life, in Proust's masterpiece, is in no way blunted by the quality of the society to which he exposed his antennae. By all means admit, as Strether himself admitted at the very end of his quest, that Mme de Vionnet herself was not equal to the task of 'transmuting' Chad: 'She had made him better, she had made him best, she had made him anything one would; but it came to our friend with supreme queerness that he was none the less only Chad.' (XII, 2).

What *is* essential to recognize, of course, is that this judgement follows immediately upon the scene where Mme de Vionnet and Strether, each exhausted and finally defeated in their so different efforts to 'save' the wretched Chad (who, for his own incapacity to profit by the sacrifice and advice of other people, deserves the kind of sympathy one feels compelled to extend to the poor lad who was the recipient of Lord Chesterfield's *Letters*), stumble upon their joint sad triumph. 'What it comes to is that it's not, it's never, a happiness, any happiness at all, to *take*. The only safe thing is to give. It's what plays you least false.' Thus the adultress, the non-transcendent Mme de Vionnet. And Strether? She 'does' him, too: 'I don't pretend you feel yourself victimized, for this evidently is the way you live, and it's what—we're agreed—is the best way.' Thus the busybody. I grant that, torn from its context, this advance statement of the deep-buried moral may look trite enough. In its all-passion-spent place—and especially amid the dangerous under-current swirl of suspicion that Marie de Vionnet is half-heartedly offering Strether himself a reversionary interest in Chad's cast-off *affaire*, which Strether is half-heartedly susceptible enough to recognize—the scene reminds the reader what all the fuss *is* about, what *are* the 'issues'. The 'offered theme' is not merely 'Strether's awakening to Life'; it is, more importantly, simply this: 'It is more blessed to give than to receive.' Any incidental infelicities of 'Impressionist aestheticizing' are certainly way off target, here.

In the following abstract, the Roman numerals represent the twelve Books of *The Ambassadors*, the Arabic numerals the sub-sections or chapters. (The astonishing long-drawn-out farce of a misplaced chapter, which for years eluded the scrutiny of readers, is a story briefly told by Professor Stallman in his note to the Everyman paperback edition of the novel, and in the Leon Edel—Dan H. Laurence bibliography.)

I, 1. The American Lambert Strether meets Maria Gostrey at Chester: she displays traces of the neat, trim, competent female arrangers and manipulators, ranging from young copyists to em-battled dowagers, who have dogged James's pages:

What had come as straight as a ball in a well played game—and caught, moreover, not less neatly—was just the air, in the person of his friend, of having seen and chosen, the air of achieved possession of those vague qualities and quantities that collectively figured to him as the advantage snatched from lucky chances.

Strether appreciates her as:

. . . the mistress of a hundred cases or categories, receptacles of the mind, subdivisions for convenience, in which, from a full experience, she pigeon-holed her fellow mortals with a hand as free as that of a compositor scattering type.

The lady herself confesses to being 'a general guide—to "Europe", don't you know? I wait for people—I put them through. I pick them up—I set them down. I'm a sort of superior "couriermaid". I'm a companion at large. I take people, as I've told you, about.'

2. Strether's American friend Waymarsh accuses him (and so informs the reader) of running away from Mrs. Newsome, a formidable American widow as yet unknown to us. Although the rôle of Waymarsh is to act merely as an excuse for half-mystifying half-expository conversation when some more competent commentator, such as Maria Gostrey, is not present, he is given a felicitously economic 'placing' as, sitting on his hotel bed,

. . . he hugged his posture of prolonged impermanence. It suggested to his comrade something that always, when kept up, worried him—a person established in a railway-coach with a forward inclination. It represented the angle at which poor Waymarsh was to sit through the ordeal of Europe.

3. At Chester, the middle-aged pair, Strether and Maria, carry on an elaborate innocent Edwardian verbal flirtation. Her own functional rôle is again underlined, in a sentence which in part (the 'dropped thread' image) takes us right back to the preliminary sketches for such women in James's earliest stories:

Wherever she happened to be she found a dropped thread to pick up, a ragged edge to repair, some familiar appetite in ambush, jumping out as she approached, yet appeasable with a temporary biscuit.

II, 1. We are told that Strether had a wife and son, both dead. He is the editor of a severely cultural review published at Woollett,

Massachusetts, and backed by the money of the formidable Mrs. Newsome. He tells Miss Gostrey of his strange mission: he has been sent on an embassy to Chad, Mrs. Newsome's son, who has overstayed his time in France and is suspected of having fallen among a circle, and formed a particular liaison, not countenanced at Woollett, Mass. All this is conveyed in an exposition brilliantly elusive and yet, step by step, seemingly obsolutely precise. As a kind of gleeful admission of obliquity, we are treated to James's famous joke about the little 'unmentionable' article, 'the little nameless object', the 'rather ridiculous object of common domestic use', on which the Newsome fortune has been founded. (This innocent if somewhat laboured example of old-fashioned jocosity, which so disconcerts some strait-laced modern readers, is merely in line with the equally tittering jest about the name of Mrs. Newsome's son-in-law—Pocock—which Strether 'sturdily confessed'.)

It becomes clear that Strether, for all his hesitations and reservations, is a man 'given over to uncontrollable perceptions'. (I hope it is not impertinent to confess that I have always pictured him, to myself, as a figure much resembling Mr. E. M. Forster.) Recalling the early set-piece demonstration of Mrs. Farrinder of *The Bostonians*, it is instructive to see how far James has developed towards a *pointilliste* subtlety of portraiture when he allows Maria Gostrey to hazard a guess at the terrible Mrs. Newsome, whom we are never to meet; a passage illustrating, at the same time, the stilted and yet curiously vivid dialogue in which so much of the plot of *The Ambassadors* is gently evolved, dialogue demanding the closest possible attention throughout if the essence of the novel is not to be lost:

'She's just a *moral* swell.'

He accepted gaily enough the definition. 'Yes—I really think that describes her.'

But it had for his friend the oddest connexion. 'How does she do her hair?'

He laughed out, 'Beautifully!'

'Ah that doesn't tell me. However, it doesn't matter—I know. It's tremendously neat—a real reproach; quite remarkably thick and without, as yet, a single strand of white. There!'

He blushed for her realism, but he gaped at her truth. 'You're the very deuce.'

'What else *should* I be? It was as the very deuce I pounced upon you. But don't let it trouble you, for everything but the very deuce—at our age—is a bore and a delusion, and even he himself, after all, but half a joy.' With which, on a single sweep of her wing, she resumed. 'You assist her to expiate—which is rather hard when you've not yourself sinned.'

2. A long presentation of Strether in Paris, reviewing his own pale wasted life; at fifty·five he feels free, in this classic place of escape, to sigh for a less ordered life: 'Everything he wanted was comprised moreover in a single boon—the common unattainable art of taking things as they come.'

III, 1. Strether admits to Waymarsh that Mrs. Newsome will marry him, but only if he succeeds in bringing Chad back safe and sound to Woollett. It begins to dawn on us that the simple joys of Paris (even 'the very taste of the soup, in the goodness . . . of the wine, in the pleasant coarse texture of the napkin and the crunch of the thick-crusted bread') may exert the stronger pull—and, 'If I'm squared, where is my marriage?' One recalls how Mrs. Lowder had to be 'squared', in *The Dove*; and the use of the word is pleasantly ominous.

2. Chad appears at last, meeting Strether and Waymarsh and Maria Gostrey at a box at the theatre. His American artist friend, little Bilham, is introduced as a kind of choric commentary from the Bohemian wings (cf. Gabriel Nash in *The Tragic Muse*); but for Strether there is a seemly 55-year-old irony between himself and any self-conscious Left Bank activities ('The ingenuous compatriots showed a candour . . . They twanged with a vengeance the esthetic lyre—they drew from it wonderful airs'), as contrasted with his whole-hearted response to the competent world of Maria Gostrey who, to his relief, was:

. . . wonderful about the delicate daubs, masterful about the way to make tea, trustful about the legs of chairs and familiarly reminiscent of those, in the other time, the named, the numbered or the caricatured, who had flourished or failed, disappeared or arrived . . .

IV, 1. Strether explains to Chad, as bluntly as the poor prospective stepfather knows how, the nature of his embassy—to drag him home from his French mistress. He cannot deny that Chad, on his side, has been immensely improved by the liaison; he has 'been made over', become polished: 'he had really, copious perhaps but shapeless, been put into a firm mould and turned successfully out'.

2. Nosing about for information, Strether learns from little Bilham that Chad's is a 'virtuous attachment'. Maria Gostrey also admits to knowing about Chad's 'two particular friends, two ladies, mother and daughter', but evades comment.

V, 1. Strether attends a party in the hope of meeting Mme de Vionnet and her daughter, and becomes involved in endless mock-questions and half-answers with various knowing guests. This is the kind of chapter that is passed over hurriedly at first reading, in the sure knowledge that its hints and clues will need further disentanglings, once one has a steadier grip on the main theme.

2. Strether meets, and is overwhelmed by, young Jeanne de Vionnet. Urging little Bilham to 'live all you can; it's a mistake not to', he groans afresh over having missed his own 'train', and now hearing its 'faint receding whistle miles and miles down the line'.

3. Still at the party, Strether obtains from Maria Gostrey an admission that she was a school-fellow of Mme de Vionnet, that her husband the Count is 'a brute', but that '*ces gens-là* don't divorce, you know, any more than they emigrate or abjure'. In an atmosphere reminiscent of the suppressed melodramatics of *Madame de Mauves*, Strether promises Chad that he will call on Mme de Vionnet. He (and the reader) is in a state of muddled obliquity, not knowing which of the two women, Jeanne or her mother, is Chad's Parisian magnet, nor even if the mother is 'bad'. But of her effect on Chad he is in no doubt: 'Chad owed Madame de Vionnet so much? What *did* that do then but clear up the whole mystery? He was indebted for alterations, and she was thereby in a position to have sent in her bill for expenses incurred in reconstruction.' The awkward *oratio obliqua* fits the mood.

VI, 1. In an atmosphere not unlike that of *The Spoils of Poynton*, Strether calls on Mme de Vionnet and admires her 'transmitted' treasures. 'The air of supreme respectability—that was a strange blank wall for his adventure to have brought him to break his nose against.' Even stranger is the way in which the charming lady commiserates with *him* on the possibility of his losing Mrs. Newsome if he should return to Woollett empty-handed. Most strange of all is his own bewildered promise: 'I'll save you if I can.'

2. 'I should like so awfully to know what you think of her.' Thus Chad, to Strether—and we are back, for a moment, in the shoes of old Mr. Longmore of *The Awkward Age*. During inconclusive chatter at another party (the least enjoyable series of entertainments, surely, in all Paris?), where everybody speaks with such mystifying hints and echoes that at times the whole company appears to be dim-witted, Strether confesses that 'I seem to have a life only for other people'.

3. Strether discusses with Mme de Vionnet her own wonderful effect on Chad, and then with little Bilham his growing admiration for the strange nobility of the friendship: but shouldn't Chad marry *somebody*, since the lady is already married? Plunging deep into treachery to Woollett, Mass., Strether believes that if Chad gives up Mme de Vionnet, 'he ought to be ashamed of himself'.

VII, 1. Strether, 'a plain tired man taking the holiday he had earned', in Notre Dame 'under the charm of a museum': a marvellous rendering of his non-religious peace of mind, his sophisticated exhaustion, like that of Milly Theale in Regent's Park after her doctor has gently condemned her to death. There he meets Mme de Vionnet ('one of the familiar, the intimate, the fortunate, for whom these dealings had a method and a meaning', observes the sadly unbelieving visitor), and over a luncheon eaten in 'costly disorder', he confesses that the situation is 'running away with him'.

2. A telegram arrives from Mrs. Newsome: if Strether's embassy is not completed, the family will follow him in the persons of daughter and son-in-law Pocock. Chad is in fact ready to sail home, but it is now Strether who begs Chad to stay on in Paris with him.

VIII, 1. A confession to Maria Gostrey that Strether, in the rôle of innocent inactive *voyeur*, is reliving his youth in the Chad-Marie situation:

'Though they're young enough, my pair, I don't say they're, in the freshest way, their *own* absolutely prime adolescence; for that has nothing to do with it. The point is that they're mine. Yes, they're my youth; since somehow at the right time nothing else ever was.'

The long-suffering *confidante* gets a consolation-prize: 'I began to be young, or at least to get the benefit of it, the moment I met you at Chester. . . .'

2. Strether and Chad await the arrival of the second embassy.

3. The Pococks arrive—and with them a refreshing interval of external descriptions, reviving in this atmosphere of breathless guesswork the sharp-eyed James of the earlier tales. Sarah Pocock, for instance, has a 'marked thin-lipped smile, intense without brightness and as prompt to act as the scrape of a safety-match'; as for young Mamie, Jim Pocock's sister, 'granted that a community *might* be best represented by a young lady of twenty-two, Mamie perfectly played the part'. Husband Jim is one of James's merciless American caricatures:

Small and fat and constantly facetious, straw-coloured and destitute of marks, he would have been practically indistinguishable hadn't his constant preference for light-grey clothes, for white hats, for very big cigars and very little stories, done what it could for his identity. There were signs in him, though none of them plaintive, of always paying for others . . .

Nevertheless, in describing his wife and mother-in-law, Jim blurts out, in language which all Strether's echoing obliquity cannot conceal, the vengeful rage of the betrayed ladies of Woollett:

'Why yes, she's prostrate—just as Sally is. But they're never so lively, you know, as when they're prostrate.'
'Ah Sarah's prostrate?' Strether vaguely murmured.
'It's when they're prostrate that they most sit up.'
'And Mrs. Newsome's sitting up?'
'All night, my boy—for *you*!'

4. After so many let-downs at busybody parties, a direct scene between Sarah and Marie de Vionnet is played out, as polite fencing, in terms of high social comedy.

IX, 1. Strether and Mme de Vionnet discuss the new arrivals: already he is her admiring co-Parisian in the face of the chill wind from Woollett, and in a conspiracy of muted assumptions very near the brink of self-parody ('It ended in fact by being quite beautiful between them, the number of things they had a manifest consciousness of not saying'), he takes without a gulp the news that Chad has found a suitable husband for Jeanne.

2. Behaving more and more like a pair of domesticated vultures, Strether and Maria Gostrey pick over Chad's relations with the two Vionnet ladies, an ambiguity as uncomfortable as that of Van's predicament in *The Awkward Age*, or, to take a modern instance, of an inverted Humbert Humbert wooing her mother behind a smoke-screen provided by Lolita.

3. Calling on the Pococks, Strether has a *tête-à-tête* with Mamie, who has already divined that Jeanne, too, is in love with Chad. The Woollett characters are already becoming bewitched, like Strether himself, into perceptions beyond their normal capacity: 'Their little interview was like a picnic on a coral strand; they passed each other, with melancholy smiles and looks sufficiently allusive, such cupfuls of water as they had saved.' Enchanted to find Mamie Pocock so 'disinterestedly tender', Strether leaves her, 'in her splendour, still waiting for little Bilham'.

X, 1. Chad gives an evening party, socially approved by Strether who had 'never known so great a promiscuity to show so markedly as picked'. In a little room off-stage from the main assembly, Strether conducts a series of conversations which give one the uncomfortable sense of communal peeping. He, who had once tried to steer little Bilham into proposing to Jeanne, now promises him all his money if only he will marry Mamie! He divines that Mamie is no longer infatuated with Chad because the operation of 'saving' him has already been performed by Mme. de Vionnet. As for Marie herself, the indefatigable ambassador learns that she in turn has already begun to make an impression on Jim Pocock.

2. Waymarsh announces to Strether the impending departure of the Pococks and himself for Switzerland, and asks him to quit Paris.

3. Sarah Pocock accuses Strether in her mother's name: 'What is your conduct ... but an outrage to women like *us*? I mean your acting as if there can be a doubt—as between us and such another—of his duty?' His mental betrayal is pin-pointed as 'just his poor old trick of quiet inwardness, what exposed him was his *thinking* such offence'. Sarah, invited at least to appreciate Chad's 'fortunate development' as a result of the liaison, pronounces it 'hideous', and departs.

4. Strether and Chad, musing at midnight on the balcony, accept the evidence that Mrs. Newsome will effectively dispossess and repudiate them both.

XI, 1. While Waymarsh and the Pococks and little Bilham go to Switzerland, Strether is left with his last chance to rescue Chad, who has given his word to follow the ambassador's advice. This is all expounded in the course of yet another session with Maria Gostrey, full of an increasingly desperate flirtatiousness on the part of this lady, who is emboldened to remark, in a flurry of 'magnificent' attributes, that Mrs. Newsome lacks Strether's own 'treasures of imagination', but with regard to the whole Vionnet business has displayed 'intensity with ignorance—what do you want worse?' Strether, as if intoxicated by Parisian air or quite entangled in the conversational web, is heard by the astonished reader to refer to his absent patroness at Woollett as 'the whole moral and intellectual being or block'.

2. Strether retires to the French countryside, and, like his creator, appreciates nature via art—in this instance, a landscape he could not afford to buy. We share his thankfulness for the fresh air, while recalling the pastoral interlude of *Madame de Mauves*.

3. In the thirty-first of thirty-six chapters, Strether reaches his climax, which after so long a frustration has all the effect of melodrama: he stumbles upon Chad and Marie de Vionnet also enjoying a *pastorale*. They dine together in 'innocent friendly Bohemia' at the village inn and all return by train to Paris—the couple minus their coats, which were evidently left behind at the unknown place where they had been staying together. The implications are obvious: Strether has been deceived; but by treating the episode as 'a wild extravagance of hazard', he smothers suspicion in assent.

XII, 1. Mme. de Vionnet sends Strether a summons to see her.

2. There follows a scene already quoted, where Strether and the lady exchange their sad confessions of secret escapes from 'the wretched self' by giving to other people. She comes near to breaking down:

She was older for him tonight, visibly less exempt from the touch of time; but she was as much as ever the finest and subtlest creature, the happiest apparition, it had been given him, in all his years, to meet; and yet he could see her there as vulgarly troubled, in very truth, as a maid-servant crying for her young man. The only thing was that she judged herself as the maidservant wouldn't; the weakness of which wisdom too, the dishonour of which judgement, seemed but to sink her lower.

3. Strether broods with Maria Gostrey, who confesses that she had 'funked' admitting the true relations between the lovers, because a woman is not obliged to lie for another woman, whereas a gentle-man is supposed to do so—as, indeed, little Bilham *had*.

4. Strether calls on Chad late at night, to tell him: 'You'll be a brute, you know—you'll be guilty of the last infamy—if you ever forsake her.' Chad admits how much his liaison has improved him as a social animal, protesting that Marie de Vionnet 'has never been anything I could call a burden'. Strether is horrified to hear that Chad has been looking into the question of returning to the family business with grand new ideas about advertising—but this is claimed to be merely a display of the full scope of the young gentleman's approaching sacrifice as a result of his *intention* to 'cleave to her to the death'.

5. A coda, with Maria Gostrey. There is a reversion to the joke about the 'article produced at Woollett'. His courtship of Mrs. Newsome is definitely over. Very delicately he rejects Maria, too, so as 'not, out of the whole affair, to have got anything for myself'. Her unique understanding of his rightness even in this, as in all his embassy throughout, condemns her to acquiescence in his with-drawal. In the chill induced by the last two chapters, it is tempting to leave the final word with a recent American critic, Mr. Quentin Anderson: 'Strether renounces nothing: he makes the most exorbit-ant claim a man can make—the claim to righteousness.' (*Scrutiny*, XV, 16). But perhaps the last word should, after all be Strether's—who, like his creator, 'had a horror . . . of being in question between women'. (VI, 3.)

Nowadays, without a doubt, such a novel needs defending. To cope with the question 'What *is* all the fuss about?' one must first examine the fuss—only to find that the termination point of a fairly con-ventional liaison has been reached amid the smothered thrills and gasps of a collection of prurient busybodies from two continents, and has been recorded with a thoroughness more in keeping, perhaps, with some such subject as the Thirty Years War. And yet one does care, at the end, what happens and how. Why is this? According to one's critical opinion, the reader has either been clobbered into subjection to the tittle-tattle level of James's stuffy characters, or else somehow been practised upon so that he finds himself educated to share the nicest shades of discrimination between the actions of intelligent people acting out the drama of social man and committing to the struggle their finest, most sensitive instincts.

It is possible, of course, to hold both views simultaneously. But one is in danger of being confined to the first view only, to sinking into the morass, without some assistance from historical imagination. Just think of the date of the novel: 1903! The date is, in many important ways, more distant from us than the Byzantine Empire. Merely to recall the physical appearance of the *beau monde* of the period, all gloved and hatted and feathered and braided, covered inches thick from neck to boots or trailing hems in clothes which, in contemporary photographs, have for our eyes the appearance of the ineradicably second-hand—this alone could set a block before an unperceptive reader. Unless—unless the recent revival of interest in the life of King Edward VII, for example, has reminded him that behind these acres of dusty silks and tweeds there lay, for the wealthy, a world of over-fed privilege which could support, at one and the same time, full-blooded fleshly pleasures conjured up better by Rubens or Boucher than by Court photographers, and a literature ranging from the self-consciously anaemic to the deliberately shocking. 1903! The year saw the appearance not only of *The Ambassadors* but also of Barrie's *Quality Street*, Butler's *The Way of All Flesh*, Shaw's *Man and Superman* and poems by Sir William Watson.

When historical allowances have been made there is—for current tastes—a still more troublesome nettle to be grasped. In most of his novels and pre-eminently in such hot-house affairs as *The Sacred Fount*, *The Ambassadors* and *The Golden Bowl*, James is dealing unashamedly with the world of wealthy dwellers in 'high society'. He echoes, lovingly, their collective mating-calls, their private cries of esoteric fashionable recognition. It is true that all such shibboleths, whether verbal or merely tonal, may easily be judged as absurd, even vulgar, from the outside. When they are contemporary, they are familiarly absurd, and hence forgiveable—like the language of Mr. Osbert Lancaster's Maudie Littlehampton. When they are out of date, unfamiliar, they sound like extremely offensive inanities mouthed by conceited imbeciles, as indicative of small minds as the jocosities of schoolboy slang. Occasionally, these herd-cries are out of date and yet still faintly familiar. The reader may perhaps have noticed, for instance, that even today the habit of repeating back a phrase in a tone of amused agreement is a habit restricted to 'U' circles—the vulgar self-consciousness of that Nancy Mitford designation being peculiarly apt, as it happens, to the self-advertising parrotry of the habit itself. The habit, at any rate, seems to have been prevalent in James's circles, and his endless fidelity to it in the later novels is, I suspect, a serious source of irritation to present-day readers. I plead, therefore, for a special effort of tolerance when these outmoded 'U' cymbals are clashed. Shudder as you will at the self-parody, but try to pass on unruffled by such passages as this between Strether and Miss Barrace (an American Parisienne):

'He has understood amazingly,' said Miss Barrace.
'It's wonderful!' Strether anticipated for her.
'It's wonderful!' she, to meet it, intensified; so that, face to face over it, they largely and recklessly laughed.

And even here there is for the tolerant, a minor instance of James's hair-breadth social 'placing': 'Nothing had yet been so "wonderful" between them as the present occasion; and it was her special sense of this quality in occasions that she was there, as she was in most cases, to feed.'

One could assemble a diverting anthology of Jamesian extra-vagances in this line (' "Ah", Sarah simply glittered'), and yet miss the cumulative point that this kind of oblique half-sympathetic half-amused reportage does manage to convey, with quite extra-ordinary fidelity, a sense of the fumbling hints and guesses by which a leisured and highly-cultivated class of inactive people, enjoying a breathless but intensely enjoyable conversational game, fed their social curiosity without ever openly expressing it. If to some readers these games are morally or even politically offensive, then 'high comedy' is not for them, and that is all there is to it. Less sourly constituted persons may profit from the reminder that although the recent past is always specially unfashionable, the conversational conventions of Edwardian London were in themselves no more (and no less) reprehensible than those of Restoration comedy or the fantasy world of Ronald Firbank. This granted, one may move on to the observation that it is usually James's *accounts* of such talk, rather than the passages of direct dialogue, that are successful in recapturing the precise tone—bantering, inflated, yet pertinacious —of the people he is describing. For as his plays only too mercilessly reveal, he could be almost farcically deaf to actual spoken language; and this for the benevolent reason that the dear good man wanted *all* his characters to speak high Jamesian comedy, the stupid with the intelligent, the *arrivistes* no less than the gentry.

You may say that in *The Ambassadors* and other late novels, James cast artificial pearls before real swine. Or you may concede that since his concentration on relations between people (e.g. Strether and Maria Gostrey meeting at Chester at the very opening of the book) is not really based on anything they say or do, then the insubstantial perceptions and apprehensions he *is* trying to convey call for a style as allusive, knowing, nudging and button-holing as he could make it. Alas, the thing had become so habitual that when the flimsiest tale with the most frankly boring theme can be equally tricked out, then the rightness—indeed, the inevitability— of this style at places where the inherently conceptual content cries out for it, is admittedly smudged. As a stylist of high comedy, James's most self-wounding fault was an inability to *stop*. His brocades are wrapped up for posting in other brocades; the very string is ridiculously golden. But if we allow the unfitness of the one to blind us to the value of the other, we shall show ourselves as even more foolish—to complete the figure—than those who enjoy shoddy conveniently wrapped *in* shoddy. That James himself was ruefully aware of the economic consequences, stylistically, of such prodigal behaviour, is demonstrated only too cruelly in his story *The Next Time*.

When all such allowances have been made, certain obstinate objections to *The Ambassadors*, as an example of what (following the late Professor Matthiessen) has come to be known as James's 'major phase', undoubtedly remain. For long passages (as, for example, Chapters V, 1 and 2), James can hardly be absolved from the charge of writing *about* what he should, so to say, have been *writing*; there are hesitations and adulterations which invite Dr. Leavis's charge of 'senility' and 'thinness'. Again, many readers will find the *dénouement* hard to swallow—until they reflect that in spite of his sacrificial gestures, Chad's over-protestation that he is not yet 'tired' of Marie, combined with her own admission that she has already been the giver and hence technically the loser, has prepared us for the inevitable cooling-off period and imminent rupture, which may be imagined as taking place once Strether is safely on board his Edwardian Cunarder. But most of all, a present-day reader has been conditioned to expect that a story like that of Chad and Marie, where human beings expose themselves, raw, to the joy and anguish of personal life, should be told either by them or with them as the main stark protagonists. Not all the special pleading of a James Preface will convince such a reader that to have the tale told by an impotent go-between, be he never so noble, never so intelligent, never so perceptive, can be anything other than cowardice on the part of a major novelist.

Yet it is precisely this limitation, or concentration, of outlook to the imaginative possibilities of a Strether, rather than a shifting *exposé* of the passions of the prime movers of the affair in their own private sufferings or triumphs, that James himself offers as the real achievement of his novel. The Prefaces for the New York Edition of his collected works were composed in 1907, and that written for *The Ambassadors* is therefore much nearer to the novel in time—and presumably in settled attitude—than are the Prefaces to other much-revised work. In the case of these earlier novels and tales, one may often enough feel that the younger novelist was nearer the heart of the matter than the later self-appraising commentator. With the later works, one is safe in assuming an unforced resonance. And in this particular Preface, James does unequivocally admit that *The Ambassadors* is, in his view, 'quite the best, "all round", of my productions'. Furthermore, he insists on 'the major propriety ... of employing but one centre and keeping it all within my hero's compass'. His task was no more nor less than to seize 'the opportunity to "do" a man of imagination', to 'do' him so thoroughly that 'satisfactorily to account for Strether and for his "peculiar tone"', was to possess myself of the entire fabric'.

As if to forestall objections, James sallies forth from his defence into a counter-attack on 'the terrible *fluidity* of self-revelation' as any sort of sound basis for the treatment of the passions, say, of Chad and Marie as Strether actually saw or imagined them. For 'composition alone is positive beauty', and it is in Strether, not in Chad and Marie, that we are to look for the key to James's composition. Before such authority, most critics have bowed. Indeed, James's exhortations and self-exculpations, whether addressed to himself in his *Notebooks* or to his readers in the Prefaces and other literary essays, are chanted with such hieratic certainty that once one falls under the spell, he could almost persuade the reader that the drama of *Romeo and Juliet* would have been improved if Shakespeare had limited himself to the sole consciousness of Friar Lawrence. Personally, I prefer to fall under the spell of the practice rather than of the theory. Of the three 'major phase' masterpieces, *The Wings of the Dove* is in sum more moving and in detail has a greater richness of poetic truth; and *The Golden Bowl* grapples at much closer quarters with the passions it seeks to analyse. James himself had a special tenderness for *The Ambassadors* as a work of art. And however much one may dislike the machinery, the product remains incontestably a work of prodigious social intelligence. We who are nowadays broad-minded enough to applaud, in our fiction, the technical skill with which the innermost feelings of criminal morons, plain or perverted, are transmitted to the page, should not draw back snobbishly from a similar fidelity of transmission, in *The Ambassadors*, of the peripheral consciousness of a man of gentle temperament slashing out in *his* bewilderment with only his intelligence as a weapon. If Strether is a Friar Lawrence figure, he is also, a little, T. S. Eliot's Prufrock. 'No! I am not Prince Hamlet, nor was meant to be. . . ' *But:* 'I have heard the mermaids singing, each to each.'

XII

The Golden Bowl

'What is morality but high intelligence?'
The Golden Bowl

HENRY JAMES was a thorough-going humanist. He rarely attempted a religious theme or even a religious atmosphere. His excursions into the supernatural are either the half-hearted dodges of the professional story-teller, as in some early tales, or mawkish subsidences into vicarious self-pity, as in such later embarrassments as *The Altar of the Dead.*

Even so celebrated a 'mystery' as *The Turn of the Screw* is open to various interpretations: some critics treat the 'ghost' figures as hallucinations of the deranged governess, but even if they are accepted as being as substantial as the witches in *Macbeth*, their fatal fascination relates back exclusively to the effect of the dead creatures on the children when they were still alive—there is no suggestion of *extra* evil from another world.

If James had other-worldly experiences, they emerge in his fiction as the raptures or ecstasies of a rooted earthbound consciousness. The magnanimity of Milly in *The Wings of the Dove*; the misnamed 'redemption' of *The Golden Bowl* which is in effect Maggie's valorous resolve to cut emotional losses and preserve what may be salvaged for civilized adjustments after the havoc wrought by primary feelings wrongly thought to have been lying dormant; the resignation of Marie de Vionnet in *The Ambassadors*: all these gestures are unsanctified by anything recognizable as religious faith. The high-level morality of the chosen objects of James's mature admiration has no religious sanction. As the dreadful Fanny Assingham asks her husband, 'What is morality but high intelligence?' James ventured, even at his most ambitious, no further than the earthbound mysticism of a noble stoic. Mr. J. I. M. Stewart has put the matter crisply enough: 'For James the Christian religion . . . figures most frequently as a means of withdrawing unwanted members of a house-party from his scene on a Sunday morning . . .'*

I do not think of myself as a more callous reader than most, but I must confess that nowhere in *The Golden Bowl* do I find substantiation for the reading of that excessively worldly novel as a kind of tract on redemption. Nor, on the other hand, do I find it in any way akin to Restoration drama, for instance, as an example of a

Eight Modern Writers, pp. 107–8.

highly-mannered attempt to recreate in literary terms the inferior values
of an ultra-sophisticated society. *The Golden Bowl* and the other late
novels are 'worldly' only in the sense that they face the human
predicament where it may be seen most fully developed: that is to
say, among people who have both leisure and intellect enough to be
conscious of all kinds of marginal problems of belief and behaviour,
over and above the basic needs which they share with all mankind.
But these additional areas of experience and conflict supplement the
normal human expanse of intellectual and emotional activity; they
do *not* supplant them. Moreover, the most extreme case of 'abnormal'
expansion is that of the novelist himself; so that in a novel like *The
Golden Bowl* all his characters, major and minor alike, are endowed
with an articulation far beyond their own realistic resources. It
takes a James to interpret, for us the readers, how they feel. They
would, these Ververs and Assinghams, have been quite unable, one
feels, to do it themselves; yet what *is* described is true in that they
were all mutely capable of such activities and interpretations.

To seize upon one example only: the American millionaire Adam
Verver represents that social summit of amiable nullity which in
older cultures was occupied by royalty, but which in vigorous
republican states is, paradoxically, the prize reserved for the toughest
survivors of the financial free-for-all contest. His status (like that
of Christopher Newman, way back in *The American*) implies a hard
toughness which in the novel itself is manifest only in a sustained if
passive emotional egotism. There is no sense of either shame or
exultation in Verver's millions. He ruminates over the possibilities
inherent in his money with as unruffled a conscience as that of
another man contemplating the outlay of a guinea. Curiously enough,
Adam Verver is a prophetic type. The amateur social psychologist
may nowadays note among wealthy Americans a new disposition
to move towards the position of eminent anonymity. They will
eschew open opinions, disguise their shrewdness of judgement in
large platitudes, providing a royal nullity for themselves by acting
like so many mirrors reflecting commonly accepted views. They are
no longer so anxious to 'return to the group' or preside at boosters'
clubs. Like Adam Verver, they may even spend some of their money
in collecting old china—and (until they die) keeping it.

A novel constructed with the amplitude of *The Golden Bowl*

demands a corresponding amplitude of reading. It should be taken in large, deliberate and comfortable doses. It exacts a concert-pitch quickening to every reference. The following commentary can attempt merely a helicopter-view of the rich terrain.

The novel opens in splendidly assured style with Prince Amerigo musing, in Bond Street, on his approaching marriage. He shows an intelligent sociological insight into the likely consequences of an alliance between Roman aristocracy and American millions. 'He was allying himself to science, for what was science but the absence of prejudice backed by the presence of money? His life would be full of machinery, which was the very antidote to superstition, which was in its turn, too much, the consequence, or at least the exhalation of archives.' This comment, mildly ironic, is nevertheless one of many recurring reminders that Henry James, for all his personal gravity and a rigorous artistic concentration seemingly at variance with the values of the new twentieth century, was by no means an automatic *laudator temporis acti*. As in *The Sense of the Past*, his final essay in social discrimination, the very title of which misleads a reader into expecting praise for the *ancien régime*, he shows himself a sturdy, if somewhat unexpected, advocate of the contemporaneous. The Prince, at any rate, is prepared to face the values of his immensely wealthy prospective father-in-law, Adam Verver, while understanding that in Verver's world he himself would 'constitute a possession'. He had already expressed to his fiancée the ironic comment that whereas he himself was a chicken 'cooked down as a *crème de volaille*, with half the parts left out', her American father was 'the natural fowl running about the *basse-cour*'. These are elements that could have made *The Golden Bowl* a major essay in the 'international Cerberus' series of stories; but as the novel develops, its intricate pattern of intertwined marriages (*The Marriages* was James's first choice for a title) so dominates the action that the old American-European theme is quite overlaid.

Amerigo betakes himself to the London home of Fanny Assingham, the American-born wife of a retired English colonel, who had engineered his engagement to Maggie Verver. In badinage with this domineering lady he confesses, as a Roman, that 'your moral sense works by steam—it sends you up like a rocket. Ours is slow and steep and unlighted'. During their talk, they both feel that 'the unspoken had come up', which swiftly reveals itself as the Prince's former relationships with Charlotte Stant, another American girl who is visiting the Assinghams and who proposes, as an old friend of both households, to embrace the new Amerigo-Maggie ménage. Charlotte herself breaks in upon their musings, reminding Amerigo of 'some wonderfully finished instrument, something intently made for exhibition, for a prize'.

A tedious and wholly unlifelike monologue by Fanny Assingham to her long-suffering husband reveals that Charlotte and the Prince had been in love but had failed to marry because neither could produce enough cash. (We are back in the Kate Croy-Merton Densher world, and already we feel an anxiety for Maggie.) High praise is lavished on Charlotte for having 'bolted' in time and kept safely out of reach in America while Maggie the heiress was dangled in front of Amerigo. Charlotte, thinks Fanny, has returned to 'be sublime', to lend moral support to Maggie while exposing the Prince to the effect of her own bravely unbowed head. Fanny is resolved to 'see her through her sublimity' by finding her an alternative husband. (This intolerable matchmaker had not only introduced Amerigo to 'the young woman who has a million a year', but had even looked up his own illustrious family, with Maggie, in the British Museum!) As a piece of induction, this scene creaks absurdly. Not only is it completely non-dramatic, but the saving grace of wit is lacking, as if James had allowed his earlier sense of economic emphasis (expressed most successfully in epigram) to be overborne by a nagging insistence on getting every minute touch and hint photographically recorded in a relentlessly conscientious recapitulation. This is, in short, the kind of scene that a practised reader of James may read with a 'willing suspension of disbelief', but that taken by itself, cold, strays far over the border of the boringly absurd.

In token of 'the full tune of her renouncing', Charlotte asks the Prince to help her select a 'funny' inexpensive present for the approaching wedding; but she also admits, ominously, that an hour or two in his sole company had also figured in her benedictory plan. She makes a parade of her renunciation: 'Giving myself, in other words, away—and perfectly willing to do it for nothing.' At the antique shop, she expresses the wish to give the Prince himself a present, as if loading him with a perpetual obtrusive memorial to her self-effacement. But the gift she selects is a gilded crystal bowl with a small crack which brings the price within her range but frightens the superstitious Amerigo as an omen of a flaw in his forthcoming marriage. He rejects it.

Meanwhile, Adam Verver, at his great rented country house Fawns, muses on a millionaire's lack of privacy ('Everyone had need of one's power, whereas one's own power, at the best, would have seemed to be but some trick for not communicating it') and also on the fact that his prospective son-in-law has grandly interrupted the pattern of his own life with Maggie, much as if a Palladian church had suddenly been dropped into a quiet city square. He is presented as a connoisseur of forty-seven with, his fortune made, one world left to conquer and one commensurate hobby: 'to rifle the Golden Isles' of every available perfect artifact. (No cracked bowls for *him*, either!)

With extraordinary abruptness, given the snail-like narrative pace, the presence of a Principino at Fawns as Adam's most precious treasure indicates that Maggie has been married for a year or so. Fanny Assingham spots that the widower, having now officially 'lost' his daughter to a ratified domesticity, needs a new wife. Yet in the almost tangible dullness of a Sunday afternoon at Fawns, it is also made clear to the reader (as to an honorary member of the interminable house-party) that 'Maggie and her father had, with every ingenuity, converted the precious creature into a new link between a mamma and a grandpapa'.

In the desperately aimless atmosphere of 'the noble privacy' of Fawns, Maggie and her father discuss the question of a marriage for him, now that he is no longer 'married' to, and protected from other women by, his daughter. The self-absorbed pair, innocent of the mildly incestuous basis of their infatuation with one another's peace of mind, decide to invite Charlotte to stay, as it were 'on approval', both of them recognizing in her penniless life a great dignity in misfortune. Charlotte settles in admirably, and after much brooding, Adam decides that if he should in fact remarry, then indeed Maggie 'would less and less appear to herself to have forsaken him'. At Brighton, whither she accompanies him on a treasure-hunting expedition, he proposes to Charlotte. They both take it for granted that their main motive is to free Maggie from any guilt at having 'abandoned' her father for her husband. Later, in Paris, the Prince and Princess (on tour) telegraph their congratulations: Maggie's wire to her father is shared; but Charlotte's, from Amerigo, though offered for Adam's inspection, is digested by her alone. Later in the novel, we learn its contents: '*A la guerre comme à la guerre* then. We must lead our lives as we see them; but I am charmed with your courage and almost surprised at my own.'

We jump a couple of years forward to observe Charlotte, ablaze with Verver diamonds, attending in London a State reception in company with the Prince and Princess. Adam had pleaded indisposition: Maggie leaves the party to return to him, a circumstance discussed with Charlotte—who stays on with her youthful stepson-in-law Amerigo—by an officiously disapproving Fanny Assingham. Charlotte maintains that since the Ververs and the Amerigos had set up separate establishments, Maggie was actually seeing even more of her father: 'the result of our separate households is really, for them, more contact and more intimacy. She likes him best alone.' She admits that she has failed to take Maggie's place in her husband's life, that Adam's love for his daughter 'is the greatest affection of which he is capable'. The outraged Fanny, while Charlotte is being quizzed by royalty, upbraids the Prince in turn for compromising Charlotte, whose place 'is naturally in Mr. Verver's boat'—to which the feckless Amerigo replies that he, too, is in Mr. Verver's boat, but for which he would, financially, have drowned. He objects, too, that Adam is more conscientious as a father than as a husband. It is clear to the Prince, as it was to Charlotte, that Fanny Assingham, their 'fairy-Godmother', is already poised to 'give them up'. She had equally, in her ministrations, been the fairy-Godmother of Adam and Maggie. Whether from genuine repentance or from a gossipy itch to foresee the worst, Fanny recognizes her own responsibility in the dangerous affair.

While Adam and Maggie busy themselves with the Principino, the desperate and neglected Charlotte takes a cab to call on the serenely solitary Amerigo. After an interval of 'a very high level of debate', they conclude, *vis-à-vis* the relapse of the Verver father and daughter to pre-marital domesticity, that 'the thing is for us to learn to take them as they are'. In a crucial but unstressed passage,

Charlotte admits that her own marriage would have been less inept
if she and Adam, 'poor duck', had had a child: ' "It's not, at any
rate," she went on, "my fault. There it is." ' But facing the Verver
self-absorption, she adds: 'it would have taken more than ten
children of mine, could I have had them—to keep our *sposi* apart.'
By the manner in which father and daughter have in effect abducted
the Principino as their own, Charlotte and Amerigo are left 'immensely alone'. Their recourse is obvious enough, and they close
the scene with as passionate an embrace as James's erotic prose
allows.

There follows an assessment of the precise place in the highest
London society filled by the establishments at Eaton Square (Ververs)
and Portland Place (the Princely pair). Charlotte's own 'tested
facility' in social life contributes much to the peaceful non-
competitive regality of Adam and his daughter; and although
Amerigo, musing again on 'the people among whom he had married',
considered that 'one used one's imagination mainly for wondering
how they contrived so little to appeal to it' (a quintessential late-
James phrase, this!), it is made clear that in spite of Maggie's
comparative effacement when set beside Charlotte's full-blooded
enjoyment of 'the London treadmill', there was nevertheless no
doubt that when sitting as guest at the 'large, bright, dull, mur-
murous, mild-eyed, middle-aged' dinners in Eaton Square, it was
his own wife, Princess or no, who 'would still always, in that
house, be irremediably Maggie Verver'.

A short and brilliant chapter (XX) brings to a head the realization
of the equivocal position of Amerigo and Charlotte, both personally
and socially, as they find themselves exposed by the joint withdrawal
of their respective spouses. They are attending, each unaccompanied
by his or her Verver, a great house-party at Matcham, the Prince's
appraisal of which provides for Henry James yet another occasion to
demonstrate how amusedly critical he could be—even while enjoying
it—of the Edwardian social high summer which rested so blatantly
upon 'a bottomless bag of solid shining British sovereigns'. Amerigo,
Roman Prince that he is, falls effortlessly into place in the 'great
bright house' where 'every voice ... was a call to the ingenuities
and impunities of pleasure'. Yet he feels obliged, in the company of
'the bravery of youth and beauty, the insolence of fortune and

appetite so diffused among his fellow-guests', to keep out of sight his own extra personal acquirements, namely 'a restless play of memory and a fine embroidery of thought'. (One can readily imagine James, especially in one of his *The Sacred Fount* moods, in a similar plight.)

What Charlotte and the Prince spot in one another at stately Matcham, in short, in addition to their odd exposure by reason of the withdrawal of Adam and Maggie to nursery nostalgia, is simply a superior and enjoyable cleverness—superior, that is, not only to the nullity of their puzzling yet radically innocent American spouses, but also to the clutter of marchionesses and Assinghams, so to say, through whom they must tread their amused way. It is this, as much as their memory of their pre-Verver love affair in Italy, that gives them 'an exquisite sense of complicity'. And since their half-guilty situation is caused not by action on their part but by mute defection on the part of the Ververs, they are able to feel half-innocent as they enjoy its fruits. This exposure of Amerigo and Charlotte is effected in prose which, after the tedious *longueurs* of chapters to which the Assinghams lend not only their gruesome presence but also their nagging style, glows with a sudden baroque imagery reminiscent of the ebullient entertaining James of ten or twenty years earlier. A single mock-epic image must suffice to illustrate this welcome reversion to an earlier vitality of writing, even if wordy to the point of self-parody:

What anyone 'thought' of anyone else—above all of anyone *with* anyone else—was a matter incurring in these halls so little awkward formulation that hovering judgement, the spirit with the scales, might perfectly have been imagined there as some rather snubbed and subdued, but quite trained and tactful poor relation, of equal, of the properest, lineage, only of aspect a little dingy, doubtless from too limited a change of dress, for whose tacit and abstemious presence, never betrayed by a rattle of her rusty machine, a room in the attic and a plate at the side-table were decently usual.

It is at moments like these, in the midst of much laboured 'late James' writing, that one recalls Proust's dictum about 'that grotesque touch which belongs to all great works', which itself, in turn, suggests the odd scraps of Coleridgean Fancy lying about in the workshops of great literary artists, ready for use when the craftsman is temporarily unvisited by Imagination. But it is, alas, a small oasis in the desert of the tireless *voyeur* speculations of the Assinghams, the nature and presentation of which are equally unconvincing.

Amerigo grasps, at any rate, the truth that the social English—who 'called it themselves, with complacency, their wonderful spirit of compromise'—had a great distaste for *'les situations nettes'*. He and Charlotte remain at Matcham for 'luncheon' after the rest of the house-party (including the Assinghams) has departed; their presence —'which really meant the absence'—providing a useful smoke-screen for their hostess Lady Castledean, who has persuaded her own young lover, a Mr. Blint, to remain on for some unchaperoned hours at the house. Amerigo and Charlotte, by a brazen use of railway time-tables, find a way of popping off to Gloucester for the afternoon at an inn ('I've chosen the right one', adds the efficient Charlotte in tones vividly reminiscent of Kate Croy) and still getting back in time for the scheduled Verver–Amerigo foursome at dinner at Eaton Square. We are left to imagine a minutely timed daylight adultery tacitly condoned by their *louche* infatuated hostess who, glad of their official presence and actual absence, 'knows for herself', as Charlotte impudently puts it, 'that we like cathedrals'.

It is left to the Assinghams (to whom, by the way, Maggie is a 'poor duck' just as Adam was a 'poor duck' to his wife) to dot every 'i' and cross every 't' in one of their ghastly bedtime colloquies. Fanny does make the point that Amerigo and Charlotte had been at least 'guileless' in letting Maggie keep her father, and also that if the Ververs are 'quaint' it is with a specifically American 'dear old quaintness'. She also spots that Amerigo doesn't really 'care' for Charlotte, but treats his conquest of her 'like a Prince'. Most perceptively of all, she grasps that Maggie's real aim is to protect her father from suspecting his wife's faithlessness: it is significant that one has so accepted Adam and his daughter as the true 'pair' of Eaton Square that it has to be Fanny who reminds the reader that the colourless cuckold Adam, no less than the 'heroic' Maggie, has been at least technically betrayed.

And there, at the end of Book First (entitled 'The Prince'), the novel could well have ended, for all that concerns 'plot'. It is in the almost equally lengthy Book Second ('The Princess') that the consequences of the Gloucester crack, the flaw in the golden bowl, are worked out and the opportunity afforded for critics to read (or, to my mind, misread) into the thick tangle of 'ifs' and 'whys' and 'buts' and 'neverthelesses' a Jamesian concern for 'redemption'. Book Second opens with Maggie musing on the 'high felicity' of a marriage in which she had 'surrendered herself to her husband without the shadow of a reserve or a condition, and yet she had not, all the while, given up her father by the least little inch'. Into this meditation is introduced so elaborate an image of a 'strange tall tower' or 'outlandish pagoda' in 'the garden of her life' that one stirs uneasily at the suggestion that father-fixation and convenient princely substitute are being equipped with an outsize phallic symbol. A reader accustomed to Jamesian circumlocution may stir uneasily, yet again, at Maggie's reflexion that in her marriage with Amerigo 'her faculties had not for a good while been concomitantly used', and her determination, in a fresh resolve to assuage the renewed feeling for her husband that had begun 'to vibrate with a violence', to behave like a person who, having forgotten how to dance, 'would go to balls again'. So, on the fatal day of the expedition to Gloucester, she awaits the return of Amerigo at home at Portland Place instead of with her father at Eaton Square, and on his eventual arrival there she greets him with unaccustomed warmth, as if '*testifying*, that she adored and missed and desired him'. It is a chapter in the full Jamesian opaque, with next to no dialogue and a host of unspoken inferences; but it glows with a strange humanity, a sense of tender understanding, immensely superior to the chapters in which there is merely a series of theories by the author—or, worse, by the Assinghams—about what *might* be going on. In the following chapter, with Maggie still introspective, we learn that on the same evening of Amerigo's return from Matcham and Gloucester, after dining with her husband *tête-à-tête*, Maggie had 'somehow been lifted aloft, floated and carried on some warm high tide beneath which stumbling-blocks had sunk out of sight'. This revelation comes just after a passage in which the Princess reminiscently sees the advent of Charlotte in the Verver–Amerigo world as having been 'ever so smoothly and beautifully' the addition of a fourth wheel to the awkward family coach. A reader in these franker days may be forgiven for observing that James, with a sort of submerged insight, was in a guarded way admitting that Amerigo's sexual infidelity had, as is so often the case, had the immediate effect of making his own wife the residuary legatee, so to say, of his aroused passion.

A similar vigorous handling of the same difficult 'late' style carries us through another lengthy assessment by Maggie of various tensions and relaxations within the quartet which tended either to distort or ratify 'the perfection of their common state'. The two men, and the two women, continue to cultivate pleasantly parallel friendships, as if to indicate that in their strange parallelogram there were two perfectly acceptable sets of social straight lines, one pair linking husbands and wives and the other pair linking the two men and the two women. We, the readers, are mainly conscious, of course, of a disruptive diagonal line linking Amerigo and Charlotte; and it is, designedly, made difficult for us to see quite how much Maggie herself is conscious of that extra geometrical possibility. What she *does* see, sometimes gratefully and sometimes with apprehension, is that 'they were *treating* her, that they were proceeding with her—and, for that matter, with her father—by a plan that was the exact counterpart of her own'. Again:

> Ah! Amerigo and Charlotte were arranged together, but she—to confine the matter only to herself—was arranged apart. It rushed over her, the full sense of all this, with quite another rush from that of the breaking wave of ten days before; and as her father himself seemed not to meet the vaguely clutching hand with which, during the first shock of complete perception, she tried to steady herself, she felt very much alone.

There had been some talk of Adam and Maggie, stewing as they all were in their leisured juice, taking an art-collecting trip to Spain; but Verver postpones the expedition. Maggie is instantly alerted. Why does he want to stay in London with the other members of the quartet? She proposes various other alternatives to Amerigo, such as that he and his father-in-law should share a little trip together. The longed-for response that *they*, husband and wife, might slip off alone, fails to materialize. And it is upon such delicate hesitances and silences, in the muted sociability of their idle days, that pages and pages of difficult and very careful prose are expended, with hardly a touch of direct dialogue. The interim solution, that Maggie should ask Amerigo to suggest to Charlotte to propose to Adam to invite Amerigo to accompany him, which sounds so much like a parody of the whole business, is merely a symbol of the cat-and-mouse game in which all four participants seem to be endlessly forestalling the possibilities of obscure affronts to the other three. Illustrative instances of Maggie's own alternating small gains and losses in this curious emotional competition are: (i) her original view that a month's absence by herself and Adam would demonstrate 'an ecstasy of confidence' in the other guilty pair; (ii) her consciousness of the 'inscrutable companionship' formed by Amerigo and Charlotte at the Matcham Party from which she and Adam, in their own self-sufficiency, had absented themselves; (iii) her suspicion that Amerigo's polite tolerant behaviour towards Adam represents a balefully significant desire not to hurt him: 'With their stillness together so perfect, what had suggested so, around them, the attitude of sparing them?' The reader finds difficulty in maintaining sympathy with a heroine so determined to suffer in a kind of 'heads-you-win, tails-I-lose' toss-up of emotional alternatives. But there is one attitude she strikes, out of the whole series of possible and attempted postures, that seems to betray to us where her own basic natural (and, equally, perverse) feelings lie; and that is when (iv) she has a fantasy of her devoted child-parent Adam saying to her: 'Sacrifice me, my own love; do sacrifice me, do sacrifice me'. To which the un-Jamesian response might be a straight 'Wow!'

Similar minor adjustments to or awarenesses of the larger social scene are by this time presented merely as hints as to the current state of mind, or imagination, of the different members of the quartet, so that a reader hoping for fresh instances of James's social comedy is being continually forced back into a fusty atmosphere of collective incest. Thus, a brilliant Proust-like description of a dinner party at Portland Place, which offers promise of another reversion to James's great vein of social comedy based on fresh and essentially affectionate observation, peters out lifelessly, like a stream drying up in the desert. Again, when Maggie and her father sit for a moment in Regent's Park and their talk turns to their 'consciousness of our general comfort and privilege', with suggestions that they are all 'a wee bit languid' in spite of the earlier plan that Charlotte should be imported to 'give us a life', any hope that the bemused pair may be roused from their sleep-walking trance-like wonderment to a consideration of what they might actually *do* with all that money, soon dwindles away when they turn back to petting or ruffling the satisfactory notion that, as a quartet, 'we're selfish together—we move as a selfish mass'.

Yet still, combing the sands of this exasperating but potentially fertile desert of speculation, one comes, every now and then, upon a human insight which is, given the extraordinarily limited area in which it is permitted to operate, on a par with some of Proust's most glittering elucidation. Take, for example, this passage describing Maggie's unspoken mental confrontation of Fanny Assingham:

'You've such a dread of my possibly complaining to you that you keep pealing all the bells to drown my voice; but don't cry out, my dear, till you're hurt—and above all ask yourself how I can be so wicked as to complain. What in the name of all that's fantastic can you dream that I have to complain *of*?' Such inquiries the Princess temporarily succeeded in repressing, and she did so, in a measure, by the aid of her wondering if this ambiguity with which her friend affected her wouldn't be at present a good deal like the ambiguity with which she herself must frequently affect her father. She wondered how she should enjoy, on *his* part, such a take-up as she had but just succeeded, from day to day, in sparing Mrs. Assingham and that made for her trying to be as easy with this associate as Mr. Verver, blessed man, all indulgent but all inscrutable, was with his daughter.

Here, although the actual phrasing of the observation reads cruelly like a clever parody of 'late James' (especially the characteristic teasing let-down when we are merely informed of the question which Maggie had *not* asked), nevertheless the realization by the Princess that her own determination not to break down before Fanny Assingham's all-too-reluctant pity may be but a parallel to her betrayed father's resolve not to show *her* any wound—all this is as subtly observed as it is clumsily worded. Indeed, at such moments one is confronted by the outrageously unexpected notion that so far from being —as most readers have complained—a super-subtle writer dealing with limited subject-matter, there are times when Henry James is a man of most delicate and far-reaching human perceptions, who is hampered only by gross clumsiness of expression.

Unable to consume her own smoke indefinitely, Maggie communicates her suspicions to Fanny Assingham when, on the occasion of another opportunity perversely presented to them by the stay-at-home

Maggie and Adam, the Prince and Charlotte are once again sharing a week-end in the country. One gains the impression that Amerigo and Charlotte—in a curious sense the victims, rather than the beneficiaries, of the lucky situation—are now almost afraid *not* to go off together, so heavy is the atmosphere of bogus confidence in which all the movements of the quartet are now taking place. Fanny, at any rate, gamely tells a lie when she roundly declares herself free of any suspicion of misconduct between Amerigo and Charlotte. Maggie lives *her* lie, by pretending to believe her. And the sophisticated Fanny retails both sets of sacrificial perjuries to her husband: it is with this knowledge that they are to arm themselves for attendance at another full-scale party at Fawns.

Apropos Maggie's outburst, Fanny is cynical enough to know in advance that 'there's no imagination so lively, once it's started, as that of really agitated lambs'. (The reader recalls that the worst depravities are said to be customarily committed by lapsed Methodists.) Nevertheless, she admires Maggie for striving so hard to furnish herself with officially acceptable '*dis*proof' of the evidence of guilt she has discerned by 'natural perception' and 'insurmountable feeling'. She has gone so far as to make her humiliated 'scream' of jealousy in Fanny's presence, simply in order to have it officially denied: she is prepared, in short, to enact the part of a suspicious simpleton, if by so doing she may persuade the world to take the view that the existence of a love affair between her husband and her father's wife is quite out of the question. As an exercise in genteel masochism, it is hard to fault this display.

Part Fourth (there are three Parts divided between the two Books) ends with two highly charged scenes, after so much unspoken speculation. They are based on the coincidence of Maggie's happening to buy, as a birthday gift for her father, the very bowl which Amerigo had rejected four years or so ago. Maggie does not spot the flaw, but the second-hand dealer, smitten with remorse, visits her on the morrow in order to point out the defect in the object for which she had overpaid (a fable which, incidentally, even if good consistent symbolism, is on the surface plane of meaning far more difficult for an antique-hunting reader to swallow than any number of shopping coincidences). In her room, the dealer recognizes photographs of Amerigo and Charlotte as being the lady and gentleman who had first admired, then rejected, the bowl some years earlier. The fateful date of that shopping expedition, just a few days before her wedding, makes undeniably clear to Maggie the fact that the now condemned pair had concealed from her not only the degree of their relationship before she herself had met Amerigo, but also its resumption both before and after her marriage. Maggie first summons Fanny Assingham to announce to her that she is now convinced that the Prince and Charlotte have been consistently deceiving her, and indicates—but without explaining why—the 'golden bowl' as the proof of her new knowledge. Fanny, herself implicated by the concealment both of her own knowledge of the earlier, Roman, entanglement of the poverty-inhibited lovers and also of her suspicion of their later lapse at Gloucester, dashes the bowl to pieces on the floor. At which point Amerigo enters, to face in turn a more fully documented accusation.

Maggie's exquisitely effective moral blackmail is now given full rein. In vain does the Prince plead, of the time of his quite innocent visit with Charlotte to the antique shop, that 'you've never been more sacred to me than you were at that hour—unless perhaps you've become so at this one'. In the full flush of her triumphant virtue, the Princess points out that looming larger even than the question of her own ignorance or knowledge of the exact relationship between Amerigo and Charlotte, is the question of her precious father's unruffled serenity. Only Charlotte, she implies, can sense how successfully (or not) *he* has been deceived—and the guilty husband and son-in-law is left to discover *that* if he may, from his partner the guilty stepmother-in-law and wife. Amerigo is left almost as speechless, throughout this scene, as was Macbeth on hearing for the first time his wife's plans for Duncan. And Maggie, immaculate in her injured innocence, is hardly more appealing, at this moment of the novel, than Lady Macbeth was at that moment of the play.

There are two small hints, in the speculative chapter (XXXII) leading up to these stirring confrontations, that James was slyly preparing the reader for a presentation of Maggie which, while on the surface all righteousness and forbearance, yet leaves room for an appreciation of her whole campaign of aggressive forgiveness as being in effect a vengeful strategem against the woman who had dared to marry her father. The first hint is a direct one, an ironic aside by the author himself about 'that wonderful reunion of the couples, in the interest of the larger play of all the virtues of each, which was now bearing, for Mrs. Verver's stepdaughter at least, such remarkable fruit'. It is the exact tone of voice of the author's comment, years earlier, about Isabel Archer's 'remarkable soul'. The second hint comes closely enough. Maggie wishes that Charlotte's betrayal 'could only have been *worse*!'—so that her father would not have been falsely enjoying, at Fawns, 'under the beautiful old trees and among the dear old gardens . . . fifty kinds of confidence and twenty kinds, at least, of gentleness'. And there follows a truly remarkable passage showing that Maggie's instinctive feeling for her father is very much stronger than any feelings she may conjure up—whether 'sublime' or long-suffering or even vindictive—about her technical betrayal by Amerigo:

> Gentleness and confidence were certainly the right thing, as from a charming woman to her husband, but the fine tissue of reassurance woven by this lady's hands and flung over her companion as a light, muffling veil, formed precisely a wrought transparency through which she felt her father's eyes continually rest on herself. The reach of his gaze came to her straighter from a distance; it showed him as still more conscious, down there alone, of the suspected, the felt elaboration of the process of their not alarming or hurting him.

It is surely in line with this reading that we are intended to take, at the very climax of her confrontation of Amerigo, Maggie's 'vision' of Adam at Fawns and her resolve to make 'her care for his serenity, or at any rate for the firm outer shell of his dignity, all marvellous enamel, her paramount law'.

There are two more Parts during which the consequences of Maggie's confrontation will be unfolded, and it is in these concluding sections of the novel that the reader who has come so far will find himself forced to take sides, to deal judicially with concepts such as redemption, renunciation, revenge, triumph, and the like. At Fawns, Maggie tells Fanny that she is convinced that Amerigo has not told Charlotte of the scene with his wife and the shattered bowl; he merely acknowledges the 'change' that such knowledge has wrought in her, and he leaves Charlotte alone and will, Maggie is sure, refuse point blank to admit that Maggie 'knows'. She wants him, in short, to behave *as if* the bowl of their marriage had never been cracked. By this token, it is she and the Prince who are now linked in a new deception, and Charlotte who is their dupe. The tables have indeed, and very rumly, been turned.

And then, in Chapter XXXVI, comes—unbelievably, after so many pedestrian approaches—a superb vindication of James's method, a chapter as taut, powerful, tensely intelligently moving, emotionally exciting to the point of torment, as anything in fiction. One may describe it, perhaps, to readers already familiar with James, as being, in effect, the missing confrontation of Milly Theale and Kate Croy in *The Wings of the Dove*. In it, the tension between Maggie and Charlotte is first screwed up to an extraordinary pitch as they stalk one another in the gathering darkness on the terrace at Fawns, while inside the lighted room Verver and Amerigo, with the Assinghams, bend over the bridge-table. No summary can do it justice. It should be possible to cite Chapter XXXVI of *The Golden Bowl* as a *locus classicus* for the display of James's mature powers in full confident operation, much as one might cite, say, Chapters XII–XV of the *Biographia Literaria* or Chapter XV of *The Decline and Fall of the Roman Empire* to a reader who wished to sample at their least adulterated the qualities of Coleridge and Gibbon as critic and ironist respectively. Yet, *could* such a chapter communicate its full force to a reader who had not, even if he made heavy weather of it, read up to it? When one is steeped in James, it is impossible to guess. I should dearly love to learn the experience of any reader who, interested in the project of tackling *The Golden Bowl* but not having yet done so, had turned to Chapter XXXVI to see what, by itself, it had to offer. It is one of the sad results of systematic reading that one cannot play such a trick on oneself.

In this chapter, at any rate, James takes the plunge and creates a major scene, *not* by use of 'reflectors' or other dodges with which he sought to persuade himself, and others, that the indirect presentation was superior to the direct, but by the physical confrontation of the major protagonists. It is true that the actual dialogue between the two women, apart from Maggie's ambiguous 'I accuse you—I accuse you of nothing', is not particularly dramatic; but the gathering excitement of the moments during which they converge, each wrapped in her own preoccupation with what policy to follow in the cumulative confusion of pride, jealousy, guilt, forgiveness, force, weakness, anxiety, release—this excitement has vitalized the prose in a manner altogether unknown in those chapters where Assinghams or mute mystifications are supposed to act as 'reflectors' or 'filters', or whatever. To Maggie's eyes, as they watch Charlotte approaching, 'the splendid shining supple creature was out of the cage, was at large . . .' The image is quickly repeated: 'Her face was fixed on her, through the night; she was a creature who had escaped by force from her cage, yet there was in her whole motion assuredly, even as so dimly discerned, a kind of portentous intelligent stillness.' In precisely the same way, the surface of the Jamesian prose may wear its accustomed 'portentous intelligent stillness', yet there is a sharpness of outline, a vividness of interpretation, a positive thrill at the prospect of naked intellectual combat between all the forces in these two exceedingly complicated characters, which charge the writing with an immediacy of effect as if the novelist, too, had escaped by force from *his* cage.

The very spaciousness of Fawns, hitherto so pretentious a setting for languid musings, comes to significant life as Maggie, at first from a neighbouring sofa and later from the terrace, watches the card-players in the lighted smoking-room and is conscious of 'the relation of the whole group, individually and collectively, to herself—herself so speciously eliminated for the hour, but presumably more present to the attention of each than the next card to be played'. As 'the light came out in vague shafts and fell upon the old smooth stones', Maggie watched the bridge-players as if they had been 'figures rehearsing some play of which she herself was the author'. Most of all, she watches her unconscious father, seeking from him a sign he, absorbed as a gracious host, cannot give:

It throbbed for these seconds as a yearning appeal to him—she would chance it, that is, if he would just raise his eyes and catch them, across the larger space, standing in the outer dark together. Then he might be affected by the sight, taking them as they were; he might make some sign— she scarce knew what—that would save *her*; save her from being the one, this way, to pay all. He might somehow show a preference—distinguishing between them; might, out of pity for her, signal to her that this extremity of her effort for him was more than he asked.

When, finally, Charlotte asks 'Is there any wrong you consider I've done you?' and Maggie issues her denial, she feels amid all the 'coldness of their conscious perjury' that by not betraying to her rival the secret of her real accusation of Amerigo to his face, 'they were together thus, he and she, close, close together—whereas Charlotte, though rising there radiantly before her, was really off in some darkness of space that would steep her in solitude and harass her with care'. It is not so much a matter of forgiveness, or redemption, as of sheer superior diplomacy. The thrill the reader receives is one of shared accomplishment with the American worm who had, in this corrupt European situation, so sinuously turned.

It is now simply a matter of time before the quartet breaks up. The intolerable strain of uncertainty passes, like a virus, from Maggie to Charlotte. Maggie still clings to her paternal life-line:

They were husband and wife—oh, so immensely!—as regards other persons; but after they had dropped again on their old bench ... it was wonderfully like their having got together into some boat and paddled off from the shore where husbands and wives, luxuriant complications, made the air too tropical.

Their determination to go on sparing each other the knowledge each has suffered at the hands of the more actively guilty pair wraps them in the security of a kind of double negative. It is Charlotte's ignorance of what lies behind their passivity, coupled with the new correctness of Amerigo's behaviour, that causes *her*, now, to come near the point of cracking. There follows a wonderfully perceptive scene when Maggie, overhearing Charlotte bravely acting out her part as wife and châtelaine, spinning out a conscientious piece of guide's patter for the benefit of visitors intent on exploring the art treasures of Fawns, detects a note of hysteria in her voice 'like the shriek of a soul in pain'. Things are shaping up for a new confrontation. It takes place in the garden, and this time it is Maggie who swoops down, as if to comfort her, on Charlotte. Charlotte announces that she is intending to return with Adam to America. 'Our real life isn't here,' she says, and adds the heavily charged words: 'I want, strange as it may seem to you ... to *keep* the man I married.' Now it is Charlotte's turn to accuse instead of offering a brazen defence: 'How I see that you've loathed our marriage!' A few words of open hostility bring Part Fifth to a close.

The coda, Part Sixth, is a near-miraculous *tour de force*, sustaining in muted form yet in a subtly changed key all the major tensions of this truly symphonic novel. As if to prove that the *longueurs* have been overcome and that the prose has recovered its vitality even through the long sustained *andante*, there are even occasional glimpses of the old Jamesian humour. We have had a long time to wait for it, it is true; but it is singularly rewarding to feel that the author can afford to join us for a moment, so to say, in an ironic aside as if indicating that he, too, has all along taken the measure—*our* measure—of the Assingham pair. With the impending departure of the Ververs, Fawns

... was to be peopled for a month by porters, packers and hammerers, at whose operations it had become peculiarly public—public that is for Portland Place—that Charlotte was to preside in force; operations the quite awful appointed scale and style of which had at no moment loomed so large to Maggie's mind as one day when the dear Assinghams swam back into her ken besprinkled with sawdust and looking as pale as if they had seen Samson pull down the temple.

It remains only for Maggie to walk the tightrope of her triumph, praising Amerigo's masterly inactivity to a Fanny Assingham ever at hand for domestic revelations, or noting with nicely tempered sympathy the truth that 'Charlotte was hiding neither pride nor joy—she was hiding humiliation; and here it was that the Princess's passion, so powerless for vindictive flights, most inveterately bruised its tenderness against the hard glass of her question'. The 'foredoomed ingenuities of her pity', as she divines the misery of Charlotte who has in effect been jilted by a lover whose conduct has every official claim to admiration, and who is herself held in bondage to Adam by a 'silken noose' that has every official sanction of happy propriety—these exercises of Maggie's penetrating forgiveness bear, too, all the marks of sadistic satisfaction. She hugs the consciousness that Amerigo is not availing himself of many opportunities of seeing Charlotte, in London, on the quiet. She is even confident enough, now, to boast to Fanny that the guilty pair have made one crucial mistake: 'They thought of everything but that I might think.'

She has thought to good purpose. The shattered bowl of her marriage is being repaired, after a fashion. From long back, we seem to hear the echo of the shopman saying to Charlotte, when she is bargaining with him over the flawed bowl: 'But if it's something you can't find out, isn't it as good as if it were nothing?' There have been so many other possibilities hovering—that Maggie (and her father) would not have noticed the flaw in the bowl of her (and his) marriage; or that, once noticed, the bowl would have been shattered as irretrievably as the impulsive Fanny had shattered its actual symbol. The one solution that could silence and outwit the transgressors was, in effect, Maggie's own solution: to accept the bowl *as if* it were sound and to see it, in the end, become so.

Maggie's own price, of course, is the expulsion of her father. This—if one wants to draw up the moral balance-sheet—is the price she has had to pay, with him, for their original self-absorbed fancy in bringing about the Adam–Charlotte marriage mainly as a sop to Maggie's pity for his lonely state, a pity which might have brought a sour taste to her own marriage. For Maggie, has, throughout the novel, sought consistently to have her cake and eat it. She has sought to establish first claim on the affections and attentions of *both* men, father and husband. Luckily for her, both sets of claims were socially acceptable. Charlotte, whose more impulsive greed had a similar object, finds herself with only one sanctioned bond—to her husband. So if, as Amerigo's wife, Maggie has trumped, so to say, Charlotte's card as Amerigo's lover; so, too, Charlotte finally, as Adam's wife, trumps Maggie's card as Adam's daughter.

All this would no doubt be highly satisfactory to the conventionally-minded reader, if it were not for James's insistence that these peaceable results are the outcome not of knowledge but of ignorance, not of candour but of deception. The grand total of ignorance is triumphantly totted up by Maggie for a panting Fanny, who has just admitted 'that I know absolutely nothing'.

'Well—that's what *I* know,' said the Princess.

Her friend again hesitated. 'Then nobody knows—? I mean,' Mrs. Assingham explained, 'how much your father does.'

Oh, Maggie showed that she understood. 'Nobody.'

'Not—a little—Charlotte?'

'A little?' the Princess echoed. 'To know anything would be, for her, to know enough.'

'And she doesn't know anything?'

'If she did,' Maggie answered, 'Amerigo would.'
'And that's just it—that he doesn't?'
'That's just it,' said the Princess profoundly.
On which Mrs. Assingham reflected. 'Then how is Charlotte so held?'
'Just *by* that.'
'By her ignorance?'
'By her ignorance.'
Fanny wondered. 'A torment—?'
'A torment,' said Maggie with tears in her eyes.

The Ververs come to London to take leave of the Prince and Princess, and of us, before setting out for what the American Fanny at least considers to be their long exile in America. Amerigo, in dutiful attendance, is seen by his wife in a new spirit of security; he is 'caged' and he is 'the man she adored'. Just before the Ververs arrive, they come near the point of full physical reunion, but the Prince, with instinctive gallantry, proposes a postponement until the Ververs have actually disappeared: it is the one chivalrous gesture he makes, silently, to Charlotte. The reunited pair can now sing alternately the praises of Charlotte, mainly for her bravery in hiding her own unhappiness. Even the easy-going Amerigo is prompted to say: 'Everything's terrible, *cara*, in the heart of man.' Maggie still insists that Charlotte be left in absolute ignorance of her own discovery of the affair with Amerigo, even at the cost of her thinking Maggie a 'fool'. At the leave-taking, Charlotte's 'resplendent . . . show of serenity' prompts Maggie to cry to her father that 'Charlotte's great', to which the enigmatic Adam agrees 'how right I was . . . to do it for you', 'it' being the marriage undertaken for Maggie's peace of mind—and we are all back at the point of departure, *apparently* none the worse. On a final note of admiration for the departed Charlotte, Maggie and her Prince embrace.

There is no denying the *longueurs* of such a book. It has become irritatingly 'social' in what is, for James, a tedious sense of the word. For long stretches, the reader loses his underlying interest in the 'real' as seen through social eyes (as remains true even of *The Ambassadors*) and feels instead that he is called upon to do little more than *share* the social prying of the intolerable Assinghams. We have lost all hope, certainly, of being encouraged or even permitted to see the real intimate relationships, of say, Charlotte and the Prince.

At times there is even something insulting in being fobbed off with the mock bating of breath at the wonder of 'what other people think of them'. This is the kind of uneasiness, I imagine, that prompted Dr. Leavis (*Scrutiny*, V, 403–4) to write: 'Actually, if our sympathies are anywhere they are with Charlotte and (a little) the Prince, who represent what, against the general moral background of the book, can only strike us as decent passion; in a stale, sickly and oppressive atmosphere they represent life.' But I believe Dr. Leavis goes too far when he adds: 'James's development was towards over-subtlety, and . . . with this development we must associate a loss of sureness in his moral touch, an unsatisfactoriness that in some of the more ambitious later works leads us to question his implicit valuations.' What does happen, I think, is that we are in danger of losing our proper grip—the moral grip no less than the physical one, so to say. James can be extremely perverse in his construction. Sudden passages of years are almost lost in parenthetical verbiage. It is a constant effort to recognize, at the begining of any chapter, where one is, what time of day it is, and even—so baroque is *all* the dialogue (with its wilful obfuscations of such circumlocutions as 'our young friend', and so on)—who is speaking. Again, all the people, like those in *The Wings of the Dove*, seem to be immensely older than their actual ages: the troubles of the three young members of the two couples seem at times to be the last-gasp exhausted intricacies of a trio of elderly libertines.

The reader's moral grip must be even tighter, if he proposes to enjoy *The Golden Bowl*. Perhaps one may leave the last words with a professional moralist, Dr. Dorothea Krook, in her book *The Ordeal of Consciousness in Henry James*. At moments and on matters seemingly trivial in themselves, James splits the moral hair so finely that the blade cuts down through the hair into the scalp, through the scalp into the skull itself. Probing with the narrator in *The Sacred Fount*, Dr. Krook applauds 'a ruthlessness, a "sacrifice of feeling", which is the heaviest price that has to be paid for the artist's fullness of knowledge'. I confess that I find Dr. Krook's reading of *The Golden Bowl* far too much preoccupied with the penalties and rewards of emancipated human behaviour, much as if one had discovered in the study of a sophisticated humanist the old embroidered framed text on the wall: 'Thou God seest me.' Yet at the end of her thorough analysis of the novel, this moralist has provided a wholly acceptable valedictory notion that: 'in Henry James's total vision, the sense of the grimness and bitterness of human life is inseparably fused with the sense of its beauty and blessedness; that neither cancels out the other; and that the ambiguity is intended to express precisely this experience of their permanent, inseparable fusion.'

XIII

Tales of the Uncanny

. . . a well authenticated goblin is, as things go, a feather in a quiet man's cap.

The Ghostly Rental

A wraith proves faithless to her marriage vow, elopes with a bogie in a cloud of words.

F. L. Colby: '*In Darkest James*' (*1904*)

IT HAS always seemed to me a pity that Henry James's best-known story should be *The Turn of the Screw*. The great bulk of his major work reveals a magisterial concern for conscious behaviour. I find little evidence, even in his most ambitious symphonic masterpieces, for any settled tendency to relate human experience to a world outside itself. His occasional experiments in dabbling with those 'things in heaven and earth' that are not 'dreamed of in your philosophy' range, for the most part, from a few youthful creepy stories to a group of mawkish late tales in which, temporarily dispirited by affronts suffered by an ageing body and a still unabated sensibility, he toyed, never very convincingly, with notions of supernatural compensation. Only in that one story, *The Turn of the Screw*, written at the height of his creative powers, did he bring off a *tour de force* of undeniable hallucinatory fascination. It is a splendid achievement—but it is uncharacteristic.

Several of the early tales have a tinge of the supernatural. The one real experiment in ghost stories is *The Ghostly Rental* (1876), a story James never bothered to collect in book form. It is a contrived little commercial tale, in which the not unaffecting climax occurs when a wronged daughter, who has been masquerading as a ghost to her penitent father, sees the 'real' ghost of her father when he dies suddenly. The narrator is a New England divinity student who has been 'explicitly cultivating cheerful views of the supernatural'—an ironic phrase which tells one more about the young James's earthbound temperament than all his efforts to create the atmosphere of a haunted house. Not, indeed, that one could ever have taken very seriously a ghost the sight of which, as 'a well-authenticated goblin, is, as things go, a feather in a quiet man's cap'. There is even an explicit avowal, in so slight a potboiler, that a writer's true imagination plays with material far less flimsy than ghosts, when an incidental character is made to remark: 'Shut me up in a dark closet and I will observe after a while, that some places in it are darker than others. After that (give me time), and I will tell you what the President of the United States is going to have for dinner.' It is as good a germ as any one may wish to find, among James's early trivia, for the kind of propaganda for the speculative non-participant which was linked by Mr. Tanner, a propos *The Sacred Fount*, with the idealistic views of a Shaftesbury.

Four tales of the years 1891 and 1892 also show traces, more or less, of the uncanny. They are in other respects quite unlike, ranging from James at his subtlest to James at his silliest. In *The Pupil* (1891), one of James's best-known stories, a slightly creepy relationship between a tutor and his adoring pupil turns sour when, with a chill of horror not unlike that of *The Turn of the Screw*, the boy dies for no apparent physical reason; in *Sir Edmund Orme* (1891), the ghost of a rejected suitor haunts his cruel lady in a highly conventional manner; in *Owen Wingrave* (1892), a rootedly civilian young man is haunted by military ancestors; in *The Private Life* (1892), yet another parable of life and art is given the melodramatic aid of hallucinatory manifestations.

The Pupil is in essence a tender study of sympathy. The parents of young Morgan Moreen are, like the parents of Verena Tarrant of *The Bostonians*, revealed as dim social frauds and financial failures. The weakly boy sees through them. His young tutor, Pemberton, loves him and stays on and on as his tutor, unpaid by his fraudulent employers. Driven away at last, he returns when informed that Morgan is ill. Even this turns out to be a Moreen trick, and little Morgan implores Pemberton to take him away. When the Moreens are driven from their lodgings, Morgan is offered to Pemberton. The shock of happiness, followed by dismay when Pemberton momentarily wavers, kills the boy. It is not exactly uncanny, except in so far as canny boys do not suffer heart attacks at such junctures. The tale is powerful, complete in itself, and strangely moving. It is also, for all its uncomfortable ending, amusing. James is merciless and sympathetic at the same time, as he watches the manoeuvres of broken-down expatriates trying to live, in Europe, on pretensions alone. 'Wandering about Europe at the tail of his migratory tribe', it is small wonder that little Morgan views life with a 'small satiric face'. (Dr. Edel, in his introduction to the story, pertinently suggests that Henry James may here be drawing upon his own childhood reactions to the nomadic James family in Europe.) We are made to feel that the possibility of real affection is too much for him to hope for, yet too crushing a disappointment if denied. So the 'precociously intelligent and incorruptibly nice child', in Dr. Leavis's phrase, is snatched away by the introduction of Death itself (*almost* personified) from the full implications of his awakening happiness. With little Miles of *The Turn of the Screw*, the experience unacceptable to life had come via the influence of the corrupt Peter Quint; in *The Pupil*, it comes to Morgan via the high-principled amiable Pemberton. The result is the same. The story is, as Professor Jefferson's commentary makes very clear, a 'mixture of reserves and confidences and evasive pleasantries'. It is also a terrible little fable—and herein lies its uncanniness—of the inability of certain pure tender natures to survive at all among the values of our flawed but less vulnerable world.

In *The Pupil*, then, a vague hint of the unnatural invests a human situation memorable in itself; in the other three 'creepy' stories of the period, old hackneyed Jamesian themes are not made more significant by supernatural additions. *Sir Edmund Orme*, a supernatural *nouvelle* with a low-pressure Jamesian patterned situation, is notable for a ghost that actually beckons *towards* marriage, instead of discouraging it. Mrs. Marsden is 'haunted' by Sir Edmund, whom as a young woman she had rejected. The narrator, courting Mrs. Marsden's daughter, also 'sees' him. Is the curse passing to him, too? Just before the distraught Mrs. Marsden dies, the daughter also for the first time 'sees' Sir Edmund—but only to seek comfort in her lover's arms. Sir Edmund's charitable work is done, and he does not reappear. This 'feeble, uncharacteristic effort' (Mrs. Q. D. Leavis, *Scrutiny*, XIV, 223) is matched by *Owen Wingrave*, the morbid tale of a brilliant young man of a military family who, on the brink of Sandhurst, refuses to adopt a military career. He is reviled by his family and by the young dependent of the family who is thought of as his possible fiancée. One of his ancestors had killed his son in a fit of passion and now haunts the room in which he, too, had died. Owen spends the night there, haunted by cumulative accusations of cowardice. He is found dead. (All that is lacking is an ironic white feather on his heroic corpse.) In *The Private Life*, the earlier Jamesian 'cousin' or 'twin' theme is pursued, in the succeeding Jamesian world of dedicated artists, across and beyond the borders of the supernatural. The statesman Lord Mellifont is all public façade—and so, invited to the extreme in denunciatory fantasy, we are to imagine that when he is alone he simply doesn't exist. The novelist Clare Vawdrey, on the other hand, is all private consciousness—he is a socially dull man, and at the same hotel graced by Lord Mellifont the narrator 'sees' him in his room, writing busily in the dark, while the man's body is still downstairs, bored and boring, among the Philistines. It is perhaps the most dismal of all James's self-pitying tales, calling in the supernatural to support his long-sustained claim that it is the observer, and not the envied player, who sees most of the game of life.

A far more significant glimpse of the darker side of James's experience, as he faced the human losses and professional discouragements of a self-driven author floundering in his touchy egotistical fifties, is to be found in *The Altar of the Dead* (1895). Except for an irresistible vitality of its external reference and a sustained eloquence even in its melancholy, the tale might merely earn the phrases 'significant badness' and 'morbidly sentimental and extremely unpleasant tale' bestowed upon it by Dr. Leavis (*Scrutiny* V, 407)—who nevertheless made the point (unsupported, then, by biographical collaterals) that it 'illustrates poor James's weary, civilized loneliness of spirit'. Dr. Edel, in some impressively convincing pages of biographical conjecture (III, 319–24), links the mood of the story with James's guilty distress at the suicide of his faithful friend Constance Fenimore Woolson and with the ever-hovering wraith of Minny Temple. The necrolatrous gloom is so pervasive that it may be well, before attempting to study James's deeply personal treatment of his theme, to be reminded that the freshness of direct observation which never failed to redeem some corner of his work is present even here. The very dinginess of wintry London suburbs is conveyed in phrases showing all the old economy of effort: 'by day there was nothing, but by night there were lamps'; the dusk is relieved by 'a shopfront which lighted the dull brown air with its mercenary grin'; while 'the pairs of shabby little houses, semi-detached but indissolubly united', strike the death-obsessed hero, in an indomitably lively simile, as being 'like married couples on bad terms'. With these incidental touchstones in mind, a reader may find evidence, even in the morbid self-pity of the 'uncanny' plot, of the toughness and resilience of James's conscious mind.

The 'plot' is simply a highly melodramatic and wildly incredible parable, complete with vague eerie flirtations with the spirit-world, of a perfectly normal (indeed, universal) experience of the elderly: the sad consciousness that more of their dear friends are dead than remain alive. The James-like hero, Stransom, had formed the habit of observing the anniversary of the death of his betrothed, even though 'he had needed no priest and no altar to make him for ever widowed'. His brooding was at first wholly mundane. He imagined his betrothed, and his other departed friends, as being 'there in their simplified, intensified essence, their conscious absence and expressive patience, as personally there as if they had only been stricken dumb.' At first, any suggestion of the supernatural is quite explicitly excluded, except in so far as, recalling the dim memories of childhood church parades, he realized that 'the religion instilled in his earliest consciousness had been simply the religion of the Dead'. The pain left by his own losses is intensified by disgust when he happens to meet an old friend who, having lost a wife as admirably sensitive as his own defunct fiancée, has become married again to a vulgar American wife fit only 'for foreign service or purely external use'—but the disgust is moral, *not* 'religious'; it has its basis in James's own peculiar sensitivity to social aesthetics: 'the frivolity, the indecency of it made Stransom's eyes fill.' And when, later, he decides to externalize his own mental tributes to his dead friends by endowing, in a Roman Catholic church, an altar to be kept aglow with candles each representing a vanished soul-mate, his involvement in the full religious implications is minimal indeed: 'it struck him as good that there should be churches.'

It is only when he notices, on his regular visits to his private altar, another—female—worshipper that he begins to yearn for the possibility of a closer identification with her faith: 'He wished he could sink, like her, to the very bottom, be as motionless, as rapt in prostration.' It is a preview of that deeply significant scene in *The Ambassadors* where Strether, a more extended portrait of James himself, feels in Notre Dame the limitations of an earthbound mind.

There can hardly be a better example than *The Altar of the Dead* of the point I find myself repeating so often in these commentaries— the immense superiority of James's natural gifts as a writer over his self-lauded tricks of parallel plotting. If the story is 'unpleasant', it is because James, lacking conviction in his marvellous capacity to convey a mood, felt it necessary to inject a silly tit-for-tat sub-plot into the story. Stransom had never been able to forgive a particular dead friend who had wronged him, and he had therefore shrunk from dedicating to his memory a candle on his private altar. And so, of course, it must be *he* to whom the unknown lady, whom the dead man had also wronged, is devoutly and forgivingly making *her* spooky tribute. The winding-up and working-out of this dispirited clockwork coincidence, which alone injects 'creepiness' and 'unpleasantness' into an otherwise acceptable fable of human grief, distracts a reader's attention from James's real achievements in the story. Chief among these is no less than a heart-arresting statement, years before Proust grappled with the subject, of the inescapable sorrow of human time and the fortitude supplied by the operation of human memory. For Stransom, as for Marcel some quarter of a century later, there is a horror in facing 'the period of life . . . when, after separations, the dreadful clockface of the friend we meet announces the hour we have tried to forget'. It is in this mood that he gives vent to the thoroughly 'morbid' sentiment:

There were hours at which he almost caught himself wishing that certain of his friends would now die, that he might establish with them in this manner a connection more charming than, as it happened, it was possible to enjoy with them in life. In regard to those from whom one was separated by the long curves of the globe such a connection could only be an improvement: it brought them instantly within reach.

It was from this mood that he was rescued, not by the foolish subplot of ghostly comradeship with the unknown female, but by a wholly Proustian and wholly secular treasuring of the resources of earthly memory:

It was in the quiet sense of having saved his souls that his deep, strange instinct rejoiced. This was no dim theological rescue, no boon of a contingent world; they were saved better than faith or works could save them, saved for the warm world they had shrunk from dying to, for actuality, for continuity, for the certainty of human remembrance.

Once one can forget the silliness of the plot, in short, there remains in the essential mood of *The Altar of the Dead* a portrait of a man who, like his creator, had resolved to make, in the face of mortality, the best of a bad job: 'His own life, round its central hollow, had been packed close enough.'

A return to the old symmetrical habit and to the anti-marriage theme, rather than any new treatment of the ghostly, is the mark of an unimportant tale *The Way It Came* (1896; the title was changed to *The Friends of the Friends* in the New York Edition). A man and a woman have each had a similar psychic experience when young— that of 'seeing' their mother and father respectively at the instant of their deaths in distant places. They have never met, and efforts by their mutual friends to bring them together have always failed. The man's fiancée (who tells the tale in a diary) arranges a meeting and then, suddenly jealous, keeps her fiancé away. But he 'sees' the other woman in his own room. She dies that night. He falls in love with what he 'saw'. His engagement to the diarist is broken off and we are to suppose that his union with his wraith will take place, safely, only after his death. It is as if James is making up for the atypical behaviour of Sir Edmund Orme, by producing another ghost who intervenes to prevent, rather than sponsor, an earthly marriage.

The Real Right Thing (1899), like *The Private Life*, merely invests with a creepy twist yet another effort to produce in fiction a professional problem of the writer. George Withermore is charged with writing the life of his dead friend, the author Ashton Doyne, who himself had firmly held the view that 'the artist was what he *did*—he was nothing else'. But Withermore and Doyne's widow nevertheless feel his ghostly presence as the work proceeds (the biography is being composed in Doyne's own study), 'drawing many curtains, forcing many doors, reading many riddles, going in general, as they said, behind almost everything'. The biographer feels conscious of being helped, of papers being shifted and chosen for him by the dead hand of his friend. Then the presence disappears, and Withermore feels 'it was stranger, somehow, that he shouldn't be there than it had ever been that he *was*'. Later, he feels that Doyne is 'making dim signs out of his horror'—horror at having his life written. The shade of the discreet author finally appears to both biographer and widow, and they agree, interpreting its forbidding aspect, to give up the project.

Much fresher and slighter is *The Third Person* (1900), the one really entertaining comedy among the uncanny tales, It is an ingenious story, tenderly and humorously done, of how two maiden ladies find their house haunted. They first grow frightened, then secretive and jealous as each treasures her own enjoyment and the titillation of 'a man in the house'. (He is the ghost of a man who had been hanged for smuggling.) In their several ways, each seeks to placate the friendly ghost, in farcical solemnity and naïveté: one sister sends anonymous 'conscience money' to the Chancellor of the Exchequer; the other, bolder, takes a trip to Paris and, greatly daring, herself smuggles in a Tauchnitz volume!

In each of the nine 'uncanny' tales so far considered, James has added a widely variable dose of the mysterious or unexplained to several different types of tale already well established in his past output. In *The Turn of the Screw* (1898) he produced his one story in which the uncanny or supernatural was undeniably the main ingredient. It has become the most widely read item in all his vast range of fiction. Its plot is known (until they read the critics' commentaries!) to hundreds of thousands of readers and theatre-goers. Its interpretation has become a battleground for scores of critics. An extremely useful *Casebook* on this one story, edited by Gerald Willen in 1959 (a seventh printing had been called for by 1964), reprints no less than fifteen sizeable studies, dating from 1924 to 1959 and including the seminal essay by Mr. Edmund Wilson, 'The Ambiguity of Henry James', published in 1934, plus two postscripts dated 1948 and 1959, in the latter of which he declares: 'Since writing [the first postscript], I have become convinced that James knew exactly what he was doing and that he intended the governess to be suffering from delusions.' To read these fifteen contradictory interpretations, in any order one chooses, is to assent to each of them in turn: they are all as momentarily convincing, and as mutually exclusive, as a set of party manifestoes at the time of a General Election. Whatever else they prove, they certainly indicate that *The Turn of the Screw*, like Stonehenge or the Sphinx, is still able to baffle the most learned expert no less than the first casual observer.

With a story so likely to be well known to every reader of this book (whatever such a reader, like the fifteen essayists and their unnumbered colleagues, may *make* of it), it is necessary to give only the briefest reminder of a plot that can be told either in a sentence or two, or, if closely studied, in almost as many as the story itself required. A young governess, sent to a secluded country house to take charge of two children, Flora and Miles, sees (or thinks she sees) the ghosts of a valet (Peter Quint) and another young governess (Miss Jessel) who had formerly lived there and had recently died. The governess is convinced, by the strange strained behaviour of the children, that they, too, see the ghosts—that Flora has seen the apparition of Miss Jessel and Miles has seen that of Quint. By questioning the housekeeper (her only adult companion in the house), she gathers the impression that both of the dead servants had been evil, corrupted persons. She also knows that little Miles, who looks as innocent and behaves as sweetly as his sister, has nevertheless been temporarily expelled from his school. She convinces herself that it is her duty to protect the children from the influence (unguessed, but presumed evil) of their former playmates: both Miss Jessel and Quint, having been raffish or worse when alive, must surely have infected the children with whom, in the absence of their uncle and guardian, they must have become intimate? The climax of the story occurs when the governess, interrogating Miles on the cause for his expulsion from school, sees (or thinks she sees) Peter Quint at the window, gazing in at them. She tries to shield Miles from seeing Quint, but foolishly betrays Quint's presence (or imagined presence) by addressing and pointing to him, whereupon Miles, in unexplained terror, dies in her arms. *H* NEXT PAGE

To the volumes of contradictory explanations of this perennially fascinating story, interpretations Freudian and common-sensical, pro-ghost and pro-hallucination, pro-governess (as an agent of redemption) and anti-governess (as an hysterical busybody), I will add only a note on the final scene. The background to the pious and maidenly governess's fears is fairly obviously the suspicion that the laxities of Miss Jessel and Quint must have included sexual licence, into which she fears her present charges may have been indoctrinated during the servants' lifetime. If this is so, is it significant that the governess suspects the ghost of Miss Jessel of seeking to haunt the little girl, and the ghost of Quint of seeking out the boy? What kind of corruption *does* she fear? It should be recalled that the tale is placed well back in the nineteenth century, when spinster governesses were not to be credited with pre-knowledge of Freudian psychology or experience of even what may be called the sexual norm, let alone deviations from it. It is fairly clear, at any rate, that she attaches no special significance to the odd terms in which Miles replies to her questions about his expulsion: he admits that he had only 'said things', and when pressed to say to whom, he replies: 'only a few. Those I liked.' Upon which the poor lady 'seemed to float not into a clearness, but into a darker obscure, and within a minute there had come to me out of my very pity the appalling alarm of his being perhaps innocent ... if he *were* innocent, what then on earth was *I*?' Recovering herself, she probes again: 'And did they repeat what you said?' Miles admits that his words were probably repeated, by his 'liked' schoolfellows, 'to those *they* liked'. It is at the very moment when she probes deeper into *what* Miles had said to his friends that she sees (or thinks that she sees) Peter Quint at the window. In her inept attempt both to denounce the apparition and to prevent Miles from seeing it, she terrifies him into thinking, at first, that it is the presence of Miss Jessel she is trying to chase off. The governess then points to the window: 'It's *there*, the coward horror——' The boy asks: 'It's *he*?' The following lines deserve quotation:

I was so determined to have all my proof that I flashed into ice to challenge him. 'Whom do you mean by "he"?'
'Peter Quint—you devil!' His face gave again, round the room, its convulsed supplication. '*Where*?'
They are in my ears still, his supreme surrender of the name and his tribute to my devotion. 'What does he matter now, my own?—what will he *ever* matter? *I* have you,' I launched at the beast, 'but he has lost you for ever!' Then, for a demonstration of my work, 'There, *there*!' I said to Miles.

But by the time she has completed her demonstration, she finds that she is clutching Miles's lifeless body. /to paper
It seems clear to me that Miles's words 'you devil!' are addressed not to Peter Quint, real or imagined ghost, but to the governess. It is certainly clear that her claim to have won the boy from Quint for herself does nothing to restore him—indeed, it kills him. Dozens of earlier young gentlemen in James's tales had sought and found various ways of eluding such encompassing engulfment as the governess offers to her little charge. A boy—like Miles or like Pemberton's Morgan Moreen—has no such resources when confronted by wild emotional claims that he wishes either to accept (if they are his own, like

Morgan's) or deny (if they are another's, like the governess's). He can only make the ultimate withdrawal of himself, in death. For what it is worth, it is my own view that the governess, having stumbled all unknowing upon childhood sensibilities in Flora and Miles (with or without supernatural aid from the persons who had first, in their life-times, excited them)—sensibilities of which she is totally ignorant—seeks in hysterical stupidity to trap and absorb spirits she cannot begin to understand. The story is full of horrors, in all conscience, but nothing is more horribly uncanny, to her vexed and harried charges, than the poor distracted governess herself. They could live with bad memories, or even bad ghosts, but not with her. She is no protectress, but a vampire. She is the most dangerously self-deluded, and Miles is the most pitiful victim, of all James's long list of emotional cannibals.

XIV

Unfinished Novels

The Ivory Tower and *The Sense of the Past*

> I will do such things,
> What they are yet I know not, but they
>   shall be
> The terrors of the earth.
>
> *King Lear*

THE foregoing chapters, and especially those dealing with the three late masterpieces, have covered a literary output vast enough to have exhausted enormous resources of mental and physical strength. And even they have omitted reference to another whole range of James's creative activity—the plays (there are fifteen complete pieces, of varying length, in Dr. Edel's collected edition); the many substantial volumes of travel essays which include much of his most perceptive writing; the critical essays and reviews which are now recognized as containing some of the most deeply intelligent literary theorizing since Coleridge and Arnold; and the Herculean toil of revising his fiction and writing the Prefaces for the New York Edition, the first of whose twenty-four volumes began to appear in 1907. Yet when James died in 1916, there remained among his papers two unfinished novels which, when issued after his death together with the notes he had dictated for their future development, already ran to some 350 pages apiece, but which were planned to embrace the full amplitude of another *Golden Bowl* or another *The Wings of the Dove*.

The surviving three of the intended ten books planned to contain *The Ivory Tower* (1917) show that recurring illnesses and deeply felt bereavements had not sapped James's amazing creative vitality. The very incompleteness of the work focuses attention on qualities which, prompted by the author's own insistence on symmetries and balances, we are in danger of overlooking in the finished work of the late period. There are, for example, many passages which recall Marcel Proust, whose genius James had saluted with customary generosity after reading *Du Côté de Chez Swann*.* Like Proust, James is at his richest when there *is* no immediate 'plot' to channel the flood of his awareness. The splendid fluency of the opening narrative of *The Ivory Tower*, the very atmosphere of seaside Newport, with its local American 'aristocracy' of wealth living out a highly complicated existence against the innocent background of beaches and promenades—all this does irresistibly evoke the atmosphere of pre-1914 Balbec and remind the reader that James and Proust, with all their differences of generation and experience, all their wild disparity of personal

*George D. Painter, *Marcel Proust* Vol. 2 (1965), p. 252.

habits and demeanour, were in fact shouldering for a long period of time, each unknown to the other, a similar burden of creative devotion. Even if only one of them had lived, the novel could never have been the same again. The combined effect of the two writers of genius has been incalculable.

The scene of *The Ivory Tower* is set with one of the best instances in all the long series of James's essays in elaborate economy. Rosanna Gaw, a large hoydenish young woman who 'lived in wrappers and tea-gowns', has been effecting a last-minute reconciliation between her father, the sick millionaire Abel Gaw who 'had dispossessed himself ... of every faculty except the calculating', and his former partner and now dying defrauder, the equally aged Frank Betterman. There is unflagging energy in the initial presentation of old Gaw,

... like a ruffled hawk, motionless but for his single tremor, with his beak, which had pecked so many hearts out, visibly sharper than ever, yet only his talons nervous; not that he at last cared a straw, really, but that he was incapable of thought save in sublimities of arithmetic, and that the question of what old Frank would have done with the fruits of his swindle ... was one of the things that could keep him brooding, day by day and week by week, after the fashion of a philosopher tangled in some maze of metaphysics.

With a mere handful of such devastating scaling-down demonstrations, we are plunged at once into the world of the robber barons, of grossly rich denizens of fashionable Newport, Rhode Island, where wizened old millionaires contrive to look as quiet as Adam Verver of *The Golden Bowl* after a lifetime of remorselessness calling for the brash effrontery of Christopher Newman of *The American*. Gaw's old face is compared to 'the hard ice of a large pond at the end of a long day's skating', and we are invited to imagine the 'amount of obstreperous exercise that had been taken on that recording field'. We are made, with miraculous obliquity, to feel the full distaste of the expatriate Henry James—a distaste recently fortified by visits to his homeland in his sixty-first and sixty-seventh years—for 'so scant a range of intrinsic tone'. It is precisely as if the Ververs had settled down again, after regaining American City, to come to terms with the life they had hoped to exchange for the inherited and non-transmittable subtleties of Europe. And when the other characters of the next generation are introduced, including the putative hero Gray Fielder who returns to attend the deathbed of his great-uncle Betterman, we are given a last whiff of the old European magic awaiting, in places like Dresden, the avidity or sensibility of James's long line of passionate pilgrims.

As the story begins to unfold, in the leisurely pace of late Jamesian prose which seems perfectly suited to the overburdened overstuffed world of Newport in all the ostentatious wealth of the new-dawned century, we are reminded again and again of themes he had treated earlier. It is as though he were making an effort, in that doomed summer of 1914 when the chapters were composed, to show that he could have managed on his native soil, after all, the treatment he had for so long reserved for American characters only after they had been transplanted to Europe. Yet there is no suspicion of exhausted self-plagiarism. The new cast of characters may remind us of other figures, but they all possess an independent life that promised to blossom in great profusion. The work was laid aside not from exhaustion but at the onset of the Great War. Percy Lubbock, who saw the fragments through the press, tells us that James 'could no longer work upon a fiction supposed to represent contemporary or recent life'. His world was being shattered in Flanders and he turned, sick at heart, to devote his still powerful energies to more routine work or to the deliberate—and itself disillusioned—withdrawal into *The Sense of the Past*. But even in the opening books of *The Ivory Tower* there are marvels of ripe observation cheek by jowl with set-piece confrontations more reminiscent of his earlier novels than of the nearer world of, say, *The Golden Bowl*.

Rosanna has induced her father's old enemy to receive the great-nephew, Gray Fielder, who had earlier disappointed him by remaining in Europe with his mother and stepfather instead of accepting an offer to return as heir-presumptive to the financier's spoils. Shortly after Gray has experienced a macabre sight of old Gaw squatting outside the vulgar mansion wherein his old enemy lies dying (a speechless encounter developed, again, in the baroque exactitude that would bring renown to Marcel Proust), the young man—for all the world like a more serious Felix Young of *The Europeans* confronted by a much more formidable Mr. Wentworth—has an interview with Betterman in his sickroom. In a daring scene of forthright verbal legacy (for even James's characters normally observe Dr. Johnson's view that imminent demise wonderfully concentrates a man's thoughts), the old American brigand explains that he wants his young heir to 'make the difference' to 'our great public'; to make decent use, in short, of the capital he had amassed but could not himself spend with imagination. 'Now you're the blank I want, if you follow —and yet you're not the blatant ass,' the old villain remarks, with native shrewdness sustaining him to the end. By a queer twist, as in *The Jolly Corner*, it is as though James is giving himself another chance—but this time as a young man and not as the world-weary Spencer Brydon—to grapple on American soil with the responsibility of American business prosperity from which he had fled so long ago.

It had been Rosanna herself, years ago when they were both American adolescents in Europe, who had influenced the young Gray to renounce Betterman's bribe in favour of staying in Europe. She loves him now with an accumulated infatuation. But his dramatic return to Newport and his new rôle as millionaire (for old Betterman dies shortly after Abel Gaw, as related in passages of great narrative skill, has himself died in chagrin at the fear that Frank Betterman will after all outlive him) make Gray the object of attention of much less innocent eyes than those of Rosanna. Another group of Jamesian characters are ready for deployment—figures by no means shadowy replicas but threatening to equal or even surpass in richness of reference the earlier versions of whom they remind the reader. There is Cissy Foy, sexually attractive 'poor dependent' of rich Newport neighbours, who now sets her cap at the new possesser of Betterman's fortune; there is Howard Vint, who had once been rejected by Rosanna and is now in love with Cissy.

Already the reader can guess, without any aid from James's notes for the chapters still to be written, that we are being manoeuvred into position to watch the corrupting influence of great wealth, to be stretched with the tensions and possibly rewarded with the unearned generosities of another and perhaps even more remarkable version of *The Wings of the Dove*. For Howard Vint and Cissy Foy have an understanding that is already made evident in their freedom of speech when they enjoy a conspiratorial *tête-à-tête* on the dusky Newport shore, a freedom reminiscent of that marvellous scene in *The Portrait of a Lady* where Gilbert Osmond and Madame Merle are first seen, unmasked, together, and a freedom markedly in contrast with the high mannered speech which on other occasions they are made to share with the Newport social set. They are casting themselves, with an equally irresistible fascination for the lure of riches, in the rôle of Kate Croy and Merton Densher. But this time the victim destined to be sucked dry will be a man, not a woman. It is Gray Fielder who, one can foresee, will enact the rôle of Milly Theale; though it is already obvious that it is Rosanna who will be called upon to do the active suffering on his behalf and perhaps even find moral reasons for finally renouncing him. And because the compromised Howard Vint will have to reduce his victim by a more elaborate campaign of deception than ever Merton Densher was called upon to use for the reduction of poor Milly's citadel, then it is also obviously necessary that he in turn must be built up as a character far more substantial than Densher. Howard is, in short, to figure not only as a menacing agent of greed but also as a figure in his own right, a figure commensurate with Gilbert Osmond of *The Portrait of a Lady*.

The Ivory Tower remains as a teasingly truncated masterpiece. I can see no reason, short of its mutilated incompleteness, for writing it off as a work of James's weary overripe maturity. It must be admitted that many paragraphs of musing *oratio obliqua* have all the tormented complexity of similar tracts in *The Golden Bowl*; but at the same time I suspect that in the great scenes of confrontation which he was plotting for the later books, James might well have broken through to a triumphant outspoken justification for the deep-laid subtleties of the novel's surviving opening books. For one thing, there was lying in reserve, awaiting release like some great dammed-up reservoir, Henry James's long-harboured hatred of the wicked selfishness underlying 'high society'. There is a virulent vitality, even in the context of his elaborate fumbling self-communing notes for the novel's development, whenever this theme works its way to the surface. To produce only one example: James notes that he is resolved to make his young hero 'definitely and frankly as complete a case as possible of the sort of thing that will make him an anomaly and an outsider alike in the New York world of buiness, the N.Y. world of ferocious acquisition, and the world there of enormities of expenditure and extravagance, so that the real suppression for him of anything that shall count in the American air as a money-making, or even as a wage-earning, or as a pecuniarily picking-up character, strikes me as wanted for my emphasis of his entire difference of sensibility and of association'. I am even persuaded that if *The Ivory Tower* had been worked out to its conclusion, James might have brought to the surface his own deep social 'commitment' in scenes so inescapably powerful that his entire reputation as a novelist might have had to be radically reviewed. I suspect, for example, that there would have been an overt demonstration, probably by Rosanna and Gray in wounded but happy harmony, in favour of some great philanthropic enterprise. I believe, at any rate, that a completion of *The Ivory Tower* would have drawn the image of Henry James the novelist out from the murky shadows cast by the misunderstood and elaborately understated subtleties of *The Ambassadors* or *The Golden Bowl* and would have revealed him, in all his magisterial maturity, as the same profoundly outraged political moralist who, years before in *The Princess Casamassima*, had tilted with feebler weapons against the standards of a world less stubbornly entrenched in egotistic complacency. We might even, with a completed *The Ivory Tower*, have seen James recruited as the eldest and greatest of the post-war novelists of social realism!

An interested reader of *The Ivory Tower* will find Dr. Cargill's chapter on the novel particularly helpful, with its recapitulation of an earlier discarded plot which had been cannibalized in this new work, destined itself to be discarded, and its restatements of various attempts to descry, through the maze of James's own notes, how the novel might have ended. Meanwhile, the three completed books, plus one chapter of the fourth, yield plenty of examples both of James's unabated power of intelligent description and also of his old disposition to toy overmuch with symbols and geometrical pairings. Matching the symbol of the flawed crystal of *The Golden Bowl* there is the exquisite oriental casket in the form of an ivory tower, 'a wonder of wasted ingenuity', in which Gray Fielder puts away, unread, the letter from Abel Gaw which that doomed old man had asked Rosanna to give him. It is fairly clear that the letter contains an exposure of the financial speculations of old Betterman, to taint Gray's new inheritance; it is equally clear that we should have found the more commonplace meaning of an 'ivory tower' used as a label for Gray's personal disinclination to use the money or live up to its social implications. There is enough vitality in the characters as already presented to suggest that they could have been carried over such needless symbolic obstacles with little loss. Even Howard Vint, whose rôle it would have been to set out systematically to rob the only too willingly gullible Gray of his fortune, has enough decency to remark to his confederate Cissy Foy: 'He shan't become if I can help it as beastly vulgar as the rest of us.' The whole treatment of Vint, even to the precision of his physical description, fits him for more than a purely mechanical rôle. Rosanna herself is conscious enough of his intelligence to wonder 'would any man ever look at her so for passion as Mr. Vint had looked for reason?'.

Rosanna's own 'functional' rôle would have been much complicated by the fact that she was herself, as Abel Gaw's heiress, worth a fortune vaster even than Betterman's. She may well have said of her father: 'He's just dying of twenty millions . . . The effect has been to dry up his life.' Now she was herself none the less doomed to the suspicion that nobody could love her for herself alone. One feels that all the early skirmishes for possession of Gray would have been won by Cissy Foy, who had been attractive enough even as a little girl to fascinate the boy's admired stepfather. There was, in short, a 'situation' quite as promising as that of *The Wings of the Dove*; a situation equally susceptible of treatment in James's later prose, which would circle endlessly, like a bird of prey, before pouncing with such swiftness that a reader's eye, bleary with watching the long drawn-out hoverings, might have found it difficult to spot just how and where the end came. One can surmise, at any rate, that Gray would be almost grateful to Howard Vince for despoiling him. He had already made it clear to his creepy business consultant just where he stood with regard to his financial position:

'You seem all here so hideously rich that I needn't fear to count as extraordinary; indeed I'm very competently assured I'm by all your standards a very moderate affair. And even if I were a much greater one'— he gathered force—'my appearance of it would depend only on myself. You can have means and not be blatant; you can take up, by the very fact itself, if you happen to be decent, no more room than may suit your taste. I'll be hanged if I consent to take up an inch more than suits mine. Even though not of the truly bloated I've at least means to be quiet. Every one among us—I mean among the moneyed—isn't a monster on exhibition.'

In his youthful self-sufficient attractiveness, the developing character of Gray Fielder suggests that James may well have modelled him on one of those 'decent' young men, like Rupert Brooke or Hugh Walpole, to whom as an elderly 'Master' he had come to feel he could now offer an affectionate solicitude. Whether, in shedding his fortune, Gray would have felt obliged to rid Rosanna, too, of *her* crippling twenty millions, must remain a matter for conjecture.

I am in complete agreement with Professor Cargill that 'no partially finished work by a great artist is capable of inspiring more regrets for its incompleteness than *The Ivory Tower*'. I do not, alas, have the same feeling about *The Sense of the Past* (1917). It is an unfinished novel, started as long ago as the turn of the century, which James took up again (having laid aside the more promising work) when the shock of the Great War sickened him as all the violence and brutality which he had long seen lying under the surface of the late nineteenth- and early twentieth-century life burst to the top in one ravaging holocaust. I have already commented (in Chapter II) on one particular significance of *The Sense of the Past* as the last disillusioned yet still utterly fascinated flirtation of the 'passionate pilgrim' side of James's make-up with the notion of the Old World he had dreamed of as a child. He had made more than one attempt to get this unwieldy novel moving. It had originally been conceived as a simple ghost story— but, like so many other of James's simple stories, it had run into immense verbose expansion, irradiated by splendid patches of fresh observation and clouded by the shadows cast by invented and contrived schematic motivations. Dr. Cargill makes a very important point when he writes: 'Since the latter portion of the completed version is livelier and more dramatic than the earlier portion, the faults of *The Sense of the Past* can no longer be ascribed to failing powers, but must be assigned to the difficulties for James of the unusual subject which he had chosen. Weakness is shown only in his allowing so much of the early composition to stand.'

The central theme, that of a young man exchanging places with the subject of an ancestral portrait and stepping into the world of a hundred years before his own, has echoes as fanciful as Wilde's *Dorian Gray* and as frivolous as Gilbert's *Ruddigore*. James's elaboration of this motif into a substantial essay on the idea that human beings were as rapacious in the early years of the nineteenth century as they are in the early years of the twentieth, was also a justifiable expansion of the original gimmicky idea. What is *not* justifiable, to my mind, is the wholly incredible 'outer plot' in which this fantasy is set. Whereas a reader may be prepared to indulge a willing suspension of disbelief when Ralph Pendrel exchanges places with his young forebear in the portrait, simply on the acceptable grounds that this *is* a fantasy and we know it to be so, that same reader may well turn rebellious when perfectly non-fantastical characters are made to behave, in the interests of a 'symmetrical' framework, as no human beings ever do behave. And yet this is precisely how the novel opens. In Book First, Ralph Pendrel, a romantically minded young New Yorker, is shown wooing a wealthy widow, Aurora Coyne. She herself had enjoyed her fill of European culture, but she is so sure that Ralph would succumb entirely to its charms that she jealously makes it a condition that before marrying her he shall expose himself alone to its dangerous fascination, and only if he is strong enough to return to claim her hand will she eventually marry him. Now, this kind of love-test is much harder to swallow than the coincidence of Pendrel's unexpected inheriting of a gracious old house in London; indeed, it is quite as much in the tradition of fairy tales as the portrait-come-to-life or the stepping-into-the-past themes.

As a supposedly normal setting for a designedly ghostly story, then, the opening section of *The Sense of the Past* is so unreal that a reader can only glumly observe that 'people in love just don't behave like this', and all the carefully elaborated 'modern' standards, against which the 'historical' part of the tale was intended to be significantly measured, are wasted—or, worse, become a definite stumbling-block. This point is of importance for two reasons, one local to the book itself, the other sadly relevant to the whole of James's fiction. First, it suggests that one's uncomfortable lack of *rapport*, when reading *The Sense of the Past*, is due less to the 'unreal' main subject than to the unreality of its apparent basic touchstone of actuality. Secondly, it shows that James never did succeed in freeing himself from the habit of manipulating into absurdly contrived melodramatic postures a set of characters who are themselves presented, as living people, with extraordinary fidelity to observed truth. It is one final reminder, in short, that James the superb recorder of mood and the subtlest critic of human and cultural values, could at the same time be woefully deficient, yet tiresomely proud of his efforts, in the subsidiary craft of plot-construction.

Once Pendrel reaches London, sap begins to flow in the prose. He was not, in himself, a very lively hero; he has nothing of the human promise of Gray Fielder of *The Ivory Tower*. 'He was by the turn of his spirit oddly indifferent to the actual and the possible; his interest was all in the spent and displaced. . . . It was when life was framed in death that the picture was really hung up.' But he was quick to observe such things as 'a background of cosy corners or photographs framed in leather, of tailor-made ladies doing tricks with little dogs and gentlemen in tweed mixtures tilting back "good" chairs'—which convicts him not so much of prim Edwardian snobbery as a share of his creator's constantly disappointed search for real quality in places where the supposed 'quality' forgather. Then comes his strange experience with the portrait, after which Pendrel is convinced that the 'other person' separately exists and has changed places with him, that *he* is indulging his sense of the past while his young ancestor is indulging *his* sense of the future. It is, again, this maddening device of parallelism, so weak and stupid an addition to a story already sufficiently straining one's credulity, that is harder to swallow than the 'ghostly' trick itself. We can 'believe', for the purposes of a promising tale, the ghostly exchange; what we certainly cannot believe is that the ghostly figure should be so pat and neat a Jamesian complement to the living Pendrel. It is failure of imagination in the author, and not lack of it in the reader, that squanders any 'belief' one may ever have invested in the story.

Later, the original Pendrel, now in the form of his young ancestor, meets at his house in Mansfield Square (it was to become Berkeley Square in the play later founded on the story) a gradually increasing family of his ancestral but now present relations. As an ex-loyalist and wealthy American, this returning Pendrel is cast, in 1820 terms, as the future husband of his cousin Molly, with whom there are some laboured scenes of cousinly flirtation (shades still, perhaps, of Minny Temple?). He takes the measure, too, of her fantasy mother and brother, the latter an insolent boor who calls forth the American's full determination not to be excluded: 'Perry would have to *take* him, and to show that he had taken him.' (Is there still, here, some remembered rankling of the excluded trans-Atlantic cousin?) Later still,

when other English types of 1820 appear, we are plunged into tedious
and stilted social gabble in which James shows himself to be utterly
uninterested in the various opportunities open to him, in so curious a
narrative situation, either from the world of fantasy or from the
historical past. When the youngest cousin Nan appears, she is
greeted by the puzzled and transported Pendrel as 'modern' in tone:
we feel certain that this bright young girl of 1820 will be shown to be
yearning for the future, just as her 'cousin' of 1910 had been yearning
for the past. We feel equally certain, in a fantasy so feebly unexploited,
so heavily overborne by James's habitual later style, that our attention will be diverted to the struggles of Pendrel (whether the Pendrel
of 1820 or the Pendrel of 1910 doesn't in the least matter, in this
humdrum unfantastic context) to disentangle himself from the
designs of the elder sister Molly. We learn from the notes James
made in 1914 that Ralph would be shown to us as feeling 'the horror
of the growing fear of *not* being saved, of being lost, of being *in* the
past to stay'. Alas, the four books James completed of this novel
never for an instant convince us that Pendrel ever *was* 'in the past', so
little use has been made of the transposition, once effected. And even
the promise of Pendrel's 'dawning anguish' at the 'brutalities, etc.' of
1820 fades away when one recalls that sooner or later, to make the
creaky pattern work, he will have to present himself to—had the
reader forgotten?—Aurora Coyne!

XV

Henry James, Man and Legend

My exile was not like the barren tree,
Which beares his fruitlesse head up to the
skye,
But like the trees whose boughs o'erladen
be,
And with self-riches bowed down to die.
                              Fulke Greville

The artist was what he *did*—he was nothing
else.
                    The Real Right Thing

WHEN an author is steadily prolific and enjoys a substantial writing life, the ground one surveys is so richly covered with foliage that one tends to forget the soil underneath. One neglects, in other words, to relate the writing to the writer or the writer to even the basic facts of his biography. And this is specially true in the case of a writer like Henry James, who—once one develops a taste for him—is so eminently quotable and re-readable that one would sooner squeeze a little more juice out of another reading of *The Spoils of Poynton*, so to say, than work out just how old he was at the time of composition and where he wrote it, and whether he was to outward appearances gloomy or cheerful at the time.

With less prolific writers, or with writers who have certain clearly marked watersheds in their private or public lives, one does not forget this life–work relationship. It is when one reads the *minor* Elizabethans that one turns to notes on the construction of the theatre or which side the dramatist happened to take in some political or religious controversy of the time. When one is reading *Richard II*, on the other hand, reminders of the Essex revolt are simply an interruption; reading *King Lear*, one ceases to be conscious even of the century in which it was written. The thick sprawling profusion of James's fiction, the increasingly familiar drone or beguilement of the tone of his writer's voice, similarly distract the reader's attention from the state of the author's heart or arteries. His youngest tales, in any case, have a mature magniloquence; and even his least attractive later morbid tales of self-pity are never devoid of delightful phrases or a thumb-nail sketch to surprise the reader to open laughter; so that an engaged reader is more conscious that 'this is James and nobody else', rather than 'this is early James and not late James'. Finally, to tackle such a massive work of fiction as, say, *The Golden Bowl*, is to take on a whole new country: the reading is itself a sufficiently formidable task, and one forbears to inquire how, why or when it came to be written.

These conclusions are the more acceptable for two excellent reasons. The first is that James himself was tireless in pointing out, to himself and to his readers, that 'the artist was what he *did*—he was nothing else'. Those who agree with him, may leave it at that. Those who consider that such an attitude is more likely to be the pose of a man abnormally anxious to conceal his inner self, have already made, by their own lights, a major biographical discovery. The second reason is that Dr. Edel's splendid biography (of which three volumes were in print in 1953, and a fourth will appear shortly) has already provided so richly documented a study of James's working life that, taken together with his own three autobiographical volumes, they provide all one needs. The main virtue of such biographical collateral, in scanning a life so outwardly unadventurous, so inwardly in constant turmoil, is to separate James the man (or even James the artist) from James the forbidding mandarin of literary legend. To seize upon one obvious example: the James of legend was a hidebound and snobbish Tory. James the man considered himself to be (in the England of Radical reform) an 'ardent Liberal'. Much of James's best-known fiction is concerned with those who considered themselves to constitute Victorian and Edwardian 'high society'. To proceed from this fact to the view that he shared their standards is as stupid as to believe that Pope, because he exposed corruption in Augustan London, actively supported it. A closer study of James's letters and autobiographies will reveal a similar liberality of outlook at a deeper and more significant level. As F. O. Matthiessen put it, 'his gradation of characters according to their degree of consciousness may be validly translated into terms of social consciousness, and thus serve as a measure in a more dynamic world than James ever conceived of'. This is but the direct application of a truth that shines out through all James's work—in passages of *The Bostonians* and *The Princess Casamassima*, in moral-aesthetic discrimination in such works as *The Spoils of Poynton*, *The Portrait of a Lady* and the three late masterpieces— that no man can be trusted to make important contributions to public causes until he has first learned how to be honest with himself.

Was Henry James honest with *him*self? The question is relevant, because although his writing life may well have been, as he so often insisted, a lonely one, nothing can really be more 'public' than the launching upon the world of a great host of books. One receives, it must be admitted, little help on this score from his surviving working notebooks (see Bibliographical Note). Their prevailing tone is that of measured self-communion, occasionally running over into a direct observation of people and places, but mainly a self-colloquy on the problems of a writing career. In them, Henry James goads himself, argues with himself; sometimes, in a moment when ideas flow free and he thrills to a conviction of mastery over his medium, he positively hugs himself: 'Oh, divine old joy of the "Scenario", throbbing up and up, with its little sacred irrepressible emotion, WHENEVER I give it again the ghost of a chance!' But this intriguing collection of notes on the tricks of his trade, these lengthy chastisements of long-windedness, these jig-saw-puzzle scenarios and unravellings of self-tied knots —all these jottings are, in the end, no more than a personal application of the rule he laid down in *The Real Right Thing*: 'The artist was what he *did*—he was nothing else.' The notebooks are certainly disappointing if one confuses them with diaries. Life—not the art of fiction—was the *subject* of his work, and of his direct reactions to living we learn more from his letters than from the notebooks. It can even be vexing to find him peering into the mechanism of his craft when we should have preferred to overlook him while he was privately examining the springs of the emotions. Instead of talking to himself about this raw material—the nature of man's life—we find him musing on the construction of *nouvelles*, on some new way of making a fictive pattern out of withdrawals from life. A study of these notebooks could provide, indeed, a plot for one of his own sad, valorous, inhibited later stories about authors—the story of a novelist who, failing to 'let himself go' in a private journal, discovers that instead of laying bare his secret heart he has only laid bare the mechanism of his craft.

There is something both pathetic and eloquent in the 'professional' notes of this most articulate of men who can nevertheless feel it necessary to record: 'I have only to let myself *go*! So I have said to myself all my life—so I said to myself in the far-off days of my fermenting and passionate youth. Yet I have never fully done it. The sense of it—of the need of it—rolls over me at times with commanding force: it seems the formula of my salvation, of what remains to me of a future ... Go on, my boy, and strike hard; have a rich and long St. Martin's summer.' His self-knowledge shows him his chief fault as clearly as his many virtues as a writer: 'a strange nervous fear of letting myself go. If I vanquish that fear, the world is mine.'

As private papers, then, the notebooks are unrewarding. We learn that when he talked to himself, James liked to call himself '*mon bon*'

—but of the self that talked we learn little that is new. What the note-books do provide is a supplement, more practical and more intimate, to the published Prefaces. In the words of the editors, they contain discussions of 'all his finished novels and all but a handful of his stories', a record of 'upwards of eighty victories in completed stories and novels, and of thirty or forty more skirmishes with themes that he abandoned, for one reason or another'. As we watch him con-templating, year after year, his work in hand, elaborating his drama-tic symmetry, playing with his counters, patting and petting his themes, teasing out the last essence of some tiny *donnée*, it is difficult to resist a feeling of embarrassment in face of his maddening, gar-rulous, self-conscious reticence. It is not even as if he could ever for long make up his own mind. The precise nature of his self-communi-cated ambition changes again and again. We find him sighing for '*short* things' and 'something *great*' (these words from the same para-graph); for 'scenic, constructive, "architectural" effects' and for 'rapid, concrete action' (these, too, from the same paragraph). 'A truce to all subjects that are not superior!' he can cry, or hesitate with some trifle in the words: 'Can I catch hold—if it be in the least worth the effort?—of a very small fantasy that came to me the other month in New York?' One consoles oneself with the reflection that in a writer of such swarming fecundity there is nothing necessarily incon-sistent about these kaleidoscopic enthusiasms. Where the notebooks *are* consistent is in harping on three or four recurring themes (such as the urge to present a whole novel via one central consciousness; the eternal struggle against overshooting the mark in the matter of length; the itch for neat symmetry; the obsession with the notion of too little and too late: '*That* was what might have happened, and what *has* happened is that it didn't') which are already familiar enough to readers of the Prefaces. We ought to have guessed that Henry James would be the last person to whom to apply if we wanted the result of a lifetime's devotion to the art of fiction concentrated in two or three epigrammatic words.

As for Henry James the man, the notebooks simply tell us that, for better or worse, his professional view of himself was the same in private as in public.

There will always, of course, be speculation about Henry James's secret private life—for if he had a personal life in the usual sense of the phrase, it has remained a secret. Dr. Edel's biography shows him to have been mildly flirtatious at times, but always with 'safe' ladies whose age or married respectability kept them, literally, at arm's length. The degree to which a repressed hope for more than friendship may have contributed to drive to suicide his female friend Constance Fenimore Woolson is problematical: his own shocked reaction to her death seemed merely to have been tinged with the uncomfortable but certainly non-criminal guilt of a man who suspects he is more loved than loving. In his later years, he gloried in the adulation of a few young admirers such as Hugh Walpole, whose ebullient letters (as quoted in Mr. Hart-Davis's biography) called forth from 'the Master' a flood of verbal warmth which, as was his epistolary habit, seemed to serve in lieu of physical embraces. In a notebook entry of 1881, James described himself 'as an artist and as a bachelor; as one who has the passion of observation and whose business is the study of human life'. It was the mask he chose to wear to the world. He seems to have worn it, too, in solitude. One remembers, of course, that there is no more effective and intriguing disguise than the mask that perfectly fits the face beneath.

The prime sources for James's *essential* biography remain his own three volumes: *A Small Boy and Others* (1913), *Notes of a Son and Brother* (1914), and the posthumous fragmentary sequel *The Middle Years* (1917). Just as the published novels absorb and transmute the working drafts committed to his notebooks, so in these grave yet immensely lively books he presents, as a finished product, the art of self-revelation—an art of which his scattered written or spoken confessions, or even his regular overflowings into personal letters, often of superlative quality, are at best but imperfect preliminaries. That something is deliberately omitted from these finished and self-censured products, one cannot doubt. But with Henry James, one's curiosity about that hidden part is transcended, to a quite extraordinary degree, by one's certainty that the face he showed to the world, a face at once bland and ravaged, sensitive and stoical, was essentially more 'real' than anything that has already been disclosed or may in future be discoverable from the haphazard actualities of the 'candid camera'. The novels are vastly superior to their drafts and scenarios. The autobiographies are crammed to concentration with the sights and sounds and smells and perceptions of a lifetime: at the expense of discarding the thorns and leaves, so to say, they release, like attar of roses, the 'real' secret of the flower. Just so, the James one learns to revere from a study of his fiction, the Henry James one learns to cherish from the evidence of compassionate understanding in the autobiographies and letters, is nearer to the true man than any figure, however amusing or provocatively stimulating, pasted together from even well observed records of the passing moment.

Why he spent a lifetime fashioning an immense *persona* for himself is a problem for the psychologist. The critic, the man of letters, can only express a grateful wonder that he *did*. One must guard, of course, against that soppy adulation which has harmed his reputation far more than the jibes of H. G. Wells or the exasperation of Mr. Maxwell Geismar. Those who still adopt the '*cher maître*' attitude to James, watchful with esoteric glee for his pathetic mannered slang or his obfuscating parentheses, are applauding the frail means and ignoring the noble ends. *Cher maître* he certainly became, but only as a result of his own admitted failure to break through the limitations of '*mon bon*'. We are at liberty to pry for the spiritual secret (the physical is anyone's guess) of his magnificent impotence. The notion that James himself was *unaware* of his own psychology has only to be stated to be dismissed as an absurdity. If his working notebooks show him to us at closer professional range than had hitherto been permitted, shrinking still from the direct forthright, then *let* that be his tone, his own perfect communication. Other writers have sought to demonstrate our active impulses; he has made himself the poet and scholar of passive states of consciousness.

One can more readily accept the limitations of James's life and art —and without the danger of joining those who, like foxes without tails, revere him just *because* of those limitations—if one grasps that from his very childhood it was quality of vision, rather than range of vision, that obsessed him. Bundled from house to house and from country to country in accordance with the whims of their brilliant erratic father, the young James boys were confronted with a changing kaleidoscope of impressions. But the whirligig was for their young minds a purely domestic affair, and the value of the impressions thus formed depended entirely upon the individual perception of the viewer. Even so, from the evidence of the autobiographies, there is no need to think of the young Henry as a boy of too injured or broody a personality. Henry James Senior was no doubt, as 'father-figure' and father in one, irritatingly authoritarian and capricious at the same time. No doubt, too, William James was an object of brotherly jealousy as well as of brotherly love. The two younger brothers who fought in the Civil War may well have acted as an unspoken reproach to the stay-at-home Henry, suffering as he was from his obscurely inglorious back injury. But when all allowances are made, there can have been nothing seriously wrong about the psychological health of a united family in which, when father brought out a book entitled *Substance and Shadow*, or *Morality and Religion in their Relation to Life*, son William 'amused himself and all the family by designing a small cut to be put on the title page, representing a man beating a dead horse'.* That Henry himself was the most 'introverted' of the James boys is not in question. But all the biographical, as well as literary, evidence shows that even in the bewilderment of his formative years, an unsettlement alike domestic and geographical, the young novelist-to-be had already developed that hard core of objective sanity, irradiated by humour, which was to distinguish all his best work.

The temptation is strong to illustrate these sadly foreshortened conclusions by quotations from James's autobiographies and letters; but my guide has been to the fiction only, and any reader who has reached this final chapter will surely wish to pursue the matter for himself. The point to be made here, in a strictly literary guide, is simply that the *style* of the conscious man and writer is everywhere consistent. If asked to distinguish the qualities that most strike me in what we now know of Henry James the man, I should nominate kindness, sanity and wit. Those same qualities ooze from all his writing. The man who could dash off, in a social scrawl rejecting a last-minute invitation to dinner, the self-parodying phrase 'for I shrink from the brutality of a telegram', was the same man who devoted several shelf-loads of stories to the exposure of non-physical brutality in lives only outwardly decorous. His letters overflow with affectionate tributes to his friends, but the style is still ceremonious, for even affection was a quality not to be rudely thrust upon his intimates like some quack's nostrum from the cheapjack world, so long

*Retold by Percy Lubbock (*Letters* 1, 9) from an account by the James family friend, Thomas Sergeant Perry.

ago, of *Professor Fargo*. To select one example from hundreds: when James assured Robert Louis Stevenson that 'the mere thought of you is better company than any that is tangible to me here, and London is more peopled to me by your living in Samoa than by the residence of almost anybody else in Kensington or Chelsea', literal truth and self-parody and verbal relish are all equally present. There is, too, something quintessentially revealing in his greed for facts, his power of self-implication, his long-memoried courtesy, as he follows the truant Louis 'with an aching wing, an inadequate geography and an ineradicable hope'. Indeed, I recommend Henry James's letters (whether in the Percy Lubbock two-volume edition, Dr. Edel's one-volume selection, or samples of individual correspondence such as that with Stevenson, edited by Miss Janet Adam Smith, or John Hay, edited by Dr. George Monteiro) as a perfect modern equivalent of Castiglione's *Il Cortegiano*—for they teach the aspirant to humane understanding that wit cohabits with consideration and that the seat of any worth-while discrimination is the heart.

BIBLIOGRAPHICAL NOTE

BEFORE the war, the novels and tales were most readily available in the
pocket version of the 'New and Complete Edition' edited by Percy
Lubbock for Macmillan, 1921–23, and based for the most part on the
revised New York Edition of 1907–9. These and other handy reprints, such
as the 'Uniform Tales' published by Martin Secker, 1915–20, tended
during the post-war years of the Henry James boom to disappear from
second-hand bookshops, whither they will presumably be driven back
for a new generation of beginners, from the shelves of purchasers of Dr.
Leon Edel's admirable edition of the 'Complete Tales' in twelve volumes
(Rupert Hart-Davis, 1962–64). The same publishers, for the most part
served by the same devoted editor, have also re-issued, at different dates
since 1946, the novels *Watch and Ward*, *Roderick Hudson*, *The Tragic
Muse*, *The Reverberator*, *The Other House*, *The Sacred Fount*, together
with *The Complete Plays*, *Selected Letters*, and collections of essays under
the titles *Parisian Sketches*, *The Painter's Eye*, *The House of Fiction* (essays
on the novel) and *The Scenic Art* (notes on acting and drama). Hart-Davis
also publishes the masterly four-volume biography by Dr. Edel, the first
three volumes of which had appeared before this book was completed:
The Untried Years, *1843–1870* (1953), *The Conquest of London*, *1870–1883*
(1962) and *The Middle Years*, *1884–1894* (1963).

The noble New York Edition is being reprinted by Scribner's. Meanwhile, a surprisingly large but scattered selection of James's novels has
been offered by different publishers in paperback form, too numerous
and diverse to be listed here. Considering the long-held popular view of
Henry James, it is astonishing how many of his books may now be
encountered at American drug-stores and among the post-card racks at
British seaside resorts. In the 1940's, *Roderick Hudson*, *Washington
Square*, *What Maisie Knew*, *The Princess Casamassima* and *The Spoils of
Poynton* were all reprinted in John Lehmann's Chiltern Library, together
with one of several selections of stories, of which another is included in
the O.U.P. World's Classics series.

James's three autobiographical volumes (*A Small Boy and Others*,
Notes of a Son and Brother and *The Middle Years*) were reprinted in 1956
(London: W. H. Allen) with an introduction by F. W. Dupee. A useful
two-volume selection from James's *Letters* was edited by Percy Lubbock

(Scribner's) in 1920. The *Prefaces* from the New York Edition were reprinted, with an introduction by R. P. Blackmur, as *The Art of the Novel* (Scribner's, 1934). The *Notebooks* were edited by F. O. Matthiessen and Kenneth B. Murdoch (O.U.P., 1947). A selection from James's *Literary Criticism* was edited by Morris Shapira (Heinemann, 1963). Of the many other non-fictional works recently reprinted, British readers will find *English Hours* (Heinemann, 1960) of special interest.

Indispensable to scholarly readers is the *Bibliography* by Dr. Edel and Dan H. Laurence (Hart-Davis 1957, second edition 1961). Readers who sometimes lose themselves in the jungle may be rescued by Robert L. Gale's *Plots and Characters in the Fiction of Henry James* (Archon Books, U.S.A., 1965). Professor Oscar Cargill's *The Novels of Henry James* (Macmillan, New York, 1961) provides, in addition to his own valuable commentaries, a convenient reference to a mass of biographical and critical material (up to about 1960), collected under sections relating to each of the novels proper (except *Washington Square*). Samples of earlier biographical and critical material have also been collected in two anthologies: *The Legend of the Master* by Simon Nowell-Smith (Constable, 1947) and *The Question of Henry James*, edited by F. W. Dupee (Allan Wingate, 1947). Among individual examples of this early work on James, the short essays by Ford Madox Ford (Secker, 1913) and Rebecca West (Nisbet, 1916) give a flavour of critical opinion during his lifetime; the Hogarth Essay by Theodora Bosanquet, *Henry James at Work* (second edition, 1927) offers a brief glimpse of his declining years. Another short but perceptive study by a contemporary may be found in Desmond MacCarthy's *Portraits* (Putnam, 1931; reprinted by McGibbon & Kee, 1949).

From the flood of recent studies on both sides of the Atlantic I would select Professor D. W. Jefferson's *Henry James and the Modern Reader* (Oliver & Boyd, 1964) for the stress it lays on the enjoyment of reading James, and Dorothea Krook's *The Ordeal of Consciousness in Henry James* (O.U.P., 1962) as a serious (at times solemn) analysis of the later novels which supplements F. O. Matthiessen's *Henry James: The Major Phase* (O.U.P., 1946). The early novels are treated in *The Comic Sense of Henry James* by Richard Poirier (Chatto & Windus, 1960). The reprinting by the C.U.P. (1963), in twenty volumes, of the critical quarterly *Scrutiny* has made readily available in their original form not only several important critical essays and reviews which have been subsequently embodied in book form (notably in Dr. F. R. Leavis's *The Great Tradition* of 1948 and *The Current Pursuit* of 1952), but also many other valuable references. A mainly unsympathetic view of James from the American standpoint was voiced in Van Wyck Brooks's *The Pilgrimage of Henry James* (Cape,

1928), which pales beside the full-scale irascible onslaught, entertaining but often wilfully dead-pan, by Maxwell Geismar in *Henry James and his Cult* (Chatto & Windus, 1964). Some of the most perceptive recent criticism, especially of difficult novels like *What Maisie Knew* and *The Sacred Fount*, is to be found in the three chapters on James in Tony Tanner's *The Reign of Wonder* (C.U.P., 1965).

INDEX

The detailed treatment of each novel and tale is indicated by italic figures.

I. HENRY JAMES

II. OTHER REFERENCES

Book references are by author only; for titles, see Bibliographical Note.

432